The Church and the Jews in the XIIIth Century

1254-1314

The Church and the Jews in the XIIIth Century

SOLOMON GRAYZEL

Volume II
1254–1314

Edited and arranged, with additional notes, by
KENNETH R. STOW

THE JEWISH THEOLOGICAL SEMINARY OF AMERICA   AND THE BUSH זתסבה WAS NOT איננו CONSUMED אכל   New York

WAYNE STATE UNIVERSITY PRESS   Detroit   1989/5749

Grateful acknowledgment is made to the following:

Dropsie University: For permission to reprint "Popes, Jews, and Inquisition from 'Sicut' to 'Turbato,'" by Solomon Grayzel, from *Essays on the Occasion of the Seventieth Anniversary of Dropsie University*, pp. 151–188. Ed. Abraham I. Katch and Leon Nemoy. Philadelphia, 1979.

Hebrew Union College Annual: For permission to reprint "References to the Jews in the Correspondence of John XXII," by Solomon Grayzel. *HUCA* 23, pt. 2 (1950–1951): 37–80.

Jewish Book Council: For permission to reprint "Solomon Grayzel, 1896–1980," by Kenneth R. Stow. *Jewish Book Annual*, Vol. 39 (5742 = 1981–1982): 158–163.

Oxford University Press: For permission to reprint excerpts from *Councils & Synods with Other Documents Relating to the English Church, II: A.D. 1205–1313, Part II: 1265–1313*, pp. 955, 959, 961–963. Ed. F. M. Powicke and C. R. Cheney. Oxford, 1964.

Library of Congress Cataloging-in-Publication Data

Grayzel, Solomon, 1896-
     The Church and the Jews in the XIIIth century / by Solomon Grayzel;
    edited and arranged, with additional notes by Kenneth R. Stow.
         p.   cm.
    Bibliography: p.
    Includes indexes.
    Contents: — v. 2. 1254-1314.
    ISBN 0-8143-2254-9
    1. Catholic Church—Relations—Judaism—Papal documents.
    2. Judaism—Relations—Catholic Church—Papal documents.   3. Jews—
    Legal status, laws, etc.—Papal documents.   4. Jews—
    History—70-1789—Sources.   5. Church history—13th century—
    Sources.   I. Stow, Kenneth R.   II. Title.
    BM535.G7   1989
    261.2'6'09022—dc20   89-8941
                                       CIP

Book design by Stephan O. Parnes and Miles B. Cohen
Composition by Bet Sha'ar Press, Inc.

Manufactured in the United States of America
9 8 7 6 5 4 3 2 1

To the Memory of Sophie Grayzel

Contents

Solomon Grayzel
1896–1980

KENNETH R. STOW

PENCILLED IN THE MARGIN of a page in Solomon Grayzel's personal copy of his *The Church and the Jews in the XIIIth Century* is the two-word comment, "wrong analysis." That, remarked a colleague of mine, who also had the pleasure of knowing him, is just the kind of person Dr. Grayzel was. Never, in fact, have I met anyone so unassuming as Solomon Grayzel, nor do I recall knowing a person so ready to rethink his ideas and revise his conclusions. These qualities enabled Dr. Grayzel to leave a lasting mark not just in one field, but three. He was, at once, a scholar, a teacher and a servant of the Jewish community.

In his own eyes, Dr. Grayzel was always the teacher and scholar. Thus, while he served as the first rabbi of Congregation Beth-El in Camden, New Jersey, from 1921, he also pursued his doctoral studies at the then Dropsie College. These studies led him to explore a field which Jewish scholars previously had not dealt with analytically. The relations of the medieval popes and the Jews had, of course, already been studied at length by L. Erler and Moritz Stern. But Stern's work, despite its value, was confined to the unannotated collection and publication of documents. Only the German Catholic, Erler, had engaged in analysis. In the early 1880s he published a series of articles in the *Archiv für Katholischen Kirchenrecht* in which he essayed an overview of papal Jewish relations. However, Erler could not free himself of contemporary prejudices, and, rather than seek the explanation for the vicissitudes of papal policy within the Church and Church teachings, he stressed the need of the popes to restrain what he termed Jewish pride and insolence.

Following Erler a number of brief essays appeared, most notably those of F. Kayser on Nicholas V (*AKKR*, 1885) and L. Lucas on Innocent III (*REJ*, 1897). E. Rodocanachi's 1891 monograph on the period of the Roman ghetto also deserves note. Nevertheless, a systematic answer to

Erler was still unavailable. Beyond that, Jewish historiography in general had been heavily colored by the opinions of Graetz, who had identified the papacy as the main source of Jewish suffering in the Middle Ages. This view clearly needed refocusing, as well as refinement. Solomon Grayzel was, therefore, responding to two major desiderata when, in the brief preface to the 1933 edition of *The Church and the Jews*, he stated that "the (study of the) relations between the Church and the Jews offered the best starting point" for a series of Dropsie monographs devoted to elucidating the essence of medieval Jewish life.

To produce his work, Grayzel first gained admission to the Vatican Secret Archive, becoming perhaps the first Jew to enter the Archive for exclusively Jewish research purposes. A large proportion, if not all of Moritz Stern's labors were carried on through the intermediary of a Roman monk who copied texts and sent them off to Stern in Germany. By electing to work in the Vatican itself Dr. Grayzel was unwittingly performing a piece of Jewish diplomacy. To this day, a Jew researching Jewish issues in the Vatican Archive cannot help but feel that the staff is especially ready to give him its fullest aid. This attitude was certainly engendered by Dr. Grayzel's modesty, studiousness, friendship and warmth. And it is no accident that in the Vatican Archive the recollection of the Grayzel name evokes smiles of pleasant memories, as well as the feeling that those who count themselves among Grayzel's students are more than welcome there to continue his work.

Corpus of Texts

What lies within the *Church and the Jews* is known to all. The texts, the translations, and their critical apparatus are a model for every researcher. They display the patience and diligence without which the transcription and publication of textual manuscripts is a useless endeavor. Indeed, if Dr. Grayzel had a weakness, it lay in his unmitigated insistence on perfection in the presentation of textual materials. At the time of his death he still had in his hands hundreds of manuscripts in various stages of transcription. For no amount of urging during his last years could move him to violate a lifetime of self-discipline and publish prematurely. He preferred to leave the publication of these manuscripts to someone else, with the provision, of course, that his own rigid standards be maintained. Typically, moreover, he never once asked that his continuator share publication credits with him.

In the analytical portions of *The Church and the Jews*, Grayzel worked a mild revolution. For while he spoke forthrightly, as on one occasion when he declared that certain papal attitudes moved "in the direction of eliminating the Jew from Society," he was equally prepared, unlike his predecessors, to point to consistent efforts made by the popes on behalf of the Jews. He was even ready to view a number of Jewish actions as potentially threatening to Christian society and thus to concede that various stringent measures were enacted by the popes in "the defense of Christianity." Grayzel, in other words, had at last made serious academic study possible in a field which hitherto had invariably been investigated more by the heart than by the mind.

Dr. Grayzel saw in *The Church and the Jews* only a beginning, and he had every intention of carrying his studies, especially of the thirteenth-century papacy, much farther. Accordingly, it comes as no surprise that without exception, every piece of ancillary literature to be cited by future scholars in discussing the popes and the Jews of this period is already mentioned in Grayzel's copious footnotes. Dr. Grayzel's plans are also evident in the studies he produced in the 1940s and 1950s: a discussion of Jewish life under the fourteenth-century Avignonese popes (*Historia Judaica*, 1940); the publication, albeit in a somewhat abbreviated format, of the letters of John XXII pertaining to Jews (*HUCA*, 1950–51, part 2); the analysis of references made to the Jews in a thirteenth-century papal formulary (*JQR*, 1955); and the translation of the confession wrought by the papal inquisition from a southern French convert who had reverted to Judaism (*HJ*, 1955).

Communal Service

Grayzel's next major publication, his well-known study of the *Constitutio pro Judaeis*, the bull *Sicut Judaeis*, was not to appear, however, until 1962 (A. A. Neuman Festschrift). The cause for this delay was, of course, Dr. Grayzel's untiring labors on behalf of the Jewish community. Between 1929 and 1945 he both taught Jewish history and served as registrar at Gratz College in Philadelphia. The latter was an especially taxing position, given its centrality in the administration of the College. It was, however, in 1939 that Grayzel became a full-time servant of the community. In that year he joined Isaac Husik as an editorial assistant at the Jewish Publication Society. But Husik died shortly after, and Grayzel was immediately promoted to the post of the Society's editor, a post he was to retain until 1966, a full twenty-seven years. During this time, he also served as president of the Jewish Book Council and was closely linked with the *Jewish Book Annual* from its initial appearance in 1942.

There is perhaps no way to measure the service rendered by Dr. Grayzel to the entire English-reading Jewish public through his work at the JPS. It is literally impossible to have a library of Jewish scholarly works produced in the past forty years that does not contain books issued by the JPS. Even more important, through such outstanding joint publication ventures as Salo Baron's *Social and Religious History of the Jews,* which bears the imprint of both the Columbia University Press and JPS, books of enduring worth were made both accessible and affordable to a wide audience. And books that otherwise would have been purchased by only a scholarly readership now found their way into numerous private libraries. In addition, there were the significant translation projects, most notably Yitzhak Baer's *History of the Jews in Christian Spain.* For Baer was induced to make additions and to update the work which, in Hebrew, had first appeared a number of years earlier. But no project overshadows the new translation of the Bible, an undertaking which pooled the collective resources of the greatest contemporary Bible scholars and demanded the kind of firm but reserved guidance and direction which Grayzel was so unusually equipped to give. Dr. Grayzel made this Bible project into one of the pillars of his life, participating in and attending the meetings of the translation committee until just a few months before his death, long after he had left JPS itself.

The JPS also published Grayzel's own *History of the Jews* (1947, revised 1968). Dr. Grayzel was undoubtedly motivated to produce this volume through his experiences in meeting the needs of the broader public at JPS. But, so too, as he once wrote in a private correspondence to one of his nephews, his *History* was written in order to stimulate Jewish youth to develop an appreciation of the Jewish past and a pride in its achievements. Indeed, in 1947, a modern Jewish educational system had only just begun to flourish in America and the shattering events of the Holocaust were also fresh at hand. Hence, there was a pressing need for a work of this kind, as its success in fact testifies.

Scholarly Studies

And still, Grayzel remained at his core the scholar. The period toward the end of his tenure at JPS and then the years spent as professor of Jewish history at Dropsie University, from 1966 (when he was already seventy) until 1979, witnessed a remarkable series of articles expanding on the themes he had first proposed in *The Church and the Jews* in 1933. Thus, in 1962, his article on the bull *Sicut Judaeis* attempted to show that the popes maintained a firm position throughout the Middle Ages and into the Renaissance on the question of Jewish protection. This article was balanced in 1968 (*JQR*) by a study of Roman Law. Here Grayzel argued that while Roman Law complemented papal protection, it also possessed strongly ambivalent features, so that, at best, the protection it offered was limited and counterpoised by the harsh limits it placed on Jewish civic freedoms.

A few years before, in 1964 (Solomon Freehof Festschrift), Grayzel produced an important review of the specific issue of papal involvement in the burnings of the Talmud. Apart from a thorough examination of earlier literature on the subject, he carefully noted the active role played by such groups as the Franciscans and, especially, the Dominicans in anti-Talmud procedures, thus showing that the question of the Talmud was one which absorbed various groups within the Church and was not simply a papal operation. At this time, Grayzel also wrote an interesting study of the twenty-one Ecumenical Councils, from the earliest days of the Church through Vatican II in 1965, and their attitudes toward the Jews.

Despite all this, Grayzel was not yet fully satisfied with his conclusions. And thus in 1975 (Baron Festschrift) he published an article on the Jewry legislation of Alexander III, the first pope since Gregory the Great in the late sixth century to produce a quantity of materials on the Jews. Reigning just prior to the period of Innocent III, Alexander III tried to draw together the strands of earlier papal and conciliar legislation to produce a harmonious structure of protection and limitation for the Jews. This structure, however, tended—in Grayzel's view—to point to the greater difficulties which the Jews would confront from the thirteenth century and onward.

It was this idea which then bothered Grayzel in succeeding years. He felt that he could not rest on the findings of his earlier days and that he must rethink his position—hardly a normal procedure for a man nearing his eightieth birthday. But this he did, and in 1979 (*Essays on the Occasion of the Seventieth Anniversary of Dropsie University*) there appeared "Popes, Jews and Inquisition from 'Sicut' to 'Turbato,'" a penetrating study of papal dealings with Jews especially in the second half of the thirteenth century. Here Grayzel came to the conclusion, which, in fact, he had already begun moving toward in his 1972 "Changes in Papal Policy toward the Jews in the Middle Ages" (Fifth World Congress of Jewish Studies, vol. 2), that while the popes formally adhered to the principles of *Sicut*, they were not fully devoted to the ideals they were espousing. Rather, they were concerned primarily with restraining the Jews and keeping their potentially threatening ways in check. Through such bulls as *Turbato Corde*, which permitted the papal inquisition to inquire into the activities of converted Jews—most or all of whom Grayzel saw as forced converts—the popes opened the door which enabled the inquisition to interfere in the activities of the Jews themselves and so cause them no little distress.

Solomon Grayzel thus leaves a legacy of no little distinction. For he was not only a scholar of great knowledge, a teacher of great devotion, a servant of the Jewish community and a leader of rare modest qualities. He was, beyond that, a man who, throughout his long and successful career, was never afraid to confront his work, his ideas, and his very self anew. He was a man who kept the injunction to choose life before himself at all times.*

*A fine biography of Dr. Grayzel, including the milestones in his career and listing specific publication data, was written by A. Alan Steinbach and appeared in *Jewish Book Annual*, vol. 28 (1970), 110–115. It should be consulted by interested readers.

Preface

ONE OF THE LASTING CONTRIBUTIONS to medieval Jewish historiography in the past half century has been Solomon Grayzel's *The Church and the Jews in the XIIIth Century.* Its careful presentation of scores of papal and conciliar texts, together with translations, notes, and a thorough introduction, has served the historian of the popes and the Jews for nearly fifty years as the one repository of source materials for the important period 1198–1254. Grayzel, however, viewed this work as only a beginning. He knew that until the nuances of papal teachings were understood through the insights gained from a continued revelation of new texts, the perception of papal policies toward the Jews would remain incomplete, and inaccurate. Thus, he spent years collecting additional documents. These he hoped to publish in a second volume in the tradition of his first work. At the time of his death in August 1980 he had nearly readied for publication the collection of texts that appears on the following pages. At Dr. Grayzel's request, I have gone over the fine points of the material, provided a full Latin text in every possible instance, and on occasion added a clarifying and, sometimes, questioning note. The format of this volume varies somewhat from that of the first volume; detailed summaries of the Latin texts are given rather than translations. Apart from this, this is the second volume that Grayzel projected.

Dr. Grayzel bequeathed his primary materials to the Library of the Jewish Theological Seminary for safekeeping. The aid furnished me by the Librarian of the Seminary, Dr. Menahem Schmelzer, in working on these materials and completing Solomon Grayzel's labors has been inestimable. I am also indebted to Harriet Catlin and Shari Friedman for supervising and editing the manuscript in its early stages. I owe a special debt of gratitude to my former student Rabbi Stephan O. Parnes for his care and diligence in the final editing of the manuscript and for his role in supervising the production of the book. Without the support of Chancellor Gerson D. Cohen and, later, of Chancellor Ismar Schorsch this book would not have been published.

The period chosen for this study is a logical one. It stands between that of the monarchical papacies of the first half of the thirteenth century and the more timid and administratively minded papacies of the Avignonese era. Perhaps the best-known expression of the period, apart from the brevity of most papal reigns, is the sharp contrast of the monkish, otherworldly papacy of Celestine V followed, suspectly, by the machinations, ideological extremes, and finally the arrest of Boniface VIII. His grandiose notions of *unam sanctam* Christian world monarchy eventually led to a trauma from which the papacy never fully recovered.

Boniface VIII was not alone among thirteenth-century popes in being guided by a vision of a unified Christian world. Yet, if scholars have outlined the shape of that vision in the thinking of earlier thirteenth-century popes, such as Innocent III and Innocent IV,[1] they have failed to do the same for the popes of the later thirteenth century. The reason may simply be that scholars have not been attracted by the brief and unexciting pontificates of the popes who reigned between 1254 and 1294. Still, judging by the stances assumed toward the Jews by Clement IV and Nicholas III, to name but two of them, there is no doubt that these later popes too possessed a vision of a properly ordered world. And if this present study of Jewry policies helps to reveal in any modest way the shape of that vision and, even more important, the degree to which the popes were able to implement it, then this study will be able to claim for itself the merit of having contributed not only to the specific question of policy toward the Jews, but also to the broader problem of the nature and direction of the pontificates of the later thirteenth century as a whole.

Solomon Grayzel was especially aware of papal ideals and, in particular, of the theology underlying papal attitudes in dealing with Jews. As he argued in his essay "Popes, Jews, and Inquisition from 'Sicut' to 'Turbato,'" which follows this preface: The popes of this time were motivated foremost by theological concerns; and these concerns led directly to threatening repression. Indeed, the popes went so far as to abandon the humanitarian doctrine of Jewish protection embodied in the canon *Sicut Judaeis*.

This new turn manifested itself in the great emphasis now placed on restrictions—and not only traditional ones. In particular, the popes had to find ways of controlling what *they* perceived as the phenomenon of conversion and apostasy: the backsliding of Jews who had been baptized, whether of their own volition or through the use of force. There was, in addition, the problem of the so-called Jewish blasphemy of the Talmud, although to judge by the number of references to the Talmud and by the lack of a formal and perpetually binding canon, it was a problem that disturbed the popes only on a limited number of occasions. The same may be said of a third area of difficulty, the attendance of Jews at missionary sermons. This was a particularly complex issue for the popes to regulate, and its specifics will be discussed in the notes to the bull *Vineam sorec* (no. 42, below).

Grayzel, of course, was correct in insisting that the popes were acting on the basis of theology and the principles of canon law. And it should be seen that when it came to the conception of the nature of the Jews and their social role, the canons and theology shared essentially identical views, as a perusal of Thomas Aquinas's *Summa Theologica* (II^a,II^{ae}, 10, 1–12) will easily bear out. Nevertheless, the shared outlook of the canons and theology was not limited to an enumeration of *restrictions*. Both the canons and theology were explicit in defining the nature and the particulars of Jewish *rights* as well. In theory, these rights were intended to coexist in balance with the various restrictions. In practice, however, the hoped-for coexistence expressed itself, at best, as a most awkward equilibrium that could easily be tilted to its extremes. For example, the insistence (*Sext.* 5,2,13) on fidelity to Christianity *after* baptism, even if the baptism was clearly the product of force, was deemed not contradictory to a sharp warning (X.5,6,9) against using force *before* the fact.

There was, it must be stressed, no cynicism here. This overfine equilibrium reflects only the medieval belief in the possibility of attaining the complete harmony that is described in the *Decretals* of Gregory IX and the *Summa Theologica* and is expressed in the wish that the structure of the earthly Church Militant should mirror perfectly that of the heavenly Church Triumphant. One should, moreover, not expect anything different. This was, after all, the post-codification period of the Church that immediately succeeded the completion of the great legal compendia and theological *summae* of the early century and their subsequent magisterial exploration and interpretation by such luminaries as Henry of Segusia (Hostiensis) and Sinibaldo Fieschi (Innocent IV).

Interpretation, however, often multiplies rather than reduces complexities. The problem besetting the later thirteenth-century popes in dealing with the Jews, therefore, may have been just that overrefined rigidity and overdelicate exquisiteness that contemporary law and theology had achieved. Precision in theory could not help but yield contradictions in practice, whence, irrespective of personal whim or predilection, the popes were forced in their dealings with Jews to apply an expanse of laws and principles that proved functionally inharmonious and incompatible, no matter how much the canonists and theologians who drafted them believed otherwise. In plain terms, the goal of perfect structure and equilibrium could not be reached. Thus, it was not a conflict between humanitarianism and theology, but the competition of one theology with another and one law with another that bedeviled decision making concerning the Jews and ineluctably caused so many problems.

The Jews were quite aware of these contradictions and discords, and they knew well that the challenge they faced was, in the words of the old cliché, "to make the best of a bad situation." This they did by stressing on every possible occasion and especially in appeals to the Roman Curia their right to "due process,"[2] a principle that medieval jurists fully recognized. Thus, in 1354 the Jewish delegates who convened at Barcelona could at one and the same time effectively admit the right of the Papal Inquisition to have jurisdiction over Jews in certain matters but still insist that this jurisdiction had carefully defined limits. The Jews had come to understand that the popes' scrupulous observance of law, no matter how repressive the law may have been, meant that there would be a powerful voice speaking on behalf of their physical safety and their right to practice Judaism.[3]

Nevertheless, the Jews could do no more than hope that the papal declarations, whatever their nature, would be heeded. There was no guarantee that those within the formal bodies of the Church would follow the papal lead, and how much the less those outside the Church. This was truly frightening. For the Jews also understood that real threats to their safety and existence arose at just those moments when papal policy was subverted by more radical, and eventually disastrous, policies. To name but one of them, royally initiated and popularly supported expulsions (including the support furnished by clerical purists and extremists) were movements too strong for the popes to oppose effectively. Indeed, opposition to such royally initiated actions might have proved dangerous for the papacy itself in the long run. And this was so even if canonistic and theological doctrines argue directly against expulsions in almost every instance.

Still, as Solomon Grayzel himself would have added at this point, only the texts themselves will reveal where the popes really stood and explain the issues in full. Grayzel, in fact, was never content with his own conclusions, and he exerted so much labor on the publication of texts just because he believed that readers and students should be able to make their own decisions about papal activities and purposes on the basis of firsthand knowledge. It is in this tradition that Grayzel began work on a collection of texts to form the bulk of his second volume. The following pages make this collection available. Since, however, Grayzel summed up his feelings about the meaning of the documents found in the collection in his article "Popes, Jews, and Inquisition from 'Sicut' to 'Turbato,'" it seemed only proper to use this article as the true introduction to the volume. Similarly, it made sense to close the volume by reprinting the study Grayzel prepared thirty years ago detailing "References to the Jews in the Correspondence of John XXII." John's reign commenced immediately after that of Clement V, the first of the Avignonese popes and the last pope whose letters are included here.

The collection itself contains ninety-two letters. Each one is fully summarized, and the complete Latin original has been made available in all but two instances, and even then the essential Latin text has been printed. Three of the entries (nos. 36, 37, and 90) are not papal letters but texts from ecumenical councils held at Lyons in 1274 and Vienne in 1311. As papal councils, however, they supplement the letters.

The decrees of provincial and local councils also reflect papal policy. Thus the collection of papal letters is followed, as in Grayzel's first volume, by the texts of the decrees issued at these councils. Their local and, strictly speaking, non-papal nature, however, made it appropriate to present them separately. Grayzel, it should be noted, made a rudimentary collection of these texts. The collection has now been expanded, and English summaries and an introduction have been added.

The texts of the papal letters are accompanied by Grayzel's lengthy notes referring to parallel texts and containing a full secondary bibliography, now updated as much as possible. Grayzel's knowledge of parallel texts was nothing short of thorough, even astounding, and the notes and bibliography they contain provide an inexhaustible source of reference for scholars. In some cases, I have made additions to the notes. The additions are enclosed in square brackets and are followed by the letters "KS."

All that remains to be said or expressed is my hope that the completed collection in its present framework will honor the memory of Solomon Grayzel and the traditions of his scholarship. I take the final liberty of dedicating the book to the memory of Sophie Grayzel, Dr. Grayzel's companion of many years.

KENNETH R. STOW

Haifa University
December 19, 1988

NOTES

1. See the brief but striking, "A New Conception of the Christian Commonwealth in Innocent IV," by J. A. Kemp in the *Proceedings of the Second International Congress of Medieval Canon Law* (Vatican City, 1965), pp. 155–59.

2. On this, see J. A. Watt, "*'Plenitudo Potestatis'* in Hostiensis," in *Proceedings of the Second Congress of Medieval Canon Law,* pp. 161–87 and esp. p. 174.

3. For a full discussion, see my *The "1007 Anonymous" and Papal Sovereignty: Jewish Perceptions of the Papacy and Papal Policy in the High Middle Ages* (Cincinnati, 1984).

Abbreviations

Aronius	Julius Aronius et al., eds., *Regesten zur Geschichte der Juden im fränkischen und deutschen Reiche bis zum Jahre 1273*
AKKR	Archiv für katholisches Kirchenrecht
ASV	Archivio Segreto Vaticano
ChJ	Solomon Grayzel, *The Church and the Jews in the XIIIth Century*
CJ	*Codex Justinianus*
CJC	*Corpus Juris Canonici*, ed. Friedberg
CTh	*Codex Theodosianus*
HUCA	*Hebrew Union College Annual*
Mansi	J. D. Mansi et al., eds., *Sacrorum conciliorum nova et amplissima collectio*
MGH Capitul. Epist. Saec. XIII	*Monumenta Germaniae Historica* *Capitularia Regnum Francorum* *Epistolae Saeculi XIII*
MGWJ	*Monatsschrift für Geschichte und Wissenschaft des Judentums*
Potthast	A. Potthast, *Regesta Pontificum Romanorum*
Reg. Vat.	Regesta Vaticana
SRH	Salo Baron, *A Social and Religious History of the Jews*, 2d ed.
VR	H. Vogelstein and P. Rieger, *Geschichte der Juden in Rom*

Key to Roman and Canon Law References

Canon law references (*Corpus Iuris Canonici,* edited by E. Friedberg) and Roman law references (*Corpus Iuris Civilis,* edited by Krueger Mommsen) will be cited by the traditional abbreviations. For example:

Canon Law

Gratian's *Decretum:*
     Part 1:   D.1,c.1 (Distinctio 1, canon 1)
     Part 2:   C.1,q.1,c.1 (Causa 1, quaestio 1, canon 1) Causa 33, q.3 is known as *De Penitentia.* It is divided into distinctions and canons.
             D.1,c.1, *de pen.*
     Part 3:   D.1,c.1, *de cons.* (Dist. 1, can. 1, *De Consecratione*)

Decretales of Gregory IX (*Liber Extra*): X.1,1,1 (*Lib. Extra,* book 1, title 1, canon 1)

Liber Sextus of Boniface VIII: *Sext.* 1,1,1 (book 1, title 1, canon 1)

Constitutiones of Clement V: *Clem.* 1,1,1 (book 1, title 1, canon 1)

Roman Law

Institutes: Inst. 1,1 (book 1, title 1)

Digest: D.1,1,1 (book 1, title 1, law 1) (ff. = D. in medieval citations)

Codes: C.1,1,1 (book 1, title 1, law 1)

Novels: Nov. 1 (number 1)

The editions of both Roman and Canon law are arranged according to the above system, and texts may be located by means of it.

Popes, Jews, and Inquisition
From "Sicut" to "Turbato"

Popes, Jews, and Inquisition
From "Sicut" to "Turbato"

SOLOMON GRAYZEL
The Dropsie University

T HIS ESSAY[1] deals with the status of the Jews in western and central Europe in relation to the Church, as that relationship evolved in the course of the 12th and 13th centuries. It attempts to show 1) how the effectiveness of the more or less permissive and clearly defensive bull *Sicut Judaeis* was eroded, since it no longer fitted the conditions that came into being during the 12th century; 2) that the new spirit, essentially suspicious and aggressive was reflected in the discussions of the theologians of these two centuries as they formulated and defined the theory of "the plenitude of power" which they claimed for the papacy; 3) that this new spirit animated the bull *Turbato corde,* issued and re-issued in the second half of the 13th century at the request of the Inquisition of the Middle Ages;[2] and that 4) nevertheless, something of the *Sicut* attitude remained, and the popes occasionally continued the policy of protecting the Jews, sometimes even restraining the Inquisition. On the whole, however, the new attitude was to characterize Christian-Jewish relations for centuries to come.

Sicut represented the attitude of the Church as that attitude evolved in the early Middle Ages. Ever since the days of Constantine, the Jews occupied an anomalous position in Christendom. On the one hand, since they denied the essential Christian belief in Jesus as Savior, they had to be considered heretics, more dangerous than pagans.[3] On the other hand, their right to live among Christians had been recognized by the early Christian emperors and by almost all the early theologians. The emperors found them economically useful,[4] and the theologians assigned to them a prominent place in the drama of Christian salvation. Augustine himself defined their position in terms of limited toleration:[5] they were not to be killed, but they were to be dispersed and degraded.

In actual fact, the situation worked out almost as Augustine had suggested. Efforts to convert the Jews did not cease, and such efforts were sometimes accompanied by force. They were deprived of some of the rights they had enjoyed under the pagan emperors, but enough remained to maintain them in their Jewishness during the turbulent era of the barbarian invasions. Pope Gregory I (590-604) enunciated a policy on this aspect of the situation. In a number of letters to various princes and prelates,[6] he expressed the view that conversion by force was contrary to the divine will; suasion alone was the proper method and kindness the proper expression of Christian faith; that within the limitations of Roman Law, Jews were entitled to live their lives and observe their religion in peace.[7] On the whole, except for the Visigothic experience of the 7th century[8] and a few other instances of intolerance during the next four centuries,[9] the Jewish condition remained more or less in accord with the views of Gregory.[10] Local councils and a number of churchmen continued to urge further restrictions on Jewish life; but even they never thought of introducing such repressive measures without the consent of the civil government.[11]

Equally significant was the attitude following the attacks upon the Jews in the Rhineland at the beginning of the First Crusade. There were bishops who were ready to protect the Jews, until it became obvious that the mob of crusaders could not be stayed. The attackers left behind a considerable number of dead and a number of forced converts. The following year, in 1097, Emperor Henry IV permitted the converts to return to Judaism.[12] Pope Urban II, who had initiated the crusade, had not spoken out against the rioters and now voiced no objection to the return to Judaism of the forced converts. The one who did object was the so-called Clement III, the anti-pope of the day: he declared the reversion to Judaism to be contrary to Canon Law.[13]

The need of the Jews for additional protection was so patent at the beginning of the 12th century that Emperor Henry IV included them in the country-wide peace proclaimed in 1103 at Mainz.[14] The Jews must have appealed to the pope as well, perhaps through the Jewish community in Rome. But it was not until some twenty years after the *Landfrieden* of Mainz that Pope Calixtus II (1119-1124) issued the famous Bull of Protection, *Sicut Judaeis*.[15]

The entire introductory sentence of Pope Calixtus' *Sicut* echoes the Gregorian attitude, thereby indicating that the pope of the 12th century was following in the footsteps of the pope of the sixth. Moreover, Pope Calixtus did not address his Bull to any one bishop or to any specified local authority; he addressed it "To all the Christian Faithful," urging them in effect to recognize the right of the Jews to live peacefully in their midst. The introductory statement made two points: 1) Since there were limits to what was permitted the Jews, there should be limits to what was forbidden them. 2) The pope says, that, although they remain obstinately insistent on their Jewish beliefs, nevertheless he, the pope, out of Christian kindness, grants the protection for which they asked.[16] The Bull then goes on to enumerate the areas in which protection is extended: No one must be converted to Christianity by force, for a conversion which is not voluntary is not trustworthy.[17] No Jew should be put to death excepting by decision of the local judicial authorities. Nor must a Jew be harmed in body or property.[18] The prevailing good customs regarding the Jews in any land ought not to be changed.[19] There had apparently been frequent instances of desecration of Jewish cemeteries; the miscreants must be punished.[20] The Bull concludes, however, on a disturbing note, namely, that it applies only to such Jews as are not guilty of plotting to subvert the Christian faith.[21] Reasonable enough under the then prevailing circumstances, the clause, perhaps unintentionally, suggested a method for counteracting the spirit and content of the entire document.

There can be little doubt that, as an exhortation to Christian piety, *Sicut* prevented many a riot and some hostile legislation. Yet it seems clear in retrospect that the Bull spoke to a state of affairs that did not long continue. The 12th century witnessed many changes in European society. It saw the growth of cities and the rise of a Christian middle class. It saw, consequently, the reduction of the Jews to a lower economic status and their increasing reliance on moneylending as an occupation.[22] In the religious aspects of 12th century life, changes were also in the making. There was no let-up in crusade preaching, with its concomitant stirring of religious fervor,[23] one indirect consequence of which was the myth of Ritual Murder. Above all, for the purpose of this discussion, it must be noted that the Church became better organized and more centralized. In the course of the 12th century, theologians and canonists were deeply involved in the discussion of the proper relationship between the pope and the secular rulers, that is, between Church and State. A corollary of that relationship was that between the Church and the Jews.[24]

It may be well to speculate, at this point, on the spirit in which *Sicut* was issued by succeeding popes. One has the feeling—it can be no more than that at present—that, judging merely from the paucity of other defensive papal statements in the second half of the 12th century, the re-issuance of *Sicut* was still considered an effective defense of the Jewish population. In the 13th century, on the other hand, the need for fairly frequent defensive utterances appears to indicate that *Sicut* could no longer be considered effective. Its re-issuance by most 13th-century popes seems to be a gesture, a formality, part of the ceremonial connected with the official entrance of the pope into the Eternal City. This impression is strengthened by the fact that three of the 13th-century popes considered it necessary, probably at the urgent appeal of the Jews, to add a statement to the official wording of *Sicut* dealing with the Ritual Murder charges.[25] In the 14th century, in the Avignon period, the issuance of *Sicut* went out of style. Only two popes of that period issued it: Clement VI (July 4, 1348) in its original form, while a few months later he issued a longer, more specific letter of protection to warn Christians that Jews must not be accused of causing the Black Death by poisoning the water.[26] On June 7, 1365, Pope Urban V likewise issued the traditional *Sicut,* directed to the Jews of Avignon, for reasons which cannot be specified.[26a] It was issued in the 15th century by Pope Martin V, on February 20, 1422.[27] It began with the usual wording, and went on to warn the monks to stop arousing the populace against the Jews. Finally, a *Sicut* was issued by Pope Eugenius IV (January 25, 1432), which turned into an order that the Jews in the State of the Church must not be burdened to excess with exactions of all kinds.[28] Clearly, the document on which popes and Jews at first relied as a means of protection lost its efficacy sometime during the 13th century. When and how did this change take place?

The turning point seems to have been the *Sicut* issued by Innocent III (September 15, 1199). He made no changes in the by then already traditional text; he did, however, add a prefatory statement. He thought it necessary to explain that he took the Bull seriously because it reflected the theological principle enunciated by Augustine, namely, that the Jews should not be oppressed too severely, since they bear witness to the truth of Christianity.[29] Even more than the need for the appendices mentioned above, this statement by Innocent III shows that, barely eighty years after its origin, the *Sicut* bull was reduced to little more than an exhortation that for the sake of tradition, Christians ought not to kill the Jews in their midst, even though their presence is intolerable.[30] The same view was taken by most of Innocent's successors. They saw no contradiction between issuing *Sicut* and urging action directly contrary to its letter and spirit. For to their minds there was no contradiction: they were acting in the spirit of their age, which—as we shall see—did not tolerate religious deviation and which some moderns have, for that very reason, admiringly called "The Age of Faith." People of that age did in fact consider the mere repetition of *Sicut* as an act of grace, an example of *mansuetudo* or *pietas Christiana.*

The primary appeal of *Sicut* was for the safety of the Jews in life and property and for their privilege of observing their religion unless they chose to abandon it of their own free will.[31] Decretalists and popes continued to insist that conversion must be voluntary, but with a difference. Gratian (*ca.* 1140), who laid the foundation for official Canon Law, chose to emphasize, not the nature or the degree of force used in converting Jews, but rather the sanctity of the formula spoken while they were being baptized. He said:[32]

> . . . Therefore they are not to be induced to conversion by force, but by the use of their judgment. Those, however, who had already been compelled—as happened in the days of the very religious prince, Sisebut—inasmuch as by accepting the grace of baptism they had become associated with the divine sacraments, . . . it is only proper that they be compelled to retain the faith they had accepted, whether by force or necessity, lest the name of the Lord be blasphemed and the faith they had assumed be considered vile and contemptible.

Gratian's ruling was, of course, not yet official. But whatever doubts remained on the subject of the converts' reversion to their original faith were removed by Innocent III in 1201.[33] The Archbishop of Arles, apparently faced with an actual situation, was not sure that Gratian's decision was correct; he may have recognized the conflict between Gratian and the statement in *Sicut*. He therefore turned to Pope Innocent with a series of questions on doubtful baptisms: of a person baptized while asleep, of an infant baptized without the consent of its parents, and of a baptism under compulsion. To the last instance the pope replied practically in the words of Gratian and of IV Toledo. A distinction should be made, he said, between people, who, when under compulsion, objected vocally and continuously, and such as objected inwardly or not insistently: the baptism of the latter is valid and they must be compelled to remain Christians. "It is better to object unmistakably than to consent in the slightest degree." Considering that, at that time, almost all conversions from Judaism were the result of riots, with the knife literally at the Jew's throat, it is difficult to see how Innocent's view, and its ultimate inclusion in the *Corpus Juris Canonici*,[34] can be anything but a negation of *Sicut*. Indeed, it all but made rioting a holy endeavor. For every riot took its toll, both of those who protested insistently, even unto death, and of those who refused martyrdom and soon became subject to inquisitional investigation.[35]

A related problem, one on which Church opinion varied through the years, concerned the infant children of Jews. *Sicut* said nothing about children; the subject had not been broached at the time of the Bull's first issuance. Perhaps humaneness was then more important than theology. In the 13th century it occurred to some theologians that to leave children under the authority of unbelieving parents was to endanger their souls.[36] Consequently, they suggested that, since Christian princes claimed the Jews as their slaves, they could and should take away their children and have them baptized. Thomas Aquinas, however, after listing the arguments for doing so, rejected the idea on several interesting grounds.[37] Nothing of the kind had ever been done by important Christians, either emperors or theologians.[38] If the baptized children remained with their parents, there was always the possibility that the parents might influence them and that their Christianity might become doubtful. Above all, Aquinas argued in a long introduction to his objections, the removal of children from their parents was contrary to Natural Law which is equivalent to Divine Law.[39] Duns Scotus, in the generation following that of Aquinas, took issue with him on this point: God's rights over the child are superior to the rights of the parents.[40] As for those who argued that to take children away from their parents was to use force in conversion of the parents, the answer was that only the Church could define the meaning of the term "force."

It may be noted in this connection that one of the popes in the second half of the 13th century—it may have been Clement IV (1265-1268)[41]—took a stand against the baptism of a child. He wrote to a certain bishop ordering him to have a child that had been abducted returned to its parents. He offered two reasons for the return of the child, a girl of seven: a) the father offered to let her remain a Christian; b) not to return the child would give some critics an opening for maligning the Church.

The imposition of the Jewish Badge by the IV Lateran Council was also contrary to the urging of *Sicut,* which states that no change ought to be made in the customs of a land which Jews inhabit.[42] No one could have taken seriously the charge of immorality by which the imposition of the Badge was justified. Instances of immorality between Jews and Christians no doubt occurred, but to involve all the Jews was patently absurd.[43] It was more likely to have been intended, as both Jews and Christians understood it from the first, to further social and commercial separation, exactly the sort of thing the early *Sicut*s were meant to prevent. Since the enforcement of the Badge was not in the hands of the Church, the civil governments sometimes did and sometimes did not enforce it, depending apparently on the personal and financial influence of the Jews concerned.[44]

Still another indication of the waning influence of *Sicut* were the two attacks on the Talmud during the 13th century. There is no need to go into the oft-told story of the charges against the Talmud, its trial, condemnation, and its burning in Paris in 1242. Gregory IX's widely circulated letter in 1239[45] made no secret of his hope that the elimination of the Talmud would expedite the conversion of the Jews and of his horror at the blasphemies it contained.[46] But it was the aftermath of the trial that showed the erosion of *Sicut*. More copies of the Talmud and of other rabbinic works seem to have been found and confiscated in the years that followed. Thereupon the Jews managed to persuade Pope Innocent IV (1243–1254) that these books were essential for their understanding and observance of Judaism, a right which *Sicut* conceded. Certainly the books were no danger to Christendom, since very few Christians could read them. The pope, in general not unfavorably disposed to the Jews, was ready to order the books returned to them. But Odo of Châteauroux, his legate to France, voiced strong objection. "The Jewish teachers of the Kingdom of France," he said, "told a falsehood to Your Holiness and to the venerable fathers, the cardinals, when they claimed that, without these books, which in Hebrew are called Talmud, they could not understand the Bible and other ordinances of their faith."[47] It was perhaps not to be expected that Bishop Odo, considering the mentality of his day, would not realize the effrontery of his remark that he knew better than the Jews what they needed for the practice of their own religion. But Pope Innocent knew better; yet he too failed to realize that, by changing his mind about the return of the books, he was interfering with the rights of the Jews to observe Judaism, which had long been theirs and which *Sicut* granted.

The results of the Paris disputation were not lost on the Dominicans of Aragon. King James I of Aragon (1213–1276) had not reacted to the papal letter about the Talmud in 1239; indeed, he was getting along very well with the Jews of his dominions. It seemed clear to the Dominicans of Aragon that they should do no less than had been done at Paris. But to arrange a trial on Aragonese soil, they needed a learned ex-Jew like Nicolas Donin. About 1260, they were joined by a convert named Paul, and he assured them that he could surpass Donin's achievement, that he could prove that the Talmud, not only contained blasphemies against Christianity, but also contained proof of the truth of Christianity.[48] The most respected Dominican of that day was Raymond of Peñaforte,[49] an experienced polemicist, an expert in Canon Law, and a person highly regarded by King James. Pressure was therefore brought on the king to arrange a public disputation on the Talmud.[50] To oppose Paul Christian the monks prevailed on the king to compel the participation of Nahmanides (Moses ben Nahman), at the time the foremost talmudic scholar in Aragon. The disputation took place in Barcelona on July 20 to 27, 1263.[51]

Again the course of the disputation is less important for our purpose than its aftermath: the efforts made by the monks to curtail the freedom of the Jews to observe their religion as they used to. The Dominicans naturally proclaimed the result of the disputation as a victory for their side.[52] Shortly thereafter, undoubtedly at the insistence of the friars, the king issued a number of edicts. One was addressed to the royal officers, commanding them to aid the Dominicans by compelling Muslims and Jews to listen to conversionary sermons.[53] Another royal command ordered the Jews to erase or remove from their books whatever blasphemies the Dominicans might point out to them or which they themselves knew to be there.[54] It is noteworthy that Maimonides' *Mishneh Torah* merited a separate edict—it was to be burned wherever the monks found it, since it spoke of the messiah in terms unacceptable to Christianity.[55]

The Jews, in their turn, reacted by pointing out to the king the effect that these decrees were having on their persons and on their faith. In a matter of months, the king modified his decrees. Since the Jews were physically endangered when they left their own quarters to listen to the Christian sermons, the king agreed that they did not have to go outside their district. Moreover, if the friars came into the Jewish quarter to preach, they should be accompanied, not by a mob, but by only ten respectable men.[56] Also, the Jews did not have to erase passages that they themselves deemed blasphemous; they could wait until the monks pointed out such passages to them, and they could then defend such passages and take an oath they were not meant in the sense in which the monks understood them.[57] Such was the royal compromise; it did not deny censorship, but set limits to it; it did not abolish conversionary preaching, but curtailed its use for stirring riots.

But the greatest disappointment for the Dominicans was connected with Nahmanides. He disappeared from view for over a year following the disputation, perhaps for safety's sake. He had, in the meantime, composed a book in which he gave his version of the argument; and according to it he had had the better of it.[58] This infuriated the Dominicans, and they complained to the king, who apparently gave them little satisfaction.[59] Thereupon, they sent Paul Christian to Rome to submit their case to the pope.

Late in the year 1266, Pope Clement IV wrote to King James in what must be described as highly critical terms.[60] After recalling the king's great services to Christendom in having conquered so much territory from the Muslims, the pope enumerates the king's misdeeds: first in permitting so much freedom to the conquered Muslims, and, secondly, giving so much leeway to the Jews. With papal claims to supreme authority clearly in mind, Pope Clement asserts that it is for the pope, not the king, to decide what privileges Jews are to enjoy.[61] The letter concludes with a demand that the king punish the man who, after the disputation with Brother Paul, wrote a book full of falsehoods and had it widely distributed. Such insolence deserves chastisement, though not such as might endanger life and limb.[62] Since this last phrase was the one used by the Inquisition when it relaxed a condemned heretic to the secular arm, it seems to suggest that the punishment was to be most severe. In any event, Nahmanides, warned—possibly through the king— of impending trouble and perhaps unwilling to embarrass the friendly king, left his native country and spent his few remaining years in the Holy Land.

The above-mentioned letter had been dispatched to King James by the hand of Paul Christian. It produced no results. The king's relaxation of his various edicts and the flight of Nahmanides deprived the Domini- cans of whatever triumph they had expected to gain from the disputation. Not only was the Talmud not burned, as it had been in Paris, but the Jews were now permitted to challenge every accusation levelled against it.[63] This is apparently why Paul was again sent to Rome, and why, barely half a year later, Pope Clement sent another vigorous letter to King James, seconded this time by one of like tenor addressed to the prelates of Aragon.[64]

This second Bull begins with invective against the Jews reminiscent of the one issued by Innocent III in 1205 about the Jews of Champagne.[65] It continues with accusations against the Talmud, as in Gregory IX's Bulls of 1239.[66] And it concludes with instructions that the talmudic books be confiscated and examined by a commission which was to include Paul, in order to make sure that the books contained no blasphemies. Only such books may be restored to the Jews as contained no falsehoods and no insults to Christianity.[67] There is no evidence that King James complied.

Whatever the two dramatic trials of rabbinic literature achieved in terms of degrading Judaism and the Jews in the opinion of Christians, they made meaningless the Church's promise in *Sicut* to leave Judaism entirely to the Jews. And if the attempt to deprive the Jews of the Talmud largely failed in Spain in 1263, it did not stop attacks on, and burnings of, the Talmud in later years.[68]

What then remained of *Sicut* in the second half of the 13th century? Practically little more was left than that living Jews, when all was peaceful around them, could not be compelled to accept baptism, and that dead Jews might remain in their cemeteries undisturbed. Even the reason why Jews were to be permitted to dwell in the midst of Christians was beginning to undergo a change of emphasis. Innocent III and his 13th century successors still relied on Augustine's remark about the need for Jews as witnesses of Christian truth; later popes stressed that part of the remark which emphasized the desirability of degrading them.[68a] If they were at all conscious of the effects of their actions, they naturally blamed everything on the Jews—their blindness, their stubbornness, their hatred of Christianity, its symbols and its beliefs.[68b]

One of the chief issues in the 12th and 13th centuries was the question of jurisdiction: did the Church or the State possess supreme authority? Could a pope have authority over an emperor, not only in the latter's status as a Christian, but also in his capacity as civil ruler?[69] One of the complicating aspects of this situation—though certainly a lesser one—was the ancient Christian tradition affecting the ecclesiastical jurisdiction over the Jews, or any other non-Christian.

It was traced back to a statement by Paul in I Cor. 5:12-13: "For what have I to do to judge them that are without *(qui foris sunt)*? Do not ye judge them that are within? But them that are without God judgeth." According to Augustine, this meant abstention from judging those who are not under Christian law, whom the Church could not discipline. The canonist Gratian quotes Augustine and accepts his view.[70] Innocent III likewise fell back on this principle in dealing with a case of divorce involving a non-Christian.[71]

On the basis of this *foris* principle, the Church could not interfere with Jews at all. Matters spiritual fell directly into this category; as to material matters, they were the concern of civil law and local civil authorities. An ecclesiastic could deal with nonreligious matters only if he was at the same time the civil ruler, as happened fairly often. Yet there was always the problem of a Jew violating a Church regulation, like failing to pay the tithe on property which had once belonged to a Christian, or treating a cleric with disrespect, or not wearing the Badge. In such cases, if the local civil ruler refused to punish the recalcitrant Jew, the Church resorted to indirect punishment, that is, to threatening with excommunication those Christians who refused to suspend their social and economic relations with the Jew or Jews involved. This method, called *judicium Judaeorum,* was so common and had been used for so long that the term came to be applied to situations that had nothing to do with Jews.[72]

It galled the decretalists and the canonists of the 13th century to see limitations placed on the authority of the pope. Even though *foris* was of Biblical origin, they sought and found a Biblical argument to supersede it. Since all God's creatures were God's flock over whom Peter has been placed as shepherd,[73] the pope, being Peter's successor, has unquestionable authority over secular rulers. Now Jews were subservient to these rulers and therefore came under ecclesiastical authority. This conclusion was drawn by Sinibaldus Fieschi (Pope Innocent IV) in the commentary which he prepared on the decretals which the learned Raymond de Peñaforte had prepared for Gregory IX. There are three situations, Pope Innocent declared in his commentary, so basic to the welfare of Christianity as to supersede the rule of *foris* and bring Jews under the direct jurisdiction of the Church: Granted that he could not force unbelievers to convert, the pope could nevertheless force them to listen to conversionary sermons intended to lead them from ignorance to truth.[74] Secondly, he could punish them when they violated the laws of nature: for example, when they led immoral lives by cohabiting with Christians.[75] Thirdly, the pope could order them punished when they acted against divine law, as when they blasphemed against Christianity, or even when they violated their own law and were not punished for it by their own religious guides.[76] It seems, however, that in all such cases the pope was willing to work through the territorial princes.

Thus, in the days of Innocent IV, the middle of the 13th century, the attempt to extend ecclesiastical jurisdiction to the Jews was still theory. Even the condemnation of the Talmud depended for its execution on the civil government. The princes were still far from willing to relinquish their full authority over their Jews. But the idea of a dominant Church was to bear fruit in time, if not in most respects, certainly with respect to lowering the status of Jews.[76a] That status fell increasingly under Church definition as the economic position of the Jews declined, as the attitude of the princes to them changed, and as the propaganda of the friars penetrated ever wider circles of the Christian population.

Broad Church jurisdiction over Jews was achieved through the Inquisition. This new organization came into being as a result of the heresies rampant in southern France at the end of the 12th and in the 13th centuries. The crusade that Innocent III organized against the Albigenses and the other heretical sects laid waste the province, but did not destroy the heresies, exponents of which now spread through Central France and Northern Italy. The Dominican and Franciscan Orders were organized for the specific purpose of combatting heresy by preaching and example; but their progress by these methods was understandably slow. Gregory IX, in the early 1230's, therefore, decided to attack the problem more directly and vigorously. The searching out of heretics was taken out of the hands of the bishops, where it had rested until then, and was transferred to investigating committees appointed from among the members of the Mendicant Orders. It was expected that these committees of inquiry, or inquisitors, under the direct control of, and responsible to, the pope, would be more effective in ferreting out the heretics and punishing them.[77] Not even the princes who were most jealous of their rights and jurisdiction could object. After all, heresy was considered equivalent to treason—worse, since it was treason against God—and treason merited the severest kind of punishment.[78] From its very beginning the Inquisition proved efficient. Whenever it wanted additional powers, it turned to the pope and was rarely refused.[79] By the 1260's, it was in full bloom.

From the first, the powers of the inquisitors extended, not only to practicing heretics, but also to those who sympathized with them, or protected them, or received them in their homes (*fautores, protectores, receptatores*).[80] The wide circle of those whom the Inquisition could consider suspect must have included many who were quite innocent of heresy. Nor did the procedures of the Inquisition inspire confidence, since there was hardly a chance for defense, and punishment was severe.[81] One must conclude that inquisitors were none too popular in any community. In the course of the 13th century, there were a few popular uprisings against the Inquisition and some assassinations of inquisitors. Pope Urban IV (1261–1264) found it necessary to declare null and void any regulation by a local authority that stood in the way of the Inquisition's work. His successor, Clement IV, required local officials to take an oath that they will not impede its work.[82] It would be hardly surprising, therefore, if Jews threatened by the Inquisition, whether as reverts to Judaism or as aids to any such, took advantage of the Inquisition's unpopularity in whatever way they could. But they occasioned thereby the issuance of a fateful Bull directed against them.

The great majority of those accused of heresy by the Inquisition of the Middle Ages were undoubtedly of non-Jewish origin. But there certainly were some Jews who, having been caught in a riot and been baptized under duress, tried to return to the faith of their fathers or to observe it to whatever extent they could or dared.[83] From the viewpoint of the Inquisition, they had "not been precisely coerced," so that their baptism was valid.[84] The convert, however, knew better, and so did his relatives and friends. They may have hidden him (or her) until he could be smuggled out to a foreign land where he might resume the practice of Judaism.[85] If that is what happened, the local inquisitor spared no effort to locate the escapee. The simplest means was to hale a Jewish relative or friend before the inquisitional court and by threat or some other means extort the required information.[86] Or a pious or hostile Christian neighbor might accuse a Jew of harboring a suspicious guest.[87] In any event, there were openings for an inquisitor to claim jurisdiction over individual Jews and occasionally over entire communities.

Still another consideration must be kept in mind when discussing reversions to Judaism. Christian princes had always been especially jealous of their control of Jews who were their *servi camerae*. The conversion of a Jew meant the loss of control over his possessions and income. Consequently the conversion of a Jew led to the confiscation of his property by the prince, who sometimes handed it back to the convert's Jewish relatives so that they might continue to make profit out of it for the prince. The Church had always protested against the resulting impoverishment of the convert.[88] Now, however, in the case of most reverts to Judaism, the property had already been lost in the riot which had brought about the baptism, or been otherwise disposed of, often to the benefit of the prince. The usual prince might, therefore, not object to action by the Inquisition against converts under suspicion of reversion, since the prince was losing nothing by it. But he would object strenuously to the inquisitor's accusing, arresting, and imposing a heavy fine on unbaptized Jews on the charge of being *fautores*. The subject will necessarily come up again. But what has to be said at this point is that this kind of interference by princes, added to the difficulties interposed by the principle of *foris*, probably prompted the inquisitors to turn to the pope with a request for further aid.

On July 27, 1267, barely two weeks after having dispatched the bull *Damnabili*[89] to King James of Aragon, Pope Clement IV issued his *Turbato corde*:[90]

> With a troubled heart we relate what we have heard: A number of bad Christians have abandoned the true Christian faith and wickedly transferred themselves to the rites of the Jews. This is obviously the more reprehensible since it makes it possible for the most holy name of Christ to be more safely blasphemed by enemies out of his own household. We have been informed, moreover, that this is not without injurious effect on the said faith, and it should therefore be countered by means of quick and appropriate remedies.
>
> We order your organization *(universitati vestrae)*, within the territories entrusted to you by the Apostolic See for searching out heretics, to make diligent and thorough inquiry into the above, through Christians as well as through Jews. Against Christians whom you find guilty of the above you shall proceed as against heretics. Upon Jews whom you may find guilty of having induced Christians of either sex to join their execrable rites, or whom you may find doing so in the future, you shall impose fitting punishment. By means of appropriate ecclesiastical censure you shall silence all who oppose you. If necessary, you may call on the secular arm.

It is not surprising that the Inquisition asked several suceeding popes for a reissue of this Bull. But it is interesting that the succeeding issues[91] were slightly but significantly modified. The Inquisition apparently felt that the above-cited form did not cover two important points: It did not specify that the chief problem was with converts from Judaism and with Jews who tried to draw them back into the Jewish faith; and it did not openly say that Jews were trying to subvert the faith of born Christians. When *Turbato* was repeated, it began as follows:[92]

> With a troubled heart we relate what we have heard: Not only are certain converts from the error of Jewish blindness to the light of the Christian faith known to have reverted to their former false belief, but even [born] Christians, denying the true Catholic faith, have wickedly transferred themselves to the rites of Judaism. . . .

There were thus four categories of person over whom the Inquisition sought and was given authority: born Jews who had been baptized and the Jews who presumably helped them to return to Judaism, and born Christians who were attracted to Judaism, and the Jews who allegedly lured them into the Jewish religion. There was, to be sure, a fifth category, of Jews who laid themselves open to the charge of blasphemy by retaining copies of the Talmud in their possession. But at least in the 13th century the Inquisition did not bother with these or other acts of alleged blasphemy by Jews, such as the charge of desecrating the Host levelled against them in Paris in 1290.[93] Local clergy and friars were active in Host desecration charges. As to the Talmud, that charge continued to be raised sporadically, whenever the Church reminded itself of the subject.[94] Besides, it involved entire communities, whereas for the time being the Inquisition was concerned only with individual Jews.

Before turning to the charge that Jews aided baptized but repentant Jews, it is necessary to examine the charge that they actively engaged in the proselytization of born Christians. It is impossible to estimate the number of Christians who adopted Judaism in the course of the centuries when the Inquisition of the Middle Ages was active.[95] Such action was fraught with great danger for both convert and converter.[96] Consequently when it did take place, it was either kept secret or became notorious. Certainly there were more instances of this than became known. Yet even if the actual number was tenfold that known, it would hardly have justified the frequency and the expressions of outrage with which several popes made the charge in terms that lead one to believe that conversions of born Christians was a real problem for the Church.

What appears to have been really involved was the matter of social contact between Christians and Jews. An explicit illustration of how Jews led Christians to "Judaize" may be seen in the letter which Pope Honorius IV (1285–1287) addressed to John Peckham of Canterbury and to other English prelates in 1286.[97] Among the misdeeds of which the Jews were accused—teaching the Talmud to their children, employing Christian domestics, cursing Christianity in their prayers, luring ex-Jews back to Judaism—was the charge that they[98] miss no opportunity to invite followers of the orthodox faith to attend services in their synagogues on Sabbaths and on other solemn occasions, when they observe their rites in accordance with their customs, when they show reverence to their parchment scroll in which their Law is written. On such occasions many Christians Judaize along with the Jews. . . .

In the same letter one finds additional information—doubtless also given the pope by the archbishop—that Christians in the England of that day visited Jewish homes, where they ate and drank. This too was considered dangerous, because it was bound to lead to discussions of religion, an action forbidden by Canon Law except to those especially equipped for it.[99] This Bull, and others which charge deliberate proselytization efforts by Jews, leave the clear impression that the term "to Judaize" meant to associate with Jews, and not necessarily to become one of them. The danger was a potential one.[100]

Other papal pronouncements fortify this impression. Thus the bull *Damnabili*[101] sent to the prelates of the Provence and Toulouse in December, 1267, begins the list of Jewish misdeeds with a statement that the Jews lure simple Christian souls into their damnable rites, and proceeds to illustrate the charge by listing their employment of Christian domestics, not wearing the Badge, and failing to obey other canonical restrictions on Jewish life. Two other papal letters, both sent by Nicolas IV on January 28, 1290, urged the prelates of southern France and the civil authorities of the Comtat Venaissin to cooperate with the inquisitors in their search for baptized Jews who reverted to Judaism and for Jews who came to their aid. Such Jews, the pope said, were also active among born Christians and made every effort to infect them with heresy.[102] A month later, the pope wrote to the inquisitors of the same provinces, instructing them vigorously to pursue these destroyers of the faith, be they Jews or Christians.[103]

It is not difficult to understand why the cooperation of the bishops had not been forthcoming. They had, from the first, resented the Inquisition's intrusion into an area which had previously been theirs, not to mention the matter of income from fines and confiscations. The inclusion of the Jews in the Inquisition's range of activity made for further dissatisfaction. Indeed, the quarrel between the episcopal and inquisitional branches of the Church were to continue to occupy the attention of the Ecumenical Council of Vienne in 1311–1312.[104] As to the differences between the Inquisition and the civil governments, it has been spoken of already and will be again below. These differences may have reached a critical stage about 1290. In any event, the Inquisition found that its hold could be strengthened on suspected converts from Judaism, especially if its attack could be fortified by an accusation that Jews were carrying on active propaganda among born Christians.[105] It was self-serving propaganda, and it resulted in increasing hostility between Christians and Jews.

There can be little doubt, however, that under the definition of "force" which the Church had adopted, the problem posed by converts from Judaism was real. They would not, or could not, completely and suddenly break with the faith of their fathers. A number of papal letters illustrate how this problem manifested itself. One such letter[106] speaks of a riot which occurred in the county of La Marche, in central France, about 1280. A number of Jews chose baptism rather than death, and they naturally asked that their infant children also be baptized. Subsequently, the riot over, they wanted to return to Judaism. The inquisitors thereupon imprisoned them and kept them in their jail for over a year. But the Jews steadfastly refused to adhere to Christianity. The inquisitors, perhaps impressed by such persistence, turned to the pope for guidance. The pope replied that they should be treated as heretics. For they had not been strictly speaking forced into conversion *(non precise coacti)*, as seemed clear from the fact that they had of their own free will offered their children for baptism.[107]

Another letter[108] of Pope Nicolas IV lists the activities by which the disloyalty of the converts might be recognized. Addressing the inquisitors of the provinces whose prelates he had urged a few months earlier[109] to cooperate in the search for secret Judaizers, he speaks of their suspicious actions. In times of personal crisis, they bring candles and lamps to the synagogue and make special offerings there. They hold vigils, especially on the Sabbath, that the sick may regain their health, that the ship-wrecked may reach a safe port, that women in childbirth may come through safely, that the sterile may be blessed with children. They show reverence to the Scroll of the Law as though it were an idol. Against these the inquisitors were granted permission to proceed as against heretics and idol worshipers.[110]

In fact, one might spend a lifetime unsuspected of judaizing and reveal his true inclinations when on the point of death. This was the case in Southern Burgundy (the later Franche Comté). On the surface it appeared that the Inquisition had nothing to do in that province; no Jews lived there, nor any known ex-Jews. Yet in 1267, the inquisitors, while searching the neighborhood for Waldensians, were informed about residents of the province who, on their deathbed, had confessed to their Jewish sympathies. The inquisitors promptly informed Pope Clement IV; he in turn wrote to Jean de Salins, Count of Burgundy, to say that it was his duty to let the inquisitors operate in his territory.[111] Not only was it probable that there were Judaizers among the living, but according to the rules of the Inquisition, it could disinter the dead, confiscate what property they had bequeathed to their children, and impose serious penalties and restrictions on them.[112]

As already mentioned, the attitude of suspicion toward converts spilled over into suspicion of any Jew who might have been in contact with a convert.[113] Such a Jew, accused of aiding an ex-Jew to revert to Judaism, was more defenseless against his accusers than any outright heretic, who could conceivably obtain favorable testimony from a credible Christian. A Jew accused of being a *fautor* had only one recourse: he could appeal to his overlord. Not that the princes were lacking in piety—they were simply protecting their rights and, quite directly, their property. For if found guilty, the Jew's property would, in large measure, be taken by the Inquisition in fines or outright confiscation.[114]

Instances of such protection can be cited for almost every country after the issuance of *Turbato*. Even before the issuance of this Bull, as already noted, King James I of Aragon took all matters connected with the Barcelona disputation out of the hands of the Church.[115] In 1275, the same king threatened to impose a heavy fine on anyone, layman or cleric, who cited the Jews of Perpignan (then part of his domain) before an ecclesiastical court, as long as they were willing to appear before a royal court.[116] A day later, he informed the Jews of Southern France—those under his rule—that, unless his officers agreed to the contrary, they were under no obligation to change their places of residence because of an ecclesiastical order.[117] He even took the charge of blasphemy out of the hands of the Church.[118] James' son, Peter III, in September 1284, ordered his officials to make the inquisitors stop investigating certain Jews on a charge of having opened their doors to some converts. If these Jews are to be punished, he said, he will do the punishing.[119] Peter's son, James II, expressed himself in the same vein to inquisitors in 1292: "Since," he said, "Jews are not of the Catholic faith or under Catholic law, if they do anything against the law, he will punish them, not they."[120]

The French royal attitude was essentially no different. There were few differences between king and Inquisition under the pious Louis IX; the king sympathized with the Inquisition, and the inquisitors were careful with the king. But the situation took a different turn under the self-willed Philip IV (the Fair), Louis's grandson. Philip repeatedly opposed the claims of the Inquisition where Jews were concerned. Not that he had any special affection for Jews—he was to expel them from his territory in 1306 because he badly needed their confiscated money and property. His interest in them was purely financial, and his personal authority and jurisdictional rights were more important. In 1287, he ordered his officers and his seneschal in Carcassonne not to permit the molestation of his Jews, whose synagogue and cemetery were endangered.[121] He was furious when, in 1288 in the city of Troyes, thirteen Jews were haled before a clerical tribunal, tortured and executed on a charge of Ritual Murder, all of this being done without informing him or his officers.[122] In 1293, he again ordered his seneschal in the Provence not to permit the molestation of Jews without the civil authority's consent. To be sure, he included in this order a copy of the *Turbato* Bull and ordered the seneschal to observe its contents, though without pemitting this to result in the arrest and punishment of Jews.[123] The obvious double-talk can only be explained by assuming that the king wold tolerate Inquisitional jurisdiction over baptized Jews if their baptism could be proved, but not the imprisonment or fining of Jews on the charge of having been *fautores*. In 1299, however, King Philip's sentiments appear to have undergone a marked change. This was in the midst of his quarrel with Pope Boniface VIII, when the king wanted to appear more papal than the pope. He now accused the Jews of everything that the most zealous inquisitor could have thought of. But in 1302, he reverted to his original stand and would not permit inquisitors to molest his Jews in matters which were no concern of theirs, such as usury, blasphemy, or magic. Four years later, he expelled the Jews for reasons which had nothing to do with Church or Inquisition.

Still another example of protection against the Inquisition extended to the Jews by their princes is the attitude of Charles I, king of the Two Sicilies, and duke of several provinces in South-Eastern and Western France. He obviously had a freer hand in his French territories than in his Italian kingdom, where he was the vassal of the pope. That he could use his income from France to maintain himself in Italy may serve to explain his actions. But he yielded to his Jewish subjects by freeing them from the Badge, probably in return for a substantial payment. In 1276, he took a strong stand against the inquisitors in the Provence who had imprisoned a number of Jews, extorted money from them in fines, imposed an unusually large Badge on them, and subjected one of them to torture. He warned the inquisitors in no uncertain terms that they must not exercise any jurisdiction over his Jews.[124] In his Sicilian kingdom, on the other hand, Charles could not but encourage the anti-Jewish activities instigated by Manoforte in 1267.[125]

Charles I's son, Charles II, however, either out of personal ineptitude or, because, as a vassal of the pope he could not oppose the Inquisition, did not even try to defend the Jews. Under the pressure from the inquisitors, and perhaps also of the townsmen of his French provinces of Maine and Anjou, he expelled the Jews from these provinces,[126] though not from the Provence. At the same time, the inquisitors proved too much for him in Naples as well. Here conversion was soon followed by regret, and regret by inquisition, so that a flourishing Jewish community was almost totally destroyed.[127] Before long, churches in Southern Italy were complaining of impoverishment due to lack of income from Jewish sources.[128]

To summarize: whether inquisitors would have much or any authority over unbaptized Jews depended on the sovereign's character and on the local political and economic situation. To be sure, the sovereign was unreliable and could change his attitude from day to day; but at least he could not be suspected of malevolence, since the presence of Jews as his *servi camerae* was to his advantage. The dread which the Inquisition inspired, by the end of the 13th century, is evident from the fact that a certain Arnold Déjean, newly appointed inquisitor in Pamiers, felt called upon to reassure the Jews, as some of his predecessors had done. It is not the condescending tone of the brief document that calls for comment—the Jews must already have been used to *hauteur*—but the very need for assurance. In effect, the document promised nothing; it said only that, if they conducted themselves "acceptably," they would be treated acceptably. The body of the document reads as follows:[129]

> In view of the fact that the Catholic Church, hopeful and confident that God will remove the veil from your hearts, supports your presence and tolerates your rites, therefore, we, following in the footsteps of our predecessors, grant the following to your collectivity (*universitati vestrae*): You may live and conduct yourselves acceptably in manner and custom, just as the Jews of Narbonne are permitted to live and conduct themselves. We, for our part, have no intention of imposing upon you any serious or unusual innovations. We grant you this by these letters, and we affix our seal in witness of the above.

There were occasions when the popes themselves had to restrain the zeal of the inquisitors, and sometimes of other clerics and lay Christians as well. When a Jewish community pressed its complaint—whatever form that pressure might have taken, since it was never easy and always expensive to get the pope's attention—the complaint was investigated and, if found justified, the guilty party was ordered to desist. That the first order was not always effective is proved by the fact that later popes had to repeat it. One source of complaint was that Jews—sometimes even converted Jews—would be summoned to answer charges against them, not before the court in the place where they lived, but before one at some considerable distance. Sometimes this was done out of malice, to annoy or to increase the defendant's expense; usually it was done to get him to appear in a court away from the customary civil jurisdiction. A number of popes recognized the unfairness of such action, and they tried to stop it.[130]

A much more serious situation was that connected with witnesses to charges of Ritual Murder. The number of such accusations, with all their murderous consequences, increased appallingly during the German interregnum (1250–1272) and continued thereafter. In 1272, Pope Gregory X issued a *Sicut* to which he appended a long statement refuting the charge and accusing enemies of the Jews of trumping it up in order to extort money from the Jews or profiting otherwise.[131] Since this papal exhortation obviously was doing no good, Pope Martin IV, issued in 1281 a *Sicut* the most important part of which was not its stereotyped wording, but a paragraph designed to limit inimical and inquisitional activity. It made the following points: Witnesses against Jews must take a solemn oath; they must be made to understand that, if they failed to substantiate their charges, they would suffer the fate their victims would have suffered if the charges had been proved. Finally, Pope Martin said that a Jew should not be accused of encouraging a convert to return to Judaism if all that was known was that the two had been engaged in conversation.[132] Neither Gregory's refutation nor Martin's suggestion is known to have served its purpose; accusations of Ritual Murder have continued down into modern times.[133]

A part of the inquisitional procedure which some of the popes recognized as unfair to Jews (and to others) derived from the right of the inquisitors not to divulge the names of witnesses hostile to the accused. The right had been granted as far back as Innocent IV and Alexander IV, that is, in the 1250's. The excuse for secrecy in so delicate a situation was the danger to the accuser and to his witnesses, since the accused might be a "powerful person" and might be able to cause harm to his opponents.[134] But the withholding of such crucial information obviously put the accused at a great disadvantage. He had to guess who his accusers might be, what they could have said about him, and why. But this very guessing was useful to the inquisitors; as a result of it they could spread their net ever wider. The inquisitors' powers in this respect was somewhat limited later, as a result of complaints from non-Jewish sources, by a requirement that the names of witnesses should be revealed to a number of reliable persons, though still not to the accused. The limitation was imposed as a possible answer to the widespread charge that the Inquisition, by causing the accused to reveal the names of his possible enemies, was really on a perpetual "fishing expedition" for more accusers and witnesses against him.

Down to the end of the 13th century the Jews were still considered *potentes*. Any Jew could be forced to appear before the inquisitional court, and without being told of any specific charge or by whom it had been lodged, be put on trial, with his life or at least his possessions in jeopardy. One cannot tell how long or how often the Jews had protested. At long last, Boniface VIII, in 1299, issued a Bull[135] by which he granted that Jews, even the wealthy ones among them, could hardly be called "powerful." The Bull tells the Jews of Rome, to whom it was addressed, that they may demand that the inquisitors reveal to them the names of the witnesses against them. If there is any suspicion that the Jew in question is unduly influential, the matter should be referred to the pope.

A reputable Jewish historical work connects Pope Boniface's action with the tragic incident that had taken place in Rome the year before.[136] The entire Jewish community was endangered by an accusation, presumably of having tried to persuade converts to return to Judaism. The converts could well have been from among those who had fallen victim to the riots and pressures of some years previously in Southern Italy. Whatever the accusation and whoever was involved, Elias de Pomis, a highly respected leader of the Roman Jewish community, took the blame upon himself and as a result was burned at the stake.

It was clear by the end of the 13th century that failure to protect the weak from one threatening danger lays them open to others. The reign of Pope Nicholas IV (1288–1292) is instructive in this respect. In 1288, and again in 1290, he reissued *Turbato*,[137] the first time to the Inquisition in general, the second to the inquisitors in the Romagna, which was more directly under his control. In that same year 1290, he urged Churchmen in France to cooperate with the Inquisition, and he repeated the charge that Jews were actively proselytizing among born Christians.[138] For a century now, Judaism was being called a threat and the Jews a malicious lot. Should the pope have been surprised when laymen and clerics anywhere made Jewish life as difficult as they could?[139] This dual and contradictory approach to their Jewish problem should have been clear to the popes long before this. In 1290, Pope Nicholas IV felt constrained to address to his vicar in Rome an eloquent appeal for moderation on the part of the Roman population. Mother Church, he said, prays for the evil to be lifted from the hearts of the Jews; yet Churchmen are guilty of making Christianity odious to them. Pope Nicholas therefore asks his vicar to make sure that justice is done to the Jews.[140]

But that was the spirit of *Sicut*. Unfortunately for both sides the spirit of *Turbato* had replaced it.

NOTES

1. This essay is concerned mainly with the 12th and 13th centuries. It is my hope, God willing, to continue the discussion into the 14th century in another study. Research for this essay was made possible by funds provided by the generosity of

Mr. D. Hays Solis-Cohen, the Fred J. Rosenau Foundation, and the A. L. and Jennie L. Luria Foundation. I am very grateful for their help. I offer my thanks also for the courtesies extended to me by the Archivio Segreto Vaticano and by the authorities at the Library of the University of Pennsylvania, especially by its Lea Library.

2. One cannot, in the course of writing a brief essay on an important subject, refer to all the books consulted. Yet these may be the very books that stimulated interest and provided basic information. I therefore list a few of them here:

> S. W. Baron, *A Social and Religious History of the Jews,* 2nd edition, Columbia University Press and the Jewish Publication Society, 1962 ff., vols. IX to XI = Baron, *History.*
>
> Peter Browe, *Die Judenmission im Mittelalter und die Päpste,* Rome 1942 = Browe, *JM.*
>
> James Parkes, *The Conflict of the Church and the Synagogue,* London 1934 = Parkes, *Conflict; idem, The Jew in the Medieval Community,* London 1938 = Parkes, *Community.*

Other works, dealing with the Inquisition of the Middle Ages, are listed below, in n. 77.

Some other volumes, the names of which occur frequently in abbreviated form, are the following:

> Baer I = F.(Y.) Baer, *Die Juden in Christlichen Spanien, Aragonien.*
>
> Baer II = *idem, Die Juden in Christlichen Spanien, Kastilien.*
>
> ChJ = S. Grayzel, *The Church and the Jews in the 13th Century,* Philadelphia 1933.
>
> CJC = *Corpus Juris Canonici,* ed. E. Friedberg, Leipzig 1879–1881.
>
> *MGH = Monumenta Germaniae Historica.*
>
> Potthast = *Regesta Pontificum Romanorum,* 2 vols., Berlin 1874–5.
>
> Raynald. = Raynaldus, Odoricus, *Annales ecclesiastici.*
>
> Stern, *UB* = Moritz Stern, *Urkundliche Beiträge über die Stellung der Päpste zu den Juden,* Kiel 1893.

The customary abbreviations have been used for periodicals:

> JJS = *Journal of Jewish Studies.*
>
> JQR = *Jewish Quarterly Review.*
>
> HUCA = *Hebrew Union College Annual.*
>
> MGWJ = *Monatschrift für die Geschichte und Wissenschaft der Juden.*
>
> PAAJR = *Proceedings of the American Academy for Jewish Research.*
>
> REJ = *Revue des Etudes Juives.*

3. Ambrose, in his commentary on Psalm 37 (Migne, *PL* 14, col. 1062), argues that the Jews, having rejected Jesus, ceased to be. *Cf.* Jean Juster, *Les Juifs dans l'Empire Romain* (Paris 1914), I, 177 ff.; 272, n. 1.

4. Juster, *ibid.,* I, 209 ff., points to the numerical importance of the Empire's Jews, and pp. 235 ff. to the maintenance of the privileges which had been granted them by the pagan emperors. *Cf.* Grayzel, "The Jews and Roman Law," *JQR,* 59 (1968), 93–117.

5. *Cf.* Augustine's comment on Ps. 59 (58):10-12; also *City of God*, Bk. 18, ch. 46 (Everyman's Library edition, II, 221):

> Some may say that the sibyl's prophecies which concern the Jews are but fictions of the Christians. But that suffices us which we have from the books of our enemies . . . that they preserve it for us against their wills . . . in every corner of the world, as that prophecy of the psalm which they themselves do read foretells them: . . . *Slay them not, lest my people forget it, but scatter them abroad with Thy power.* . . . So it were nothing to say, *Slay them not,* but that he adds, *scatter them abroad;* for if they were not dispersed throughout the whole world with their scriptures, the Church would lack their testimonies concerning those prophecies fulfilled in our Messiah.

6. For the text of Gregory's letters see *MGH*, Epistolae, I and II. Their Jewish references are discussed by Solomon Katz, "Pope Gregory the Great and the Jews" *JQR* 24 (1933-4), 113-36; and by Parkes, *Conflict*, pp. 210-20; see also the summaries provided by B. Blumenkranz, *Les auteurs chrétiens latins du Moyen Age* (Paris 1963), pp. 73-80.

7. *MGH*, Reg. Greg. I, Bk. I, 34, March 16, 591; Jaffe 1104:

> . . . Hos enim qui a Christiana religione discordant, mansuetudine, benignitate, admonendo, suadendo ad unitatem fidei necesse est congregare. . . .

His letter to the Bishop of Palermo, *ibid.*, Bk. 8, 25, June 598; Jaffe 1514, is the one that begins with the words *Sicut Judaeis.* Only its first sentence and the sentiments were copied later.

8. For the Visigothic experience of the Jews in Spain see Bernard S. Bachrach, "A Reassessment of Visigothic Jewish Policy, 580-711," *American Historical Review*, 78 (1973), 11-34; also Parkes, *Conflict*, pp. 345-70.

9. A number of anti-Jewish outbreaks occurred in various parts of Western Europe in the course of these centuries down to the First Crusade. They are described by B. Blumenkranz, "The Roman Church and the Jews," *The Dark Ages*, ed. by Cecil Roth (Tel Aviv 1966), pp. 69-99; Cecil Roth, "Italy," *ibid.*, pp. 100-121; S. Schwarzfuchs, "France and Germany under the Carolingians," *ibid.*, pp. 122-42; *idem*, "France under the Early Capets," *ibid.*, pp. 142-61; Blumenkranz, "Germany," *ibid.*, pp. 162-74.

10. Pope Leo VII (937-939) was asked by the Archbishop of Mainz what to do with the Jews who refused to join the Church. The pope replied, in what he must have considered to be the spirit of Gregory—expulsion was apparently then not considered an act of compulsion—that he must first try to persuade: ". . . si autem credere noluerint, de civitatibus vestris cum nostra auctoritate illos expellite. Per virtutem autem et sine illorum voluntate nolite eos baptizare." Migne, *PL*, 132, col. 1083; Aronius, *Regensten zur Geschichter der Juden im fränkischen und deutschen Reiche bis zum Jahre 1273* (Berlin 1902), no. 125; Jaffe 2766: *Diebus vitae.* There is also the story of Pope John XVIII (1004-1009) sending a special emissary to save the Jews of Normandy: *cf.* V. Zimmermann, *Papsturkunden*, no. 1018. Above all, we have the expressed gratification of Pope Alexander II in 1065 that the prince of Benevento refused to force Jews into Christianity (S. Loewenfeld, *Epistolae Pontificium Romanorum ineditae* (Leipzig 1885), p. 52, no. 105), and to Viscount Berengarius of Narbonne (Jaffe 4528), as well as to other bishops,

for defending the Jews against the knights on their way to aid in the reconquest of Spain (Migne, *PL*, 146, col. 1386; Mansi, XIX, 964).

11. On the efforts of Bishops Agobard and Amulo of Lyons and their colleagues to have the Carolingian emperors impose further restrictions on the Jews, see *Agobardi Lugdunensis Archiepiscopi Epistolae, MGH,* Epistolae, V, 164, 199 f., 239 f.; Arthur J. Zuckerman, "The Political Uses of Theology, the Conflict of Bishop Agobard and the Jews of Lyons," *Studies in Medieval Culture,* III, ed. by J. R. Sommerfeldt for the Medieval Institute, Western Michigan University, 1970, pp. 23–51; Blumenkranz, *Les Auteurs,* pp. 152 ff. *Cf.* also Aronius, *Regesten,* nos. 84–97.

12. Reversion to Judaism was permitted by the early Christian emperors: *cf.* Theodosian Code (*CTh*) XVI.8.23. In later centuries, down to the First Crusade, there is also little evidence that reversion was punished, although it was of course frowned upon, except in Visigothic Spain (see next note). Even a century later, when, at the time of Richard's coronation, Benedict of York was forcibly converted, the archbishop of Canterbury permitted his reversion to Judaism (*cf.* Joseph Jacobs, *The Jews of Angevin England* [London 1893], p. 106). Henry IV's permission to revert to Judaism is discussed by Parkes, *Community* (2nd ed., New York 1976), pp. 79 f.; Aronius, *Regesten,* no. 203. *Cf.* Browe, *JM,* pp. 252 ff. Sara Schiffmann, "Heinrichs IV. Verhalten zu den Juden zur Zeit des ersten Kreuzzuges," *Zeitschrift für die Geschichte der Juden in Deutschland,* 1931, 39–58, esp. p. 50.

13. "Relatum est nobis a quibusdam quod Judaeis baptizatis, nescio qua ratione . . .": Philip Jaffe, *Monumenta Bamburgensis* (vol. V of Bibliotheca rerum Germanicarum), p. 75, no. 90; Aronius, *Regesten,* no. 204; Jaffe 5339 [4013]. The reference to this being prohibited by Canon Law—"secundum canonicam sanctionem"—can refer only to the IV Council of Toledo (Dec. 633) and to the inclusion of the same attitude in subsequent canons of various Church councils. No papal expression and no universally accepted code of Canon Law was as yet in existence to prohibit reversion to Judaism.

14. For the Landfrieden of Mainz in 1103, see Aronius, *Regesten,* no. 210. The Jews were taken under imperial protection, along with churches, clerics, monks, laymen, merchants, and women. This automatically deprived them of the right of self-defense, that is, the right to carry weapons. In a sense this had social disadvantages: *cf.* Kisch, *The Jews in Medieval Germany* (Chicago 1949), pp. 140 ff. It led before long to the evolution of the concept of the Jews as *servi camerae.*

15. For a discussion of *Sicut* see Grayzel, "The Papal Bull *Sicut Judaeis,*" *Studies and Essays in Honor of Abraham A. Neuman,* ed. by Meir Ben-Horin, Bernard D. Weinryb, and Solomon Zeitlin (Philadelphia 1962), pp. 243–280. There, on pp. 244 ff., the Bull is given in full. It is also given in Grayzel, *ChJ* (2nd ed., New York 1966), p. 92, no. 5, with the addition by Pope Innocent III (Potthast 834, *Licet perfidia*). *Cf.* Baron, *History,* IV, 7 f.; J. R. Marcus, *The Jew in the Medieval World,* (Cincinnati 1938), pp. 152 f., with the addition by Gregory X.

16. "Sicut Judaeis non debet esse licentia in synagogis suis ultra permissum est lege presumere, ita in his que eis concessa sunt nullum debet prejudicium sustinere. Nos ergo licet in sua magis velint duritia perdurare quam prophetarum

verba et suarum scripturarum arcana cognoscere atque ad Christianae fidei et salutis notitiam pervenire, quia tamen defensionem nostram et auxilium postulant, ex Christianae pietatis mansuetudine [At this point, succeeding issues of the Bull mentioned the names of all or most of the predecessors who had issued it.], ipsorum petitionem admittimus eisque protectionis nostre clypeum indulgemus."

17. "Statuimus etiam ut nullus Christianus invitos vel nolentes eos ad baptismum per violentiam venire compellat. . . . Veram quippe Christianitatis fidem habere non creditur qui ad Christianorum baptisma non spontaneus sed invitus cognoscitur pervenire."

18. "Nullus etiam Christianus eorum personas sine judicio potestatis terrae vulnerare aut occidere vel suas pecunias auferre presumat."

19. "aut bonas quas hactenus in ea qua habitant regione habuerint consuetudines immutare."

20. ". . . decernimus ut nemo cemetarium Judeorum mutilare vel minuere audeat, sive obtentu pecunie corpora humata effodere."

21. "Eos autem dumtaxat huius protectionis presidio volumus communiri qui nihil machinari presumpserint in subversionem fidei Christianae."

22. *Cf.* Robert S. Lopez, *The Commercial Revolution of the Middle Ages, 950–1350* (New York, Prentice-Hall, 1971), esp. pp. 121 f.

23. During the Second Crusade, 1144 and for a few following years, Pope Eugenius III was not heard from when the Jews of Germany were again in danger, but Bernard of Clairvaux did intervene in their behalf. See his letter to Henry, Archbishop of Mainz (1146) in Bruno James, *The Letters of Bernard of Clairvaux* (Chicago 1953), pp. 465 f., no. 465.

24. *Cf.* S. W. Baron, "Plenitude of Apostolic Power and Medieval Jewish Serfdom" (Hebrew), *Sefer Yobel leYitzhak Baer* (Jerusalem 1960), pp. 102–124; *idem,* "Medieval Nationalism and Jewish Serfdom," *Studies and Essays in Honor of Abraham A. Neuman* (Philadelphia, Dropsie College 1962), pp. 17–48; Kisch, *Germany,* 145–53. *Cf.* also Walter Ullmann, *The Growth of Papal Government in the Middle Ages,* I (London 1962), ch. 13, pp. 413–446.

25. Innocent IV in 1247; Gregory X in 1272; Martin IV in 1281. The additions are noted in the essay in the Neuman *Studies,* pp. 258– 61. They are also discussed below.

26. Reg. Vat. 187, 20v–21r has the two Bulls: *Quamvis perfidiam* as no. 105, and *Sicut* as no. 106. Raynald, a.a. 1348 #33, runs them together. Both were occasioned by the charge that the Black Death was due to the Jews poisoning the drinking water, and *Quamvis* urges the prelates to fight against the charge. *Quamvis* is given in full in A. Lang, *Acta Salzburgo-Aquilajensia,* I (Graz 1903), pp. 300 f.

26a. Reg. Vat. 254, fol. 34r.; *Bull. Rom.* III, 22, 327. Clement VII of the Avignon succession issued a Bull on October 18, 1379, which begins like a *Sicut* but continues as a defense of the Jews of Avignon against a compulsory change of residence (Reg. Avin. 215, fol. 158r–v). He issued the usual *Sicut* on November 12, 1393 (Reg. Avin. 273, fol. 354r.).

27. Félix Vernet, "Le Pape Martin V et les Juifs," *Revue des questions historiques,* LI (1892), 373–423, lists a number of Bulls issued by Pope Martin that began

with the phrase *Sicut Judaeis,* and even listed preceding popes who issued a *Sicut,* but soon went off into matters of immediate moment to the Jews. So no. 9 of his appended list (p. 411) is given by Raynald, a.a. 1419 #2. So too no. 24, given at Rome on February 20, 1422, is the one cited by Moritz Stern, *UB,* pp. 31 ff., and quoted by Raynald, a.a. 1422 #36.

28. The Bull is given in full in Stern, *UB,* p. 43, no. 34.

29. The few lines read as follows: "Licet perfidia Judaeorum sit multipliciter reprobanda, quia tamen per eos fides nostra veraciter comprobatur, non sunt a fidelibus graviter opprimendi. . . . quam ipsi non intelligentes, in libris suis intelligentibus representant." *Cf.* Neuman, *Studies,* p. 256; *ChJ,* p. 92; Potthast, 834.

30. Innocent III, *Etsi Judeos,* to the Archbishop of Sens and the Bishop of Paris, July 15, 1205: ungrateful and untrustworthy as they are, "pietas Christiana receptet et sustineat cohabitationem illorum." Potthast 2565; *ChJ,* pp. 114 ff., no. 18; Decr. Greg. IX, Lib. V, tit. 6, c. xiii (Friedberg, II, col. 775).

31. See above, nn. 16 and 17.

32. "Ergo non vi, sed libera arbitrii facultate ut convertantur suadendi sunt, non potius impellendi. Qui autem jampridem ad Christianitatem coacti sunt, (sicut factum est temporibus religiosissimi principis Sisebuti), quia iam constat eos sacramentis divinis associatos et baptismi gratiam suscepisse, et crismate unctos esse, et corporis Domini extitisse participes, oportet ut fidem, quam vi vel necessitate susceperint tenere cogantur, ne nomen Domini blasphemetur et fidem quam susceperunt vilis ac contemptibilis habeatur." Gratian, *Decreti,* part I, distinctio XLV, c. 5 (Friedberg, I, col. 162).

This is a quotation from IV Toledo (633), as transmitted by Ivo of Chartres (Mansi, X, 633). It is to be noted that the council took place after Sisebut's death. He had tried to convert the Jews by force, without benefit of a council, about 613. The IV Toledo was more lenient than "the very religious" Prince Sisebut had been. *Cf.* S. Katz, *The Jews in the Visigothic Kingdoms of Spain and Gaul* (Cambridge, Mass. 1937), p. 12.

33. *Maiores ecclesiae:* Potthast 1479; *Decr. Greg. IX,* Lib. III, tit. 42, c. iii. *ChJ,* p. 100, no. 12: ". . . Verum id est religioni Christiane contrarium ut semper invitus et penitus contradicens ad recipiendam et servandam Christianitatem aliquis compellatur. Propter quod inter invitum et invitum, coactum et coactum, alii non absurde distinguunt, quod is qui terroribus atque suppliciis violenter attrahitur, et ne detrimentum incurrat Baptismi suscipit sacramentum (sicut et qui ficte ad Baptismum accedit) characterem suscipit Christianitatis impressum, et ipse tamquam conditionaliter volens, licet absolute non velit, cogendus est ad observantiam fidei Christiane, in quo casu debet intelligi decretum Concilii Toletani . . . habeatur. Ille vero qui numquam consentit, sed potius contradicit, nec rem nec characterem suscipit sacramenti; quia plus est expresse contradicere quam minime consentire. . . ."

34. The reference to *CJC* was given above, in the preceding note. How unquestioningly the attitude was accepted is clear from its surprising defense by Thomas Aquinas (*Summa,* Bk. II, pt. II, qu. 10, art. 8). One should remember, however, that Aquinas was not justifying the existing Canon Law as much as setting it forth rationally. It may be considered subjective on the part of a Jew to feel that

Aquinas' argument on this point is unconvincing, but it does appear unworthy for a man of his intellectual stature to offer the following comparison: "sicut vovere est voluntatis, reddere autem est necessitatis, ita accipere fidem est voluntatis, sed tenere iam acceptam est necessitatis." Making a voluntary promise and choosing between life and death are not comparable situations. In time, of course, force itself came to be justified. See Browe, *JM*, pp. 237–51, esp. 239.

35. A number of instances will be cited below, notably the one in Southern Italy, the one at La Marche in France, and the one in Rome in 1290. *Cf.* respectively nn. 125, 127, and 107. The pious prospect of making converts could serve as an excuse.

36. The statement in Gratian reads: "Judeorum filios vel filias, ne paren-tum ultra involvantur erroribus, ab eorum consortio separari decernimus, deputatos . . ." either to monasteries or to God-fearing Christians from whom they might learn the ways of Christianity. It seems to apply to Jewish children of whatever age and already converted under whatever circumstances. *Decreti*, II, Causa XXVIII, qu. 1, c. xi. This statement, too, is traceable back to Visigothic precedent, that of King Reccared and III Toledo (589); *cf.* Mansi, IX, col. 996 #14. For a discussion of the subject see Mario Condorelli, *I fondamenti giuridici della tolleranza religiosa* (Milan 1960), pp. 103–04; Guido Kisch, "Toleranz und Menschenwuerde," *Judentum im Mittelalter* (Miscellanea Mediaevalia, 4), (Berlin 1966), 1–36, esp. 17 ff.

37. *Summa*, Bk. II, pt. ii, qu. 10, art. 11.

38. Aquinas properly omits the Visigothic examples, since Reccared's edict was directed against children of a mixed relationship, and that of Egica (XVII Toledo, 694; Mansi, XII, 101–03) represented a conversion by force of both children and adults.

39. *Ibid.* : "Alia vero ratio est quia repugnat iustitiae naturali. Filius enim naturaliter est aliquid patris. . . . Unde contra iustitiam naturalem esset si puer, antequam habeat usum rationis, sit sub cura patris, vel de eo aliquid ordinetur invitis parentibus." The third point in his refutation is, therefore, "quod Iudaei sunt servi principum servitute civili, quae non excludit ordinem iuris naturalis vel divini."

40. Duns Scotus said, "Nam in parvulo Deus habet maius jus dominii quam parentes." *Cf.* the Kisch essay mentioned above, p. 18. Ultimately this view prevailed over that of Aquinas, at least in practice. No one raised his voice in criticism of King Manoel of Portugal when, in 1497, he took all Jewish children away from their parents and had them baptized in order to retain the parents in Portugal.

41. The document on which this is based comes from the Vatican Archive, Armarium XXXI, no. 72, fol. 232r., no. 2360. It was published in full by me, "Jewish References in a 13th Century Formulary," *JQR*, XLVI (1955), pp. 61–63. The attribution to Pope Clement IV is conjectural, since offhand it strikes one as out of character. In the Formulary, however, it is located following a number of other Bulls by that pope. The Formulary does not identify the authors of the Bulls. This Bull *(Cum de tam)*, says in part: "Verum sicut interdicta est eis seducendi Christianos audacia . . . sic ad fidem non sunt inviti cogendi. . . . Sane lacrimabili nobis Eleazar-Judaeus cum quaestione monstravit quod clericus tuae

diocesis filiam suam septennem par pedisecam eius seduci faciens at abduci, eam renitentem ad quondam monasterium asportavit; et cum a domino terre, ad predicti Judei querimoniam, quereretur, idem clericus ad partes alias transferri fecit eandem; et sic pater querens eam et non inveniens paterno discruiatur affectu. Quare nobis humiliter supplicavit ut eam sibi liberam restitui faceremus, non curaturus si demum ad religionem transire voluerit fidei Christiane." The pope orders the guilty cleric's superior to see that the child is brought back and restored to her father.

42. Above, n. 19. There is no convincing evidence that a Badge had been imposed on the Jews anywhere in Europe before the IV Lateran Council in 1215.

43. The justification offered at the IV Lateran Council for the imposition of the Badge, implying that Moses had ordered the Jews to be distinguishable in their clothing and that therefore Jews ought not complain about it, was obviously merely a turn of the screw: the Badge was hardly equivalent to *tsitsit* as described in Num. 15:37–41. The justification for the Badge from the Christian point of view was apparently meant to be insulting. The idea that Jews were prone to fornication may have been derived from the Vulgate translation of the Hebrew word *zonim* as *fornicatores*. For the canons of the Council cf. *Decr. Greg. IX*, Lib. V, tit. 19, c. v; Mansi, XXII, 1055; *ChJ*, pp. 308 f. *Cf.* Kisch, *Germany*, p. 205 and notes on the punishment of fornication between Jews and Christians; but it does not help in estimating its frequency.

44. After 1215, there was a steady flow of papal letters to various princes to remind them of their new obligation to enforce the rule of the Badge. For the first half of the 13th century see *ChJ*, s.v., "Badge." The Jews naturally tried to free themselves from the degrading sign; they at first succeeded by bribing or otherwise prevailing upon the local governments to lower their visibility. Their economic usefulness was crucial in this respect: *cf.* Robert Anchel, *Les Juifs de France* (Paris 1946), p. 120. On September 3, 1258, Pope Alexander IV reminded the Duke Hugh of Burgundy and Count Charles of Anjou and the Provence, brother of King Louis IX, of their obligation to impose the Badge, to refrain from appointing Jews to public office, and to burn the Talmud. *Cf. In sacro generali*, among the documents published by I. Loeb, *REJ*, I (1880), 116 f. A similar letter was sent also to King Louis (Archives Nationales, L 252, no. 178), which speaks of the Badge and of the appointment of Jews to office, but not of the Talmud, probably because King Louis had been zealous enough in that regard. *Cf.* the Council of Beziers, May 6, 1255, Mansi XXIII.882; *ChJ*, 336–37.

45. *Si vera sunt*, June 9 and 10, 1239; Potthast 10759, 10776, 10768; *ChJ*, pp. 239 ff. See also *ibid.*, no. 95, ordering the Bishop of Paris to distribute the letter among the French prelates. Among princes, the letter was sent to the kings of France, England, Aragon, Navarre, Castile, Leon, and Portugal.

46. ". . . in qua tot abusiones et nefaria continentur quod pudori referentibus et audientibus sunt horrori. Cum igitur hec dicatur esse causa precipua que Judeos tenet in sua perfidia obstinatos. . . ." The best contemporary outline of the accusations and of the Paris manuscript Latin 16558 is to be found in Ch. Merchavia, *Ha'talmud b're'i ha'natsrut* (Jerusalem 1970), chs. 12 and 13, pp. 249–315. See also Isidore Loeb, "La Controverse de 1240 sur le Talmud," *REJ*, I (1880), 247–61; II (1881), 248–70; III (1881), 39–57. *Cf.* Baron, *History*, IX, 66 ff.

47. For Innocent's attitude see Walter Ullmann, *Medieval Papalism*, p. 122. For Pope Innocent IV's change of mind, see his letter to the King of France, *Ad instar*, August 12, 1247, Denifle, *Chartularium*, I, 201, no. 172; with the argument of Odo of Châteauroux attached, in *ChJ*, pp. 275-80: "Unde manifestum est magistros Judeorum regni Francie nuper falsitatem Sanctitati vestre, et venerabilibus patribus dominis cardinalibus, suggessisse dicentes quod sine illis libris, qui Hebraice Talmut dicuntur, Bibliam et alia instituta sue legis secundum fidem ipsorum intelligere nequeunt."

48. For changes in the approach to Christian-Jewish polemics see Amos Funkenstein, "Changes in the Patterns of Christian anti-Jewish Polemics in the 12th Century," (Hebrew with English summary), *Zion*, XXXIII (1968), 125-44; and *idem*, "Basic Types of Christian anti-Jewish Polemics in the Later Middle Ages," *Viator*, II (1971), 375-82.

49. For Raymond of Peñaforte see A. Lukyn-Williams, *Adversus Judaeos* (Cambridge Univ. Press, 1935), pp. 241-48.

50. Martin A. Cohen, "Reflections on the Text and Context of the Disputation of Barcelona," *HUC Annual*, XXXV (1964), 157-92, speaks of the political intrigues by which the king was forced to permit, and participate in, the disputation.

51. In addition to the references given above, attention must be called to the following: Heinrich Denifle, "Quellen zur Disputation Pablos Christiani mit Mose Nachmani zu Barcelona 1263," *Historisches Jahrbuch der Goerres Gesellschaft*, VIII (1887), 225-44, containing many of the documents connected with the disputation and its aftermath; Cecil Roth, "The Disputation of Barcelona (1263)," *Harvard Theological Review*, 43 (Apr. 1950), 117-44; Y. Baer, "A Review of the Disputations of R. Yechiel of Paris and of R. Moses ben Nachman," (Hebrew), *Tarbits*, II (1931-2), 172-87; Jose M. Millas Vallicrosa, "Sobre las fuentes documentales de la controversia de Barcelona en el año 1263," *Anales de la Universidad de Barcelona, memorias y comunicaciones*, 1940, 25-43.

52. The official Latin report in Denifle, *op. cit.*, pp. 231 ff.

53. On August 26th, just about a month after the end of the disputation, the king addressed the bailiffs, judges and other local officials: "Dicimus et mandamus vobis quod cum fratres ordinis fratrum predicatorum venerint ad vos et Judaeis vel Sarracenis voluerint predicare, ipsos fratres benigne recipiatis, et inducatis Judeos et Sarracenos, tam pueros quam senes viros et mulieres et, si necesse fuerit, compellatis, ut coram ipsis fratribus, ubi et quando et quomodo ipsi voluerint, conveniant et verba ipsorum sub silencio audiant diligenter . . . :" *ibid.*, pp. 234 f., no. 2. *Ibid.*, pp. 235 f., no. 4 is a special order to the Jews to give close attention to the preaching and the arguments of Brother Paul the Christian whenever he comes to them to argue against Judaism.

54. *Ibid.*, p. 236, no. 5: ". . . mandamus universis Judeis . . . quod quascunque blasfemias contra ipsum Dominum nostrum Jhesum Christum et matrem suam beatam Mariam virginem gloriosam in libris vestris vel quibuscunque scriptis inveneritis, per vos ipsos vel qui vobis significati fuerint vel hostensi per fratrem Paulum Christiani ordinis fratrum predicatorum viva voce vel litteris, cum consilio fratris Raymundi de Pennaforti et fratris A. Segarra eiusdem ordinis, scindatis omnino de libris vestris intra spacium trium mensium. . . ." If this is not done, the books are to be burned and the Jews heavily fined.

55. *Ibid.*, p. 235, no. 3: ". . . libros qui vocantur Soffrim, compositos a quondam Judeo qui vocabatur Moyses filius Maimon egipciacus, sive de Alcayra, Jhesu Christi blasfemias continentes. . ." If they do not hand these books over for destruction, the Jews are to be punished severely. The word *soffrim* is an obvious misreading of *Shofetim*, the last book in the *Mishneh Torah* of Maimonides which concludes with a description of the Jewish concept of the Messiah and the Messianic Era completely at variance with the Christian idea.

56. Francisco de Bofarull y Sans, *Jaime I y los Judios* (Barcelona 1910), pp. 76 f., no. lxxiii: ". . . quod non teneamini ire ad abscultandam predicationem alicuius fratris . . . extra vestra calla judaica. Et si predicti fratres vel alii intus synagogas vos voluerint predicare non veniant ad ipsas synagogas cum multitudine . . ." (Oct. 1268). *Cf.* Denifle, p. 237, no. 6.

57. Denifle, *ibid.*, p. 238, no. 7: ". . . quod non teneamini aliquid de ipsis libris levare nec dampnare per penam . . . donec per fratrum Paulum vel per alium sint vobis ostensa capitula dictarum blasfemiarum, . . . si ea excusare potestis non fore blasfemia . . . ad cognitionem et iudicium super hoc assignatorum a nobis . . . non teneamini dampnare aliquid vel levare de eisdem. . . ." This was issued as early as March 1264; in 1268 another royal order freed the Jews from taking cognizance of accusations of blasphemy in rabbinic literature not agreed to by the royal court: Bofarull, *ibid.*, p. 78, no. lxxv, "quod non teneamini respondere alicui vel aliquibus personis in aliquibus petitionibus quas vobis moneant super aliquibus que asserant in libris vestris ebrayicis contra fidem nostram continere. . . . Et quod de hoc simus Nos vel nostri, et non alii. . . ."

58. The essays cited above (n. 51) discuss the relative trustworthiness of the official Latin report (given in Denifle, *ibid.*, pp. 231 ff.) and the report composed by Nahmanides. Denifle naturally says that Nahmanides lied. Baer (and *cf.* Millas Vallicrosa) points out that the official report puts into Nahmanides' mouth words that he could not possibly have said: e.g., admitting that the Messiah had already come. Roth argues that 1) the claim of victory by both sides was to have been expected; 2) Nahmanides could express himself in writing more openly and more forcefully than he could during the debate when he, of necessity, had to guard his speech.

59. The meeting is described in Bofarull, p. 67, no. liii. Raymond de Peñaforte, A. de Segarra, and Paul Christian formed the committee of Dominicans come to accuse Nahmanides of having committed blasphemy by the publication of his report. King James told them that the punishment he had fixed was a two-year exile and the burning of the report: ". . . volebamus ipsum Judeum per sentenciam exiliare de terra nostra per duos annos et facere comburi libros qui scripti erant . . . quam quidem sentenciam dicti fratres predicatores admittere nullo voluerunt." Thereupon, the king in effect dismissed the case.

60. *Agit nec immerito*, Potthast 19911; E. Jordan, *Les Registres de Clement IV*, p. 334, no. 848; Denifle, *ibid.*, pp. 240 ff., no. 9.

61. ". . . ipsos in aliquo non extollas, sed in quantum concessa eis a Sede Apostolica privilegia patiuntur. . . ."

62. ". . . Sed illius precipue castiges audaciam qui de disputatione quam in tua presencia cum dilecto filio, religioso viro, fratre Paulo de ordine predicatorum habuerat, multis confictis adjectisque mendaciis librum composuisse dicitur, . . .

Cuius ausum temerarium sic debite censura iustitie, absque tamen mortis periculo et membrorum mutilatione, castiget ut quid excessus meruerit districtionis severitas manifestet. . . ."

63. *Cf.* n. 57 above. The Jews were apparently willing to grant that some passages in the Talmud could be interpreted in a sense offensive to Christians and agreed to expunge them.

64. *Damnabili perfidia,* July 15, 1267; Potthast 20081; Coll. Doat 32, fol. 11r–15r; Sbaralea, *Bullarium Franciscanum,* III, 123 f.; Ripoll, *Bullarium Ordinis FF. Predicatorum,* I, 487.

65. *Etsi Judeos,* addressed to the Archbishop of Sens and the Bishop of Paris; Potthast 2526; *ChJ,* pp. 114 ff., no. 18. See above, n. 30.

66. *Si vera sunt,* addressed to the prelates of France; Potthast 10759; *ChJ,* pp. 240 ff., nos. 96 ff. See above, n. 45.

67. ". . . ut a Judeis tibi et eis (i.e., his barons and officers) subditis totum Talmud cum suis additionibus et expositionibus, et omnes eorum libros, ipsis faciatis liberaliter exhiberi, quibus exhibitis, illos ex eis qui de textu Biblie fuerint et alios de quibus nulla sit dubitatio quod blasphemias vel errores contineant, seu etiam falsitatem, Judeis restituant supradictis." Other books are to be kept under seal in a safe place until the pope decides what is to be done with them. Great care should be taken that the confiscation is carried out "ita prudenter et caute quod id ubicumque contingat fieri simul et eodem tempore fiat, ne Judeorum ipsorum fallacia dictos libros quomodolibet valeat occultare." Paul is to have a voice in deciding about the books: "Ad hoc autem dilectus filius Frater Paulus, dictus Christianus . . . lator presentium . . . tum quia ex Judeis trahens originem et inter eos litteris hebraicis competenter instructus linguam novit et legem antiquam ac illorum errores, tum etiam quia de sacro fonte renatus zelum habet fidei Catholice . . ." It is noteworthy that nothing is said in this Bull about burning the rabbinic books. Conceivably Paul presented to the pope his case in favor of bargaining with the Jews for the degree and the nature of a censorship that would be favorable to him—and to Christianity.

68. A Christian scholar's report on Christianity and the Talmud is Peter Browe, S.J., "Die religiöse Duldung der Juden im Mittelalter," *Archiv für katholisches Kirchenrecht,* 118 (1938), 1–76, esp. 42 ff.

68a. *Cf.* Kenneth R. Stow, *Catholic Thought and Papal Jewry Policy, 1555–1593* (New York 1977), pp. 92 and *passim.*

68b. *Cf.* Browe, *Judenmission,* pp. 267–310, summarizing the failure of the missionary policy.

69. The problem has naturally produced an extensive literature. Among the books which touch upon the Jewish aspect are: R. W. and A. J. Carlyle, *A History of Medieval Political Theory in the West* (London 1928), V, esp. ch. V, 318–54; John A. Watt, *The Theory of Papal Monarchy in the 13th Century,* London 1965; Walter Ullmann, *Medieval Papalism* (London 1949), and his *Growth of Papal Government in the Middle Ages* (London 1953). On the Jewish aspect, see the Baron essays cited above, in n. 24.

70. ". . . ab his qui non sunt sui juris, in quos nequit disciplina exerceri." Causa XXIII, qu. 4, 17: quoted from Mario Condorelli, *I fondamenti giuridici della tolleranza religiosa,* Milan 1960, p. 24, n. 13.

71. Innocent III, in *CJC*, Lib. X, tit. 8, c. 4, 19, *de divortiis.*

72. A number of such instances are offered in *ChJ*, s. v., "Boycott." See *ibid.*, pp. 250 f., no. 103. The earliest use of this method appears to have been mentioned by Raoul Glaber in the 11th century; *cf.* B. Blumenkranz, *Les auteurs Chrétiens Latins du Moyen Age* (The Hague 1963), p. 258; see also Urban IV, on May 2, 1262, in the case of a quarrel among Christians, in Jean Guiraud, *Les registres d'Urbain IV*, no. 2900. But no case can be found of a reigning prince being excommunicated solely because he violated a Church law in connection with Jews: *cf.* the long-drawn-out argument with Alfonso III of Portugal: E. Jordan, *Les registres de Clement IV*, 236, no. 669, c. 1265, and Raynaldus, a.a. 1273 #26. The method was more effective when applied locally.

73. John 21:16-17; *cf.* Ezek. 34:16-17. From the fact that Jesus entrusted his sheep to Peter, "apparet quod papa (as Peter's successor) super omnes habet jurisdictionem et potestatem de jure, licet non de facto." God's sheep includes all His creations, believers as well as non-believers. Quoted from Condorelli, *op. cit.*, p. 25, citing Sinibaldus Fieschi (Innocent IV) in his *Decretalium Commentaria. Cf.* Pietro Gismondi, *Ephemerides Juris Canonici*, III (1947), p. 21. n. 4, Ullmann, *Med. Papalism*, p. 119; Carlyle, *op. cit.*, V, 323, n. 2.

74. "Licet non debeant infideles cogi ad fidem . . . tamen mandare potest papa infidelibus quod admittant predicatores Evangelii in terris sue jurisdictionis . . . si ipsi prohibent predicatores predicare peccant, et ideo puniendi sunt." Condorelli, p. 125.

75. ". . . si contra legem naturae facit, potest licite puniri per papam." The example offered is that of the city of Sodom, in which, according to the story of Lot (Genesis 19), immorality prevailed. The immorality indicated among Jews is cohabiting with Christians. Condorelli, *op. cit.*, p. 126.

76. "Item Judaeos potest judicare papa si contra legem Evangelii faciunt in moralibus, si eorum prelati eos non puniunt, et eodem modo si hereses circa suam legem inveniant; et hac ratione motus papa Gregorius et Innocentius mandaverunt comburi libros talium in quibus multe continebantur hereses . . ." Condorelli, *op. cit.*, 127 f.; Carlyle, *op. cit.*, V, 323, n. 2.

76a. For a description of the Church attitude toward the Jews when the attitude reached its nadir, in the late 16th century, when the divine purpose in keeping the Jews alive was interpreted as meant solely to test the zeal of Christians in working for their conversion, *cf.* Kenneth R. Stow, *Catholic Thought and Papal Jewry Policy, 1555-1593* (JTSA, New York 1977). The book reached me too late for more extensive use. The only echo of *Sicut* that one finds in it is the continued frowning on outright physical force.

77. The following, among a great many other works on the subject, offer the essential information on the establishment and functioning of the Inquisition of the Middle Ages: Henry Charles Lea, *The Inquisition of the Middle Ages*, 3 vols. (New York 1887). The introduction to an edition published in 1963, by Walter Ullmann, is very useful. Jean Guiraud, *Histoire de l'Inquisition du Moyen Age*, 2 vols. (Paris 1935). C. Douais, *Documents pour servire a l'histoire de l'inquisition dans le Languedoc*, 2 vols. (Paris 1900). M. J. Vidal, *Bullaire de l'inquisition française au XIVe siecle* (Paris 1913). Useful shorter works are: R. W. Emery, *Heresy and Inquisition in Narbonne* (New York 1941); A. C. Shannon, *The Popes*

and Heresy in the 13th Century (Villanova 1949). Useful as a summary of the Inquisition's evolution is the chapter by Tuberville in *Cambridge Medieval History*, VI. The following are of special interest to the Jewish aspect of the Inquisition's activities: L. I. Newman, *Jewish Influence on Christian Reform Movements* (New York 1923). J. H. Yerushalmi, "The Inquisition and the Jews of France in the Time of Bernard Gui," *Harvard Theological Review*, 63 (1970), 317–76. S. W. Baron, *A Social and Religious History of the Jews*, IX (1965), 1–134 and the notes to these pages.

78. The trend to severity began in the 12th century. In 1220, Frederick II's constitution for his Sicilian kingdom decreed, "ut vivi in conspectu populi comburantur." The attitude was adopted and repeated by a number of popes. As is generally known, the Church condemned and, if the condemnation involved a sentence of death, handed the guilty persons over ("relaxed") to the State for execution. *Cf.* Ullmann, *Med. Papalism*, p. 252; Lea, I, 541 ff.; *Cambridge Med. Hist.*, VI, 716 ff. Lea, *ibid.*, 549 ff., points out that actual executions were comparatively few; the terror which the Inquisition inspired was due rather to the confiscations, the torture, and the imprisonment. On heresy as treason, see also Kisch, *Germany*, pp. 199, 203.

79. The entire series of papal regulations in *Sexti Decret.* V, tit., ii, *de Hereticis*, extending from Gregory IX to Boniface VIII, is of this nature. Several areas of activity were apparently omitted deliberately: e.g., the enforcement of the Jewish Badge was, for practical reasons, left to local civil authorities: *cf.* Ullmann, *Med. Papalism*, pp. 122 f. The war against the Talmud, like the two public disputations discussed above, was left to the Mendicant Orders; at least in the 13th century the Inquisition took no direct part in it. The practice of usury was a difficult subject to class with heresy, even where Christians were concerned. Alexander IV, in 1260, in answer to a question of the extent of their jurisdiction, replied to inquisitors in Italy that they could consider it heresy if the accused claimed that Christianity permitted usury, but not when they merely practiced it. Eventually, however, the Inquisition did find ways of prosecuting Jewish moneylenders. *Cf.* Alexander IV, *Quod super nonnullis*, Potthast 17745.

80. H. C. Lea, I, 461, defines the concept as "Receivers and defenders—those who showed hospitality, gave alms, or sheltered or assisted heretics in any way, or neglected to denounce them to the authorities."

81. H. C. Lea, I, 360 ff. G. G. Coulton, *Inquisition and Liberty* (London 1938), ch. 18, pp. 192–99. Innocent IV, in 1243, Potthast 11083; Ripoll, I, 118, no. 2, urged the inquisitors to act: "sicut eidem negotio expedire videretis, tam contra hereticos, credentes, fautores, receptatores, et defensores eorum quam contra alios ipsi negotio adversantes." Also in 1254: Potthast 15473; Ripoll, I, 252, no. 342, to Inquisitors in Lombardy. Their aids included the "familiars," who spied and informed. The interrogations were carried on in secret and torture was permitted. Names of informers and witnesses were not revealed.

82. Urban IV, *Sexti Decr.*, V, tit. 2, c. ix; Clement IV, *ibid.*, c. xi.

83. The problem was, of course, not new. Jews had reverted to Judaism before and the State had them severely punished. *Cf.* Bouquet, *Recueil des Historiens*, XVI, 8: Louis VII in 1144, during the period of the Second Crusade: "Statuimus igitur . . . ut deinceps quicumque Judeorum per baptismi gratiam in Christo

renati ad suae vetustatis errorem revolare presumpserint, in toto regno nostro remanere audeant, et si capi poterint, vel capitali damnentur judicio vel membrorum portione multentur." Louis VII was a contemporary of Gratian (see above n. 32). But there is no record of the frequency with which this edict was applied; there was as yet no Inquisition to enforce it.

84. *Cf.* Innocent III's *Maiores*, above, n. 33.

85. Pope Honorius IV, in his *Nimis*, addressed to John Peckham, Archbishop of Canterbury, in 1285, Potthast 22290-1; M. Prou, *Les registres d'Honorius IV*, cols 76 f. and 88 f., nos. 96–97, did not know which was worse, a converted Jew continuing to practice Judaism in the very parish where he had been baptized or one going to places where he would not be recognized in order to revert to Judaism there, always with the aid of other Jews. Such organizations for mutual help and assistance in escaping to foreign parts functioned among non-Jewish heretics in various countries: *cf.* Jean Guiraud, *Histoire de l'Inquisition de Moyen Age*, II, 251 ff.

86. A case in point is the Inquisitional document discussed by Joseph Shatzmiller, "L'Inquisition et les Juifs de Provence au XIIIe Siecle," *Provence Historique*, fascicles 93 and 94. The family of Abraham de Grasse is accused of aiding his step-daughter to revert to Judaism after her baptism. He had to clear himself of this accusation twice, and did so apparently at considerable cost.

87. *Cf.* Nicolas IV in 1288: Potthast 22846; Douais, *Documents*, I, xxxi. It addresses all Christians, urging them to confess to their priests if they become aware of a heretic or of anyone extending aid to a heretic. The names of witnesses against them were not divulged to the accused: Gregory X, 1273: *Prae cunctis*, Ripoll, I, 512, no. 12. On the nature of some witnesses, see Lea, I, 434; Tuberville, *Camb. Med. Hist.*, VI, 722.

88. The III Lateran, in 1179, c. 26: ". . . principibus vel potestatibus eorundem locorum sub poena excommunicationis injungimus ut portionem hereditatis et bonorum suorum ex integro eis faciant exhiberi." Pope Innocent IV; in 1245, praised James of Aragon for having done just that; at least, he ordered it done in an edict which Pope Innocent repeated: *Ea que*, Potthast 10822, *ChJ*, pp. 254, no. 105. For a discussion of the subject, *cf.* Browe, *Judenmission*, pp. 185 ff.

89. See above n. 64. This proximity in time may have prompted Cecil Roth's assertion that *Turbato* was an outgrowth of *Damnabili* and the situation there described. If there was such a relationship, it was not necessarily close. *Cf.* Roth's essay in *HTR*, XLIII (1950), p. 143, discussed above.

90. The Bull, addressed to the Dominican and Franciscan friars now, or in the future to be, appointed as inquisitors of heresy, reads:

> Turbato corde audivimus et narramus quod quamplurimi Christiani, veritatem Catholice fidei abnegantes, se ad ritum Judaicum damnabiliter transtulerunt; quod tanto magis reprobum fore dignoscitur quanto ex hoc nomen Christi sanctissimum quadam familiari hostilitate securius blasphematur. Cum autem huic pesti damnabili, que, sicut accepimus, non sine subversione predictae fidei nimis excrescit, congruis et festinis deceat remediis obviari: Universitati vestrae per apostolica scripta mandamus quatenus, infra terminos vobis ad inquirendum contra hereticos auctoritate

Sedis Apostolicae designatos, super premissis, tam per Christianos quam
etiam per Judaeos inquisita diligenter et solicite veritate, contra Christianos
quos talia inveneritis commisisse tanquam contra hereticos procedatis,
Judaeos autem, qui Christianos utriusque sexus ad eorum ritum execrabilem
hactenus induxerunt aut inveneritis de caetero inducentes poena debita
puniatis. Contradictores per censuram ecclesiasticam, appellatione postposita, compescendo; invocato ad hoc, si opus fuerit, auxilio brachii
secularis.

Datum Viterbii, vi Kalendas Augusti, anno tertio.

Potthast 20095; Sbaralea, *Bull. Francisc.*, III, 126; Fond Doat XXXI, fol.
328r–333v; Browe, *Judenmission,* p. 258; also Armarium XXXI, 72, fol. 238r. In a
general way, the contents of *Turbato* had been covered by Alexander IV in what
we have in *Sexti Decret.,* Lib. V, tit. II, c. 2.

91. By Gregory X on March 1, 1274; and by Nicolas IV on September 5, 1288, and
September 9, 1290. It is possible that it was also issued by Martin IV, as indicated
in Fond Doat 37, 193 ff., and consequently by Ulysse Robert, "Catalogue d'Actes
Relatifs aux Juifs," in *REJ,* III (1881), 218, no. 53. The difficulty is with the date,
March 1; a coincidence with the date of issue by Gregory X; besides, March 1,
1281, was only a short time after Martin's election and before his coronation. The
Bullaria and the *Registres* compiled by Olivier-Martin do not list a *Turbato* by
Pope Martin. Conceivably, a copy of the Gregory Bull could have been forwarded
to some French inquisitors in 1281, with the consent of the newly-elected pope.
See the next note.

92. The Gregory X issue: Potthast 20724, 20798; Ripoll, I, 517, no. 19; Sbaralea,
III, 213. Nicolas IV issue: Potthast 23391, *cf.* 22795; Sbaralea, V, 234; Fond Doat
32, fol. 193r–194v; *Registres de Nicolas IV,* by E. Langlois, p. 62, no. 322, and
p. 511, no. 3186, Wadding, *Annales Minorum,* a.a. 1290 #7, explains the re-issue
by saying that the pope was concerned about similar conditions in Germany. *Cf.*
Kisch, *Germany,* pp. 463 f. A summary, credited to Boniface VIII, in *CJC,* Sixt., V,
tit. II, c. 13.

Turbato corde audivimus et narramus quod non solum quidam de Judaicae
caecitatis errore ad lumen fidei Christianae conversi ad priorem reversi
esse perfidiam dignoscuntur, verum etiam quamplurimi Christiani, veritatem Catholicae fidei abnegantes, se damnabiliter ad ritum Judaicum
transtulerunt. . . .

93. Boniface VIII, July 17, 1295: *Petitio dilecti,* Potthast 24139; D. Michel
Félibien. *Histoire de la Ville de Paris* (Paris 1725), III, 296 f.; G. Digard *et al.,*
Registres de Boniface VIII, col. 156, no. 441. Raynald, a.a. 1290 #54, tells the story
of the Host desecration by a Jew whose house was thereupon destroyed by a mob.
A number of other accounts of the miracle are given in the *Recueil des Historiens,*
XX, 658; XXI, 127, 132; XXII, 32–33; also *MGH,* XXV, 578. The papal letter
speaks of the Jew trying to stab the wafer and then putting it in boiling water.
The pope grants the request of a citizen of Paris to establish a chapel in the place
where the Jew had resided. This Host desecration is discussed by Peter Browe,
"Die Hostienschändungen der Juden im Mittelalter," *Römische Quartalschrift,*
XXXIV, 167–97, esp. pp. 180 ff. In another essay—"Die Eucharistenwunder des
Mittelalters," *Breslauer Studien zur historischen Theologie,* n.F., 4 (1938),

128–39, 162–65—Browe described the annual procession which took place in Paris, in honor of the miracle, down to the 15th century, *ibid.*, 131 ff. There is no evidence that the Inquisition had any part in this.

94. There is no indication that the Inquisition was concerned directly with the Talmud during the second half of the 13th century. It has already been shown above that it had no direct share in the public disputations. The Inquisition is not mentioned in the Bulls which Alexander IV sent on September 3, 1258, to Hugh IV, Duke of Burgundy, and to Charles, Count of Anjou and the Provence: *In sacro generali:* Archives Nationales, L 252, no. 178; *cf.* Isidore Loeb, in *REJ,* I (1880), 116, no. 2. A similar letter was sent at the same time to Louis IX of France, which, Loeb failed to notice, did not contain any reference to the prohibition of the Talmud. The omission was probably due to the fact that the pious king was himself very much concerned with this matter. (*Cf.* the Council of Beziers in 1255, in *ChJ,* p. 336.) Nor was the Inquisition directly involved in the attack on the Talmud in Southern Italy by the greedy convert Manoforte, ca. 1270, of whom we shall speak later. The Inquisition was not mentioned in the orders sent by Philip IV in 1299 to his officials in Southern France, which included an attack on those *libros damnatos:* Fond Doat 37, fol. 246v–247v; Saige, *Les Juifs de Languedoc,* p. 235, no. 20.

95. Louis I. Newman, *Jewish Influence on Christian Reform Movements* (New York 1925), esp. pp. 393–430, seems to exaggerate the influence. Benzion Wacholder, "Cases of Proselytizing in Tosafoth Responsa," *JQR,* 51 (1961), 288–315, offers no specific instances. Both cover a good many generations. See also B. Blumenkranz, "Jüdische und Christliche Konvertiten," *Judentum im Mittelalter* (Berlin 1966), pp. 264–82; and Baron, *History,* IX, 57 and 266, n. 3. A. Paschovsky, *Der Passauer Anonymus* (*MGH SS,* vol. 22, Stuttgart, 1968) p. 152, mentions two clerics who adopted Judaism. One of them was the brother of a prelate, who had become a Jew for love of a Jewish woman. He returned to Christianity after having been castrated by order of his brother. This can hardly be called a case of Jewish proselytization. Moreover, the story sounds like an *exemplum* used in a sermon, not a real case.

96. From early times proselytization of Christians by Jews was punished severely (*CTh,* 16.8.6). The cases of Bodo-Eleazar ca. 840 and of Andreas-Obadiah ca. 1102, indicate that a Christian convert to Judaism had to fear for his life if he did not flee to Muslim territory (*cf.* Blumenkranz, *op. cit.,* pp. 266 ff. and 269 ff.). Cecil Roth, *History of the Jews in England* (Oxford 1941), pp. 41 and 83, speaks of two cases in England, both of which ended in execution. The *Siete Partidas* of Alfonso X of Castile, VII, tit. 24, *ley 7,* speaks of a Christian who converts to Judaism and ordains that he is to be executed for it, as one would execute a heretic, and his property is to be dealt with as the property of a heretic. One must assume that this law included also ex-Jews who had reverted to Judaism, since the *Siete Partidas* does not mention this contingency elsewhere. That the problem of reversion to Judaism was not unknown is evident from a number of measures taken by previous kings of Castile. (*Cf.* Browe, *Judenmission,* p. 165.)

97. *Cf.* n. 85 above; also Grayzel, "Bishop to Bishop I," in *Gratz College Anniversary Volume* (Philadelphia 1971), 131–45.

98. "Non omittit Judaeorum ipsorum nequitia quin fidei orthodoxae cultores quolibet die Sabbati ac aliis solempnitatibus eorundem invitet ac instanter

inducat ut in synagogis suis ipsorum officium audiant, illudque juxta sui ritus consuetudinem sollempnizent, rotulo involuto membranis . . . reverenciam exhibentes, quamobrem plerique christicole cum Judaeis pariter judaizant. . . . "

99. The prohibition of eating with Jews goes back to the Council of Elvira (ca. 306): Mansi, II, 14, par. 50. The prohibition for laymen to discuss religion publicly or privately is recorded, in the name of Pope Alexander IV, in *CJC, Sexti Decret.*, Lib. V, tit. ii, c. 2, #1. An example of the fast spreading attitude against socializing with Jews out of fear for Christianity is the order of an English bishop (1286) forbidding his parishioners to accept an invitation to a Jewish wedding: "ut sic fidei Christianae, cuius hostes gratis existunt, detrahere valeant et sinistra simplicibus predicare": *Registrum Recardi de Swinfield*, ed. W. W. Capes (London 1909), pp. 120 ff. Baron, in his *History*, IX, 57 f., brings another example of how Christians felt the Jews were corrupting Christianity. Louis I. Newman, *Jewish Influence on Christian Reform Movements*, esp. 360–430, and 393 ff. on proselytization, makes some exaggerated claims. But the fears of the Christians cannot be completely discounted.

100. "Cum itaque non sit tam pestilens et periculosus morbus aliquatenus contemnendus, ne, quod absit, relictus neglectui tractu temporis invalescat." On Judaism as "contagious," see also Ullmann, *Med. Papalism*, p. 254.

101. This *Damnabili*, not the one sent earlier in 1267 to the king of Aragon, was addressed to the prelates of Poitou, Toulouse, and the Provence. It is to be found in Fond Doat, 32, fol. 4r–7r; for some of the background see Emile Camau, *La Provence à travers les siecles*, III, 466–75. The relevant sentence is: "Nam, ut dolentes audivimus et penitus reprobamus, Christianos utriusque sexus simplices ad suum ritum dampnabilem retrahere moliuntur. . . ."

102. *Attendite fratres*, addressed to the prelates and abbots of Aix, Arles, and Embrun: Potthast 23170; Sbaralea, IV, 131, no. 209; Reg. Vat. 44, fol. 284r–v; *Inter innumerabiles*, Reg. Vat., *ibid.*; Langlois, *Les registres de Nicolas IV*, no. 2029. Since a good part of both documents is identical, the same sentence occurs in both: ". . . ac ipsi Judaei, nostrae fidei corruptores, conversos et baptizatos de ipsis ad fidem nostram, immo ipsos etiam Christianos, inficere et apostatare pro posse nituntur, in contumeliam fidei Christianae."

103. *Ad augmentum*, addressed to the iniquisitors of Aix, Arles, and Embrum, on February 20, 1290: Potthast 23185; Reg. Vat. 44, fol. 294v: Langlois, *Registres*, nos. 2124–5; Raynald, vol. XIV, a.a. 1290 #49. "Et si quos tales inveneritis Christianos, cuiuscumque conditionis aut status existant . . . etiam si Judaei vel Christiani esse noscuntur, qui eis talia suadeant. . . ."

104. *Cf*. Council of Vienne, 1311–1312, *Conciliorum Oecumenicorum Decreta*, 1962, pp. 356 ff., 26; *cf*. Lea, II, 96.

105. There is evidence that, after *Turbato*, the Inquisition extended its activity concerning Jews, for example, the prosecution of Jews on a charge of mistreating converts: G. Opitz, "Ueber zwei Codices zum Inquisitionsprozess," in *Quellen u. Forschungen aus italienischen Archiven*, 8 (1937–38), p. 103. Wadding reports for 1290 that Pope Nicolas became so concerned about the spread of heresy and Judaism in Palestine that he ordered the patriarch of Jerusalem to appoint a special inquisitor there (a.a. 1290 #2). In the second half of the 13th century, the belief became widespread that the time of the Antichrist was approaching,

partly as a result of Jewish and heretical activity in subversion of Christianity: A. Paschovsky, *Der Passauer Anonymus*, p. 158.

106. *Sicut nobis* by Pope Nicolas IV, May 7, 1288. Fond Doat 37, fol. 191r–192r gives it as by Nicolas III, also dated as of the nones of May, in his first year, while fol. 206r–208r gives it again, presumably for Nicolas IV. The document is therefore listed twice in Ulysse Robert's catalogue in *REJ*, III (1881), 217, no. 50 and 219, no. 62. Consequently, Joshua Starr (*Speculum*, XXI [1946], 205, n. 15) and Guido Kisch, (*Germany*, pp. 463 f., n. 101), and myself as well (*ChJ*, p. 15, n. 15) credited it to Nicolas III, re-issued by Nicolas IV. But there is nothing in the document that would call for a re-issue. The date, moreover, is suspicious on several counts. On the whole, it appears more reasonable to attribute the Bull to Nicolas IV.

107. "Dudum in Comitatu Marchiae contra [Judaeos] inibi commorantes per Christianos illarum partium persecutionis insurgente procella, plures ex dictis Judaeis metu mortis . . . non tamen absolute seu precise coacti, se baptizari fecerunt; aliqui ipsorum quibusdam infantibus lactantibus filiis suis et consanguineis baptismum conferri per huius metum illatum ipsis modo simili permiserunt . . . Postmodum vero predicti taliter baptizati sacramentum baptizatis . . . dampnabiliter contempnentes . . . ad caecitatem Judaicam redierant; propter quod inquisitores hereticae pravitatis tunc in Regno Francie . . . eos capi fecerunt et carcerali custodiae mancipari. . . . Sed sibi predictam excommunicationis sententiam et squalores carceris per annum et amplius contemptibiliter sustinuerunt animis induratis ad Christianam fidem redire penitus denegantes." The pope concludes that the inquisitors must proceed against them "as against heretics."

108. For references see n. 103 above: *Ad augmentum*.

109. *Attendite fratres*. For references see n. 102 above.

110. ". . . quamplures sacri baptizatis fonte renati . . . dum languorum afflictionibus et tribulationum periculis a Domino visitantur, ad Judaici ritus vanum auxilium errando recurrunt, in synagoga Judaeorum lampades et candelas tenentes accensas et oblationes inibi facientes, vigilias quoque die precipue sabbati protrahunt, ut infirmi recuperent sanitatem, naufrangantes ad portum salutis pervenissent, existentes in partu absque periculo pariant, et steriles prolis fecunditate letentur; ibi pro his et aliis suffragia implorantes dicti ritus, rotulo quasi per idolatriae modum nefarium devotionis et reverentiae signa patentia exhibendo. . . ."

111. Clement IV, *Professionis Christianae*, August 17, 1267, addressed to Jean de Salins: Jean Delois, *Speculum Inquisitionis Bisuntinae* (Dôle 1628), pp. 229–31. Another letter about aid to the Inquisition had been written on July 6, 1267: *ibid.—Prae cunctis*, pp. 165–72: Potthast 20064; but it makes no mention of Jews. In *Professionis* the Pope says he had been informed "quod multos in locis tibi subjectis et adjacentibus crimen heretici pravitatis infecit . . . tamquam in tenebris et umbra mortis positi caecitatis Judaice veteram et corruptam damnabiliter induunt." In a note, Delois says that there were no known Jews in that province at that time. *Cf.* J. Morey, "Les Juifs en Franche Comté au XIVe siecle," *REJ*, VII (1883), 3; also Leon Gauthiers, *Memoires . . . du Jura*, 9me serie, III, 91.

112. *Cf. Sexti Decret.*, Lib. V, tit. ii, c. 2. Confiscation was part of the regular punishment for heresy: *cf.* Lea, I, 501 ff. It naturally became desirable to condemn a heretic *post mortem*, so that his property might be confiscated.

113. *Cf.* above, nn. 80 and 86.

114. The Inquisition of the Middle Ages was never established in England. The bishops did not want it—with the possible exception of Archbishop Peckham of Canterbury—because they were aware of the resentment against it on the part of the continental bishops. Nor did Henry III or Edward I want to have it interfere with their subjects, especially with the Jews, whose property they considered their own. Edward's attitude is revealed in the discussion of it in H. G. Richardson, *The English Jewry under Angevin Kings* (London 1960), pp. 223 ff., especially in his relations to the Jews of Gascony which was then under his rule.

115. *Cf.* above, n. 59. See the very interesting and, for the time, very liberal charter which King James I of Aragon gave to the Jews of Lerida in 1268 (reprinted by James Parkes in his *The Jew in the Medieval Community*, pp. 403 f.). He there unmistakably asserts his authority as against interference by Church and Inquisition. He would enforce the Church's viewpoint regarding blasphemy in Jewish books, the erection of new and ornate synagogues, or the preaching of conversionary sermons, but it must all be done under his direction and with his consent. He concludes by saying: "Concedimus etiam vobis et vestris quod super aliquibus non possit vobis fieri aliqua innovatio."

116. Regné, "Catalogue des Actes," etc., *REJ*, 62 (1912), 62, no. 625.

117. *Ibid.*, p. 63, no. 630.

118. In this respect he emulated and outdid Edward I of England: *Calendar of Close Rolls*, 1272-9, 529-30, 565-6. There blasphemy was a capital offense. James I of Aragon, not only claimed it as under his own jurisdiction, but also pardoned a number of Jews, although the evidence against them might elsewhere have been considered strong. *Cf.* F. de Bofarull y Sans, *Los Judios en el territorio de Barcelona* (Barcelona 1910), no. 49, which is understandable if it really refers to a charge of blasphemy (in 1265) against Nahmanides in connection with the disputation, but no. 60 presents a more puzzling case. No matter what the antecedent quarrels within the family of the accused, and no matter how valuable the accused was as a royal official, he would scarcely have been freed by an ecclesiastical court when his own family accused him of blasphemy against the cross. *Cf.* Regné, *REJ*, 61 (1911), p. 24, no. 354.

119. Regné, "Catalogue," *REJ*, 65 (1913), p. 76, no. 1101: the rights of the Jews and their property must be protected; p. 204, no. 1206: the Dominicans must not prosecute the Jews of Barcelona on the charge of having aided ex-Jews to revert to Judaism.

120. On June 20, 1292, James II ordered the inquisitors not to concern themselves with the Jews of Gerona, since they were not subject to Catholic law: "cum non sint de fide seu lege catholica; et si aliquo excesserint contra legem, sint per nos puniendi." *Cf.* Baer, I, 148, no. 133. He also promised to see to it that converts are not harmed or persecuted by their former coreligionists; *cf.* Rubio y Lluch, *Documentos per la historia de la cultura Catalana*, II, no. 12. But anyone accused of aiding a convert to return to Judaism had to be brought before his court: Baer, *ibid.*, nos. 164 and 168. *Cf.* also J. L. Shneidman, *REJ*, 121 (1962), 49-58.

121. Gustave Saige, *Les Juifs de Languedoc anterieurement au XIVe Siecle*, p. 249, no. 6.

122. Arsène Darmesteter, "L'autodafé de Troyes," *REJ*, II, 199–247, esp. p. 246. The court that tried the 13 unfortunate Jews may not have been inquisitional, but it probably consisted of monks and clerics. This may have resulted in the order forbidding Churchmen to take money from Jews as fines or to imprison them. Boutaric, *Actes de Parlement*, I, 414; Saige, *op. cit.*, pp. 233–6. *Cf.* Robert Chazan, *Medieval Jewry in Northern France* (Baltimore 1975), pp. 180 ff.

123. Douais, in his *Documents*, I, 228, was so eager to show that Philip IV cooperated with the Inquisition that he failed to note the king's tergiversations in accordance with his political needs. In 1291, the king ordered his seneschal, Simon Brisetête, to protect the Jews in all their privileges regarding synagogues, bodily injury, and excessive fines (Saige, *op. cit.*, 223 f.). In 1293, when his quarrel with the pope had not yet gone very far, Philip appeared willing to follow *Turbato*, though certainly not all the way, for he ordered his seneschal, at the same time: "et si sit super his aliquid dubium vel obscurum, ad captionem predictorum (accused Jews) nostra curia inconsulta non procedatis" (Saige, *ibid.*, 231 f.; Fond Doat 37, 239v–240v; 241r–245r). In 1299, Philip IV charged that they build new synagogues, protect heretics, sing too loudly at their services, study the Talmud, and seduce simple-minded Christians into having themselves circumcised (Saige, *ibid.*, 235 f.). In 1302, the quarrel with the pope practically won, the king reverted to protecting his Jews (*Ordonances des rois de France*, I, 346; *REJ*, 2 (1881), 31, no. 15; Chazan, *op. cit.*, p. 177).

124. Charles I of Sicily to his officials in the Provence, March 26, 1276: He had heard that Brother Bertrand Rocca and his fellow inquisitor in the Provence "plura gravamina indebite et injuste Judaeis nostris Provinciae intulerunt, auferendo illis magnam pecuniae summam, que nostra erat et ad nostram curiam pertinebat; imponendo quoque aliquibus ex eisdem magna signa et insolita, et quosdam ponendo in carcere, et alia plura mala et gravia fecerunt eisdem et cotidie facere moliuntur." He had consulted some of his learned friends—he was in Rome at the time—and they told him that he was within his rights to put a stop to all this. *Cf.* Papon, *Histoire Générale de Provence*, III, Preuves, pp. XXXII- XXXIII.

125. Manoforte of Trani was a convert who, in 1267, initiated a conversionary campaign and a confiscation of rabbinic books. As a reward King Charles I assigned to him a substantial sum from the income of the Jewish dyeing establishments, a Jewish monopoly. *Cf.* G. del Giudice, *Codex diplomaticus del regno di Carlo I* (Naples 1863), pp. 314 ff.; D. A. Cassuto, "Destruction of the South Italian Yeshibot in the 13th Century," *Studies in Memory of Asher Gulak and Samuel Stern* (Hebrew) (Jerusalem 1942), pp. 137- 52, esp. 141 f.; Joshua Starr, "The Mass Conversion of Jews in Southern Italy, 1290–1293," *Speculum*, XXI (1946), pp. 203–11; N. Ferorelli, *Gli Ebrei nell'Italia Meridionale* (Bologna 1915), pp. 53 ff. It is well to remember that this was during the reign of Pope Clement IV, a firm believer in conversion of Jews and in the destruction of rabbinic literature.

126. On the expulsions from the French provinces, see Lucien Lazard, "Les Juifs de Touraine," *REJ*, 17 (1888), 210–34, esp. 225, no. VI (December 1288); also Leon Brunschvieg, "Les Juifs d'Angers et de pays Angevin," *REJ*, 29 (1894), 229–41.

127. For the events in the Kingdom of Naples from 1290 to 1294, see the essays by Cassuto and Starr, as well as the references in the volume by Ferorelli, listed in n. 125, above. They estimate the number of converts at about 8,000. Since many of these soon regretted their conversion, the inquisitors had much to do, both with the suspected neophytes and with the remaining Jews accused of aiding the former to continue their practice of Judaism in secret.

128. See the complaint of Bartholomeo, Bishop-Elect of Trani, in 1328, to which Pope John XXII replied by asking the inquisitors in South Italy to refrain from prosecuting and impoverishing the converts and the Jews for a period of two years, so that the Jews can have some means from which the Church of Trani might draw income. Since the bishop had undertaken to punish the culprits, they may move against such only at the bishop's request. John XXII, *Petitio dilecti:* Mollat, *Lettres communes de Jean XXII*, no. 40234; Eubel, *Bullarium Franciscanum*, V, 338, no. 700 ff.; Grayzel, "References to the Jews in the Correspondence of John XXII," *HUC Annual*, XXIII (1950–1); *JM*, no. 33.

129. The document is taken from *Histoire generale de Languedoc*, X, Preuves, col. 347 f. "Frater Arnaldus Johannis, de Ordine Fratrum Predicatorum, inquisitor heretice pravitatis in Appamiarum diocesi auctoritate apostolica deputatus, universis et singulis Judaeis in predicta Appamiarum diocesi commorantibus spiritum consilii sanioris et viam agnoscere veritatis. Considerantes quod Ecclesia catholica, habens spes et fiduciam quod Deus auferat velamen de cordibus vestris, statum vestrum sustinet et habet in tollerantia ritus vestros, predecessorum nostrorum vestigiis inherantes, universitati vestre tenore presentium duximus concedendum ut positis vivere, esse et conversari secundum modum et usitationem tollerabilem, sicut in Narbonensi provincia Judaei communiter conversari et vivere permittuntur; non enim intendimus vobis facere aliquas graves et insolitas novitates. Concedentes vobis presentes litteras, sigillo nostro sigillatas in testimonium premissorum. Datum Appamiis, dominica secunda in quadragesima, anno Domini MCCXCVII." *Cf.* J. M. Vidal, *Le tribunal d'Inquisition de Pamiers* (Toulouse 1906), pp. 66 f.; Fond Doat XXXVII, fol. 160r.

130. Alexander IV protected converted Jews against this kind of chicanery in his Bull *Ex parte vestra*, December 9, 1255: C. Bourel de la Roncière *et al.*, *Registres d'Alexandre IV*, no. 957. Nicolas IV protested against such violations of justice three times within six days, all the letters being addressed to officials in the Comtat Venaissin: *Sicut ad nostrum*, November 5, 1290, addressed to all the inhabitants of the Comtat (*Registres* 3574), *Intellecto dudum:* November 6, to the Bishop of Carpentras (*Registres* 3575), *Ut ex gratia:* November 9, 1290, addressed to the inhabitants, assuring them that he wants to protect their liberties (*Registres* 3578). In all cases the culprits mentioned were clerics as well as laymen, and the sufferers were Jews and non-Jews. It was evidently a common practice; for Edward I of England strongly objected to it being practiced in his French province of Gascony. *Cf. Foedera*, II (a. 1281), p. 180.

131. Gregory X's *Sicut*, with its addition on the subject of Ritual Murder, has been reproduced many times: Potthast 20915; Stern, *Urkundliche Beiträge* (Kiel 1893), no. 1, pp. 5 ff.; and *idem, Päpstliche Bullen über die Blutbeschuldigung* (Munich 1900), pp. 18 ff.; G. Bondy and F. Dworský, *Zur Geschichte der Juden in Boehmen* (Prague 1906), I, 32 ff. Grayzel, in *Studies and Essays . . . A. A. Neuman*

(Philadelphia 1962), pp. 269 f. The last-named essay also has the addition on the subject by Innocent IV (p. 258).

132. The *Sicut* by Martin IV in B. and G. Lagumina, *Codice diplomatico dei Giudei di Sicilia*, I, 117, no. 81. The pope orders that no inquisitor or any other official shall detain a Jew on the testimony of anyone: "sed ille qui eos accusaverit det et prestet ydoniam fidejussoriam . . . et si legitime non probaverit de quo accusatus est, quod accusator teneatur ad illam poenam sicut accusatus est teneretur . . . et si aliquis Judaeus baptizatus haberet aliquam familiaritatem cum aliquo alio Judaeo . . . quod non teneatur ad poenam aliquam." How much grief would have been saved had this order been adhered to!

133. *Cf. The Ritual Murder Libel and the Jew*, edited by Cecil Roth (London 1935); it contains much of the material referred to above.

134. *Sexti Decret.* Lib. V, tit. ii, c. 20: "Jubemus tamen quod, si accusatoribus vel testibus in causa haeresis intervenientibus . . . propter potentiam personarum contra quas inquiritur, videant episcopus vel inquisitores grave periculum imminere si contingat fieri publicationem nominum eorundem, ipsorum nomina non publice sed secreto . . . aliquibus aliis personis . . . exprimantur." For earlier regulations in that direction, by Innocent IV and Alexander IV, see *Layette du Tresor des Chartes*, III, nos. 4112, 4113, 4221.

135. Boniface VIII, June 13, 1299: *Exhibita nobis*, G. Digard *et al., Les Registres de Boniface VIII*, II, 412, no. 3063. On July 7, 1299, the same Bull was sent also to the Jews of the County Venaissin: *ibid.*, no. 3215. "Inquisitores tamen . . . vos asserentes potentes, publicationem huiusmodi vobis aliquando facere denegant, sicque vobis ex hoc debite defensionis facultas subtrahitur. . . . Nos autem, considerantes imbecillitatem vestram et propterea vos, etiam si divitiis habundetis, impotentum numero ascribentes, volumus ut tanquam impotentibus predicti inquisitores . . . vobis predictam publicationem faciant." In cases of doubt, the pope is to be consulted.

136. H. Vogelstein und P. Rieger, *Geschichte der Juden in Rom* (Berlin 1896), I, 256 f.

137. See note 92, above.

138. See note 102, above.

139. See note 130, above.

140. Nicolas IV, January 30, 1291: *Orat mater*, Potthast 23541, A. Theiner, *Codex diplomaticus domini temporalis S. Sedis*, I, 315, no. 486. "Orat mater ecclesia pro subducendo velamine de cordibus Judaeorum et de ipsorum oculis squamis caecitatis eductis Christum illuminati agnoscant, candorem lucis eterne; propter quod ipsa ecclesia non tolerat patienter ut Judaeos injuriis vel jacturis indebite afficiant Christiani nominis professores. Nuper siquidem sinagoga Judaeorum de Urbe nobis insinuate admodum flebili patefecit quod nonnulli clerici de predicta Urbe manus infestationis extendentes pontice in eos ipsos gravare exactionibus gravibus afficere injuriis et in bonis suis graviter molestare non cessant; quare ipsi pressi tam infestis angustiis humiliter implorarunt super hoc presidium apostolice pietatis. Nos, itaque attendentes, quod mansuetudinem christianam non decet in Judaeos molestiis et insolentiis excandere, ac propterea volentes ut ipsi apostolice clementie favore protecti contra injustitiam non

vexantur, discretioni tue per apostolica scripta mandamus quatenus prefatos Judaeos non permittas super hiis a talibus indebite molestari. Molestatores huiusmodi per censuram ecclesiasticam, appellatione postposita, compescendo. Datum apud Urbemveterem, III Kalendas Februarii, Pontificatus nostri anno tertio."

Papal Bulls
Concerning the Jews
1254-1314

Table of Papal Letters

A text published from manuscript source for the first time is indicated by asterisk (*).

Gregory X

John XXI

Nicholas III

Martin IV

Honorius IV

Nicholas IV

Boniface VIII

Clement V

Papal Bulls Concerning the Jews

1254–1314

THE PAPAL DOCUMENTS analyzed below help complete the collection of papal pronouncements for the thirteenth century I began many years ago.[1] Each document is presented in an English paraphrase or summary, followed by the Latin original and notes. Occasionally, the full translation of a passage is given in English because of its importance. In most cases, a manuscript source was consulted, either in the Doat Collection at the Bibliothèque Nationale in Paris or in the Vatican Archives, and appropriate manuscript and source collection references are provided. Eleven of the ninety-two texts are new and have never been published. The reader will identify them easily by the asterisk following the manuscript reference. The reference number to Potthast is also given when possible.

The bulls of Pope Clement V are included here to fill the gap which might otherwise exist between this register and that for Pope John XXII which I assembled in 1951[2] and which has now been reprinted as the concluding chapter of this volume.

NOTES

1. Solomon Grayzel, *The Church and the Jews in the XIIIth Century* (Philadelphia, 1933; New York, 1966).

2. First printed in *HUCA* 23 (pt. 2): 37–80.

Alexander IV

Alexander IV (December 1254–May 1261) was, like Innocent III and Gregory IX, a member of the Conti family, yet he resembled neither in energy or statesmanship. Although he continued the struggle against the Hohenstaufens bequeathed to him by Gregory IX and Innocent IV, his efforts against Manfred were inconsistent. (Cf. E. Jordan, *L'Allemagne et l'Italie aux XIIe et XIIIe siècles,* vol. 4 of *Histoire du Moyen Age,* ed. Gustave Glotz [Paris, 1939], p. 323.)

1   February 1, 1255

To the civil authorities of the Patrimony of the Apostolic See and of the Kingdom of Sicily:

NOLENTES UT . . . Angelus, Sabbatinus, Museus, Salomon and Angelus,[1] Jews, along with their associates, merchants commissioned by our camera (*curiam nostram sequentes*) and citizens of Rome, are neither to be burdened with taxes nor to be charged tolls during their journeys to and from the curia, either now or in the future.

Reg. Vat. 24, fol. 12, c. 91.
C. Bourel de la Roncière et al., eds., *Les registres d'Alexandre IV,* (Paris, 1895-1959), no. 101.
MGH, Epist. Saec. XIII, vol. 3, p. 335, no. 370.

Potestatibus, baronibus et communitatibus in Patrimonio Sedis apostolice et regno Sycilie constitutis.

NOLENTES UT Angelus, Sabbatinus, Museus, Salamon et Angelus judei ac eorum socii mercatores cives Romani cum suis mercibus Curiam nostram sequentes in terra Ecclesie exactionibus aggraventur, universitati vestre per apostolica scripta mandamus quatinus ab eisdem mercatoribus, cum ad Curiam nostram cum mercibus suis veniunt vel recedunt ab ipsa, nichil penitus ratione passagii vel pedagii exigatis. Dat. Neapoli, kalendis februarii, anno primo.

In e. m. eisdem pro Consiliolo judeo et sociis ejus mercatoribus civibus Romanis.

1. A similar letter was sent in behalf of a Jew named Consiliolus and his associates, also called Roman citizens (*MGH, Epist. Saec. XIII*, vol. 3, p. 335, no. 370) a status possessed at least technically by all Roman Jews by virtue of their standing in *ius commune* (Italian medieval Roman law). A month later (March 5), a like order was sent to the civil and military authorities of the Kingdom of Sicily, but this time without mention of the Jews (La Roncière, *Registres*, no. 101). That is, in commercial matters Jews were often not discriminated against. For a pertinent letter, dated April 2, 1264, by Pope Urban IV, see no. 19, below. E. Jordan, *De mercatoribus camerae apostolicae saeculi XIII* (1909), does not list these names, perhaps because of their slight importance. On the importance of Jewish merchants in Rome at this time, see VR, vol. 1. pp. 239, 274. A. Milano, "The Church and the Jews of Rome in the Thirteenth and Fourteenth Centuries" (in Hebrew), in *Eretz Israel (Sefer Yovel L'Moshe D. Cassuto)* 3 (1954): 224, assigns these Jews a lesser position in the Roman economy; he believes they profited from a loose arrangement with non-Jewish merchants, citing as evidence the humble place assigned them in the statute for Roman merchants issued by Senator Pandolfo in 1297. Cf. VR, vol. 1, 257, 303.

2   September 22, 1255

To the Christian Faithful everywhere:

SICUT JUDAEIS[1] . . . Pope Alexander reissues the customary Bull of Protection. He cites the copies of this bull issued by his predecessors: Calixtus, Eugenius, Alexander, Clement, Coelestine, Innocent III, Honorius, Gregory, and Innocent IV.[2]

Fidel Fita, "Privilegios de los Hebreos Mallorquinos," *Boletin de la Real Academia de la Historia* 36–37 (1900): 16–18; reprinted from *España Hebrea* (Madrid, 1891), vol. 2, pp. 87–90.

Alexander episcopus, servus servorum Dei, dilectis in Christo filiis, fidelibus, salutem et apostolicam benedictionem.

SICUT JUDEIS non debet esse licentia in sinagogis suis, ultra quam permissum est, lege presumere, ita in hiis que concessa sunt nullum debent judicium sustinere. Nos ergo, licet in sua magis velint duritia perdurare quam prophetarum verbo et suarum Scripturarum archana cognoscere atque ad christiane fidei et salutis notitiam pervenire; quia tamen defensionem nostram et auxilium postulant et christiane pietatis mansuetudinem, predecessorum nostrorum felicis memorie Calixti, Eugenii, Alexandri, Clementis, Celestini, Innocentii, Honorii, Gregorii et Innocentii summorum pontificum vestigiis inherentes, ipsorum petitionem admittimus, eisque protectionis nostre clipeum indulgemus.

Statuimus etiam ut nullus christianus invitos vel nolentes eos ad bab-tismum per violentiam venire compellat; sed si eorum quilibet sponte ad christianos fidei causa confugerit, postquam voluntas ejus fuerit pate-facta, christianus absque aliqua efficiatur calumpnia; veram quippe christianitatis fidem habere non creditur qui ad christianorum baptisma non spontaneus sed invitus cognoscitur pervenire.

Nullus etiam chistianus eorum personas, sine judicio potestatis, ferire, vulnerare aut occidere, vel suas illis pecunias auferre presumat, aut bonas, quas hactenus in ea quam habitant regione, habuerint con-suetudines immutare.

Preterea, in festivitatum suarum celebratione quisquam fustibus vel lapidibus eos ullatenus non perturbet; neque aliquis ab eis coacta servitia exigat, nisi ea que ipsi preteritis facere temporibus consueverunt.

Ad hec, malorum hominum pravitati et avaritie obviantes, decernimus ut nemo cimiterium judeorum mutilare vel minuere audeat, sive obtentu pecunie corpora humata effodere.

Siquis autem decreti hujus tenore cognito, temere quod absit, contraire temptaverit, honoris et officii sui periculum patiatur aut excommunica-tionis ultione plectatur, nisi presumptionem suam digna satisfactione correxerit. Eos autem dumtaxat hujus protectionis presidio volumus communiri, qui nichil machinari presumpserint in subversionem fidei christiane.

Ego Alexander catholice Ecclesie episcopus, subscripsi.

(Rueda). Suscipe, Domine, servum tuum in bonum. Sanctus Petrus. Sanctus Paulus. Alexander Papa IIII.

Ego Odo, Tusculanus episcopus, subscripsi.

Ego Stephanus, Prenestinus episcopus, subscripsi.

Ego frater Joannes (1), tituli sancti Laurentii in Lucina, presbiter Cardinalis, subscripsi.

Ego frater Hugo, tituli sancte Sabine, presbiter cardinalis, subscripsi.

Ego Ricardus, sancti Angeli diaconus cardinalis subscripsi.

Ego Petrus, sancti Georgii ad velum aureum diaconus cardinalis, subscripsi.

Ego Joannes sancti Nicholai in carcere Tulliano diaconus cardinalis, subscripsi.

Ego Willelmus, sancti Eustachii diaconus cardinalis, subscripsi.

Ego Ottobonus, sancti Adriani diaconus cardinalis subscripsi.

Datum Anagnie, x kal. Octobris, anno primo.[3]

1. For a discussion of the bull, see S. Grayzel, "The Papal Bull *Sicut Judeis*," *Studies and Essays in Honor of Abraham A. Neuman*, ed. Meir Ben-Horin et al. (Philadelphia, 1962), pp. 243–280. Cf. *ChJ*, pp. 76–78, 92–95. Every repetition of the bull contains the phrase that the Jews requested it (*quia tamen defensionem nostram et auxilium postulant*); but there is no indication as to the identity of those who made the request, [perhaps because the clause was, by now, purely formulaic; cf. no. 11, below—KS]. Fita ("Privilegios," p. 90) points out that the part of the bull forbidding compulsory baptism was especially applicable to the situation then obtaining in Mallorca. [See "Popes, Jews, and Inquisition from 'Sicut' to 'Turbato,'" pp. 3–45, above, for Grayzel's revised views on this bull.—KS]

2. The dates when the bull was issued by Alexander's predecessors are discussed in my essay "Sicut Judeis," mentioned above. There are some slight, probably unintentional, variations in phraseology between this reissue and its predecessors, including the omission of the prefatory statement made by Innocent III but edited out of the formal canon which made the bull into law, as well as the omission of the additional statement on the ritual-murder accusations made by Innocent IV in July, 1247.

3. [It should be noted that repetitions of *Sicut Judaeis* are, technically speaking, only for emphasis. The essence of the text was edited into the *Decretals* in 1234, thus making its principles into perpetually binding law. No one could ignore *Sicut*, yet Odo of Tusculum, a signer of this particular reissue, was a leader of the Parisian forces that engineered the assault on the Talmud in the 1240s. Apparently, *Sicut Judaeis* and the attack on books were compatible in Odo's mind, a proposition which merits some thought.—KS]

3   December 9, 1255

To all converts to the Faith from the error of Jewish blindness who reside in the city and diocese of Paris:

EX PARTE VESTRA . . . These converts had complained to the pope about certain churchmen of Paris and the archiepiscopal diocese of Sens who had been ordered to provide them with the necessities of life[1] but who had apparently become hostile and compelled them to respond to lawsuits in distant courts. The pope grants the converts relief from these hardships and indicates that if summoned, they are to appear before the court of the bishop of Paris.

Reg. Vat. 24, fol. 113v, c. 768.
La Roncière, *Registres*, no. 957.

Universis christianis de judaice cecitatis errore ad fidem conversis, in Parisiensibus civitate et diocesi commorantibus.

Ex parte vestra fuit propositum coram nobis, quod nonnunquam persone ecclesiastice Parisiensium et Senonensium civitatum et diocesium a quibus auctoritate Sedis apostolice vite necessaria debetis percipere, vobis super hiis se opponentes adeo, ad diversa et remota loca per litteras Sedis ejusdem vos trahunt in causam quod nonnulli vestrum litibus cedere in suum non modicum prejudicium compelluntur: propter quod apostolice Sedis remedium implorastis. Nos igitur, volentes tranquillitati et indempnitati vestre paterna sollicitudine providere, vestris supplicationibus inclinati, vobis auctoritate presentium indulgemus, ut per litteras Sedis ejusdem vel legatorum ipsius extra civitatem et diocesim Parisienses a quoquam trahi non possitis in causam, dummodo parati sitis coram venerabili fratre nostro . . . , Parisiensi episcopo, de vobis conquerentibus respondere. Nulli etc. nostre concessionis etc.

Dat. Laterani, V idus decembris, anno primo.

1. Mandates ordering churches and monasteries to support converts were frequent (cf. Peter Browe, *Die Judenmission im Mittelalter und die Päpste* [Rome, 1942], *passim,* esp. pp. 197 ff.). Ecclesiastical persons and institutions often tried to rid themselves of this extra burden. In a similar case, Pope Alexander III, in 1173–1174, scolded the bishop of Tournai and accused him of racism. Cf. Walther Holtzmann, "Zur päpstlichen Gesetzgebung über die Juden im 12ten Jahrhundert," in *Festschrift Guido Kisch* (Stuttgart, 1955), pp. 230 f. For other instances, see *ChJ,* pp. 48, 75, 84. The converts here are not named; in fact, we must rely on the editor of the letter to know converts are involved. They could have come from the family of that Philip who figures in document no. 124 in *ChJ,* p. 285. [Is there any relation between this letter and no. 61 of Nicholas IV, below? If so, we learn how poorly jurisdictional boundaries functioned.—KS]

4   October 13, 1257[1]

To the King of Navarre, Count Palatine of Champagne and Brie:[2]

Ex parte tua . . . Despite a royal prohibition, the Jews of Navarre continue to practice usury, a crime which violates the law of both Testaments. The pope directs the king to seize that property of the Jews which may have derived from usurious practices and to restore it to those from whom it had been extorted. If these people cannot be found, the property must be put to pious uses.[3]

Leon Cadier, ed., *Bulles originales du XIIIe siècle* (Rome, 1887), p. 54.

Alexander episcopus, servus servorum Dei, carissimo in Christo filio . . . regi Navarri illustri, Campanie et Brie comiti palatino salutem et ap. ben.

EX PARTE TUA fuit propositum coram nobis quod, licet tu olim, pruden- ter attendens usurarum crimen utriusque testamenti pagina condemp- nari, universis Judeis tue ditioni subjectis, ne usuras exerceant duxeris artes inhibendum, nichilominus tamen ipsi, contra inhibitionem tuam temere venientes, pravitatis usurarum hujusmodi se involvunt. Super quo petivisti a nobis salubri remedio provideri. Tuam igitur excellen- tiam ad executionem justitie invitantes, apprehendendi bona Judeorum ipsorum, de quibus legitime constiterit quod ex hujusmodi pravitate provenerint, et restituendi ea illis personis a quibus taliter sunt extorta, si poterunt inveniri, alioquin convertendi ea in pios usus plenam tibi et liberam concedimus auctoritate presentium facultatem.

Datum Viterbii, iii id. Octobris, anno tertio.[4]

---

1. J. Amador de los Rios, in *Historia social, politica y religiosa de los Judios de España y Portugal* (Madrid, 1876), vol. 2, pp. 22 f. (reprinted edition: [Buenos Aires, 1943] vol. 1, p. 370), dates the bull in 1256, one of the earliest of its specific genre; cf. n. 4, below.

2. Thibaut (Teobaldo) II of Navarre, V of Champagne, 1253–1270. His father had been warned by Innocent IV in June and July of 1247 (*ChJ*, nos. 115, 117) not to permit the expropriation of Jewish property on the pretext of usury. Nevertheless, there can be little doubt that when Thibaut II asked the question to which this document is the answer, he knew that the times favored him, for he had before him the examples of the confiscations of Louis IX to the north (see the document which follows) and of James I of Aragon to the south (cf. Y. Baer, *A History of the Jews in Christian Spain*, [Philadelphia, 1966], vol. 1, pp. 149 f.) A decade later, on March 1, 1268, Thibaut received from Pope Clement IV the usual crusader's privileges, which included a moratorium on the payment of all debts (Cadier, *op. cit.*, pp. 65 ff., no. 35). In September of that year, Thibaut again followed Louis IX's example by expropriating the property of the Jews in Champagne (cf. H. d'Arbois de Jubainville, *Histoire des ducs et des comtes de Champagne* [Paris, 1859–1869], vol. 4, pp. 412 f.).

3. The term "pious uses" remained vague. We shall see, in connection with the next document, how Louis IX interpreted it. A few years later, Thomas Aquinas offered a definition in his letter to the Duchess of Brabant (*Aquinas, Selected Political Writings*, ed. A. P. d'Entrèves and trans. J. G. Dawson [Oxford, 1948],

pp. 84-95, esp. pp. 86-87): "So if you can find with certainty those from whom usury was extorted, you must make restitution to them. Otherwise, such money must be put to pious use, according to the advice of the diocesan bishops and of other upright men, or used for the public benefit of your kingdom to relieve want or serve the interests of the community." The last phrase leaves the matter almost as vague as ever; but there is no evidence that Thibaut, following papal instructions, did disperse monies charitably.

4. [The paradigm for this letter was issued by Gregory IX on October 6, 1237 (*ChJ*, no. 90); it corresponds perfectly with the text of Aquinas just cited. Neither this letter, nor that of Gregory IX, may be construed as a papal rejection of moderate Jewish interest taking. No more proof of its permissibility is required than the letter of Alexander IV himself (no. 6, below), issued but months after this text: For all his anger at Jewish acceptance of church vessels as pledges, the pope still admits that normally Jews collect both *sortem* (the principal) and *lucrum* (the profit) on a loan.—KS]

5   April 11, 1258

To the illustrious King of France:

SIC ILLE LUCIFER: . . . After a highly flattering description of Louis IX's religious attitudes,[1] the pope grants him the right of applying to pious uses[2] property which had come to him from various sources,[3] and whose owners he cannot identify.

J. de Laborde, *Layettes du trésor des chartes* (Paris, 1875), vol. 3, no. 4404.

Alexander, episcopus, servus servorum Dei, carissimo in Christo filio, . . . (*sic*), illustri regi Francie, salutem et apostolicam benedictionem.

SIC ILLE LUCIFER matutinus, qui nescit occasum et qui humano generi serenus illuxit, in tui claustra pectoris luminis sui gratiam, quod referimus gaudentes, infudit, quod, omni exinde obscuritatis depulsa caligine, tuum serenavit animum claritate virtutum, tuamque mentem luce justitie ac fulgore rectitudinis illustravit. Hinc procedit, fili karissime, quod juxta tui status magnitudinem studuisti semper et studes opera exercere magnifica, teque lucidis et placidis actibus gratum reddere apud Deum, qui te apud homines et opibus et honoribus magnificentius sublimavit. Hinc procedit quod existis in augmentatione ac defensione cultus fidei orthodoxe sollicitus, in conservatione libertatis ecclesiastice strenuus, in ecclesiarum aliorumque piorum locorum constructione benivolus et benignus, in eorum dotatione ac ditatione largifluus, in gratiis et beneficiis erga personas ecclesiasticas, regulares et seculares, et in elemosinarum erga pauperes largitione valde munificus, et in devotione ad nos et Ecclesiam stabilis et accensus. Hinc etiam provenit quod conscientie puritatem et bonitatem, per quam Altissimo placeas, totis votis amplecteris, et, in ea delitiosum extimans et suave intendere ac vacare virtutibus, firmatis ad condignum et honestum affectibus maxime delectaris, ut, odore grato de tuis processibus ad Dominum asscendente, merearis sua potenti dextera ab omni nocumento corporis et anime preservari. Digne igitur super hiis ei gratias referentes, supplici apud eum deprecatione insistimus ut tuum in hiis animum regat et firmet, ac proficiendi ad melius tibi gratiam largiatur. Ex parte sane tua fuit a nobis devote petitum ut, cum tu quedam bona, que ad te diversis modis pervenisse noscuntur, personis quarum sunt restituere tenearis, et scias te teneri ad restitutionem bonorum hujusmodi faciendam, ac persone, quibus eorum restitutio fieri debeat, sciri et inveniri non possint, quamquam super hiis per viros discretos et ydoneos feceris diligenter inquiri, providere in hac parte tibi, Apostolica sollicitudine, curaremus. Nos igitur, qui salutem in te utriusque hominis totis desideriis affectamus, volentes super hoc conscientie tue, ad removendum exinde omne scrupulum, remedio consulere oportuno, tuis precibus grato concurrentes assensu, excellentie tue auctoritate presentium indulgemus ut liceat tibi hujusmodi bona pauperibus in elemosinam erogare, ac de hiis, que taliter erogaveris, liberationem et absolutionem plenariam consequaris. Veruntamen scire te volumus quod, si personas, quibus eorum restitutio fieri debeat, ad tuam notitiam pervenire contingat, te ipsis predicta bona restituere nichilominus oportebit. Nulli ergo omnino hominum liceat hanc paginam nostre concessionis infringere, vel ei ausu temerario contraire. Si quis autem hoc attemptare presumpserit, indignationem Omnipotentis Dei et Beatorum Petri et Pauli, apostolorum ejus, se noverit incursurum.

Datum Viterbii, iii id. Aprilis, anno quarto.

1. King Louis IX died in 1270 (in Tunisia, while on a crusade). He was canonized within a remarkably short time, in 1297.

2. In this connection, Robert Anchel (*Les Juifs de France* [Paris, 1946], p. 112) makes a point of King Louis's zeal for the conversion of Jews. One of the "pious uses" to which he put this money may well have been to maintain the Converts House which came into existence at this time.

Similar bulls dealing with money whose original owners could not be located, and which Louis IX had inherited, are given by Laborde (*Layettes du trésor des chartes*, no. 4405) and A. Tardif (*Privilèges accordés à la Couronne de France par le Saint-Siège* [Paris, 1885], pp. 142, no. 163; 159, no. 181; 212, no. 239).

3. The "various sources" must have included Jews, though they are not mentioned in this text. A document dated July 31, 1259, a letter to the king from the bishop of Paris (Laborde, *Layettes du trésor des chartes*, no. 4502) written in the spirit of the pope's advice, specifically mentions the Jews (*sive in bonis Judaeorum, sive in aliis quibuscumque*). Cf. H. Graetz, *Geschichte der Juden*, 2nd ed. (Leipzig, 1873), vol. 7, p. 118, and Anchel, *Juifs de France*, pp. 110 ff. A partial expulsion of Jews from the French royal domain took place, according to Anchel, in 1252 and, according to Graetz, on the basis of Solomon ibn Verga's *Shevet Yehudah* (ed. A. Shohet [Jerusalem, 1946], p. 69, no. 22), in 1254; in any event, if it occurred, it followed the return of the king from his Egyptian crusade. The Jews were permitted to return in 1257 or 1258, and King Louis restored to them property that was considered unlikely to have been gained through usury (e.g., synagogues and homes). The present letter applies to the property the king retained. For Louis's own description of his actions, see E. de Laurière et al., *Ordonnances des rois de la troisième race* (Paris, 1723-1849), vol. 1, p. 85. [And for the royal confiscations of Jewish property following the cancellation of Jewish debts at this time, see G. Nahon, "Le crédit et les Juifs dans la France du XIIIe siècle," *Annales* 24 (1969): esp. 1138-39; and W. C. Jordan, "An Unpublished *Enquête* from Picardy, *REJ* 138 (1979): 47-55. See also W. C. Jordan, *Louis IX and the Challenge of the Crusade: A Study in Rulership* (Princeton, 1979).—KS]

6   August 23, 1258

To the archbishops and bishops of France:

SI OLIM . . . "If the Israelites of the Old Testament, living under the shadow of the Law, used the vestments and vessels employed in the performance of animal sacrifices solely for that purpose, how much more then, in the time of the New Testament, ought the Christian clergy—who have seen the grace and humaneness (*benignitas et humanitas*) of the Savior and at the same time have experienced the mystery of God's Kingdom—treat with reverence and guard with solicitude those vestments of their ministry, the sacred ornaments, the chalices, and the ecclesiastical vessels with and through which they perform the unique and ever lifegiving sacrifice of the son of God. . . . Yet we have heard—and we speak of it not without bitterness of heart—that some clergy make no distinction between the sacred and the profane, that they dare leave such vestments, ornaments, and vessels as loan pledges with Jews.[1] And these very Jews, like ingrate enemies of the Cross and Christian Faith—for Christian piety through mercy alone accepts them to dwell in our midst—treat these pledges with irreverence, to the disgrace of the Christian religion, and act so nefariously toward them as is shameful to speak of and horrible to hear.[2] . . . We request Your Fraternity and order you to

command each one of the clergy of your dioceses never hereafter to
dare, under pain of excommunication and the loss of office and
benefice, to pledge vestments, ornaments, and vessels with Jews . . . .
In our behalf, you shall take good care to warn these Jews that if, . . .
after this warning, they continue to accept such articles, . . . they will
lose not only the gain accruing from the debt, but also incur the loss
of the principal."

Archives Nationales, L 242, no. 177.

Isidore Loeb, "Bulles inédites des papes," *REJ* 1 (1880): 296 f. (locating the manuscript
as no. 202).

Alexander episcopus servus servorum Dei, venerabilibus fratribus universis archiepiscopis et episcopis per regnum Francie constitutis, salutem
et apostolicam benedictionem.

SI OLIM in testamento Veteri vestimenta sacerdotalia et vasa deputata in
opus sacrificii quod tunc de brutis fiebat animalibus, apud israeliticum
populum, qui sub legis umbra vivebat, cultu celebri habebantur, multo
fortius nunc in Novo xpistianus clerus, cui et apparuit benignitas et
humanitas Salvatoris et est datum nosse misterium regni Dei, debet et
tractare venerabiliter et custodire decenter indumenta ministrorum, ornamenta, calices et vasa ecclesiastica cum quibus et in quibus illud unicum
et vivificum holocaustum semper offertur quod pro redemptione humani
generis semel in ara crucis extitit immolatum, videlicet Dei filius Jhesus
Xpistus, idem ipse sacrificium et sacerdos, cum certiora sint experimenta
rerum quam enigmata figurarum. Accepimus siquidem, et non absque
amaritudine cordis referimus, quod nonnulli prelati ac rectores et clerici
vestrarum civitatum et diocesium, inter sanctum et prophanum in hoc
minime discernentes, indumenta, ornamenta et vasa huiusmodi presu-
munt Iudeis titulo pignoris obligare, ipsique Iudei, velut crucis Xpisti et
fidei xpistiane hostes ingrati, quod ipsos ex sola misericordia pietas
xpistiana receptat et cohabitationem illorum sustinet patienter, in xpistiane religionis obprobrium, eadem sibi taliter obligata et irreverenter
tractant et in eis et cum eis talia, pro dolor, committunt nepharia que
pudori relatui et auditui sunt horrori ac dedecerent etiam in prophanis.
Nolentes igitur tantum dissimulare contagium et xpistiani nominis
iniuriam sustinere, fraternitati vestre per apostolica scripta in virtute
obedientie firmiter precipiendo mandamus quatinus singulis vestrorum
clericis per vestras civitates et dioceses sub pena excommunicationis et
privationis ab officiis et beneficiis quam ipso facto, si contra egerint,
incurrant, ut predicta vestimenta, ornamenta et vasa Iudeis obligare de

cetero non presumant, et ipsis Iudeis ne in pignore illa deinceps recipiant ex parte nostra districte curetis inhibere, predictis Iudeis expresse denunciantes et denunciari facientes quod illa ipsis, si ea post inhibitionem huiusmodi receperint, erit impune auferre licitum xpistianis, et iidem Iudei non solum lucrum non consequentur exinde, sed potius sortis amissionem incurrent. Taliter autem preceptum nostrum in hac parte studeatis ad implere quod ex vestrorum operatione studiorum fructus optatus proveniat et sollicitudo vestra exinde possit merito commendari.

Datum Viterbii, x kal. Septembris, anno quarto.

1. This may have been the first time that a pope dealt with this problem so openly (cf. Loeb, "Bulles inédites," p. 295), but the problem itself did not originate in the thirteenth century. Toward the end of the previous century, it was noted in the regulations of a French bishop, though the reference was only to sacred books and ornaments of the church; see *ChJ*, pp. 300–301, no. IV. At the Council of Trier (Trèves) in 1227, the prohibition was extended to cover church ornaments and religious articles (*ChJ*, p. 319, no. XIX); in 1229, William of Bley, Bishop of Worcester, included ecclesiastical books, vestments, and other ornaments (*ChJ*, p. 321, no. XXIII).

2. We are not told what these horrible actions were or how the pope heard of them[, although even the simple mundane storage of otherwise holy objects would constitute a disgrace in papal eyes—KS].

7   September 3, 1258

To the Duke of Burgundy:[1]

IN SACRO GENERALI[2] . . . It was decreed in the sacred General Council that Jews be distinguishable from Christians by means of the clothes they wear, for fear of sexual intermingling. The same council decreed that Jews should not be given public office, lest they use it to oppress Christians. But these regulations are not being observed in the duke's territory, and the pope expresses his chagrin. He orders the duke to command the Jews to wear a badge and to prevent them from holding office. Moreover, the duke must confiscate the books generally known as *thalmuth*,[3] which contain errors against the Catholic faith as well as horrible and intolerable blasphemies against our Lord, Jesus Christ, and the Blessed Virgin, his mother. By obeying this command, the duke will earn for himself the mercy of God.

Archives Nationales, L 252, no. 178.
Loeb, "Bulles inédites," (1880): 116 f. (locating the manuscript as no. 204).

Alexander episcopus servus servorum Dei, dilecto filio nobili viro duci Burgundie salutem et apostolicam benedictionem.

IN SACRO GENERALI concilio provida fuit deliberatione statutum ut Iudei a Xpianis qualitate habitus distinguantur, ne illorum isti vel istorum illi possint mulieribus dampnabiliter commisceri. In eodem etiam concilio fuit prohibitum ne Iudei publicis officiis preferantur, quoniam sub tali pretextu Xpianis plurimum sunt infesti. Sed sicut accepimus Iudei terre tue statutum huiusmodi non observant, propter quod dampnate commixtionis excessus potest sub erroris velamento presumi. Iidem quoque Iudei contra prohibitionem eandem huiusmodi officiis preferuntur. Cum autem per te decet super hiis salubriter provideri. Nobilitatem tuam rogamus et hortamur attente per apostolica tibi scripta mandantes quatinus predictos Iudeos ad deferendum signum quo a Xpianis qualitate habitus distinguantur, tradita tibi a deo potestate compellens non permittas quod ipsi predictis officiis preferantur. Ad hec omnibus Iudeis predicte terre auferri facias libros qui thalmuth vulgariter appellantur, in quibus continentur errores contra fidem catholicam ac horribiles et intollerabiles blasphemie contra dominum nostrum Jhesum Xpum et beatam Mariam virginem matrem eius. Super hiis autem sic provideat tua sinceritas quod exinde tibi a clementia Regis eterni proveniat quod ipsa pro piis actibus recompensat, nosque propter hoc devotioni tue grates uberes referamus.

Datum Viterbii, iii non. Septembris, anno quarto.

1. Hugh IV, duke of Burgundy from 1218 to 1272, tried hard to strengthen his authority within the duchy, a situation that may account for his lack of enthusiasm in the enforcement of the above Church legislation. He needed the financial and commercial resources of the Jews (cf. Léon Gauthier, "Les Juifs dans les deux Bourgognes," *REJ* 48 [1904]: 208–229, esp. 215 ff.). His successor continued to employ Jews in financial posts (cf. Anchel, *Juifs de France*, pp. 119 f.). On the same date, an identical letter was sent to Charles, count of Anjou and the Provence, whose failure to observe the above Church legislation is the more surprising since he was the brother of the pious King Louis. But Charles's reasons were no different from those of Hugh of Burgundy.

2. The reference is to the Fourth Lateran Council in 1215. Its 68th canon legislated that Jews must wear a distinguishing garb, and canon 69 ordered that no Jew be given public office (cf. *ChJ*, pp. 308–311). Subsequent local and provincial councils and the popes who followed Innocent III referred frequently to these two regulations. Cf. U. Robert, "Catalogue des actes relatifs aux Juifs (1183–1300)," *REJ* 3 (1881): 216, no. 42: Alphonse of Poitiers, another brother of Louis IX, ordered his Jews to wear a badge in 1269.

3. A copy of this same bull was also addressed to the king of France (Arch. Nat., L 252, no. 180; Loeb, "Bulles inédites," p. 117, gives it as no. 205). Interestingly, this copy omits the statement regarding the Talmud. The reason may have been that in the royal territory such an order was no longer needed; the burning of rabbinic literature in Paris had been quite thorough (cf. *ChJ*, pp. 240-241, 274-281). Moreover, King Louis himself had been present at the Council of Beziers, on May 6, 1255, and had insisted on legislation against Jewish usury and blasphemous books (*ChJ*, pp. 336-337; cf. Karl Hefele, *Histoire des Conciles*, trans. and aug. Henri Leclercq et al. [Paris, 1907-1949], vol. 6, pt. 1, pp. 83 ff.). The dispatch of this bull to the king would seem to imply that Jews in the royal territory were disregarding the order about the badge, not an impossible state of affairs in view of its novel, drastic, and repugnant nature (cf. Robert, "Catalogue," p. 216, no. 41). But it would also appear to imply that without the king's knowledge, some of his administrators employed Jews. On the possible extension of this order to Rome see VR vol. 1, p. 240; but the evidence there seems unsubstantiable.

[Could it also be that the pope wished mainly to call his letters to Hugh and Charles to the attention of St. Louis, hoping to gain the active support of the king in having the letters obeyed? The omission of a reference to the Talmud in the letter to the king may be a coincidence, but, in any case, presents no real problem.—KS]

8   September 17, 1259

To the Cathedral Chapter of Pampelona:

JUSTIS PETENTIUM . . . Pope Alexander announces his decision in a complicated dispute that had been going on for years. It had started with King Thibaut of Navarre on one side and the bishop of Pampelona and his chapter on the other. The king and the bishop arrived at an understanding; but then the chapter claimed that it had not been consulted. After long litigation, the chapter won. The Jews figured in two items of the agreement between the king and the bishop: (1) From the possessions which the Jews have outside of Pampelona they shall pay tithes[1] to the parish churches in which the possessions are located; and (2) whatever the bishop and the king possess or will possess in the city and its territory shall be held jointly, so that the king has half and the church of Pampelona half, whether it be in the nature of vineyards, fields, mills, or transit taxes on Jews.[2]

La Roncière, *Registres*, vol. 3, pp. 63, 64, no. 2958.

JUSTIS PETENTIUM . . . dent decimas ecclesiis parochialibus infra metas quarum sitae sunt possessiones predictae . . .

Datum Anagnie, xv kal. Octobris, anno quinto.

1. The struggle of the Church to have the Jews pay tithes to the local churches had been going on for centuries, as may be seen from the numerous references to the subject in *ChJ* (Cf. also B. Blumenkranz, *Juifs et Chrétiens dans le monde occidentale* [Paris, 1960], pp. 349 f.). The rulers of the various lands, who claimed that the Jews were their property and the like, were long hesitant about enforcing this claim of the Church. By the thirteenth century, however, the Church had pretty nearly made its claim good.

2. Jews frequently were exempted from such tolls; see Pope Alexander's demand in bull no. 1, above.

9   no date

No addressee:

DE HAERETICIS[1] . . . We forbid any lay person to dispute, either publicly or privately, about the Catholic faith.[2]

Potthast, 1815.
Sext. 5,2,2, in *CJC*, vol. 2, p. 1068.

DE HAERETICIS . . . Quicunque haereticos, credentes, receptatores, defensores vel fautores eorum scienter praesumpserint ecclesiasticae tradere sepulturae, usque ad satisfactionem idoneam excommunicationis sententiae se noverint subiacere, nec absolutionis beneficium mereantur, nisi propriis manibus publice extumulent, et proiiciant huiusmodi corpora damnatorum, et locus ille perpetua careat sepultura. §1. Inhibemus quoque, ne cuiquam laicae personae liceat publice vel privatim de fide catholica disputare. Qui vero contra fecerit, excommunicationis laqueo innodetur. §2. Haeretici autem, credentes, receptatores, defensores et fautores eorum, ipsorumque filii usque ad secundam generationem, ad nullum ecclesiasticum beneficium seu officium publicum admittantur. Quod si secus actum fuerit, decernimus irritum et inane. §3. Ad haec quoscunque viros ecclesiasticos, qui ad preces huiusmodi pestilentium personarum dignitates, personatus et quaecunque alia ecclesiastica beneficia sunt adepti, ex nunc privamus taliter acquisitis, volentes, quod tales et habitis careant perpetuo, et, si receperunt illa scienter, ad alia vel similia nequaquam in posterum admittantur. §4. Illorum autem filiorum emancipationem, quorum parentes post emancipationem etiam huiusmodi apparuerit ante ipsam a via veritatis ad haereticae superstitionis invium declinasse, nullius volumus esse momenti, velut factam de hominibus sui iuris, quum dignum sit, ut propter tanti atrocitatem delicti filii esse in parentum haereticorum desierint potestate.

1. The canon derives from a letter of Gregory IX excommunicating heretics. See L. Auvray, ed., *Les registres de Grégoire IX* (Paris, 1899-1908), vol. 1, pp. 351 f., no. 539.

2. Jews, it is noted, are not specifically mentioned in this regulation, which apparently applies only to heretics; but it was soon interpreted to apply to Jews as well, if not more so. [See especially Thomas Aquinas, *Summa Theologica* II, II, 10, 7, on public debates.—KS]

Informal private discussions must have gone on from the very beginnings of Christianity, as an inevitable result of Christians and Jews living side by side. Unlike the published debates, whose authors invariably have the better of the argument (cf. A. Lukyn Williams, *Adversus Judaeos* [Cambridge, 1935] and O. S. Rankin, *Jewish Religious Polemics* [Edinburgh, 1956]), the private discussions were less predictable. Since Jews were more conversant with the Bible than were Christians, at least until the thirteenth century, the Church sensed danger in permitting such discussion at all. A rule at a French synod around 1200 prohibited lay Christians from arguing religion with Jews (*ChJ*, pp. 300-301). Pope Gregory IX, in 1233, ordered churchmen in Germany to forbid Jews to discuss their rites and beliefs with Christians (*inhibentes ne de fide vel de ritu suo cum Christianis presumant aliquatenus disputare*), lest the simpleminded Christian be misled (*ChJ*, pp. 200-201, no. 69). None of this applied to organized public disputations, since there the Jews were under constraint not to hurt Christian sensibilities. Local church councils continued to express themselves on the subject, as we shall see below. (Cf. Browe, *Judenmission*, p. 89).

10   no date

Letter patent to Greek Churchmen[1]

ECCE ISTI . . . As part of a long list of instructions, a warning is given against summoning non-Christian physicians, who, whether Jew, Muslim, or other, are classed with magicians, diviners, and even *de schola diaboli*.[2] Such a summons would also make the Jews and Muslims the superiors of the Christians and would thus be offensive and disrespectful to the faith and its law.

Acta Alexandri PP. IV: no. 46a, in *Acta Alexandri IV*, ed. Aloysius L. Tatu (Rome, 1952), *Pontificia commissio ad redigendum codicem iuris canonici orientalis, Fontes, Series* 3:4.

"ECCE ISTI de longe venient: et ecce illi ab aquilone et mari: et isti de terra australi. Leva in circuitu oculos tuos et vide: omnes isti congregati sunt, venerunt tibi. Vivo ego dicit Dominus: quia omnibus his velut ornamento vestieris: et circumdabis eos tamquam sponsa . . . ."

10. Nil ad medicinam sumendum, quod si periculum vertat animarum: nec eundem ad sortilegos, vel divinos, nec ad medicum infidelem.

Cum autem anima sit multo pretiosior (sic) corpore, sub interminatione anathematis prohibetur, ne quis pro corporali salute aliquid infirmo suadeat, quod in periculum animae convertatur. Unde qui Christianus videri et esse voluerit, sortilegos fugiat et divinos, ne esse de schola diaboli comprobetur. Prohibemus etiam districte, ne quis christianus, sanus aut infirmus, medicum advocet infidelem, Judaeum scilicet aut Saracenum; sed nec ab eo vel de eius consilio, medicinam aliquam recipiat: quia hoc pia consideratione in sacris canonibus prohibetur. Nam ex hoc contingit, nostram fidem haberi despectui, cum ipsi Judaei vel Saraceni in huiusmodi christianorum uti ministerio dedignerentur et reputent propter hoc offendere suam legem.

1. [This text was not included in the materials that were collected by Solomon Grayzel.—KS]

2. [The prohibition against resorting to Jewish physicians is rooted in those canons which forbid social mingling with infidels, especially Gratian, *Decretum*, C.28,q.1,c.13, *nullus,* which prohibits the use of Jewish physicians, bathing with Jews, and the eating of Passover *matzot.* At the same time, no one needs reminding of the constant use of Jewish physicians made by popes and princes. Technically, it was possible to claim that only Jews knew how to treat a certain illness, thereby making it permissible to summon them to a Christian bedside. Exceptions aside, however, the present statement is exceedingly strong. Surprisingly, it is also rare from a pope. *ChJ* offers a number of references made by councils to Jewish physicians, but it contains only one such reference by a pope, Honorius III (p. 154), and that reference has nothing to do with medical practice.

It would be tempting to try to extrapolate from the present text and suggest a demonic view of Jews on the part of Alexander IV. But, most likely, this particular text must be viewed under the rubric of pure theory, for, unlike most papal letters, it was not composed in response to a particular problem or crisis. In any case, no other letter of Alexander IV would support anything more than a strict-constructionist view of the canons applying to Jews, and, even then, on matters like usury, he practiced the customary policy of allowing "not immoderate usury."—KS]

Urban IV

Urban IV (1261–1264), Jacques Pantaleon had risen from lowly origins to become the patriarch of Jerusalem. He was not a cardinal at the time of his election; but the cardinals went outside their ranks to find a man of firmness and diplomatic skill. Urban was all of that. He opposed the Hohenstaufens everywhere and invited Charles of Anjou to Sicily.

---

11   April 26, 1262

To all faithful Christians:

SICUT JUDAEIS[1] . . . Pope Urban reissues the customary Bull of Protection. As his predecessors in this action, he mentions: Calixtus, Eugenius, Alexander, Clement, Coelestine, Innocent, and Honorius.[2]

ASV, Armarium 2, tome 38, fols. 22r–24v.

SICUT JUDAEIS non debet esse licentia in Sinagogis suis ultra quam permissum est a lege presumere; ita in his que concessa sunt nulla debent preiudicium sustinere. Nos ergo licet in sua magis velint duritia perdurare, quam Prophetarum verba, et Sacrarum scripturarum arcana cognoscere, atque ad christiane Fidei, et salutis notitiam pervenire que tamen defensionem nostram, et auxilium postulant, et christiane pietatis mansuetudinem predecessorum nostrorum felicis memorie Calixti, Eugenii, Alexandri, Clementis, Celestini, Innocentii, et Honorii Romanorum Pontificum vestigiis inherentes ipsorum petitionem admittimus, eisque Protectionis nostre Clipeum indulgemus. Statuimus etiam, ut nullus Christianus invictus, vel nolentes eos ad Baptismum per violentiam venire compellas. Sed si eorum quilibet sponte ad christianos fide eam[3] confugerit postquam voluntas eius fuerit patefacta Christianus efficiatur, absque aliqua alia pena. Veram quippe Christianitatis fidem habere non creditur qui ad Christianorum Baptisma, non spontaneus, sed invictus cognoscatur pervenire. Nullus etiam Christianitatis eorum personas sine iudicio potestatis terre vulnerare, aut occidere, vel suas illis pecunias aufferre presumat aut bona, que hactenus in ea, in qua habitant regione habuerunt consuetudines immutare. Preterea festivitatum suarum celebratione quisque fustibus, vel lapidibus eos illatenus non perturbet, neque aliquis ab eis coacta seruitia exigat, nisi ea que ipsi temporibus preteritis facere consueverunt, ad hec malorum hominum pravitati, et avaritia obuiantes, decernimus ut nemo illorum Cemeterium mutilare vel diruere audeat, pretextu pecunie, Corpora humata effodere. Si quis autem, Decreti huiusmodi tenorem cognito, temere, quod absit, contraire tentaverit, honoris et officii sui periculum patiatur, aut excommunicationis ultione plectatur, nisi presumptionem suam digna satis factione purgaverit eos autem dumtaxat Judeos huiusmodi protectionis presidio volumus communiri, qui nihil machinari presumpserint in subversione Fidei Christiane.

Ego Urbanus Catholice episcopus.

Ego Odo Tusculanus.

Ego Stephanus Prenestinus episcopus.

Ego Fr. Joannes Tituli Sancti Laurentis in Lucina Presbiter Cardinalis.

Ego Frater Hugo Tituli Sancti Sabine Presbiter Cardinalis.

Datum Viterbii, vi kal. Maii, anno primo.[4]

1. For a discussion of the bull, see the notes to bull no. 2, above.

2. It is curious that he does not mention any predecessors after Honorius III, whose *Sicut* was issued on November 7, 1217 (*ChJ*, no. 35), not even his immediate predecessor, Alexander IV. Perhaps it was mere carelessness on the part of the scribe, whose copying of this text was not up to the highest standards of notarial accuracy, or perhaps the Jews who asked for it could produce only the Honorius bull for the scribe to copy. Normally the petitioners would have been the Jews of Rome, who asked for the bull as part of the by now regular procedure at the accession of a new pope. But here it might have been the Jews of Germany, who were beginning to feel the turbulence of the interregnum, or the Jews of Trani, in southern Italy, who had suffered from serious rioting in 1260 (cf. N. Ferorelli, *Gli Ebrei nell'Italia meridionale* [Turin, 1915], p. 53).

3. Other issues have *fidei causa* at this point.

4. The bull is unquestionably that of Urban IV. It is signed *Ego Urbanus, catholice episcopus*, followed by the signatures of Odo Tusculanus and others. [Once more Odo of Tusculum appears in an unexpected role; see above, bull no. 2, n. 3.

With respect to the list of predecessors, it must be recalled that once included in the 1234 Decretals, *Sicut Judaeis* became binding canon law, valid at *all* times. Any reissue served the purpose of adding emphasis. The omission of the name of a papal predecessor in a reissue, therefore, may be of note, but it is not of real moment.—KS]

12   May 2, 1262

To Cistercian Abbots:

EX PARTE SIQUIDEM . . . The pope has learned that many clerics in the neighborhood of Cistercian monasteries are trying to destroy the order's privileges. Since they could not excommunicate the Cistercians, as they wished, they decreed a boycott against them in the manner of the "judgment of the Jews"[1] (*judicari videamini judicio Judaeorum*). The pope orders the boycott lifted.

Archives Nationales, L 254, no. 25.
Jean Guiraud, ed., *Les registres d'Urbain IV* (Paris, 1901-1958), no. 2900.

Urbanus episcopus, servus servorum Dei, dilectis filiis . . . abbati Cistercii ejusque coabbatibus et conventibus universis Cisterciensis ordinis, salutem et apostolicam benedictionem.

Cum a nobis—. EX PARTE SIQUIDEM vestra fuit propositum coram nobis quod nonnulli ecclesiarum prelati, vestris libertatibus invidentes, cum eis non liceat ex apostolice sedis indulto in vos excommunicationis vel interdicti sententias promulgare, in familiares, servientes et benefactores ac illos qui molunt in molendinis vel coquunt in furnis vestris quique vendendo seu emendo vobis communicant, sententias proferunt memoratas, sicque non vim et potestatem privilegiorum vestrorum sed sola verba servantes, vos quodam modo excommunicant, dum vobis communicare fideles non sinunt; ex quo illud evenit inconveniens ut, quantum ad hoc, judicari videamini judicio Judeorum, et qui vobis communicant in predictis majorem excommunicationem incurrant quam excommunicatis communicando fuerant incursuri. Quare nobis humiliter supplicastis ut providere quieti vestre paterna sollicitudine curaremus. Nos igitur vestris supplicationibus inclinati, ne quis prelatorum ipsorum sententias easdem in fraudem privilegiorum apostolice sedis de cetero promulgare presumat, ad instar felicis recordationis Innocentii et Alexandri, predecessorum nostrorum Romanorum pontificum, auctoritate apostolica inhibemus, decernentes eas irritas et inanes, si contra inhibitionem hujusmodi fuerint promulgate. Nulli ergo—. Si quis—.

Datum Viterbii, vi nonas maii, pontificatus nostri anno primo.

---

1. The details of the dispute between the clerics are of no interest to us, but this term is of great interest. It served as a euphemism for the method used regularly to

compel Jews to obey the demands of the Church. [Its appearance in a text otherwise having no relation to the Jews means that this boycott, or indirect excommunication, was not only well known but also in frequent use. The popes were thus assertive and forceful in seeking to enforce canonical limits on Jewish behavior; not, however, in overstepping them.—KS]

13   June 29, 1262

To the people of Guarcino, diocese of Alatri:

SANE MIRANTES . . . Pope Urban withdraws a privilege granted by his predecessor, Alexander IV, to a certain Roman noble by the name of Gratianus Belmonte. The privilege had empowered Gratianus to collect a substantial portion of what the people of Guarcino were obligated to pay annually to their suzerain, the Church. Gratianus had so abused his privilege that he dared to claim full power over the town, broke into people's homes and took away what he liked. Moreover, "in contempt of our Savior, he had no qualms about bringing along a Jewish "magician"[1] who sinfully boasted that he knew everything the men and women of Guarcino were doing in secret." Under pain of a heavy fine, the people of the town are forbidden to give Gratianus anything whatsoever.

Reg. Vat. 26, fol. 26v, no. 109.
Guiraud, *Registres Urb. IV*, pp. 37–38, no. 111.
A. Theiner, *Codex diplomaticus dominii temporalis S. Sedis* (Rome, 1861–1862), vol. 1, p. 146, no. 272; with slight variants.
MGH, Epist. Saec. XIII, vol. 3, p. 490.

Populo Guarcinati, Alatrine diocesis. In nostris semper haberi—.

SANE MIRANTES audivimus, sed non utique acceptamus quod, cum felicis recordationis Alexander papa, predecessor noster, vobis dederit sub certa forma per litteras apostolicas in mandatis ut duas partes omnium proventuum et reddituum, quos ecclesia Romana in castro vestro dinoscitur obtinere, nobili viro Gratiano Belmontis, civi Romano, assignaretis, certo super hoc per alias suas litteras, ut dicitur, executore concesso, idem nobilis hujusmodi gratia ipsius predecessoris abutens, ejus pretextu omnimodam jurisdictionem in castro ipso nititur exercere, laicos quoque et, quod est gravius, clericos ejusdem castri multipliciter propter hoc aggravans et molestans, domos eorum frangere et quandoque bona ibidem inventa temere asportare presumit, illos eorum qui sibi super jurisdictione ipsa que ad eum non pertinet, obedire denegant, faciendo coram senatoribus Urbis malitiose citari. Quendam autem Judeum sortilegum illuc ducere non est veritus in nostri contumelia Redemptoris, qui se nequiter jactando cognoscere asserit universa occulta que ab hominibus et mulieribus committuntur, ibidem in nostrum et apostolice sedis contemptum ac injuriam et ipsius ecclesie Romane prejudicium et vestrum non modicum detrimentum. Quia vero sepedictum castrum ad nos et eandem ecclesiam pertinet pleno jure, nos pati nolentes ut ipsi ecclesie hujusmodi seu quecumque jura vel redditus aliquatenus subtrahantur, cum omnia bona ipsius quoquomodo distracta intendamus ad jus et proprietatem ejusdem ecclesie revocare, universitati vestre sub pena centum marcarum argenti solvendarum nostre camere si quod injungimus non feceritis, per apostolica scripta districte precipiendo, mandamus quatenus eidem nobili nec supradictas duas partes premissorum proventuum et reddituum solvere, nec ei super hiis et aliis intendere de cetero presumatis. Nos enim nichilominus prefatas ipsius predecessoris nostri litteras pro eodem nobili vobis aut cuicumque executori directas, et quamlibet concessionem per ipsas aut quascunque litteras alias de premissis et quibuscunque aliis juribus in predicto castro ad nos et supradictam ecclesiam pertinentibus, nobili factam eidem, auctoritate presentium revocamus et volumus vires aliquas non habere.

Datum Viterbii, iii kal. Julii, anno primo.

1. On the belief in magic during the Middle Ages see G. G. Coulton, *Medieval Panorama* (New York, 1955), chap. 9, "Nature and Superstition," and Joshua Trachtenberg, *Jewish Magic and Superstition* (New York and Philadelphia, 1961).

14   November 24, 1262

To the Abbot and Convent of St. Anthony in Pamier:

Ea que judicio . . . The pope ratifies an agreement arrived at in a dispute between the abbot and the convent. He had appointed Bishop Raymond de Felgar of Toulouse to look into the dispute. Jews are mentioned at two points in the long list of articles of agreement. The abbot is to receive: (1) the feudal census or tribute which the Jews of Pamier pay annually and (2) the tithes and first fruits from the produce of two parcels of land which a certain R(abbi?) David held in fee.

Reg. Vat. 26, fol. 57, anno II, no. 32.
Guiraud, *Registres Urb. IV*, p. 66, no. 170.

... abbati et conventui monasterii sancti Antonini Appamiarum, ordinis sancti Augustini, Tholosane diocesis.

EA QUE JUDICIO etc. usque communiri.

Item censum seu tributum, quod Judei de villa Appamiarum tenentur reddere annuatim. Item . . . et ecclesia sancti Martini de Oleriis, quam tenet Stephanus de Lauriaco, et exceptis decimis et primitiis de Fraxineto et de Mediana, quas tenet magister R. David, et villa sancti Amatoris cum juribus suis temporalibus, que modo Petrus Pontii tenet;

Datum apud Urbem Veterem, viii kal. Decembris, anno secundo.[1]

1. [The possession of Jewish revenues by monasteries was anything but rare. But one would like to know why these monasteries did not feel the same uneasiness about the possibly usurious origins of these revenues that was felt by royalty and other nobles, women in particular, as a number of the documents in this collection demonstrate (including that immediately following).—KS]

15   February 8, 1263

To the abbot of Aulne of the Cistercian Order, Diocese of Liege:[1]

OBLATA NOBIS . . . Girard de Marbais[2] had written to Pope Urban that his conscience was troubled about the money he had received while a counselor of the duke of Brabant.[3] The money, 1200 Louvain pounds per year, had been assigned to him by the duke as his salary. But it had come from Jews, and consequently he assumed that it had been gained through usury. He therefore had asked the pope what to do about the money. The pope minimizes Girard's personal guilt and asks that the abbot provide a penance for the peace of Girard's soul,[4] urging also that one hundred pounds of the money be devoted to charitable ends.

Reg. Vat. 27, fol. 53, no. 2.
Guiraud, *Registres Urb. IV* (Cameral.), p. 57, no. 204.

. . . abbati Alnensi, Cisterciensis ordinis, Leodiensis diocesis.

OBLATA NOBIS ex parte dilecti filii nobilis viri Girardi de Marbais, domini de Bruco, petitio continebat quod, cum nobilis vir . . . dux Brabantie, cujus tunc erat consiliarius, annis sibi singulis ducentas libras Lovaniensium de camera sua exhiberi faceret nomine pensionis ipse aliquotiens pensionem ipsam, duce ipso mandante, recepit de pecunia et manibus Judeorum. Unde, cum pecuniam ipsam credit per Judeos eosdem a Christianis extortam fuisse per usurariam pravitatem et ex hoc consciencie sue metuit, nobit humiliter supplicavit ut in hac parte sibi providere salubriter curaremus. Nos itaque attendentes, quod bonarum mentium est ibi timere culpam ubi culpa minime reperitur, discretioni tue presentium auctoritate committimus et mandamus quatinus circa prefatum G. super hoc auctoritate nostra providas et dispenses, prout secundum Deum anime sue saluti videris expedire, recepturus ab eo centum libras dicte monete nomine helemosine nostre quas ipse sponte ac devote nobis duxit in ejusdem helemosine subsidium offerendas.

Datum apud Urbem Veterem, vi id. Februarii, anno secundo.

1. Aulne-sur-Sambre in Hainaut. The abbot was probably a friend of Girard and may have initiated this correspondence on his behalf.

2. The document speaks of him as *dominus de Bruco;* not Bruge, but some minor locality.

3. Henry III became duke of Brabant in 1248. He married Alice (Alix, Aleyde), daughter of the duke of Burgundy, in 1252. He died in February 1261. Although in his lifetime he had encouraged the activities of Jewish and other moneylenders, for the good of his soul, he left instructions in his will that "Jews and Cahorsins shall be expelled from Brabant . . . so that none remain unless they do business like other merchants, without moneylending or usury" (cf. S. Ullman, *Histoire des Juifs en Belgique,* [Anvers, n.d.], p. 15). Alice, as regent for her young son, did not carry out the wish of the deceased. Instead, she sought the advice of Thomas Aquinas, who replied in the famous letter cited above (bull no. 4, n. 3), in which he said nothing about expulsion, but spoke instead of imposing no new hardships. He did, however, urge that Jews be made to wear distinguishing clothes, and he advised using monies known to have been gained through usury for pious purposes. Girard de Marbais appears to have had similar qualms of conscience. On Aquinas's letter, see also Aronius, no. 770. On Henry III as ruler, see H. Pirenne, *Histoire de Belgique,* (Brussells, 1929; reprint 1972–75), vol. 1, p. 224.

4. At the same time, Pope Urban dispatched another letter to the same abbot (Guiraud, *Registres Urb. IV,* no. 205) easing the conscience of Girard de Marbais from another burden. Henry III of Brabant had taken a crusader's vow; on his deathbed, he had asked Girard to carry it out. Girard had agreed, but there were

good reasons why he was unable to keep his word; and so, he asked to be absolved. The pope granted the request; see *SRH*, vol. 9, p. 262, n. 52.

16   February 20, 1263

To Albert, formerly Bishop of Regensburg:[1]

CUM PREDICATIONEM CRUCIS . . . The pope empowers Albert to recruit volunteers for a crusading army in the various lands of central Europe where the German language is spoken.[2] If any of the would-be crusaders are under financial obligation, or are bound to the repayment of interest-bearing loans, they are to be released from these obligations and, in accordance with the decree of the Lateran Council,[3] no one may hold them to the payment of usury. As for Jews,[4] they are to be compelled to restore usury to the crusaders, and, until they do so, they are to be denied contact with the faithful.

Reg. Vat. 27, fol. 88, no. 1.
Potthast, no. 18491 (gives the date as Feb. 13).
Guiraud, *Registres Urb. IV* (Cameral.), p. 87, no. 316.

Eidem.

CUM etc. usque monitus, fraternitati tue presentium auctoritate committimus, ut si qui crucesignati vel crucesignandi partium earumdem ad prestandas usuras juramento vel alio quocumque modo teneantur astricti, creditores ipsorum ut remittant eis prestitum super hoc juramentum vel cujuslibet generis obligationem et ab usurarum exactione desistant, ac ad solutionem usurarum nullum eorum cohercere presumant, de plano et absque judiciorum strepitu, veritate cognita, clericos, monitione premissa, per censuram ecclesiasticam, laicos vero per penam in Lateranensi concilio contra usurarios editam, appellatione remota, compellas. Judeos vero ad restituendas usuras eisdem crucesignatis vel crucesignandis volumus qua convenit, districtione compelli et donec ipsas reddiderint, communionem eis fidelium denegari.

Datum apud Urbem Veterem, x kal. Martii, anno secundo.

---

1. The famous philosopher-theologian Albertus Magnus. He was bishop of Regensburg from 1260 to 1262, when he resigned to become the papal legate to the German-speaking lands of central Europe. On his attitude to Jews and Jewish

literature, cf. J. Guttmann, "Guillaume d'Auvergne et la littérature Juive," *REJ* 18 (1889): 243–255.

2. Recruitment of crusaders went on constantly. For the dangerous situation for the Latin Kingdom and the Latin principalities in Syria and Palestine, see Steven Runciman, *A History of the Crusades* (Cambridge, 1954), vol. 3, pp. 284 ff., 306 f.

3. The Third Lateran Council, 1179, c. 25.

4. The Fourth Lateran Council 1215, c. 67 (*ChJ*, pp. 306–307, no. IX). Every crusader's privilege contained a statement to this effect.

17   July 19, 1263

To the King of Hungary:[1]

REGALIS CELSITUDINIS . . . The correct and proper duty of a king is to safeguard the liberties of the Church and of professing Christians. Yet the pope hears that Jews and Muslims crowd his city and that the king appoints them to collect his taxes and revenues. Canon law provides that in such cases a Christian must be appointed to supervise the activity of non-Christians;[2] even if the king is correct that previous popes had granted him the right to act as he does.[3] Nevertheless, it is still wrong that those who, through their own fault, are condemned to perpetual servitude and whom Christian piety permits to live by the side of Christians, should exercise authority over Christians.[4] The pope therefore asks that despite his old privilege, the king appoint only Christian officials.

Potthast, no. 18595.

Arminius Friss, ed., *Monumenta Hungariae Judaica* (Budapest, 1903), no. 24.

George Fejér, *Codex diplomaticus Hungariae ecclesiasticus et civilis* (Buda, 1829–1866), IV, 3, p. 86.

Urbanus, servus servorum dei, charissimo in Christo filio, regi Hungarie illustri, salutem et apostolicam benediccionem.

REGALIS CELSITUDINIS honori convenit et saluti ad illa intente sollicitudinis studium adhibere, per que libertati ecclesie ac christiane religionis professoribus a dispendiis utiliter caveatur. Accepimus sane, quod Tu consideracione debita non advertens, quod iudei et saraceni christianis oppido sunt infesti, eos interdum ad colligendos reditus et proventus tuos, postquam illos iudeis et sarracenis vendideris, preficis, nec ipsis aliquem christianum iuxta sancciones canonicas deputas, de gravaminibus inferendis clericis et ecclesiis non suspectum, per quem dicti iudei sive saraceni sine christianorum iniuria iura regalia consequantur, in excusacionis tue suffragium pretendendo, quod id tibi licet ex privilegio progenitoribus tuis ab apostolica sede concesso. Cum igitur ex hoc libertati predicte ac christiane fidei plurimum derogetur, serenitatem regiam rogamus, monemus et adhortamur attente, in remissionem tibi peccaminum svadentes, quatenus prudenter considerans, quod non est conveniens vel honestum, ut eisdem iudeis et sarracenis, quos propria culpa submisit perpetue servituti, exercendi vim potestatis in christianos, quorum pietas illorum cohabitacionem dignanter sustinet, possibilitas tribuatur; eosdem sarracenos et iudeos, privilegio non obstante predicto, pro nostra et prefate sedis reverencia, in colligendis huiusmodi redditibus et proventibus, nisi deputato sibi secundum sancciones prefatas aliquo christiano, de cetero non preponas, preces nostras in hac parte taliter admissurus, quod circa id fidelium iacturis et iniuriis obvietur, nosque magnificenciam tuam provide dignis in domino laudibus commendemus.

Datum apud Urbem Veterem, x kal. Augusti, anno secundo.

1. Bela IV, king from 1235 to 1270.

2. In X.5,6,18.

3. The reference is to Gregory IX's letter to the same king, December 10, 1239 (*ChJ*, no. 100). It is clear from that letter that Pope Gregory was making the concession most reluctantly. But in view of the instability of the king's position and the heterogeneous nature of the Hungarian population, the king's situation called for the relaxation of the rule. The situation had not changed by 1262, and Urban's letter, too, appears mild in tone. Cf. S. W. Baron, *SRH*, vol. 10, pp. 22 ff. Moreover, even into the 1270s there was no significant change (see *ChJ*, p. 211). [One would hope that the long-held assumption about the inevitability of using Jews in undeveloped medieval economies will someday be examined in depth.— KS]

4. [Does the pope thus imply that Muslims are, like Jews, condemned to perpetual servitude?—KS]

18   October 23, 1263

To all Archbishops, to members of the Dominican and Franciscan Orders, and to all now appointed or to be appointed for matters pertaining to the Holy Land:

CUM NEGOTIUM CRUCIS . . . In order to enumerate the privileges to be extended to anyone taking the Cross, Pope Urban repeats verbatim the bull issued at the Fourth Lateran Council by Pope Innocent III (December 15, 1216), which began with the words "Ad liberandam terram."

Reg. Vat. 28, fol. 21, no. 70.
Guiraud, *Registres Urb. IV*, p. 226, no. 467.

Universis archiepiscopis ac dilectis filiis fratribus Predicatorum et Minorum ordinum, ceterisque executoribus per diversa christiana regna mundi ad Crucis negotium pro Terre Sancte subventione, a sede apostolica deputatis et in posterum deputandis.

CUM NEGOTIUM CRUCIS, pro Terre Sancte subsidio, vobis per diversas nostras sub certis formis litteras per diversa christiana regna mundi duxerimus committendum, faciendi observari per vos vel per alium seu alios, circa crucesignatos et crucesignandos, privilegia et indulgentias et immunitates, que ipsis in generali concilio sunt concessa, et contradictores per censuram ecclesiasticam, appellatione postposita, compescendi, vobis plenam auctoritate presentium concedimus facultatem. Tenorem autem hujusmodi privilegiorum indulgentiarum et immunitatum, sumptum ex regesto felicis recordationis Innocentii pape III, predecessoris nostri, presentibus inseri fecimus, qui talis est:

"Ad liberandam Terram Sanctam de manibus impiorum ardenti desiderio aspirantes—." Et infra:

Quod si quisquam creditorum eos ad solutionem coegerit usurarum, eum ad restitutionem eorum (*sic*) simili cogi animadversione mandamus. Judeos vero ad remittendas usuras per secularem compelli precipimus potestatem, et donec illas remiserint, ab universis Christi fidelibus per excommunicationis sententiam eis omnino communio denegetur. Hiis autem, qui Judeis debita solvere nequeunt in presenti, sic principes seculares utili dilatione provideant, quod post iter arreptum, usque quo de ipsorum obitu vel reditu certissime cognoscatur, usurarum incommoda non incurrant, compulsis Judeis proventus pignorum, quos interim ibi perceperint, in sortem, expensis deductis necessariis, computare, cum hujusmodi beneficium non multum videatur habere dispendii, quia solutionem sic prorogat, quod debitum non absorbet.

Datum apud Urbem Veterem, x kal. Novembris, anno tertio.

19   April 2, 1264

To the Prior and the Canon of Troyes:[1]

DILECTIS FILIIS . . . Pope Urban requests the help of the addressees in collecting the debts owed by the archbishop of Sens to Angelo Scarsus, son of Jacob Scarsus the younger, and to Angelo, son of John *Judaeus*.[2] Both are called merchants, citizens of Rome.[3]

Reg. Vat. 28, fol. 43, no. 145.
Guiraud, *Registres Urb. IV*, p. 269, no. 542.

In e. m . . . . priori s. Bernardi, et Phylippo de Planci, canonico Trecensi, pro DILECTIS FILIIS Angelo Scarso, filio quondam Jacobi Scarsi juvenis, et Angelo Johannis Judei, civibus et mercatoribus Romanis, contra . . . archiepiscopum Senonensem, et nonullos suffraganeos, etc., usque servetur. Datum apud Urbem Veterem, iiii nonas Aprilis, anno III.

In e. m. . . . priori s. Bernardi Trecensis, pro eisdem mercatoribus contra . . . electum Lugdunensem, et nonullos suffraganeos ipsius, etc., usque servetur. Datum ut supra.

In e. m. Petro Comitis, thesaurario Tripolitano, et Petro Inglibaldi, canonico ecclesie s. Marci de Urbe, Parisius commorantibus, pro eisdem mercatoribus, contra . . . archiepiscopum Remensem, et nonnullos suffraganeos, etc.

Datum apud Urbem Veterem, iiii non. Aprilis, anno tertio.

1. Similar letters were sent to a number of churchmen to help these and other Roman merchants in the collection of debts owed by the archbishop of Sens and his suffragans, as well as by others (Guiraud, *Registres, Urb. IV*, loc. cit.). One letter mentions the archbishop of Rheims as a debtor; another, the bishop-elect of Lyons.

2. The interesting consideration in this document is the Jewishness of the merchants. A similar letter, though in an entirely different situation, had been sent by Pope Alexander IV (bull no. 1, above); but there, the merchants are distinctly called *Judaei* and they are not referred to as *dilecti filii*, a term reserved at this time for Christians only. It is possible that the Angelo mentioned here was of that fairly common type of those days whose families continued to be characterized as *Judaei* because of a conversion from Judaism one or more generations earlier. The name was not necessarily used disparagingly. On the other hand, the use of *dilecti filii* in this case may have been purely accidental. [But compare the highly derogatory remarks made in the 1130s about the

antipope Anacletus II, whose great-grandfather had converted—and married a Christian (cited in K. Stow "*Gishat ha-Yehudim le-'Apifiorut ve-ha-Doktrinah ha-'Apifiorit shel Hagannat ha-Yehudim ba-Shanim 1063-1147,*" in *Studies in the History of the Jewish People and the Land of Israel* 5 [1980]: 180).—KS]

3. [It is important to note the papally inspired collection of debts on behalf of cameral merchants; on which see Robert Lopez, *The Commercial Revolution of the Middle Ages, 950-1350* (Englewood Cliffs, N.J., 1971). If popes were willing to participate in the violation of canons by Christians, how much more would they accept the lending activities of Jews who were damned already and exempt from the canons pertaining to mortal sins? See here, K. Stow "Papal and Royal Attitudes toward Jewish Lending in the Thirteenth Century," *AJS Review* 6 (1981): 161-184.—KS]

20   July 7, 1264

To the Archbishop of Tournai:

LECTA NOBIS . . . John of Chinon and his wife Joanna, of the diocese of Tournai, came to petition the pope for an increase in their stipend. In a previous letter, the pope had asked the archbishop[1] to arrange that some church or monastery, not otherwise thus burdened, undertake the support of these converts and their daughter; all they had received was fifty solidi annually, which was hardly enough. The pope orders that the stipend be doubled.[2]

Reg. Vat. 29, fol. 202, no. 1005.
Guiraud, *Registres Urb. IV*, p. 311, no. 1955.

. . . archiepiscopo Turonensi.

LECTA NOBIS dilecti filii Johannis de Kaynone et Johanne, uxoris ejus, tue diocesis, petitio continebat quod, licet nos pro eis qui de judaice cecitatis errore ad fidem catholicam sunt conversi, tibi dederimus sub certa forma per nostras litteras in mandatis ut eis ab aliquibus monasteriis vel ecclesiis tue civitatis seu diocesis, super provisione simili de mandato apostolico non gravatis, faceres, prout expedire videres, in vite necessariis, quoad viverent, provideri, tu tamen ipsis non nisi in quinquaginta solidis turonensium annuatim providisti seu provideri fecisti auctoritate hujusmodi litterarum, propter quod dicti vir et uxor, ad benignitatem sedis apostolice recurrentes, humiliter petebant a nobis ut eis pro se ac unica ipsorum filia de sacro fonte renata, provisionem congruam de qua sustentari valeant, fieri mandaremus. Nos itaque, circa

ipsos paterne ducti benignitatis affectu, fraternitati tue mandamus quatenus, si est ita, eis a predictis monasteriis vel ecclesiis, qui super ipsorum
vel aliorum conversorum non sint simili provisione gravata, facias
auctoritate nostra, per te vel per alium, in aliis quinquaginta solidis
turonensium, supradicta provisione tua in suo duratura robore, provideri. Contradictores etc. usque compescendo. Non obstante si—.

Datum apud Urbem Veterem, non. Julii, anno tertio.

1. Vincent de Pilmil 1257–1270.

2. For the support of converts as a matter of policy, see the references cited in bull
no. 3, n. 1, above. Add here the material cited in S. Grayzel, "Jewish References in
a 13th Century Formulary," *JQR* 46 (July, 1955): 50–53. See the following
document for still another aspect of the same problem.

21   July 26, 1264

To the Patriarch of Jerusalem:[1]

NONNULLI SICUT ACCEPIMUS . . . Pope Urban had been informed that
on occasion poverty-stricken Muslims and Jews come to Acre desiring to receive baptism, yet, after it is given, many of them return to
Judaism and Islam in opprobrium of the Faith. Oppressed by
poverty, they do not have the means to sustain themselves. The pope
thus asks that at least during a very brief period of instruction,[2] the
converts be supported in monasteries.[3]

Reg. Vat. 29, fol. 198v, no. 975.
Guiraud, *Registres Urb. IV*, p. 304, no. 1925.
O. Posse, ed., *Analecta Vaticana* (Innsbruck, 1878), p. 35, no. 427.

Patriarche Jerosolimitano apostolice sedis legato.

NONNULLI, SICUT ACCEPIMUS. Sarraceni pauperes et Judei, converti ad
unitatem ecclesie cupientes, ad civitatem Acconensem accedunt et postulant baptizari. Verum licet donum baptismatis consequantur, tamen,
quia paupertatis mole depressi non habent unde possint in vite necessariis sustentari, prius quam catholice fidei doctrinam suscipiant, abire
sinuntur. Nec interdum aliqui eorum in huiusmodi proposito perseverant, quin immo ad errores solitos redeunt, in obprobrium nominis
christiani. Unde cum in exaltationem et augmentum fidei dinoscatur,

cum tales de gentilitatis errore ad Dominum convertuntur, etsi eos resilire contingat, quodammodo cedat in ipsius fidei detrimentum, fraternitati tue mandamus quatenus super hiis apponas salubre remedium illis, quos taliter converti contigitur, saltem per aliquos dies, in quibus cathecizari valeant et in fidei doctrina formari, ab ecclesiis vel monasteriis Acconensis civitatis et diocesis facias, per te vel per alium seu alios, in vite necessariis, secundum quod expedire videris, provideri. Contradictores etc. usque compescendo. Non obstante si aliquibus a sede apostolica sit indultum, quod interdici vel excommunicari nequeant aut suspendi, per litteras apostolicas non facientes plenam et expressam de indulto huiusmodi mentionem.

Datum apud Urbem Veterem, vii kal. Augusti, anno tertio.

1. William, bishop of Agen since 1247, succeeded Jacques Pantaleon (when he became Pope Urban IV) as patriarch of Jerusalem and administrator of St. John of Acre. He retained the post for two years.

2. The period of the catechumenate for Jews had been set by the Council of Agde (506) at eight months. The reason given was that Jewish habits of mind were too deeply ingrained, and one had to make certain of the prospective convert's sincerity. Gratian, in his *Decretum* (D.4,c.93, *de cons.*), prepared about 1140, repeated this rule. In practice however, exceptions were frequent. During periods of riot and persecution, conversions were performed on the spot. Here the pope effectively left it to the judgment of the patriarch to decide the length of the catechumenate.

3. See the discussion of this incident in B. Z. Kedar, "Notes on the History of the Jews in Palestine in the Middle Ages [Hebrew]," *Tarbiz* 42 (1973): 401-418, and the text, p. 416.

Clement IV

Clement IV, 1265–1268. As Gui Foulquois, he had been archbishop of Narbonne. Urban IV made him a cardinal. As pope, he favored the ambitions of Charles of Anjou, King Louis's brother, for the throne of Naples; with his help, Charles finally overcame the remaining Hohenstaufen opposition. Clement does not appear to have issued the bull *Sicut Judaeis*.

22   March 26, 1265

To the archbishop of Seville:[1]

NON SINE MISTERIO . . . Pope Clement entrusts the archbishop with the task of preaching a continuing crusade against the Muslims of Spain and those of North Africa who have come to their aid. The archbishop is empowered to free crusaders from the payment of usury, no matter to whom they are indebted. Jews must be compelled by the secular authorities to restore interest already collected and, until they do so, they are to be denied contact with faithful Christians.[2]

Reg. Vat. 29A, fol. 3, no. 13.
E. Jordan, ed., *Les registres de Clement IV* (Paris 1893–1945), p. 4, no. 15.

. . . Archiepiscopo Ispalensi.

NON SINE MISTERIO factum est quod Agar ancilla olim a facie domine sue Sare fugiendo recessit, quod in Yspania retroactis temporibus dinoscitur contigisse; quia et si proles ipsius Agar eandem pene totam horrendis spurcitiis polluisset Yspaniam, ita ut in sordibus tanquam menstruosa mulier tunc temporis haberetur, ex alto tamen digne postmodum provisum conspicitur, quod Christiane fidei veri cultores, tunc pauci numero, terre ipsius incole, ipsam ab Agarenorum, qui usurpato libere matris nomine Sarraceni dicuntur, oppressionibus in spiritus fortitudine liberarunt. Sed sic terra eadem ad inextimabilis commoda libertatis perducta, et Christiano cultui divina faciente dextera restituta, necnon fidelibus Christi, cum nullus eos, subactis 'et exterminatis taliter Sarracenis predictis ipsos vexare solitis, exterreret, vitam in Dei servitio ducentibus pacificam et quietam; ecce subito et ex insperato Sarraceni de Africa in multitudine contumaci ejusdem terre limites invaserunt; quod non absque dispensatione divina, cujus semper sunt justa, et si occulta interdum, judicia, creditur provenisse, ne forte ex longa fideles ipsi quiete torperent otio, et fortitudinis virtus per ignaviam in eis decresceret, si cum quo confligerent et se exercerent utiliter adversarium non haberent. Sed in eo quod stragem ipsis fidelibus contra eorum imprevisa jacula armis providentie non munitis nequiter intulerunt, pia mater ecclesia quasi unigeniti planctum assumit, impiorum gladiis pretioso Christi redemptos sanguine conspiciens sic prosterni. Attamen et in hoc attenuato merore, quadam consolatione respirat, dum interne considerationis oculis eorundem Sarracenorum arrogantiam et superbiam ipsorum fortitudine majorem attendit, propter quod ipsos sperat, prout verisimilis conjectura pretendit, fidelium viribus tanquam vas figuli facile conterendos, dummodo magnanimitate solita ad id ipsi velint intendere, quod utique facere debent, si volunt instantia vitare pericula, et filii degeneres non haberi. Nam ad proprii jacturam honoris procul dubio eis accederet, si tueri non possent per suos progenitores quesita, et conculcarentur ab eis de quibus eorum parentes sepius feliciter triumpharunt. Sane cogit nos caritas, qua non possumus aliorum timore non affici, et malorum eis contingentium pericula per compassionis consortium non sentire, ac pastorale officium, quo pro universali Christi grege fragilitati nostre credito vigilare jubemur, instanter exigit, ut contra pericula que possint populo Christiano accidere, si negotium quod adversus Sarracenos eosdem imminet negligenter, quod absit, sive tepide procuratum fuerit, firmamentum quod possumus opponamus. Habentes igitur plenam de tue fidei puritate et circumspecta providentia in Jhesu Christo fiduciam, predicationem crucis in regnis Yspanie et Januensi ac Pisana civitatibus et diocesibus, contra Yspanie ac Africe Sarracenos, presentium tibi auctoritate, committimus, in remissionem tibi peccaminum injungentes quatinus in commisso tibi super hoc officio juxta datam tibi a Deo prudentiam efficaciter procedere studeas, illos quibus predicandum duxeris exhortationibus oportunis inducens, ut ad refrenandos ipsorum Sarracenorum malignos impetus cum reverentia suscipiant crucem ipsam, ac eam propiis humeris affigentes, votum ipsum fideliter exequantur, ut per ipsorum sollicitudinis studium et laborem, divina suffragante clementia, ipsorum Sarracenorum malitia, ne in suis cogitationibus convalescant, protinus reprimatur. Et ut ipsi fideles tanto libentius atque ferventius prosequantur premissa, quanto ex suo labore se potiorem fructum noverint percepturos; nos de omnipotentis Dei misericordia et beatorum Petri et Pauli apostolorum ejus auctoritate confisi, et illa quam nobis Deus, licet indignis, ligandi atque solvendi contulit potestate, omnibus vere penitentibus et confessis, qui assumpto vivifice crucis signaculo ad prelium Domini adversus Sarracenos hujusmodi preliandum in personis propriis processerint et expensis, plenam peccatorum suorum, de quibus corde contriti et ore confessi fuerint, veniam indulgemus, et in retributione justorum salutis eterne pollicemur augmentum. Eis autem qui non in personis propriis illuc accesserint, sed in suis tantum expensis, juxta qualitatem et facultatem suam, viros ydoneos destinarint illic justa providentie tue arbitrium moraturos, et illis similiter, qui licet in alienis expensis, in propriis tamen personis assumpte peregrinationis laborem impleverint, plenam suorum veniam concedimus peccatorum. Hujusmodi quoque peregrinationis volumus esse participes, juxta quantitatem subsidii et devotionis affectum, omnes qui ad subventionem ipsius negotii de bonis suis congrue ministrabunt, quique ad hoc naves proprias exhibuerint, et qui eas studuerint fabricare. Personas insuper, familias et bona eorum, ex quo crucem susceperint, sub beati Petri et nostra protectione suscipimus, et sub diocesanorum suorum defensione consistant. Quod si quisquam contra presumpserit, per diocesanum loci ubi fuerit per censuram ecclesiasticam appellatione postposita compescatur. Siqui vero illuc proficiscentium ad prestandas usuras juramento tenentur astricti, creditores eorum per te vel alios, sublato appellationis obstaculo, eadem districtione compellas, ut juramenta hujusmodi penitus relaxantes, ab usurarum ulterius exactione desistant. Si autem quisquam creditorum eos ad solutionem coegerit usurarum, eum ad restitutionem earum, appellatione remota, simili districtione compellas. Judeos quippe ad remittendas ipsis usuras, per secularem compelli precipimus potestatem, et donec eas remiserint, ab omnibus Christi fidelibus tam in mercimoniis, quam aliis, sub excommunicationis pena eis jubemus communionem omnimodam denegari. Porro ut predicti crucesignati eo exequantur libentius et ferventius votum suum, quo pluribus fuerint favoribus communiti, presentium auctoritate concedimus, ut iidem eis immunitate et privilegio gaudeant, que in generali crucesignatorum in terre sancte subsidium indulgentia continentur, atque per sedis apostolice litteras, vel legatorum ipsius, extra suas dioceses, nisi ille que ab eadem sede obtente fuerint plenam de indulto hujusmodi mentionem fecerint, non valeant conveniri, dummodo parati existant coram suis ordinariis de se querelantibus respondere; quos per te tuosque commissarios ab hiis ecclesiastica defendi censura, cessante appellationis obstaculo, volumus, qui eosdem contra indultum hujusmodi presumpserint temere molestare. Ceterum ad hujusmodi ardui et salubris negotii efficaciam pleniorem, ut tu et iidem

commissarii convocare possitis cleros et populos ad quemcunque volueritis locum ydoneum, et ibidem verbum crucis proponere, ac fidelibus
vere penitentibus et confessis ad predicationem eandem convenientibus,
ipsamque audientibus reverenter, centum dies de injunctis eis penitentiis
relaxare; quodque tu ipsique commissarii vobis et vestris familiis in
ecclesiis ecclesiastico interdicto suppositis, excommunicatis et interdictis
exclusis, non pulsatis campanis, voce summissa, et clausis januis, divina
celebrare officia, et facere celebrari, ac populis proponere verbum crucis,
atque crucis caractere insignitos ab excommunicatione quam pro eo
quod sepulchrum Dominicum contra prohibitionem legatorum sedis
aspostolice visitarunt, et illos etiam qui eam pro eo quod Sarracenis
merces portaverunt et arma prohibita, vel eisdem contra Christianos
impenderunt favorem, consilium, vel auxilium, necnon tam clericos
quam laicos crucesignandos, qui pro violenta injectione manuum in
clericos seculares, virosque religiosos, vel pro incendio inciderunt, vel
durante negotio quod ad presens contra Sarracenos eosdem intenditur,
inciderint in canonem sententie promulgate, absolvere juxta formam
ecclesie vice nostra, illis exceptis, quorum fuerit excessus difficilis et
enormis, et dispensare cum clericis qui cum excommunicationis sententiam latam a canone vel ab homine incurrissent, se divinis immiscuissent
officiis, et receperunt ordines absolutionis beneficio non obtento, dummodo passis dampna vel injurias satisfaciant competenter, et negotium
hujusmodi in propriis prosequantur personis, vel ad hoc in expensis
propriis ydoneos bellatores transmittant, vel de bonis suis juxta tuum vel
dictorum commissariorum arbitrium aliquod impendant subsidium,
valeatis, auctoritate apostolica vobis ducimus concedendum. Preterea
cum nonnulli clerici et laici non ratione ecclesiarum pacifice et sine
controversia quasdam dicantur decimas possidere; quod tibi, sit liberum
de fructibus earundem perceptis hactenus quartam recipere pro ipsius
negotii subsidio portionem, dictique clerici et laici residuum fructuum
eorundem in predictum convertere subsidium per se ipsos, vel tibi si
maluerint, exhibere, in idem subsidium convertendum, ita quod ipsi ad
restitutionem aliam minime teneantur, sed inde remaneant penitus
absoluti, dummodo decimas ipsas ecclesiis dimittant in posterum ad quas
spectant, auctoritate concedimus supradicta. Concedimus insuper, ut si
aliqui crucesignatorum medio tempore ipsis a te ad votum exequendum
hujusmodi assignato decesserint, illarum indulgentiarum et gratiarum
sint plene participes, que obeuntibus in terre sancte servitio sunt con-
cesse. Ad hec credentes utiliter expedire instanti negotio, concedendi
Militie Templi, Hospitalis Ierosolimitani, Sepulchri Dominici, sancti
Jacobi, et aliis cujuscunque sint ordinis fratribus, qui personaliter ipsum
negotium prosequentur, vel ad hoc bellatores ydoneos destinarint, vel

subsidium dederint, illam indulgentiam quam consideratis circumstantiis attendendis secundum Deum expedire noveris, et commutandi ab Yspanis emissum jejuniorum et ultramarine atque cujuslibet alterius peregrinationis votum, in negotii sepedicti subsidium, plenam tibi tuisque commissariis concedimus facultatem. Volumus preterea et concedimus, ut illi qui in officio predicationis crucis pro presenti negotio per unius anni spatium duxerint laborandum, illis privilegio et immunitate gaudeant, que personaliter in terre sancte subsidium transfretantibus in generali concilio noscuntur esse concessa. Et ut premissa plenius sortiantur effectum, committendi ea personis ydoneis, non obstante aliqua indulgentia per quam excusari possent a susceptione commissionis hujusmodi, liberam habere te volumus potestatem, ac etiam per censuram ecclesiasticam crucesignatos quoslibet, cujuscunque dignitatis vel condicionis fuerint, compellendi, ut infra certum terminum prefigendum a te, vel votum crucis redimant, vel illud executuri ad locum accedere studeant destinatum.

Datum Perusii, vii kal. Aprilis, anno primo.[3]

1. Raimundus de Losana, archbishop of Seville from 1259 to 1286.

2. [It is to be noted that this text offers no innovations in policy concerning crusader debts; thus one must assume that the standard moratorium on principal and interest enjoyed by the crusaders was, as usual, valid only until the crusader returned home. See Stow, "Papal and Royal Attitudes," pp. 162–164.—KS]

3. A few days earlier, on March 23, he had issued two other bulls bearing on the same subject and presumably containing the same instructions: one was addressed "To all faithful Christians" (*Quod voluit apostolus:* Jordan, *Registres,* p. 7, no. 17), and the other went to the Archbishop of Tarragona, Benedict de Rocaberti, asking him to solicit aid for James I of Aragon and his continuing struggle against the Muslims (Potthast, no. 19156).

Another series of bulls containing, with slight variations, the same exhortation regarding debts and usury from which crusaders were to be freed is connected with the pope's struggle against the Hohenstaufens: *De venenoso genere,* on July 10, 1265 (Potthast, no. 19276, 19429, 19252; *MGH, Epist. Saec. XIII,* vol. 3, p. 637, no. 645). Finally, there were the appeals for crusading in the Holy Land. In connection with the Spanish crusade, see also *Gaudeamus in Domino,* addressed to Archbishop Sancius of Toledo, on July 11, 1267 (Potthast, no. 20075; Jordan, *Registres,* no. 500) with the standard clauses on loans and usury.

23   no date[1]

To the Pope's chaplain:[2]

ISTI SUNT ARTICULI . . . The chaplain is asked to look into the complaints[3] against the royal administration of the Kingdom of Portugal[4] made by the archbishop of Braga and the bishops of the kingdom. Among the complaints listed are:

1. The king subjects disobedient clerics to the "judgment of the Jews" (*judicio Judaeorum*).[5]
2. Persons seeking sanctuary in a church are dragged out by Muslims and Jews, or by Christians.[6]
3. The king uses Muslims, Jews, or other people "belonging to him" as executioners of condemned clergy.
4. The king appoints Jews to office in preference to Christians, thus violating ancient conciliar legislation.
5. He does not compel Jews to wear distinguishing clothes.[7]
6. He permits them to refuse to pay the church tithe[8] despite the statute of the general council.

ASV, Instr. Misc.
Reg. Vat. 29A, fol. 234, no. 66.
Jordan, *Registres*, p. 236, no. 669.

Magistro Guillelmo Folquini, capellano nostro, canonico Narbonensi.

ISTI SUNT ARTICULI exhibiti ex parte venerabilium fratrum nostrorum M. . . . et aliorum episcoporum regni Portugalie, super quibus facienda est per te inquisitio juxta formam per alias nostras litteras tibi datam. Predicti autem articuli sic incipiunt.

Item si archiepiscopus, episcopi vel eorum vicarii locum aliquem vel ecclesiam supponunt ecclesiastico interdicto, vel in homines ipsius regis excommunicationis, prout justitia exigit, ferunt sententias, dictus rex et sui episcopos vel eorum vicarios ad relaxandum hujusmodi sententias per minas et terrores et occupationem bonorum suorum compellunt; judicans eos, si sententias ipsas relaxare noluerint, judicio Judeorum, subtrahendo ipsis communionem fidelium, ac fideles ipsos, si eis in aliquo communicaverint vel receperint ipsos in castris, villis aut domibus suis, capiendo, incarcerando, et bonis propriis spoliando . . . .

Item quod personas ad ecclesias fugientes in illis casibus in quibus debent per ecclesias defensari, violenter facit ipse ac sui per Sarracenos aut Judeos vel per christianos extrahi ab eisdem, vel facit eos ibi custodiri et compediri quandoque per suos satellites, et eis cibaria denegari, ut sic exire de ecclesiis compellantur.

Item quod sepe minatur archiepiscopo et episcopis mortem, et quando-que procurat et facit eos inclusos in ecclesiis, monasteriis et alibi detineri; Saracenis, Judeis, ac aliis suis apparitoribus et meyrinis ad interficien-dum eos adhibitis circumquaque; facit etiam amputari auriculas servien-tium episcoporum, et quandoque alios capi, et alios interfici coram eis.

Item quod preficit Judeos indifferenter, contra generalis statuta concilii legemque paternam, in officiis publicis christianis; quos ad deferendum signum quo a christianis qualitate habitus distinguantur, prout in generali concilio est statutum, propter quod dampnate commixtionis excessus sub erroris potest velamento presumi, nec ad debitas decimas persolvendas compelli permittit.

1. The date of the document is not known; it is assumed to have been executed in late 1265 or early 1266.

2. William Folquinus. [Is this a relative of the pope, as seems likely?—KS]

3. The complaints numbered more than two score. The argument dragged on for years. We see it settled under Pope Nicholas IV, on March 7, 1289; and cf. Martin IV, April 1, 1284, bull no. 48, below.

4. The king was Alfonso III (1248-1279). At the time of his accession, Pope Innocent IV favored him. Cf. M. Kayserling, *Geschichte der Juden in Portugal* (Leipzig, 1867), pp. 4 f. The country had a considerable Muslim population and was in the throes of reorganization and Christianization. Even Pope Gregory IX had recognized that patience was needed and had granted a number of exemp-tions related to Jews and Muslims. See above, bull no. 17, n. 3, and *ChJ*, pp. 1190-1194, no. 64.

5. See bull no. 12, above.

6. Jewish and Muslim royal officials were used for purposes pleasant and unpleasant; but from the point of view of the churchmen, this was adding insult to injury: Violating "ecclesiastical liberties" and using infidels to do it. [Was, then, Alfonso oblivious of "ecclesiastical liberties," and did "frontier" conditions prompt him to ignore canonical precision—or was his outlook truly "pluralis-tic," at least for the Middle Ages? In other words, is it possible that Alfonso did not accept the premises of social hierarchy and exclusion as the Church expounded them concerning the correct relations between Church, kings, Jews and Muslims? If this is so, the traditional explanation for Iberian peculiar-ities, which sees royal convenience pitted against ecclesiastical zeal, must be questioned.—KS]

7. Fourth Lateran Council. Cf. *ChJ*, pp. 308-309, no. X.

8. On the struggle to have Jews pay tithes to the local churches, see *ChJ*, *passim*.

24   1266[1]

To James, King of Aragon:[2]

AGIT NEC IMMERITO . . . Pope Clement urges King James to forgo whatever advantages he derives from the Muslims in his kingdom. He points to the incongruity of fighting the Muslims outside Aragon, yet tolerating them and even favoring them inside. The pope then turns to the problems connected with the presence of Jews in Aragon. They must not be permitted to hold public office, although they should enjoy those privileges granted them by the Apostolic See.[3] In particular, the king is to punish the man who in his royal presence had a disputation[4] with Friar Paul[5] of the Dominican Order and who reportedly published a book,[6] reproduced in many copies and spread far and wide, which contains numerous lies. This man's punishment should not, however, endanger him in life and limb.[7] The pope concludes by expressing the hope that the king will take appropriate action.[8]

Reg. Vat. 29A, no. 20.
ASV, Armarium 31, tome 72, fol. 247r–v.
Potthast, no. 19911.
Jordan, *Registres*, p. 334, no. 848.

. . . Regi Aragonum illustri.

AGIT NEC IMMERITO mater ecclesia dum letanter tua magnifica gesta commemorat dies festos, iocunditatis et letitie cantica replicat tui çeli fervorem et strenuitatis merita, tam cari et devoti filii, quasi recenter cotidie delectabiliter recensendo. Exultat et iubilat in tuorum felicium commemoratione successuum, per quos contra Sarracenos, nominis sui blasfemos et catholice fidei persecutores infestos, salutem populi christiani Domini dextera virtuose in tuis manibus et data tibi ab ipso virtute direxit. Apud bonorum omnium largitorem preces devote multiplicat, ut in hac çeli rectitudine, in hac fidei puritate, te in tempora longiora conservet. Quod nos eo postulamus avidius, eo instantius imploramus, quo tibi vinculis caritatis solidioris astringimur, ad honorem tuum soliditate sincerioris dilectionis afficimur et salutem tuam sincerius affectamus. Hec quidem nos movent efficaciter et inducunt, ut serenitatem tuam paternis adeamus commonitionibus, et attentis exhortationibus excitemus adversus ea, que grandia pericula temporaliter etiam tibi et posteris tuis ingerere, tui nominis claritatem inficere, ac creatorem tuum contra te possent graviter provocare. Considera igitur, fili, considera, cum te tam experientia cogat advertere, quam familiaria etiam exempla ignorare non sinant, quam gravibus sit res plena periculis Sarracenorum in terra tua retentio, qui licet ad tempus occultent iniquitatis sue neccessitate cogente propositum, illud tamen quam avide, quam ardenter immo etiam quam inique captata oportunitate revelant. Profecto nec discreti consilii est nec tutum, tam perfidos, tam plenos nequitia inimicos habere domesticos vel tenere vicinos, non magis quam nutrire serpentem in gremio vel ignem in sinu. Quod si te forsan ad huiusmodi retentionem ipsorum aliqua ex illis proveniens inducit, ne dicamus seducit utilitas, tanto preponderet in tue magnanimitatis iudicio et recto libramine rationis acerba tui contumelia creatoris, quam assidue patitur Sarracenis eisdem inter Christicolas diebus singulis clamore publico certis horis nomen extollentibus Machometti, quanto procul dubio ferres et revera ferre deberes acerbius illatas inter tuos subditos celsitudini tue iniurias, quam inter eos, qui tue non essent ditioni subiecti. O quam debet esse detestabile, quam amarum tibi precipue, qui ab annis teneris illius cultores et cultum infra fines ipsorum totis viribus persequendo ad eorum exterminium laborasti, nunc ipsum in regnis tuis pati per culturam huiusmodi taliter exaltari! Nonne consideras, quod per hoc detractorum linguis exponeris? Qui quasi verisimiliter asserent, quod in omnibus tuis laboribus, quos nullis vitatis periculis in ipsorum persecutione ab adolescentie tue initiis pertulisti, non exaltationem fidei, sed tua venabaris comoda, tuis solummodo utilitatibus intendebas? Porro etiam amicorum forte alternabuntur iudicia, si propter utilitatem pecuniariam, sic tuis laudabilibus actibus detrahi tantum superni regis opprobrium, tantam christianitatis infectionem, quam ex eorumdem Sarracenorum cohabitatione horribili detestandis horroribus et horrendis spurcitiis non est dubium provenire, amplius patiaris. Et quidem tu vel huiusmodi obloquentium detractioni consentiens vel ipsi tibi contrarius videreris, si Sarracenos eosdem in suis partibus persequens in tuis ipsos substineas patienter. Hec si discussa debite meditationis examine in rationis consistorium introducas, ipsos nec dubium, prout excellentiam tuam decet, prorsus abiciens et profugos extra tue ditionis terminos effugabis. Ad quod magnificentiam regiam, ut tue saluti providas, ut tue fame consulas, ut consultius periculis, que tibi et ipsis posteris, ut premittitur, per eos imminere possunt, occurras, et paterno affectu et omni quo possumus studio invitamus, presertim ut reddas altissimo votum tuum, quo ad id publice diceris obligatus. Sicque oppilentur ora contra te inique loquentium, tuque prout es, et fidei çelator precipuus, et ad ipsius exaltationem labores tuos dirigere censearis. Ad quam cum ferventer intendas, regalem prudentiam, oportet attendere, quod ecclesie status et fidei earumque negotia ea sunt indivisibili unione coniuncta, ut altera, reliqua in honore non habita, honorari non possit. Nec enim potest fidei derogari, quin nimis ecclesie detrahatur, nec ipsius ecclesie honori ac libertati detrahi, quin et fidei, quantum in detrahente fuerit, derogetur. Ne igitur tu, qui eiusdem fidei vacasti semper et adhuc vacas studiose negotio, eidem, si ecclesie iniuriosus fueris, existas iniurius, decet, et nos excellentiam tuam quo possumus affectu rogamus, ut ab iniuriis ecclesiarum abstineas, quibus in partibus tuis iniuriari diceris supra modum, tam in bovaticis et albergis, quam in aliis exactionibus omnino indebitis, et in eo potissime, quod ab illis eorum, que annorum quadraginta spatio et interdum a tempore, cuius non existit memoria, possederunt, titulum sue possessionis contra rationem et legitimas sanctiones exquiris, quem nisi probaverint, possessiones occupas iuris ordine non servato. Quesumus itaque, fili karissime, ac tue salutis et honoris obtentu pietatem regiam instantius deprecamur, ut ab earumdem ecclesiarum iniuriis omnino desistas, eas, personas ecclesiasticas, iura et libertates earum manuteneas, protegas et defendas ipsasque favorabiliter prosequaris. Circa ecclesiam vero Valentinam, donum tibi a Deo tam gratiose concessum, ut concedentis et concessionis gratiam gratam ut decet videaris habere, ipsiusque mensuram de donantis magnitudine metiaris habunde, tuus favor exhuberet et in ipsam ita liberalitas regie pietatis habundet, ut eam, cum sit novella plantatio noviter divina potentia per te de gentium perfidarum manibus eruta, in paupertate arescere non permittas, sed eam regalis munificentia sic honoret et dotet, sic in suis iuribus tueatur, quod deterioris saltem conditionis, quam sunt alie vicine sibi ecclesie, non existat, immo illam a paupertatis et deiectionis opprobriis tua magnificentia liberet, que ipsam ab earumdem gentium iugo et immunditia liberavit. Ad quod etiam venerabilis fratris nostri . . . episcopi Valentini, tui et tuorum honoris et comodi seduli çelatoris, cuius ad te ac regna tua experientia instructi testamur affectum, et quem tibi propterea confidenter et affectuosissime commendamus, specialis ad personam tuam et approbanda devotio efficaciter te inducat. Ut autem, princeps inclite, çelus tuus erga defensionem eiusdem orthodoxe fidei, quam tamquam vir christianissimus indefesse prosequeris, undique contra ipsius hostes et emulos aperte reluceat, in ipsius auxilium contra Iudeos, qui pre ceteris eandem fidem persequentibus et nomen blasfemantibus christianum, et illud blasfemant amarius et illam nequissime persecuntur, favor tuus apertissime invalescat, Iudeos de cetero ad aliqua officia non admittens ipsos in aliquo non extollas, sed in quantum concessa eis a sede apostolica privilegia patiuntur, ipsorum refrenando malitiam deprimas et conculces, nec pretereas illorum blasfemias incorrectas. Sed illius precipue castiges audaciam, qui de disputatione, quam in tua presentia cum dilecto filio, religioso viro fratre Paulo de ordine predicatorum habuerat, multis confictis adiectisque mendaciis librum composuisse dicitur, quem ad sui dilatationem erroris in varia exempla multiplicans per regiones varias destinavit. Cuius ausum temerarium sic debite censura iustitie absque tamen mortis periculo et membrorum mutilatione castiget, ut quid excessus meruerit, districtionis severitas manifestet, et ipsius exemplo aliorum audacia compescatur. Super hiis igitur serenitatem regiam monemus in Domino nostro Ihesu Christo ac in remissionem tibi peccatorum suadentes, quatinus in premissis vota tua sic previo rationis iudicio et devotionis affectu dirigas, sic opere compleas, que nos paternis affatibus et sinceris affectibus suademus, quod id nobis, qui per hec salutem, honorem et utilitatem tuam querimus et tibi ac tuis contra pericula providere studemus, cedat ad gaudium, tibique perinde salutis, honoris ac utilitatis, prout desideramus, incrementa proveniant et efficax contra huiusmodi pericula munimentum. Et ut nobis quoad hec de tuo beneplacito et nostrarum exhortationum quam speramus exauditione certius innotescat, per dilectum filium . . . latorem presentium tuum circa premissa propositum plene rescribas, eidem in hiis, que circa eadem tibi ex parte nostra direxit, fidem plenariam habiturus.

1. The exact date is not known. Potthast, and others following him, including Jordan (in *Registres*), simply place it at the end of December, 1266. The chronology of events seems to require such an assumption; but see bull no. 25, n. 1, below [as well as n. 7—KS], for an alternate suggestion.

2. James I became king of Aragon in 1213, at the age of five, and reigned till 1276. He was surnamed "the Conqueror" because he greatly extended the limits of his kingdom. But with the capture of Seville in 1248, the period of the Reconquest came to a temporary end until the fall of Granada in 1492. The kings of the Iberian Peninsula felt that time was needed to absorb the reconquered territory, whereas the popes wanted them to continue the fight against Islam (see bull no. 22, above). By far the greater portion of this bull reflects this difference of opinion between pope and king. The Jewish part of it looks almost like a postscript, the result, perhaps, of the appearance at the papal court of Friar Paul Christian with his complaint against Nahmanides.

3. The statement appears to assert that royal authority could not legislate in favor of the Jews. It is thus a negative and unusual extension of the *Sicut Judaeis* bull. [Alternately, this clause may be basically formulaic, reminding the king that observance of canonical restrictions does not imply the invalidation of rights otherwise canonically granted, with the point of reference being, indeed, *Sicut Judaeis*. The intention of the pope is not altogether clear in the murky Latin syntax of his phrases.—KS]

4. The major documents connected with the disputation, which took place at Barcelona between July 20 and August 4, 1263, are available in H. Denifle,

"Quellen zur Disputation Pablos Christiani mit Moses Nachmani zu Barcelona, 1263," *Historisches Jahrbuch* 8 (1887): 225–244, who sees everything from the Christian viewpoint (in refutation of Graetz, *Geschichte,* 2nd ed., vol. 7, p. 417, n. 2), and in Isidore Loeb, "La controverse de 1263 à Barcelone," *REJ* 15 (1887): 1–18 (taking issue with Denifle). Cecil Roth reviewed the available material more calmly in "The Disputation of Barcelona (1263)," *HTR* 43 (1950): 118–144. For a novel interpretation see Martin A. Cohen, "Reflections on the Text and Context of the Disputation of Barcelona," *HUCA* 35 (1964): 157–92. The disputation is discussed more briefly by Lukyn Williams, *Adversus Judaeos,* pp. 245–247; Browe, *Judenmission,* pp. 73 ff.; and Baer, *History,* vol. 1, pp. 150–159. Other references to the entire subject and to the relevant documents are listed in Roth, "Disputation," p. 118. [More recently, see Robert Chazan, "The Barcelona Disputation of 1263: Christian Missionizing and Jewish Response," *Speculum* 52 (1977): 824–842, and Jeremy Cohen, *The Friars and the Jews* (Ithaca, 1982).—KS]

5. Paul Christianus, or Pablo Christiani, or, as Roth prefers to call him, Pablo Cristià, was a convert from Judaism and, like Nicholas Donin (cf. *ChJ,* app. A), who engineered the disputation in Paris in 1240, evidently possessed considerable Jewish knowledge. His objective, with which he imbued the Dominicans, was to undermine Judaism by destroying the authority of the Talmud. After the disputation, he at first had his way, when King James ordered the Jews to permit him to preach in the synagogue (Denifle "Quellen," pp. 234 f., nos. 2 and 3; Jean Régné, "Catalogue des actes de Jaime Ier," *REJ* 61 [1911], p. 1, no. 215), and to show him whatever books he asked for. On the same date (August 29, 1263), the king appointed a commission to investigate the Jewish books and destroy those which they found contained blasphemous statements about Jesus and Christianity (Denifle, "Quellen," p. 236, no. 5; Régné, "Catalogue," p. 2, no. 216). A few days later, however, on August 30, the king lightened the burden of the preaching (Régné, "Catalogue," p. 2, no. 217); and in March, 1264, he modified the decree on the books by agreeing to have the Jews themselves eliminate the passages objectionable to the Dominicans (Denifle, "Quellen," p. 238, no. 7; Régné, "Catalogue," pp. 7 f., no. 249). Paul is specifically mentioned at every step in these developments. The relaxation of the royal decree made him and the other Dominicans unhappy, and their anger increased when King James refused to impose a severe punishment on Nahmanides for the publication of his report wherein he claimed to have gotten the better of the argument during the disputation (see n. 7, below). This is when Paul went to Rome to put the matter before Pope Clement. In 1269, Paul is found in France, where King Louis IX commands his officials to have the Jews listen to Paul's missionary sermons and to show him whatever books he asks for (Robert, "Catalogue," *REJ* 3 [1881]: 216, no. 40). He stirred up further missionary controversy in the Provence as well (Roth, "Disputation," p. 143, n. 41; H. Gross, *Gallia Judaica,* ed. S. Schwarzfuchs [Amsterdam, 1969], pp. 4–5).

6. The contents of Nahmanides' report on the disputation are outlined in the works of Graetz, Denifle, Loeb, and Roth mentioned above. M. Steinschneider published what is presumably the entire report in *Sefer Vikhuah ha-Ramban lifné Melekh ve-Sarim* (Berlin, 1860). It was published by Wagenseil, with a Latin translation, in his *Tela ignea satanae,* though on the basis of an imperfect text (cf. Lukyn Williams, *Adversus Judaeos,* p. 245, n. 3). But see now the edition of Ch. Chavel, *Kitvei R. Moshe b. Nahman* (Jerusalem, 1971), vol. 2, pp. 302–319.

7. Pope Clement was apparently offering a compromise between the king and the Dominicans. The king had fixed Nahmanides' punishment as burning the report and exiling the author for two years. When the Dominicans objected to this as too mild, the king suspended all punishment. He argued (cf. Denifle. "Quellen," p. 239, no. 8; Régné, "Catalogue," p. 19, no. 323; dated April 12, 1265) that Nahmanides had been granted freedom of speech during the disputation, and that he had been persuaded to write the report only upon the request of the bishop of Gerona. It looks as though the Dominicans had demanded some form of corporal punishment. [This suggests a significant escalation. Previously, the Talmud alone, the object containing blasphemies, had been indicted. Now, those held responsible for blasphemies were being indicted too, a step toward making Jews directly liable to inquisitorial proceedings, as indeed occurred a few months later in Clement IV's *Turbato corde*. To be sure, the punishment may also have been intended in recompense for Nahmanides' general comportment at the 1263 debate and subsequent to it; but this is not certain.—KS]

8. The king responded by "urging" Rabbi Moses to leave Aragon, which he did, departing for the Holy Land no later than June 1267 and reaching Acre about August 12. One may assume (since no actual order of exile is extant) that Nahmanides left Aragon not only to avoid more severe punishment, but also to avoid creating a delicate situation for the king, who otherwise would have had to exact a more onerous punishment in response to the papal call.

25   July 15, 1267

To the King of Aragon:[1]

DAMNABILI PERFIDIA JUDAEORUM[2] . . . Because the reprehensible Jewish lack of faith was long ago deservedly rejected because of its vice of ingratitude, and the Synagogue given its bill of divorcement, this blind and grievously sinful people—disdaining to recognize its time of visitation, as the Prophet Jeremiah said it would—has been made to wander over the earth like the fratricide Cain, who was driven from the face of God because his crime was too great for forgiveness. This miserable people likewise denied the Son of the Eternal Father, the Lord Jesus Christ, saying in its folly that He was not God. According to the flesh, He was the seed of David, as the prophets in the Holy Scriptures had promised, and therefore he was their brother. He had come calling them—the House of Israel that was perishing like sheep—to participate in the eternal heritage; they, however, felled him, and flogged him, and impiously killed the Crucified One, calling His blood down upon themselves and their children. To this day the dispersed Jews do not want to understand, as well as they might, that sufficient humaneness is accorded them when they are permitted to dwell among the faithful without burdensome disgrace. But see how wicked is this generation (of Jews). Even while Christian piety tolerates its presence and receives it with a real kindness, it shows itself ungrateful and injurious, repaying kindness with insult, friendliness with contempt, and favor with the kind of compensation—as a popular proverb has it—[to be expected from] a mouse in the pocket, a serpent about the waist, or a fire in one's bosom.

The pope goes on to say that he was grieved to hear that the Jews of Aragon had set aside the Old Law received from Moses and had adopted another in its place, which they call Talmud, and which exceeds the Old and New Testaments in length. It contains innumerable abuses and blasphemies against Jesus and Mary, such as are unfit to mention or to hear. It also teaches the Jews to utter daily imprecations against Christians. And it is a cause of the obstinacy of this foolish and faithless people.[3]

Such abuses cannot continue without injury to the Catholic Faith and to all Catholics, and the pope, in particular, must take appropriate steps to halt them. Whence the archbishop of Tarragona and his suffragans[4] are instructed to take active measures against the Jews. The king must alert his barons and officials to make the Jews surrender the entire Talmud along with its commentaries and additions.[5] All their books must be exhibited for inspection; although those which conform to the text of the Bible and in which there is no question of blasphemies or errors or falsifications may be returned. The others shall be kept for examination and for the decision of the Apostolic See. The examination, restitution, or consignment of these books and the setting aside of those others (about which there is doubt) shall be conducted in the presence, and with the advice, of Dominican and Franciscan brothers, as well as of other educated persons. The entire pious proceedings shall be conducted with such care and prudence that all events occur at the same moment, lest the Jews in their deceitfulness succeed in hiding the said books.[6] As one of those who will carry out the investigation of the books seized, the pope strongly recommends Paul Christian, the bearer of this letter,[7] who, as a former Jew and zealous convert, has all the essential qualifications of expert knowledge of the languages and of the heresies and errors found in these books and of Christian theology as well.

The pope concludes by saying that he does not believe the king needs further persuasion to act in this matter.[8] His own mind was made up, and he pleads from the depth of his heart that the king fulfill his duty, namely: the impounding of the books and the appointment of a commission of examiners.[9]

ASV, Armarium 31, tome 72, fols. 231v–232r.

Bibliothèque Nationale, Fond Doat 32, fols. 11r–15r.

Potthast, no. 20081.

Thomas Ripoll, *Bullarium Ordinis FF. Praedicatorum* (Rome, 1729–1740), vol. 1, p. 487.

J. H. Sbaralea, *Bullarium Franciscanum Romanorum Pontificum* (Rome, 1759–1904), vol. 3, pp. 123 f.

Carissimo in Christo Filio . . . Illustri Regi Aragonum Sal., et Apost. Bened.

DAMNABILI PERFIDIA JUDAEORUM propter ingratitudinis suae vitium olim merito reprobata; et Synagogae dato libello repudii, suae visitationis tempus agnoscere contemnenti; coecus ille populus, qui peccatum peccavit juxta Jeremiae vaticinium, instabilis est effectus; immo vagus, et profugus super terram, velut fratricida Cayn, qui ejectus fuit a facie Domini; quasi major esset ejus iniquitas, quam ut posset veniam promereri. Hujusmodi namque miserabilis populus Patris aeterni Filium Dominum Jesum Christum, qui secundum carnem factus est ex semine David; prout ante in Scripturis sanctis promiserat per Prophetas, frater ipsorum erat, et ad participium haereditatis aeternae illos vocare venerat, tanquam ad oves, quae perierant domus Israel; non solum nequiter negaverunt dicentes in sua desipientia, non est Deus; verum etiam caesum, flagellatum, et crucifixum impie occiderunt, ejus sanguinem super se, ac filios suos, detestabiliter imprecantes. Verum cum dispersiones Judaeorum ipsorum adhuc nolint intelligere, ut bene faciant, cum ipsis satis humaniter agitur, quod inter Fideles absque gravibus contumeliis vivere permittuntur. Sed ecce prava ista generatio; dum cohabitationem ejus sustinet pietas Christiana; dum ipsam ex quadam benignitate receptat; se ingratam inde constituit, et nocivam; reddens pro gratia contumeliam, pro familiaritate contemptum, et pro beneficiis illa stipendia, quae mus in pera, serpens in gremio, et ignis in sinu, suis hospitibus juxta vulgare proverbium, largiuntur. Dolentes quidem audivimus, et narramus, quod Judaei de Regno Aragoniae; lege veteri praetermissa, quam per Moysen servum suum contulit Majestas omnium conditoris; quamdam legem aliam, seu traditionem, quam Talamud vocant, falso Dominum tradidisse confingunt; in cujus amplo volumine per Orbis latitudinem destinato, quod textum novi, et veteris Testamenti excedere dicitur, abusiones fere innumerabiles, ac detestabiles blasphemiae contra eumdem Dominum Jesum Christum, et Genitricem ejus

Beatissimam, continentur; quorum relatio, vel auditus sine interventu pudoris, et horroris gravissimi vix potest ab aliquo sustineri. Maledictiones quoque gravissimae, ac imprecationes horribiles, quae ab eisdem Judaeis ingratis, et perfidis contra Christianos committuntur quotidie in dicta lege, seu traditione damnabili sunt adscriptae. Quid plura? hujusmodi, et alia detestanda, quae in dicta lege, et traditione prophana sunt damnabiliter annotata, praecipua esse censentur, et causa propter quae praedictus fatuus, et infidelis populus diu in sua stetit perfidia obstinatus. Quia vero iis, et aliis eorum abusionibus, quae, ut accepimus nimis excrescunt non sine detrimento Catholicae Fidei, quosque Fideles, sed Nos praecipue, qui constituti sumus in specula, ut resistamus ascendentibus ex adverso; decet tam congruis, quam festinis remediis refragari: Venerabilibus Fratribus Nostris . . . Archiepiscopo Tarraconen., et Suffraganeis ejus, Nostris in virtute obedientiae damus litteris in mandatis, quod adversus praedictos Judaeos super praemissis prudenter, et viriliter insurgentes, te carissimum in Christo Filium Nostrum, et omnes Barones, Nobiles, et Balivos Regni, et Terrarum tuarum moneant, et inducant attente, Barones, Nobiles, et Balivos eosdem ad hoc per censuram Ecclesiasticam, si neccesse fuerit, appellatione postposita compellendo; ut a Judaeis tibi, et eis subditis totum Talamud cum suis additionibus, et expositionibus, et omnes eorum libros ipsis faciatis liberaliter exhiberi; quibus exhibitis, illos ex eis, qui de textu Bibliae fuerint, et alios, de quibus nulla sit dubitatio, quod blasphemias, et errores contineant, seu etiam falsitatem, Judaeis restituant supradictis. Ceteros vero sigillis eorum, ut expedit, consignatos, in aliquibus tutis locis, in quibus ipsis videbitur, deponant custodiendos fideliter; donec super hiis consulta Sedes Apostolica ordinet in posterum, quid de ipsis sit fieri opportunum. Volumus autem, quod tam examinationem librorum, quam hujusmodi restitutionem, consignationem, et depositionem ceterorum in praesentia, et de consilio Fratrum Praedicatorum, et Minorum, aliarumque personarum faciant, quae providae sint, et jam litteratae; Proviso attentius, ut condicto consilio tecum, et cum aliis personis idoneis, prout fuerit opportunum, commissum eis tam pium, et salubre negotium taliter ordinent; ac ita prudenter, et caute procedant in ipso, quod id, ubicumque contingat fieri, simul, et eodem tempore fiat; ne Judaeorum ipsorum fallacia dictos libros quomodolibet valeat occultare; sed Nostrum potius in hac parte mandatum, executionis votivae plenitudinem consequatur. Ad hoc autem dilectus Filius Frater Paulus dictus Christianus de Ordine Fratrum Praedicatorum lator praesentium creditur non modicum profuturus, tum quia ex Judaeis trahens originem, et inter eos litteris hebraicis competenter instructus linguam novit, et legem antiquam; ac istorum errores; tum etiam quia de sacro

fonte renatus zelum habet Fidei Catholicae; ac eruditus occurrit lauda-
biliter in Theologica facultate. Licet igitur super hiis, quae faciunt ad
gloriam Divini nominis, Serenitatem tuam non credamus indigere pre-
caminum lenimentis; eam tamen pro hujusmodi negotio, menti Nostrae
firmiter alligato, ex intimo cordis affectu rogamus, et obsecramus in
Domino Jesu Christo, in remissionem tibi peccaminum injungentes;
quatenus totum praedictum Talamud cum additionibus, et expositionibus ejus, ac omnes libros Judaeorum ipsorum ubique per tuum
Regnum, et Dominium capias, et capi facias, ac eisdem Archiepiscopo,
et Suffraganeis adhiberi; alias in hiis, quae ipsis circa Judaeorum
praesumptiones committimus, impendendo eis necessarium auxilium,
consilium, et favorem; itaquod ipsi tua fulti potentia commissum sibi
ministerium ad Divinae Majestatis honorem exequi valeant juxta votum;
ac tibi exinde felicitatis aeternae praemia, laudisque humanae pro-
econium, et favoris Apostolici proveniat incrementum.

Datum Viterbii, id. Julii, anno tertio.

1. The issuance of this bull so soon after the one that had urged the punishment
of Nahmanides may have been the result of King James's failure to inflict that
punishment and of Rabbi Moses's escape from Aragon. Once more, it appears,
Paul Christian went to Rome, this time to persuade Pope Clement to expand the
attack on rabbinic literature, and in particular to stop the practice of allowing
censorship to be carried out by the Jews themselves (see above, bull no. 24, n. 5).

2. Much of this bull, in content and wording, derives from bulls of former popes.
The introductory passage echoes *Etsi Judeos* of Innocent III in 1205 (cf. *ChJ*,
no. 18).

3. The paragraph repeats the charges first made by Gregory IX in 1239 at the
instigation of Nicholas Donin, with the incipit *Si vera sunt* (*ChJ*, nos. 96 ff.).
That text was sent to various countries; this *Dampnabili* was sent only to Aragon.
See also *Impia Judeorum* of Innocent IV, May 1244, (*ChJ*, no. 104).

4. The reference is to a letter addressed to Benedict de Rocaberti, archbishop of
Tarragona, and his suffragans; it is almost verbally identical with this bull,
except for the necessary changes of person and the omission of the final urgent
plea. It was issued on the same day as the present text, is listed as Potthast,
no. 20081, and is given in full or in part in Bibliothèque Nationale, Fond Doat 32,
fols. 7r–10r, Ripoll, *Bull. Ord.*, vol. 1, p. 488, and Sbaralea, *Bull. Francisc.* vol. 3,
p. 125. Cf. P. Browe, "Die religiöse Duldung der Juden in Mittelalter," *Archiv für
Katholisches Kirchenrecht* 118 (1938): 60.

5. Among these undoubtedly was the Code of Maimonides, which had figured
prominently in the disputation and against which King James had issued a
special condemnation (cf. Denifle, "Quellen," p. 235, no. 3). It mentions
specifically the book *Soffrim* (no doubt meaning *Shofetim*), by *Moyses filius
Maymon*, the Egyptian, which contains blasphemous remarks about Jesus.

6. Gregory IX, in 1239, ordered the books taken on a Saturday, while the Jews were at synagogue.

7. Is it unreasonable to suppose that the bull *Agit nec immerito* and this one were issued and sent by the hand of Paul at the same time (see n. 1, above) [and that the two letters must be seen as complementary—KS]?

8. Was this a subtle suggestion that King James tended to be lenient in such matters? There is, in fact, no record that the king did anything to implement the papal request. When next we hear about books in Aragon, it is, on the contrary, that Jews need not answer charges about blasphemies in their books, except only before a royal court. Cf. Régné, "Catalogue," p. 30, no. 387; Baer, *Die Juden im Christlichen Spanien* (Berlin, 1929-1936; repr. Farnborough, Eng.), vol. 1, p. 36. [Of course, the issue may have been essentially jurisdictional. James did not object to censoring the Talmud, etc., but he did insist on supervising the issue, much in the manner of Philip the Fair, who agreed to enforce *Turbato corde*, as long as he, and not ecclesiastical judges, was doing the enforcing (Gustave Saige, *Les Juifs de Languedoc, antérieurement au XIVe siècle* [Paris, 1881; repr. Farnborough, Eng., 1971], pp. 231-235).—KS]

9. [It should be noted that the discussion had shifted from the burning of books to censorship alone. Did this shift occur in Spain at the behest of Dominican Hebraists, or was censorship already under consideration by Innocent IV in Paris in 1247? (See *ChJ*, p. 274, no. 119).—KS]

26   July 27, 1267

To the friars of the Dominican and Franciscan Orders who are now or who will in the future be deputized by papal authority as inquisitors of heresy:[1]

TURBATO CORDE[2] . . . Pope Clement declares that he is deeply disturbed by reports that a number of Christians have defected to Judaism.[3] This insult to the name of Christ can only result in subversion of the Christian Faith. Within the limits of their present authority to "inquire" in matters of heresy (as established by Innocent IV in 1254), the inquisitors are empowered to seek out the guilty by using both Christians and Jews as witnesses.[4] Christians found guilty of the crime must be treated as heretics. Jews found to have induced Christians of either sex to adopt their rites must be appropriately punished. Whoever stands in the way of the inquisitors shall be subjected to ecclesiastical punishment; if necessary, the aid of the secular power shall be invoked.

ASV, Armarium 31, tome 72, fol. 233r.
Potthast, no. 20095.
Sbaralea, *Bull. Francisc.*, vol. 3, p. 126.
Browe, *Judenmission*, p. 258.

Dilectis filiis Fratribus Praedicatorum, et Minorum ordinum Inquisitoribus haereticae pravitatis auctoritate Sedis Apostolicae deputatis, aut in posterum deputandis Sal., et Apost. Bened.

TURBATO CORDE audivimus, et narramus, quod quamplurimi reprobi Christiani veritatem Catholicae Fidei abnegantes se ad ritum Judaicum damnabiliter transtulerunt; quod tanto magis reprobum fore dignoscitur, quanto ex hoc nomen Christi sanctissimum quadam familiari hostilitate securius blasphematur. Cum autem huic pesti damnabili, quae, sicut accepimus, non sine subversione praedictae Fidei nimis excrescit, congruis, et festinis deceat remediis obviari: Universitati vestrae per Apostolica scripta mandamus, quatenus infra terminos vobis ad inquirendum contra haereticos auctoritate Sedis Apostolicae designatos super praemissis tam per Christianos, quam etiam per Judaeos inquisita diligenter, et solicite veritate, contra Christianos, quos talia inveneritis commisisse, tanquam contra haereticos procedatis; Judaeos autem, qui Christianos utriusque sexus ad eorum ritum execrabilem hactenus induxerunt; aut inveneritis de caetero inducentes poena debita puniatis: Contradictores per censuram ecclesiasticam, appellatione postposita, compescendo; invocato ad hoc, si opus fuerit, auxilio brachii Secularis.

Datum Viterbii, vi kal. Augusti, anno tertio.

1. This bull represented a general extension of powers, not limited in time and place.

2. In more or less the same wording, this bull was destined to be repeated by two other popes in the course of the thirteenth century: Gregory X, in March 1274, and Nicholas IV, apparently on three occasions (March 1281, September 1288, and September 1290). See below.

3. The conversion of born Christians to Judaism was so rare during this period as to have hardly justified such attention. The reference must be to Jews converted to Christianity under pressure, perhaps under threat of expulsion, possibly during riots. [One would like to know how much conversion resulted from actual resolve and free will, or from a sense of despair and defeat, and not only from pressure and force.—KS] The danger over, some of these converts may have moved to a faroff place where they threw off the mask of Christianity. If they remained in their former homes, they may have tried to obtain the help of Jews in returning to Judaism, at least in fact, since in name this was unthinkable. The objections of the Church were of long standing. While forced baptism was theoretically considered ineffective, the difference between willing and forced conversion was almost impossible to discern (cf. Innocent III's reply to a question on the subject, in *ChJ*, pp. 100–103, no. 12). The idea that baptism, once received, was irradicable dates back to the Fourth Council of Toledo, in 633, and was sustained even by

those who voted down the use of force in making converts. (Cf. Jean Juster, *La condition légale des Juifs sous les rois visigoths* [Paris, 1912], pp. 6 f. and 37; and see the notes and translations and additions to Juster by A. M. Rabello, *A Tribute to Jean Juster* [Jerusalem, 1976].) Nevertheless there were occasions, as after the First Crusade, when forced converts were allowed to return to Judaism. Pope Urban II did not object, although the antipope Clement III was horrified that Christian tradition was thus violated (cf. Aronius, no. 207). [The decision of the Fourth Council of Toledo made its way into Gratian's *Decretum* (D.45,c.5) and was referred to by Innocent III (*ChJ*, p. 100). However it became binding law and policy only in 1298 (*Sext.* 5,2,13; bull no. 78, below.) One must, however, be careful in seeing this as a violation of *Sicut Judaeis*. No matter what papal policy and feeling about baptism was before the fact, once baptism had been effected, its rejection was unthinkable because of the obvious aspersions and insults to the Church that such an action brought about.—KS]

4. A separate office, apart from the inquisitorial powers of the local bishops, had been authorized and given power with the rise of the Dominican and Franciscan Orders, who rivaled each other in zeal. Various popes in the course of the thirteenth century granted the mendicants ever wider authority (cf. Jean Guiraud, *Histoire de l'Inquisition au Moyen Age* [Paris, 1938], vol. 2, pp. 251 f.; and see more recently, Y. H. Yerushalmi, "The Inquisition and the Jews of France in the Time of Bernard Gui," *HTR* 63 [1976]: 317-376; Joseph Shatzmiller, "L'Inquisition et les Juifs de Provence au XIIIe siècle," *Provence Historique,* Fasc. 93/94: 327-338; and M. Kriegel, "La Juridiction Inquisitoriale sur les Juifs à l'époque de Philippe le Hardi et Philippe le Bel," in M. Yardeni, ed., *Les Juifs dans l'Histoire de France* [Leiden, 1980], pp. 70-77). But none of the previous popes had granted them authority to draw Jews into their investigations, since Jews were not normally subject to ecclesiastical authority. The desire to extend church powers into a new jurisdictional sphere, rather than the supposed revelation of the crimes *Turbato corde* alleges, may have been a central motive behind its ediction. That the civil authorities objected to such direct interference with "their" Jews is evident, for example, from the order (1299) by Philip IV of France that his officials must not permit Jews to be made answerable before the inquisition unless the consent of the royal officials was first obtained (cf. Robert, "Catalogue," p. 223, no. 90).

27   August 17, 1267

To John de Salins, Count of Burgundy:[1]

PROFESSIONIS CHRISTIANAE . . . Pope Clement urges the count to exert himself in behalf of the Christian Faith, for his lands harbor persons who, after baptism, have reverted to the old and corrupt Jewish blindness. This deadly herb of heretical apostasy[2] must be uprooted in full cooperation with the Dominican inquisitors. For sometimes, through injury to a member (the individual turned heretic or apostate), the head (the church itself) is afflicted and harmed.[3]

Jean Deloix, ed., *Speculum Inquisitionis Bisuntinae* (Dôle, 1628), pp. 229-231.

Clemens episcopus servus servorum Dei. Dilecto filio nobili viro Ioanni Comiti in Burgundia, Domino Salinensi, salutem et apostolicam benedictionem.

PROFESSIONIS CHRISTIANAE magnates Catholici placent nitore syderio in orthodoxae fidei firmamento suntque nihilominus infulcimentum ipsius velut columnarum stabilium fortitudo. In virtutem igitur et decorem fidei consitutae a domino personae potentia praedictae, ac illustri prosapia praepollentes, quae dum illam fulciunt et se operosos exhibent in illius dilationem ministros, fama crescunt et meritis: sicque ipsis deperit et ponitur in eorum gloria macula, cum eadem fides vim patitur, vel infidelium maxime subiectorum eisdem morsibus lacessitur; frequenter enim ex errore membrorum caput affligitur, et nonnunquam poena principibus propter peccata plebis infertur. Inter alios namque, quos nexu paterne dilectionis adstringimus, te specialiter in sede nostri pectoris praedilectione portamus, sperantes ut sicut tuam terraeque tuae cupis salutem et gratiam sic intentis studiis foveas et dilates praedicta fidei palmites, pro cuius defensione ferventer hactenus perstitisti. Verum ad nostrum, de quo dolemus pervenit auditum, quod multos in locis tibi subiectis et adiacentibus, crimen haereticae pravitatis infecit, plerique per apostasiae vitium inconsutilem Christi tunicam, quam sacri baptismatis regeneratio contulit, [reiecientes] damnabiliter mentes induunt, tamquam in tenebris et umbra mortis positi, caecitatis iudaicae veterem et corruptam. Quare validus clamor insonuit, quod in illis partibus devotionis obnubilata sit claritas, et divini cultui nomini miserabiliter illuditur. Exurgat itaque tua quae sumus devota synceritas, et ad evellendam de tuis agris illam herbam mortiferam quae messem benedictionis extenuat, opportuna studia et opera efficaces impendat, et seges fructifer adepressa consurgat talibus spinis et tribulis radicitus extirpatis. Ut autem Christi operarii videlicet dilecti filii fratres Ordinis Praedicatorum, huiusmodi pravitatis Inquisitores in eisdem partibus per sedem Apostolicam deputati utilius proficere valeant, et commissum sibi officium ad laudem divini nominis melius et efficacius exequantur, tam eis quam aliis qui pro tempore fuerint ad disperdendum et exterminandum illos maledictionis alumnos, qui taliter iram Dei meruisse noscuntur, sicut de te specialem fiduciam obtinemus, opem et auxilium largiaris: ut eorum sic pullulata nequitia per tuum et eorundem Inquisitorum ministerium in exterminium deducatur; et eadem loca, conpurgata inquinamentum labe, reddantur Deo placabilia et accepta; tuque per hoc divinae retributionis praemium nostramque benedictionem et gratiam digne valeas uberius promereri. Super eo autem quod eisdem Inquisitoribus, sicut ipsi nobis significare curarint circa praemissa, cum opportunum extitit. Te favorabilem exhibere curasti, devotionem tuam multipliciter in Domino commendamus, et condignis prosequimur actionibus gratiarum.

Datum Viterbii XVI Cal. Sept. Pontific. Anno tertio.

1. This was the other Burgundy, later called Franche-Comté. Its count was Jean de Chalon l'Antique, Lord of Salins.

2. The bull obviously ties in with *Turbato corde* (bull no. 26, above). What makes it the more curious is that Deloix, in a note, asserts that there were at that time no Jews in this part of Burgundy: *Nullos esse pro hoc tempore in hac diocesi seu provincia Judaeos.* But, he goes on to say, there must have been some few against whom the Inquisition could take action.

3. Pope Clement had issued another bull about a month earlier: *Prae cunctis nostrae mentis,* addressed to the Dominican inquisitors in Besançon (July 6, 1267). It describes the same situation, although it makes no mention of Jews. (It is noted in Potthast, no. 20064, and given in Deloix, *Speculum,* pp. 165–172). But Léon Gauthier, "Les Juifs dans les deux Bourgognes: Étude sur le commerce de l'argent aux XIIIe et XIVe siècles," *Mémoires de la Société d'émulation du Jura,* 9me serie, 3 (1914): 91, mentions Jews and the relapsed among those whom the bull concerns. It appears, however, that in the Franche-Comté, the inquisitors had more to do with Waldensians than with Jews. Cf. J. Morey, "Les Juifs en Franche-Comté au XIVme siècle," *REJ* 7 (1883): 3.

28   December 23, 1267

To the Archbishops and Bishops in the territory of the Counties of Poitiers, Toulouse, and the Provence:[1]

DAMPNABILI PERFIDIA JUDAEORUM[2] . . . The pope laments how grieved he was to hear that the Jews wickedly try to attract simple-minded Christians to their rites. They act with greater assurance, and more boldly, because they have succeeded in flouting canonical regulations concerning clothing and mingling with Christians. Since this presents an obvious danger to the Catholic Faith, the pope orders the addressees to insure that the following statutes are enforced: No Jew is permitted to have a Christian serving maid under his charge, especially in his home, to care for his children or for any other purpose.³ Jews may not erect new synagogues.⁴ The Jews may not keep their doors and windows open on Good Friday; on days of lamentation and the Sunday of the Passion they must not be found outside their dwellings, "lest the result be blasphemy against Him who was crucified for us." They may not be preferred to public offices.⁵ And they must wear garments whose nature will distinguish them from Christians.⁶

Jews must be made to observe these regulations by the use of punishments and canonical sanctions; if necessary, the aid of the secular authorities should be invoked. If the Jews remain disobedient and stubbornly refuse to observe, "you must disregard their protests and make clear to them that, God willing, we shall proceed against them by depriving them of our guardianship and the privileges extended them by the Church, as well as by other punishments we shall deem appropriate." The pope appeals to the bishops to be zealous.⁷

Bibliothèque Nationale, Fond Doat 32, fols. 4r–7r.

Clemens Episcopus servus servorum dei, venerabilibus fratribus Archiepiscopice, et Episcopis universis in terris comitis Pictavie, et Tholosoe, ac comitatu Provincie constitutis praesentes litteras inspecturis salutem, et Apostolicam benedictionem.

DAMPNABILI PERFIDIA JUDEORUM propter ingratitudinis sue vitium olim merito reprobata, et sinagoge dato libello repudii sue visitationis tempus agnoscere contempnenti cecus ille populus qui peccatum peccavit iuxta Jeremie vaticinum infallibilis est effectus ymo vagus, et profugus super terram velut Fratricida Caym qui eiectus fuit a facie domini quasi maior eius esset iniquitas quam ut posset veniam promereri huius namque miserabilis populus patris eterni filium dominum Iesum Christum qui secundum carnem factus est ex semine david prout ante in scripturis sanctis promiserat per prophetas frater ipsorum erat, et ad participium haereditatis aeterne illos vocare venerat tanquam ad oves que perierant domus Israel non solum nequiter negaverunt dicentes in sua desipientia non est Deus verum etiam cesum, flagellatum, et Crucifixum impie occiderunt eius sanguinem super se ac filios suos detestabiliter imprecantes, verum cum dispersiones iudeorum ipsorum ad huc nolint intelligere ut benefaciant cum ipsis satis humaniter agitur quod inter fideles absque gravibus contumeliis vivere permittuntur, sed ecce prava ista generatio dum cohabitationem eius pietas sustinet Christiana dum ipsam ex quadam benignitate receptat, se ingratam inde constituit, et nocivam reddens pro gratia contumeliam pro familiaritate contemptum. Nam ut dolentes audivimus, et poenitus reprobamus Christi Christianos utrius-que sexus simplices ad suum ritum dampnabilem retrahere moliuntur eos domesticis hostilitatibus seducendo quod tanto securius ymo peri-culosius perpetrant quanto sanctionibus Canonicis adversus eos editis vilipensa in habitu et commixtu a Christianis per abusionem reprobam minime dicernunter, cum autem haec, et similia que patenter fidem subvertunt Catholicam non fuerint aliquatenus toleranda fraternitati uestra per Apostolica scripta in virtute obedientiae districte praecipiendo mandamus quatenus statuta illa videlicet quod nulli iudeo Christiana mancipia in suo dominio neque sub alendorum suorum puerorum obtenta aut pro seruitio vel alia quemlibet eam in domo propria liceat retinere, aut novas construere sinagogas quodque Christianis obstetri-cibus, et nutricibus prohibetur ne infantes iudeorum in eorum domibus nutrire praesumant seu in parasceve iidem iudei habeant aperta hostia uel fenestras, ac in Lamentationis diebus et dominice passionis in publicum minime procedant nec in contumeliam creatoris presilire audeant ne crucifixum pro nobis aliquatenus blasphemare praesumant uel publicis officiis proferantur sed habitum deferant cuius qualitate a Christianis populis distinguantur faciatis per poenas in factionibus Canonicis contra iudeos editas firmiter observari invocato ad hoc si opus fuerit auxilio bracchii secularis; si vero iidem iudei in hiis obseruandis in obedientes extiterint aut pertinaciter resistentes ipsos protestatione prae-habita intelligere faciatis quod aduersus eos per privationem tutelae, et privilegiorum Ecclesiasticorum aut alias poenas debitas sicut expedire viderimus, annuente domino, procedemus. Proeceptum igitur uestrum sic adimpleat industria vestra provida, et prudentia circumspecta ut pateat per effectum operis quod zelum fervidum circa fidei negotium habeatis; Hosque nihilominus devotioni vestre propter hoc gratiosi lavoris praemia compescemus.

Datum Viterbii, x kal. Januarii, anno tertio.

1. It seems apparent from the address—since some of the geographical names are those of archiepiscopal and episcopal provinces, although Provence was an administrative district—that the pope was addressing the churchmen of the territory under the rule of Charles of Anjou and Alphonse of Poitiers. Both were ambitious men, or so it seems, quite unlike their pious brother, Louis IX. Their primary interest in the Jews of their territories was venal. Yet it is likely that the churchmen to whom this letter was sent were the real targets for its accusations. A few years earlier (1260 or 1261), at a provincial council called by Florentius, the

archbishop of Arles, who had just returned from his experience as bishop of Acre in Palestine, Jews were prohibited from wearing the kind of round capes usually worn by Christian clerics and required to wear an easily visible badge (Mansi, 23:1007), but the decision appears not to have been enforced. At times, the bishops also appeared no more eager to interfere with the economic activities of the Jews than were the secular rulers (cf. Jean Régné, *Étude sur la condition des Juifs de Narbonne* [Narbonne, 1912], pp. 98 f.).

2. The first paragraph is practically identical with the bull of the same *incipit* addressed to James of Aragon on July 15, 1267 (see above, bull no. 25).

3. The question of Christians serving Jews and living in Jewish homes was raised by Emperor Constantine, early in the Christianized Roman Empire; it was also a subject on which Pope Gregory I rendered a decision (*CTh* 16,9,2; *MGH, Reg. Greg. I*, Bk. IX, no. 104; cf. Grayzel, "Jews and Roman Law," *JQR* 59 [1968]: 105 ff.). But these laws applied to Jews' slaves. The Third Lateran Council (1179) began to regulate domestics; and subsequent local councils repeated its prohibitions frequently (see *ChJ*, pp. 296–297, no. I; pp. 298–299, no. III; *et alibi*, esp. pp. 23–26). [But the real problem is true dominion and in-house service; in theory, some canonists might have argued that it was licit to send a Jewish child out to a Christian wetnurse, as even the present text implies.—KS]

4. The rule against building new synagogues or enlarging old ones also went back to early Christian times (*CTh* 16,8,25; Grayzel, "Jews and Roman Law," p. 99). Pope Innocent III (cf. *ChJ*, pp. 106–107) and other popes condemned the erection of new synagogues. Frequently, however, such building activity had to be permitted if the recognized right of the Jews to their own free worship was to be respected (cf. Grayzel; "Jews and Roman Law," pp. 100 ff.). The regulation was, by this time, part of canon law (X.5,6,3).

5. The reference here is to the concluding days of Holy Week, from Good Friday to Easter Sunday. The effort to isolate the Jews on these days and force them to stay indoors goes back to several councils of the sixth century (the Third Council of Orleans in 538 and the Council of Macon in 581). Earlier in the thirteenth century, the restriction was enacted at the Fourth Lateran Council (1215), where the reason stated was that Jews dressed themselves in their finery on Christian days of lamentation—as might have been expected, since these days often coincide with Passover. At the Council of Narbonne in 1227 an additional restriction forbade Jews from working publicly on Sundays and Christian holidays. All this was repeated at the Council of Beziers in 1246 (cf. *ChJ*, pp. 308–309, no. X; pp. 316–317, no. XVII; pp. 332–333, no. XXXVII; also cf. Blumenkranz, *Juifs et Chrétiens*, pp. 315 ff.). Canon law contained a briefer statement pertaining only to the closing of doors and windows at this season, citing a letter of Pope Alexander III (c. 1180): X.5,6,4. [The original letter of Alexander III is the paradigm for the present text in that it also speaks of domestics and their possible conversion to Judaism through overfamiliarity with Jews. (It does not refer at all to synagogues.) The earlier text differs from the present letter in that it lacks the strong language, the charge of blasphemy, and the sense of a real Jewish conversionary activity, which here is unmistakably present. What accounts for the change of tone may be the problem of reversion to Judaism, the same problem that evoked *Turbato corde* and brought to the surface latent, although previously

purely formulaic, anxieties about aggressive Jewish proselytizing among born Christians.—KS]

6. The first regulation about such a distinction in the nature of the clothing to be worn by Jews was made by the Fourth Lateran Council (1215). Popes and canon law did not specify how the distinction was to be made, although it was generally understood to be a colored patch, front and back, on the outer garment. But this was not the only method employed. For a fuller discussion, see the numerous references to the subject in *ChJ*, Index, s.v. Badge, and in Guido Kisch, *The Jews in Medieval Germany* (Chicago, 1949), pp. 295-298.

7. There is no evidence of immediate action taken by the churchmen as a result of this bull. At the time, Alphonse of Poitiers was too busy with other plans. In 1268, preparing to leave for a North African crusade in support of his brother Charles, he had all the Jews of his territories imprisoned, their property assessed, and a huge ransom imposed in return for their release (Jusselin, "Documents financiers concernant les mesures prise par Alphonse de Poitiers contre les Juifs," *Bibliothéque de l'École des Chartres* 40 [1907]; Emile Camau, *La Provence à travers les siècles,* vol. 3, pp. 466-475). In June 1269, King Louis issued an order compelling Jews to wear the badge. A month later, Alphonse followed this example; but no doubt seeing a way of profiting from the situation, he began making exceptions almost at once (Robert, "Catalogue," p. 216, nos. 41, 42, 43). [One would like to know how ambivalent Alphonse was; how did he juggle the needs of piety with the needs of the fisc?—KS] Charles of Anjou was too busy with his Kingdom of Naples and his trans-Mediterranean plans.

29   no date[1]

No addressee:[2]

PECCATUM PECCAVIT[3] . . . The Jewish people, like the fratricide Cain, has become a fugitive upon the earth. For the Jews killed Him who, as the seed of David, was their brother. Yet they are not to be killed, lest the law of God be forgotten; a remnant of them must be saved. They are, however, subjected to deserved servitude until, their faces covered with shame, they are compelled to seek the Lord.

The pope continues by expressing his pain over the situation in Poland: Jews living there purchase public offices, with the full knowledge of nobility and commoners;[4] favored by some churchmen, they have Christian nurses in their homes, whom they compel to cohabit with them;[5] they have more than one synagogue in a community, whose lead roofs they paint with various colors and which they build to a considerable height, with the result that the synagogues are more attractive[6] than the churches.[7]

ASV, Armarium 31, tome 72, fol. 232r.

J. Ptasnik, ed., *Analecta Vaticana*, vol. 3 of *Monumenta Poloniae Vaticana* (Lemberg, 1864–1888), p. 466, no. 515.

PECCATUM PECCAVIT populus Iudeorum propterea est factus instabilis instar fratricide Caym, qui quasi maior esset eius iniquitas, prout ipse fuit in desperationis confusione confessus, quam, ut veniam mereretur, eiectus a facie Domini vagus fuit et profugus super terram. Prefatus namque prophanus populus Ihesum Christum verum Deum Dei filium, qui factus ex semine David secundum carnem, prout ante promissum fuerat per prophetas in scripturis sanctis frater erat ipsorum et ad participationem hereditatis eterne, quantum erat in se, illos vocare venerat, missus ad oves, que perierunt, domus Israel, non solum infideliter negaverunt, dicentes in insipientia: non est Deus, verum etiam cesum, flagellatum et crucifixum impie occiderunt dampnabiliter imprecantes eius sanguinem super se ac filios suos esse. Unde, cum dispersiones illorum adhuc nolint intelligere, ut bene agant, alii Abrahe pueri cum asino expectantes, cum inhumanitate ipsorum satis humane agitur, si ab omnibus, qui eos invenerint, minime occidantur, ne obliviscantur legem Domini in eternum sed tandem reliquie salve fiant. Sunt autem ut servi dampnati iugo servitutis merito comprimendi, si forte vexacio eis periat intellectum et dum facies illorum impleta fuerit ignominia, nomen Domini querere compellentur. Ceterum, quod dolentes referimus, ad nostram noveritis audienciam pervenisse, quod Iudei quidam in partibus Polonie commorantes, ut christianis efficiant efficaciter officia publica precio a christianis participibus empta gerunt, et multis nobilibus et innobilibus participantibus indifferenter eisdem, et quibusdam eciam ecclesiarum prelatis faventibus ad lactandum pueros suos conducunt feminas christianas, que cohabitare conducentibus compelluntur in iniuriam Christi et nominis christiani. Sinagogas etiam plures quinque unam in una civitate contra edificant et plumbo tectas desuper inter diversis coloribus depinguntur, in tantam eas in altitudinem producentes, ut earum respectu decorem domus Domini perdidisse in Polonia videatur.

1. The year must have been early 1266 or late 1265, perhaps before the Council of Breslau in the spring of 1266. The resolutions passed there under the guidance of the papal legate, aimed at regulating the new Jewish settlements with regard to

residence, appearance in public on Christian holidays, limitation of synagogues to one per community, special clothing, domestics, separate bathing places, and public office. Cf. R. Hube, *Antiquissimae constitutiones synodales provinciae Gneznensis* (St. Petersburg, 1856), p. 69; also Aronius, no. 724. The bull and the council which followed were very likely intended to complement the charter of privileges that King Boleslav had granted the Jewish settlers only a year earlier in order to attract more Jews to Poland (cf. Simon Dubnow, *History of the Jews in Russia and Poland* [Philadelphia, 1916], vol. 1, pp. 45 f.). [Though granting many privileges, the royal charter created no obstacle to basic canon law legislation, and especially not to that mentioned here. What had come into being was a typical frontier situation: Jews in offices and a less than careful attitude to the canons in general. The object of the pope, council, and synod, therefore, was to remind everyone that secular and ecclesiastical law had to coexist; neither alone was sufficient.—KS] The same regulations were adopted the following year at a council held in Vienna (whose statutes also applied to Bohemia), presided over by the same legate (Mansi, 23:1174; Aronius, no. 725).

2. The addressees must have been the higher clergy of Poland, and in particular, John, archbishop of Gnesen (1258-1274).

3. The introductory paragraph resembles, in somewhat abbreviated form, the bull *Dampnabili* (no. 25, above). [Nevertheless there is one deviation of note. While maintaining that Jews do not and likely will not convert, the phrase "*Sunt* (they should live) *autem ut servi . . . et dum facies illorum repleta fuerit ignominia, nomen Domini querere compellentur,*" suggests a new approach. Somehow, the yoke of servitude is supposed to teach the Jews Christian truth. This concept would appear but once or twice in papal letters through the late fifteenth century, then reemerge in much sharpened form about 1525, whence it would become a staple of papal policy and active conversionary intent.—KS]

4. Jews in public office constituted a problem for the rulers of all underdeveloped lands (see bull no. 17, above). Here the Jews are represented as buying offices. The reference may be to those Polish Jews who were already leasing estates and managing them for the local nobility (*arrendare:* to rent; cf. Dubnow, *History,* vol. 1, p. 93). The usual reason given for preventing a Jew from holding public office was *ne vim potestatis in Christianos exerceat.* Instead, this bull has the peculiar phrase *ut Christianis efficiant efficaciter publica officia,* etc. Was this a copyist's invention? Indeed the copyist also erred (elsewhere), in one case repeating an entire sentence.

5. The charge of immorality was usually connected with the badge, not with wetnurses.

6. For the rule about synagogues, see bull no. 28, n. 4, above.

7. The bull concludes without the usual hortatory expressions.

30   no date[1]

No addressee:[2]

CUM DE TAM[3] . . . Since exceedingly few are left of the once fabled Jewish people who seek our protection, and these are dispersed among the Christian peoples in testimony of their ancestral crime— so that out of their confusion the glory of our faith may be manifest— Christian humaneness must be shown them; for, as the prophet bore witness, a remnant of them will be saved. Moreover, just as they are forbidden to have the audacity to mislead unthinking Christians away from the truth of the Christian faith into the error of Jewish unbelief, so they, in turn, must not be compelled to join the faith against their will.[4] For no one believes against his will, and God does not accept forced service; when He wills it, He can, by His breath, raise sons of Abraham out of stones.

Now Eleazar, a Jew, has pointed out in a tearful complaint that a cleric of your diocese had his seven-year-old daughter tricked and abducted by her nurse, and that he (the cleric) had transported her to some monastery and detained her there against her will. What is more, after the complaint of the said Jew, when the cleric was asked about the child by the lord of the land, he had her transferred to another place; and so the father, searching for the child in vain, has been tormented by paternal affection. Thereupon he humbly besought us to have the child restored to him, adding that he will not object if, in the future, she desires to go over to the Christian faith.

Lest those who wish to malign (the Church) discern in this affair material for so doing,[5] we herewith order Your Fraternity to search out the truth of the matter diligently. And if you find the truth consonant with the complaint, you must compel the said cleric to restore the girl to her father. You need give the cleric no warning and may impose upon him ecclesiastical punishment without appeal.

ASV, Armarium 31, tome 72, fol. 232r.

CUM DE TAM famoso quondam populo judeorum suis clypeis exignetibus non nisi modice modice reliquie sint relicte que in testimonium patrati sceleris inter christianos populos sunt disperse, ut ex eorum confusione nostre fiat fidei gloria manifesta, apud christianos saltem humanitatis gratia sunt fovendi quia testante propheta ipsorum tandem reliquie salve fient. Verum sicut interdicta est eis seducendi christianos audacia ne illos a veritate christiane religionis ad errorem judaice perfidie pertrahant improvisos, sic ad fidem non sunt inviti cogendi, quia nemo credit invitus et Deus coacta servitia non acceptat, quare ubi vult spirans potest filios Abrae de lapidibus suscitare. Sane lacrimabili nobis Eleazar judeus cum questione monstravit quod clericus tue diocesis filiam suam septennem, per pedisecam euis seduci faciens et abduci, eam renitentem ad quosdam monasterium asportavit et cum a domino terre ad predicti judei querimoniam quereretur idem clericus ad partes alias transferri fecit eandem, et sic pater querens eam et non inveniens paterno discruriatur affectu. Quare nobis humiliter supplicavit ut eam sibi liberam restitui faceremus non curaturus si demum ad religionem transire voluerit fidei christiane. Ne qui malignare volentes ut ex hoc sumant materiam malignandi, fraternitati tue per apostolica scripta mandamus quatinus inquisita super hoc diligentius veritate si rem inveneris ita esse predictum clericum ut patri filiam restituat conquerenti monitione postposita per poena ecclesiastica appellatione remota compellas.

1. The ascription of this bull to Pope Clement IV is, of course, an assumption based on the position of the bull in the formulary following others which are undoubtedly by Clement. Since nothing at all is known about this Eleazar, the incident can only be dated vaguely.

2. The addressee was a bishop, since he is addressed as "Your Fraternity."

3. The original Latin of the bull was published with notes by S. Grayzel, "Thirteenth Century Formulary," pp. 61-63.

4. The sentiment expressed echoes the bull *Sicut Judaeis*. Cf. above, bull no. 2 and notes. [In some ways this text is an excellent example of both the outer and inner limits of the *Sicut* doctrine, as the continuation of n. 5, below, argues. One may also see here the vagaries of Roman (canon) law: namely, harsh decrees and procedures, balanced by an unmitigating insistence on the doing of justice.—KS]

5. The critics about whom the pope was concerned were surely those who might argue that he was too well disposed toward Jews; thus he wanted the incident to be carefully investigated. The pope must have been inclined toward a more lenient attitude in the matter of the conversion of Jewish children, for the matter was still under discussion. Thomas Aquinas, a contemporary, argued, on the basis of "natural rights," that parents could not be deprived of their children and that conversion meant deprivation (*Summa*, II,II,2,12). John Duns Scotus, on the other hand, discounted any such approach (*Opera Omnia*, vol. 16, pp. 487 f.). Pope Innocent III, in answering a question on the subject in 1201, (*ChJ*, pp. 100-103, no. 12) had expressed himself in the stricter sense, namely, that the effect of the sacrament was indelible, and so the child remained baptized, even without parental consent and even if the baptism should not have been performed in the first place. The question was never fully resolved, although in theory a child could not be baptized without the consent of either its father or mother before the age of 12. Cf. *SRH*, vol. 9, pp. 15 f., and 247 f., nn. 13-15.

[The problem faced by the pope might best be expressed in terms of the *Sicut* doctrine. Did its guarantee of the Jews' good customs and due process extend to the paternal right of fathers (a Roman law concept)? It was on this point that Aquinas and Scotus differed. Indeed, this question would become a *locus classicus* of medieval legal argumentation, to peak in the *Three Questions Concerning the Baptism of Jewish Children*, composed by Ullrich Zasius in the sixteenth century (see G. Kisch, *Zasius und Reuchlin* [Constance, 1961]), and to continue as a real matter in the Roman ghetto. (See here C. Roth, "The Forced Baptisms of 1783 at Rome and the Community of London," *JQR* 16 [1925–1926]: 105–116; and "Forced Baptisms in Italy," *JQR* 27 [1936–1937]: 117–136; but especially Archivio di Stato, Roma, Cam. II, Ebrei, b. 1, where this letter of Clement IV is cited by many jurists arguing a similar case in the *eighteenth* century). In the present text, however, it is clear that *Sicut* was limited, although not cast aside, on the basis of the well established principle that once baptism had occurred, there was no going back (see bull no. 26, n. 3, above). Before the fact, no force could be applied; after the fact, Christianity could not be insulted through backsliding. Thus, the text tells us that although the father is now given the right of raising his underage, kidnapped, and baptized daughter, nevertheless, he had probably agreed beforehand to raise her as a Christian. He had certainly agreed to let her be taken from him when she came of age. Unless, then, there is a legal fiction here, (i.e., the pope understands that the father will send the child far away, to some unknown place), it must be assumed—and surely this is what did occur—that the future whereabouts of both father and child were going to be continually monitored. Would not the father, should he violate his agreement, be subject to inquisitorial trial under the rules of *Turbato corde:* aiding an apostate to Judaize?

What emerges from all this is a view of the tension generated by the *Sicut Judaeis* doctrine and of the attempt by the popes to remain faithful to both it and the needs of the Church as a whole. The specific solutions which emerged were not always elegant, as here: The child is returned, preserving the Jewish right to due process (This, incidentally, is precisely as the important canonist Panormitanus [d. 1445] would have had it [*Lectura super libros V Decretalium* (1559), vol. 4, fols. 95r–99v, on X.5,6,9]. He said *Sicut Judaeis* placed limits on the concept of Jewish "perpetual servitude"; whence, in cases of the baptism of children without parental consent, the children must be returned.) At the same time, the baptism is held valid, respecting the purity of the Church. It is thus all the more amazing that the doctrine of *Sicut Judaeis* remained in force, with but one effective (although still not absolute) hiatus under Benedict XIII, in 1415, until the period of the Catholic Restoration. Then it indeed did suffer true violence at the hands of Paul IV and others.—KS]

Gregory X

Teobaldo Visconti was not a member of the College of Cardinals; at the time of his election, he was in the Holy Land with the crusaders. For two years and nine months the Church had been without a head, because the cardinals were unable to resolve the differences among them (Jordan, *L'Allemagne et l'Italie*, pp. 394 f.). It took the newly elected pope another half year to arrive in Rome, so that he was not consecrated until March 27, 1272. There is general agreement that he was one of the most pleasing personalities ever to ascend the papal throne (cf. VR, vol. 1, p. 244; F. X. Seppelt, *Papstgeschichte* [Munich, 1940], pp. 148 f.).

31   October 7, 1272

To faithful Christians, now and in the future:

SICUT JUDAEIS . . . que ipsi preteritis facere temporibus consueverint.[1] Within the standard format of the *Sicut Judaeis* bull, the following two innovations are inserted:[2] (1) The testimony of a Christian shall not suffice to condemn a Jew unless a Jewish witness appears in corroboration, "for Jews (alone) cannot bring (convicting) testimony against Christians."[3] (2) Although Jews have frequently, and falsely, been accused of abducting and murdering a Christian child in order to use its heart and blood as a sacrifice, this charge is unfounded and must not be believed. Those imprisoned for such a charge must be set free.[4] Indeed, testimony was given before the pope by Jewish converts to Christianity that the Bible prohibits Jews from using the blood of even cloven-hoofed animals, let alone from drinking human blood.[5] Nevertheless, since Jews have often been imprisoned on charges of this kind, it is decreed that in the case of such a charge, those Christians who allege the crime "ought not to be given a hearing," and Jews held captive for this frivolity should be freed. Such an empty charge should not serve as an excuse to hold Jews in captivity, unless—although it is preposterous to think it possible—they are caught in the act.

The letter then continues with the customary wording of the *Sicut Judaeis* bull about not subjecting Jews to unusual regulations and not desecrating their cemeteries. It concludes with the standard formula decreeing punishment for disobedience.[6]

Potthast, no. 20915.

M. Stern, *Urkundliche Beiträge über die Stellung der Päpste zu den Juden* (Kiel, 1893), pp. 5 ff., no. 1.

M. Stern, *Päpstliche Bullen über die Blutbeschuldigung* (Munich, 1900), pp. 18 ff.

G. Bondy and F. Dworský, *Zur Geschichte der Juden in Böhmen, Mähren und Schlesien von 906 bis 1620* (Prague, 1906), vol. 1, pp. 32 ff., 110, 27.

Gregorius episcopus, servus servorum Dei, dilectis in Christo filiis fidelibus Christianis presentibus videlicet et futuris salutem et apostolicam benedictionem.

SICUT JUDEIS in sinagogis suis non licet ultra quam permissum est lege presumere, ita in hiis, que concessa sunt, nullum debent preiudicium sustinere. Nos ergo, licet in sua magis velint duritia perdurare, quam prophetarum verba et suarum scripturarum archana cognoscere atque ad Christiane fidei et salutis notitiam pervenire, quia tamen defensionem nostram et auxilium postulant, ex Christiane pietatis mansuetudine predecessorum nostrorum felicis memorie Calixti, Eugenii, Alexandri, Clementis, Celestini, Innocentii et Honorii Romanorum pontificum vestigiis inherentes ipsorum petitionem admittimus eisque protectionis nostre clypeum indulgemus. Statuentes etiam, ut nullus Christianus seu invitos vel nolentes eos vel aliquem ipsorum ad baptismum venire compellat; sed si eorum quilibet sponte ad Christianos fidei causa confugerit, postquam voluntas eius fuerit patefacta, efficiatur absque aliqua calumnia Christianus, veram quippe Christianitatis fidem habere non creditur, qui ad Christianorum baptisma non spontaneus, sed invitus cognoscitur pervenire. Nullus etiam Christianus eorum personas capere, incarcerare, vulnerare, tormentare, mutilare, occidere, violentiam eis inferre vel bonas eorum etiam consuetudines in ea, in qua habitant regione, pro pecunia vel bonis eorum auferendis ab eis vel aliis absque iudicio potestatis terre immutare presumat. Preterea in festivitatum suarum celebratione nocte dieque quisquam fustibus vel lapidibus vel aliis quibuscumque eos nullatenus non perturbet neque aliquis ab eis coacta servitia exigat, nisi ea que ipsi preteritis facere temporibus consueverint. Statuimus etiam, ut testimonium Christianorum contra Judeos non valeat, nisi sit Judeus aliquis inter eos Christianos ad testimonium perhibendum, cum Judei non possint contra Christianos testimonium perhibere. Quia contingit interdum, quod aliqui Christiani perdunt eorum pueros Christianos et impingitur in Judeos ipsos per inimicos eorum, ut pueros ipsos Christianos furtim subtrahant et occidant, et quod de corde et sanguine sacrificent eorundem, ac patres eorundem puerorum vel Christiani alii Judeorum ipsorum emuli clam abscondunt ipsos pueros, ut possint Judeos ipsos offendere et pro eorum vexationibus redimendis possint a Judeis ipsis extorquere aliquam pecunie quantitatem, asseruntque falsissime, quod Judei ipsi pueros ipsos clam et furtim subtraxerunt et occiderunt et quod Judei ex corde et sanguine eorum sacrificent puerorum, cum lex eorum hoc precise inhibeat et expresse, quod Judei ipsi non sacrificent, non comedant sanguinem neque bibant nec etiam comedant de carnibus animalium habentium ungues scissas, et hoc per Judeos ad Christianam fidem conversos in nostra curia pluries probatum, hac occasione huiusmodi Judei plurimi pluries contra iustitiam capti fuerunt et detenti: statuimus, quod Christiani in casu et huiusmodi occasione contra Judeos audiri non debeant, et mandamus quod Judei capti huiusmodi occasione frivola a carcere liberentur nec deinceps huiusmodi occasione frivola capiantur, nisi forte, quod non credimus, in flagranti crimine caperentur. Statuimus, ut nullus Christianus novitatem aliquam exerceat in eosdem, sed in eo statu serventur et forma, in qua fuerunt predecessorum nostrorum temporibus hactenus ab antiquo. Ad hoc malorum hominum pravitati et avaritie obviantes decernimus, ut nemo cimiterium Judeorum mutilare vel minuere audeat seu obtentu pecunie corpora humana effodere. Si quis autem decreti huius tenore cognito temere, quod absit, contraire temptaverit, honoris et officii sui periculum patiatur aut excommunicationis ultione plectatur, nisi presumptionem suam digna satisfactione correxerit. Eos autem dumtaxat Judeos huiusmodi protectionis presidio volumus communiri, qui nichil machinari presumpserint in subversionem fidei Christiane.

Ego Gregorius catholice ecclesie episcopus subscripsi.

Ego Simon tituli sancti Martini presbyter cardinalis.

Ego Antonius tituli sancti Praxedis presbyter cardinalis.

Et ego Oddo Tusculanus episcopus subscripsi.

Ego frater Johannes Portuensis et sancte Ruffine episcopus subscripsi.

Ego Johannes sancti Nicolai in carcere Tulliano diaconus cardinalis subscripsi.

Ego Matheus sancte Marie in Porticu diaconus cardinalis subscripsi.

[Rota: Sanctus Petrus, Sanctus Paulus, Gregorius papa X. Perfice congressus meos in semitis eius].

Datum apud Urbem Veterem, non. Octobris, anno primo.

1. For earlier promulgations of the bull see above, bulls no. 2 and 11 and the references cited in both. Like the text of Urban IV (bull no. 11), the *Sicut Judaeis* of Gregory X also stops in the enumeration of his predecessors with the name of Honorius III.

2. A translation of the entire bull into German is to be found in the collection by Bondy and Dworský cited above, as well as in Stern, *Päpstliche Bullen.* A translation into English of the Gregory addition is found in *SRH*, vol. 9, pp. 40 f. and in Grayzel, *"Sicut Judeis,"* pp. 259 f. A complete translation into English is found in J. R. Marcus, *The Jew in the Medieval World* (Cincinnati, 1938), pp. 152–154.

3. The credibility of Christian witnesses against Jews and of Jewish witnesses against Christians was already a subject of disagreement between State and Church in the Carolingian era (cf. Blumenkranz, *Juifs et Chrétiens*, p. 357). A more even treatment, calling for the use of Christian testimony against Jews, while accepting the fact of Jewish testimony, was advocated by the Third Lateran Council in 1179 (cf. *ChJ*, p. 296, no. I, par. 2, and X.2,20,21). A further refinement was made at the Council of Vienne, in 1312, as will be seen below (*Clem.* 2,8,1).

[The text of Gregory X, however, if taken literally, argues that Jews may not testify against Christians at all. No such canon existed prior to 1272 or afterward, but canonists did discuss whether, in fact, this should be the case. Most felt there were times when Jewish testimony was valid, although, following the lead of Roman law (*CJ* 1,5,21), there was a desire to repress all Jewish evidence, if possible (See Marq. de Susannis, *De Iudaeis et aliis Infidelibus* [Venice, 1558], II,5). In the present context such a limitation would be out of place. The pope wanted to establish the need for Jewish testimony to prevent blood libel-induced lynchings. The correct reading, therefore, is that just as Jewish testimony *alone* is insufficient for conviction, so, too, is Christian testimony *alone* insufficient. Indeed, this reading is explicitly supported by the statement of Rudolph I cited in n. 6 below.—KS]

4. The accusation that Jews were guilty of ritual murder was not new. Pope Innocent IV spoke of it in two of his protective pronouncements (*ChJ*, nos. 113 and 116, and cf. pp. 79–80). Innocent IV's *Sicut Judaeis*, issued in July 1247, also had an additional paragraph dealing with the subject (*ChJ*, no. 118), and no. 116 mentions the cannibalistic charge. Cf. the same type of story, plus a miracle, in *Shevet Yehudah* (ed. Shohet) p. 126, no. 61. The ritual murder accusation was made with particular frequency at this time, the period of the German interregnum: cf. e.g., Aronius, nos. 597, 728.

5. Some forty years earlier, a similar commission of Christian converts from Judaism had been called by Frederick II, and it testified to the same effect (Aronius, no. 497; cf. *ChJ*, p. 79 n. 19 and the reference there cited).

6. For a discussion of this bull's effectiveness, see Grayzel, *"Sicut Judeis."* It is clear that Jews in various parts of central Europe had occasion to produce copies of the bull and bring it to the attention of the authorities. The newly elected king of the Romans, Emperor Rudolph I, ratified it on July 4, 1275. Addressing all his subjects, he announced that he had examined the bull of Gregory X as submitted to him by Albert (Albertus Magnus), formerly bishop of Regensburg. The bull is quoted in full, and King Rudolph adds a warning that no one may condemn Jews for this crime unless they had been found guilty on the testimony of both Jewish

and Christian witnesses (*nisi legitimo iudaeorum et christianorum testimonio convincantur*); cf. Bondy and Dworský, *Zur Geschichte*, vol. 1, p. 35; Count Edward of Savoy took official note of the bull on July 20, 1329, and so did the authorities of Turin about the same time (cf. Stern, *Päpstliche Bullen*, p. 23; and M. Esposito, *Revue D'Histoire Ecclésiastique* 34 [1938]: 785–801). King Boleslav of Poland, however, had anticipated the pope, prohibiting the accusation as early as 1264. The crime had to be proved by three Jewish and three Christian witnesses; and if the one bringing the charge failed to prove it, he was to suffer the fate he had intended for the Jews (Aron Eisenstein, *Die Stellung der Juden in Polen im XIIIten und XIVten Jahrhundert*, pp. 34 ff.). Despite all this, the charge continued to be raised in Poland, in Germany, and elsewhere. One may recall, although cautiously, the apt remark made by D'Blossiers Tovey, in his *Anglia Judaica* (Oxford, 1738), that "*Jews are never said to have practiced this crime but at such times as the king was manifestly in need of money.*" He should not have limited it to Kings. [Perhaps.—KS]

32   May 28, 1273

To the King of Portugal:[1]

SCIRE DEBES[2] . . . On the complaint of the clergy of Portugal, Pope Gregory takes the king to task for his diverse violations of canon law and the rights of the Catholic Church, to wit: the king confiscates the property of Jews and Muslims who undergo baptism;[3] if Muslim slaves of Jews undergo baptism, he forces them to return to their masters;[4] he does not compel Jews or Muslims who acquire land from Christians—either by purchase or as the result of an unpaid debt—and work it with their own hands or hired labor to pay tithes or first fruits to those churches which had once received these payments from Christian owners.[5]

Potthast, no. 20742.

O. Raynaldus, *Annales Ecclesiastici*, ed. J. D. Mansi (Lucca, 1738–1756), *a.a.* 1273, no. 26.

Sbaralea, *Bull. Francisc.*, vol. 3, p. 202 , no. 23.

Regi Portugalliae illustri.

SCIRE DEBES, fili charissime, sicut necessario scire te convenit, ut regni tui negotia per circumspectionis directa prudentiam prosperis successibus convalescant, quod prae caeteris rebus, quibus Christiana regna fundantur solidius est tutela ecclesiasticae libertatis, ita ut omnia tam tempora quam loca considerationis oculo percurrendo, nullus ignorat, quod eadem libertate convulsa, sceptra regalia tenere non possunt aliquam firmitatem.

Praeterea si quando Judaei vel Saraceni liberi divina inspiratione, veniunt ad baptismum, tu bona ipsorum facis protinus confiscari, et eos in novam redigi servitutem. Et si Saraceni servi Judaeorum per baptismum Christi fidem acceperint, eos reduci facis in servitutem pristinam Judaeorum. Si Judaei quidem vel Saraceni emptionis vel pignoris titulo Christianorum possessiones obtineant, vel acquirant, non permittis, edicto generali super hoc edito, ut de hujusmodi possessionum fructibus, quas dicti Judaei vel Saraceni propriis manibus, vel sumptibus excolunt, ecclesiis in quarum parochiis possessiones ipsae consistunt, decimae ac primitiae persolvantur.

Datum apud Urbem Veterem, v kal. Julii, anno secundo.

1. Alphonso III. Cf. bull no. 23, above, esp. n. 4.

2. This text reflects a continuation of the ongoing argument between the king and the clergy of Portugal, already evident in the letter mentioned above. Each of the charges enumerated here represents a clear violation of canon law.

3. The economic problem faced by converts from Judaism is discussed by Browe in his *Judenmission*, pp. 183-195. He traces the problem back to the Theodosian Code and points out the financial considerations which motivated medieval rulers to confiscate the property of Jewish converts. Pope Alexander III had spoken out on this subject to the prelates of Spain in 1171 and at the Third Lateran Council in 1179 (Browe, *Judenmission*, pp. 187 ff.; *ChJ*, pp. 296-297, no. 1). Discussion continued as long as secular authorities stood to gain more from these confiscations. For a reference to the subject in the correspondence of Pope John XXII, in 1320, see below, pp. 301-340.

4. Legislation on the subject of the ownership of slaves by Jews goes back to the days of Constantine (*CTh* XVI.9). Its main concern was the possibility of the slaves' becoming converts to Judaism. The first to concern themselves with pagan slaves who adopted Christianity and with the compensation subsequently to be paid to former Jewish owners were the Fourth Council of Orleans (541) and the Council of Macon (583). Pope Gregory I discussed this subject in a number of letters, once stating (*MGH, Reg. Greg. I*, Bk. VII, no. 21, in May 597): *omnino grave execrandumque est Christianos esse in servitio Judaeorum*, "they must all be redeemed." On the subject of slaves owned by Jews, see B. Blumenkranz, *Juifs et Chrétiens*, pp. 184 ff. In *ChJ*, the subject is discussed with special reference to the first half of the thirteenth century on pp. 23 f.

5. For a discussion of the tithes imposed on Jewish owners of land previously in Christian hands and from which local churches had once drawn part of their income, see *ChJ*, pp. 36 ff. In the eastern parts of Christian Europe, an attempt was made to extend such taxation to Jewish-owned town dwellings in which Christians used to reside. Cf. the synod of Bratislava (Breslau) in 1266 (Hube,

Antiquissimae Constitutiones, p. 70, and conciliar text no. VI, below) and the Council of Vienna in 1267, c. 15 (Mansi, 23:1174, and conciliar text no. VII below.)

33   March 1, 1274

To the friars of the Dominican and Franciscan Orders who are or will be deputized by the Holy See as inquisitors of heresy:

TURBATO CORDE[1] . . . Gregory is deeply disturbed. Not only had certain Jews who had converted to Christianity reverted to their former unbelief, but a number of others, born Christians, had converted to Judaism, and so blasphemed the name of Christ. Since a plague of this sort must be quickly stopped by appropriate means, the addressees are ordered to proceed against (suspect) Jews and Christians in the prescribed manner for seeking out heretics and their fautors. Jews responsible for leading Christians to their execrable rite must be punished as is fitting. The aid of the secular arm may be invoked if necessary.

Potthast, no. 20798.
Ripoll, *Bull. Ord.*, vol. 1, p. 517.
Sbaralea, *Bull. Francisc.*, vol. 3, p. 213.

TURBATO CORDE audivimus, et narramus, quod non solum quidam de Judaicae coecitatis errore ad lumen Fidei Christianae conversi ad priorem reversi esse perfidiam dignoscuntur; verum etiam quamplurimi Christiani veritatem Catholicae Fidei abnegantes se damnabiliter ad ritum Judaicum transtulerunt; Quod tanto magis reprobum fore cognoscitur, quanto ex hoc Christi Nomen Sanctissimum quadam familiari hostilitate securius blasphematur. Cum autem huic pesti damnabili congruis, et festinis remediis deceat obviari; Universitati vestrae per Apostolica scripta mandamus, quatenus infra terminos ad inquirendum contra haereticos auctoritate Sedis Apostolicae designatos super praemissis tam per Christianos, quam etiam per Judaeos, inquisita diligenter, et solicite veritate, contra eos, quos talia invenietis hactenus commisisse; ac committere etiam in futurum, tanquam contra haereticos, contra fautores quoque, receptatores, et defensores eorum procedere studeatis: Judaeos autem, qui Christianos utriusque sexus ad eorum ritum execrabilem induxerint, aut inveneritis de cetero inducentes, poena debita puniatis:

Contradictores per censuram ecclesiasticam, appellatione postposita, compescendo: invocato ad hoc, si opus fuerit, auxilio brachii secularis.

Datum Lugduni, kal. Martii, anno secundo.

1. Unlike the first issue of this bull in July 1267 (no. 26, above), this text emphasizes the conversion to Judaism of born Christians. [The reference to reprobate Christians in the 1267 text doubtlessly refers to apostate converts. Why Gregory X believed real proselytism was going on is a bit mysterious; yet, see above, bull no. 28, n. 5. Perhaps the bull reflects the striking fact of the spontaneous conversions to Judaism which, although rare, did occur? One must appreciate the awfulness of these conversions and acts of apostasy in the eyes of contemporary churchmen—no matter how morally reprehensible the persecutions they evoked may appear today. There is finally another possibility: The "born Christian" converts to Christianity were the *children* of converts from Judaism, returning, as did the sons of the New Christians in the seventeenth century, to the original faith of their parents, an act in which Jews sometimes played an active role.—KS]

A bull of almost similar content, beginning *Prae cunctis mentis*, had been issued to the inquisitors of France and repeated a few days later to the inquisitors in Paris, without specifically mentioning Jews (Potthast, nos. 20720 and 20724; Ripoll, *Bull. Ord.*, vol. 1. p. 512, no. 12; E. Martène et U. Durand, *Thesaurus novus anecdotorum* [Paris: 1817, 1822], vol. 5. The document given here also appears in Bibliothèque Nationale, Fond Doat, 37, fol. 241–245, repeated as part of the 1293 command given by King Philip IV to Simon Bristête, his seneschal in southern France, ordering royal officers in Carcassonne and Beziers to cooperate with the Inquisition in ferreting out heretics, but insisting that they not permit the arrest and punishment of a Jew without prior royal consent. In 1299, the Jews of Carcassonne were told that they could refuse to appear before the Inquisition if royal officials were not present. Bibliothèque Nationale, Fond Doat, 37, fols. 161r–163r; cf. Saige, *Les Juifs de Languedoc*, pp. 232 ff.). U. Robert, "Catalogue," p. 218, no. 53, omits reference to the *Turbato* of Gregory X and cites that of Martin IV in 1281 (see below).

34   July 7, 1274

To all the Christian faithful:[1]

On behalf of the Jews in German lands, Pope Gregory reissues the bull previously addressed to the German episcopacy and enacted by Innocent IV (July 5, 1247). The vellum of the original document had begun to disintegrate.[2]

To all the faithful:

LACHRYMABILEM JUDAEORUM . . . Pope Innocent made the following points: Some princes, both ecclesiastical and lay, plot against the

Jews in order to deprive them of their property. They accuse the Jews of sharing the heart of a murdered child in their Passover celebration, saying that Jewish law commands this, although it is in fact contrary to Jewish law. When a dead body is found, it is thrown into the Jews' midst, and, without proper trial, they are despoiled of their property, imprisoned, afflicted with all sorts of penalties, and shame fully executed. The remaining Jews are then compelled to go into exile from places where they and their ancestors had lived from time immemorial.

The pope orders the archbishops and bishops of Germany to look into this matter and not permit the Jews to be undeservedly molested in the future.

Potthast, no. 20861.

T. J. Lacomblet, *Urkundenbuch für die Geschichte des Niederrheins* (Dusseldorf, 1840-1857), vol. 2, no. 305.

L. Ennen and E. Eckertz, eds., *Quellen zur Geschichte der stadt Köln*, vol. 3, p. 62, no. 88.

Gregorius episcopus servus servorum dei. Universis christifidelibus presentes litteras inspecturis, salutem et apostolicam benedictionem.

Tenorem litterarum, quas felicis recordationis Innocentius papa quartus predecessor noster venerabilibus fratribus nostris archiepiscopis et episcopis per Alamaniam constitutis in iudeorum Alamanie favorem direxit, pro eo quod incipiebant nimia vetustate consumi, de verbo ad verbum fecimus presentibus annotari, qui talis est:

Innocentius episcopus servus servorum dei. Venerabilibus fratribus archiepiscopis et episcopis per Alemanniam constitutis, salutem et apostolicam benedictionem.

LACRIMABILEM IUDAEORUM Alemannie recepimus questionem, quod nonnulli tam ecclesiastici quam seculares principes ac alii nobiles et potentes vestrarum civitatum et diocesium, ut eorum bona iniuste diripiant et usurpent adversus ipsos impia consilia cogitantes ac fingentes occasiones varias et diversas, non considerato prudenter, quod quasi ex archivis eorum christiane fidei testimonia prodierunt, scriptura divina inter alia mandata legis dicente: "non occides," ac prohibente illos in sollempnitate paschali quicquam morticinum non contingere, falso imponunt eisdem, quod in ipsa sollempnitate se corde pueri communicant interfecti, credendo id ipsam legem precipere, cum sit legi contrarium manifeste, ac eis malitiose obiciunt hominis cadaver mortui, si contigerit illud alicubi reperiri, et per hoc et alia quam plura figmenta sevientes in ipsos eos super hiis non accusatos, non confessos nec convictos contra privilegia illis ab apostolica sede clementer indulta spoliant contra deum et iustitiam omnibus bonis suis et inedia carceribus ac tot molestiis tantisque gravaminibus premunt ipsos diversis penarum affligendo generibus et morte turpissima eorum quam plurimos condempnando, quod iidem iudei quasi existentes sub predictorum principum, nobilium et potentum dominio deterioris conditionis quam eorum patres sub Pharaone fuerunt in Egypto, coguntur de locis inhabitatis ab eis et suis antecessoribus a tempore, cuius non extat memoria, miserabiliter exulare, unde suum exterminium metuentes, duxerunt ad apostolice sedis providentiam recurrendum. Nolentes igitur prefatos iudeos iniuste vexari, quorum conversationem dominus meseratus expectat, cum testante propheta credantur reliquie salve fieri eorundem, fraternitati vestre per apostolica scripta mandamus, quatenus eis vos exhibentes favorabiles et benignos, quicquid super premissis contra eosdem iudeos per predictos prelatos, nobiles et potentes inveneritis temere attemptatum, in statum debitum legitime revocato non permittatis ipsos de cetero super hiis vel similibus ab aliquibus indebite molestari, molestatores huiusmodi per censuram ecclesiasticam appellatione postposita compescendo.

Datum Lugduni, iii non. Julii, anno quinto.

1. Cf. *ChJ*, pp. 268–271, no. 116.

2. It was not unusual for a pope to reissue the bull of a predecessor; see, for example, no. 32, above. Normally, however, the reissuing pope adopted the bull of his predecessor as his own. In distinction, Pope Gregory here simply repeated Innocent's bull, without personal acceptance. The reason given for the reissue, that the vellum of the document was deteriorating after only twenty-seven years, may indicate that it had been "needed" on numerous occasions during the interregnum in Germany and that the Jews expected it would be needed again, and frequently, in the future. The pope may also have argued that it would be pointless to reissue the bull in his own name since it so closely resembled the *Sicut Judaeis* he had issued less than two years earlier (see above, bull no. 31). In fact, when taking cognizance (*vidimus*) of Gregory's *Sicut Judaeis*, Rudolph of Hapsburg (July 4, 1275) also confirmed Gregory's repetition of *Lachrymabilem* (cf. n. 6 to bull no. 31, above). The city of Frankfurt took cognizance of the *Lachrymabilem* on July 26, 1287 (J. F. Böhmer, *Urkundenbuch der Reichsstadt Frankfurt* [Frankfurt a. M., 1836], vol. 1, pp. 232–233), as also did Cologne in the same year (Ennen and Eckertz, *Quellen*, vol. 3, p. 62, no. 88). In some instances, when both the *Sicut Judaeis* and the *Lachrymabilem* were ratified together, the shorter form of the *Sicut Judaeis* was used, without Gregory's additions as given above. Ernst Weyden, *Geschichte der Juden in Köln am Rhein* (Cologne, 1867), p. 357, *Urkunde* 10, gives the entire bull, dated the nones of July, 1273, and issued at Lyons. Yet, the bull appears to have helped little, even after its ratification by

Rudolph of Hapsburg. Cf. Weyden, *Geschichte*, p. 157. During the German interregnum many German cities witnessed blood accusations and riots.

35   September 17, 1274

To the Archbishop and Bishop of York:[1]

SI MENTES FIDELIUM[2] . . . Pope Gregory issues an urgent call for volunteers for a crusading army, as decided at the recent Council of Lyons.[3] The volunteers are offered the usual privileges, including the remission of interest on all debts. The Jews (as is the norm) must be compelled by the secular authorities to remit the interest they have already collected.

Reg. curiales (Reg. Vat. 37), no. 94, f. 195.
Potthast, no. 20920.
J. Guiraud and L. Cadier, eds. *Les registres de Gregoire X et de Jean XXI*, p. 226, no. 569.
Friss, *Monumenta Hungariae Judaica*, pp. 45 f., no. 28 (esp. p. 49).

Gregorius episcopus, . . . venerabilibus fratribus . . . archiepiscopo Strigoniensi et universis episcopis sue provincie salutem etc.

SI MENTES FIDELIUM, terrenis abdicatis illecebris, recolendis immensis beneficiis nostri redemptoris intenderent, si ea celesti lumine illustrate diligenti scrutarent examine, si frequenter mediacionis attente conspectui presentarent, profecto eorum corda concalescerent intra ipsos, igne in meditancium animis ardescente. Cuius etenim pectus saxeum non emolliret considerata illius humanacionis humilitas, in qua dei filius factus homo exinanivit semetipsum formam servi accipiens, in simili-tudinem hominum factus, et habitu inventus ut homo? Cuius viscera non inflammaret caritatis ardore pia consideracio illius humiliacionis extreme, in qua ipse idem factus obediens usque ad mortem, ad expro-brancium obprobria coram tondente se velut agnus obmutuit, et sicut ovis ad occisionem ductus, post contumelias et terrores, post spinas et sputa, post flagella varia, post diversa denique genera tormentorum, innocens sine causa dampnatus, et demum saturatus obprobriis clavis affixus, aceto et felle potatus, confossus lancea, in crucis patibulo tam dire mortis subiit passionem, misterium redempcionis nostre perficiens, sine qua parum nobis nativitas profuisset? Quis igitur hec et alia largitatis divine carismata, infra pectoris claustra debita et frequenti meditacione revolvens, non intus fervide zelo devocionis accensus ferveat, foris ebulliat, exclamet et dicat: Quid retribuam domino pro omnibus que retribuit mihi? et non expectato monitoris vel sollicitatoris officio subiungat ultroneus: Calicem salutaris accipiam et nomen domini invocabo?

Si qui vero illuc proficiscencium ad prestandas usuras iuramento tenentur astricti, creditores eorum per vos vel alios, sublato appellacionis obstaculo, districcione simili, ut iuramenta huiusmodi penitus relaxantes ab usurarum alterius exaccione desistant: si autem quisquam creditorum eos ad solucionem coegerit usurarum, ipsum ad restitucionem earum eadem districcione, sublato appellacionis obstaculo, compellatis. Iudeos quoque ad remittendas ipsis usuras per secularem compelli precipimus potestatem et donec eas remiserint, ab omnibus Christi fidelibus tam in mercimoniis quam aliis sub excommunicacionis pena iubemus communionem illis omnimodam denegari. Porro ad huiusmodi ardui et salubris negocii efficaciam pleniorem, ut vos convocare possitis cleros et populos ad quemcumque volueritis locum ydoneum et ibidem verbum crucis proponere.

Datum Lugduni, sexto kalendas Octobris, anno tercio.

1. This is the address in the *Registres;* the Archbishop of York at the time was Walter Gifford. The original bull was addressed to all churchmen. The copy in Friss, *Monumenta Hungariae Judaica,* the text appearing here, is addressed to the Archbishop of Gran (September 26, 1274.)

2. For similar calls for crusader volunteers see *ChJ, passim,* and bull no. 17, above.

3. Cf. J. Alberigo, ed., *Conciliorum Oecumenicorum Decreta* (Basle, 1962), Constitutiones, p. 285.

36   Second Council of Lyons, 1274[1]

Extractiones de Libro quem fecit . . . Humbertus de Romanis,[2] magister quondam ordinis Praedicatorum.

PRIMUM QUIDEM . . . In his discussion of the three struggles of the Church (against the infidel—including heretics, the schismatic, and the criminal), Humbert, (writing a conspectus of the items to be discussed at the council at the *express directive* of Gregory X) reiterates (chaps. 5 and 15) the principle that Jews are passive and do not threaten Christianity (*nihil ultra sciunt aut* possunt *contra populum Ch[r]istianum*). Thus, they are to be tolerated.[3]

Mansi, 24:109, 115

Prima pars agit de negotio ecclesiae contra Sarracenos, et habet XXVII. capitula.

CAP. I.

Quod ad summum pontificem pertinet vigilare diligenter super populum Christianum.

Ad omnes siquidem praelatos pertinet vigilare, secundum illud Lucae 2. Pastores erant vigilantes et custodientes vigilias noctis super gregem suum. Nam latro ex improviso superveniens gregi, transjugulat pastorem quem invenit dormientem; et Dominus dicit Apocal. 3. Si non vigilaveris, veniam ad te tanquam fur; sed hoc summe seu maxime pertinet ad summum pastorem, tum quia habet maximum gregem, tum quia grex suus est omnibus periculis expositus, tum quia ipse habet maximam mercedem, non solum aeternam, sed etiam temporalem, quia Dominus universorum est. Unde ceteris dormientibus, Petrus specialiter increpatur Marci XIV. Simon dormis, non potuisti una hora vigilare mecum? Maxime ad illum, ait papa Gregorius, hoc est vigilans quodam praesagio futurorum.

CAP. II.

Quod populus Christianus subjacet triplici incommodo, sicut olim populus Israeliticus.

Sicut enim populus Israeliticus primo a tempore Abrahae usque ad finem fuit quasi continue ab infidelibus impugnatus. Secundo sub Roboam et Jeroboam circumbiliter divisus. Tertio, pars illa quae veri Dei cultui adhaesit, majoribus sceleribus se involvit; sic populus Christianus semper a foris infidelium persecutionem habuit et habebit. Secundo, patitur divisionem inter Graecos et Latinos, qui in ventre Rebeccae, ecclesiae, colliduntur, ex quo regnum ecclesiae in se divisum miserabiliter desolabitur. Tertio, ecclesia Latinorum, salva fide, quoad mores pluribus foeditatibus implicatur.

CAP. III.

Quod ad summum pontificem pertinet contra praedicta tria remedium adhibere.

Sicut enim pastor nititur oves a lupis defendere, dispersas congregare, aegras sanare; sic ad summum pastorem pertinet contra hostes forinsecos ecclesiae defensionis bravium providere, dispersos schismate reunire. Latinos aegros moribus reformare, implendo illud Ezechielis, Quod pingue et forte custodiam etc.

CAP. IV.

Quod christianitas impugnata fuit a sui initio usque nunc a VII. generibus hominum.

Primi impugnatores fuerunt Judaei a Stephano inchoantes. Secundi fuerunt idololatrae persequentes apostolos et martyres. Tertii fuerunt philosophi gentiles, de quibus act. XVII. Disserebant cum Paulo; alii dicebant: Novorum daemoniorum videtur annuntiator. Quarti sunt haeretici diversarum sectarum. Quinti fuerunt imperatores ante Constantinum magnum, qui moverunt decem generales persecutiones significatas per decem cornua bestiae monstruosae, de qua habetur Apocalypsis XVI. Septimi fuerunt barbari, videlicet Wandali, Gothi, et Huni, qui et Hungari dicuntur, et Tartari. Septimi fuerunt et sunt Saraceni, quorum seductor Mahometus finxit se esse prophetam a Deo missum ad exponendum et corrigendum legem Judaeorum et Christianorum. Isti septem gentes Israel impugnantes, de quibus habetur Deuter. VII. et septem capita bestiae, de quo habetur Apocalyps. XVI.

CAP. V.

Quod ista septem genera persecutorum jam pene enervata sunt praeter saracenos.

Primum quidem Judaei scientia convicti, potentia subacti, nihil ultra sciunt aut possunt contra populum Christianum. Secundo idololatria cum crucis vexillo exsufflata, tantum in partibus Aquilonis apud Prucinos et quosdam alios paucos exsultat. Tertio, philosophia per veram sapientiam destructa est, immo obsequium fidei per viros excellentis ingenii explanata. Quarto haeretici olim contra ecclesiam palam latrantes sua latibula sunt ingressi. Quinto, imperatores ecclesiam quam olim conculcabant, a multo tempore jam exaltant. Sexto, barbari non comparent praeter Tartaros, qui etsi solos Hungaros persequantur, contra tamen Saracenos praebent auxilium Christianis. Septimo autem, Saraceni semper in malitia perseverant.

CAP XV.

Responsio contra quintum.

Quinti oblocutores dicunt, quod non debemus Saracenos persequi, sicut nec persequimur Judaeos, nec Saracenos nobis subditos, nec idololatras, nec Tartaros, nec Barbaros. Quibus respondendum est, primo de Judaeis, qui tolerantur, quia reliquiae Israel salvae fient. Item, quia crudele esset mactare subjectos. Item propter prohibitionem prophetae dicentis; Ne occidas eos, ne quando obliviscantur populi mei. Saraceni autem nobis subditi tolerantur, quia nocere non possunt. Item, quia in multis servitiis utiles sunt, et facilius converti possunt. De idololatris autem qui sunt in partibus Aquilonaribus, sicut sunt Phiteni, speratur eorum conversio, quia omnis lingua serviet ei, nec ipsi nos infestant, quare dimittuntur: Tartaros autem nec sic leviter invadimus, quia inter nos et eos medii sunt Saraceni, et ideo primitus expugnandi. Item, certas mansiones non habent, in quibus possunt semper inveniri, sicut nec Cumani.

CAP. XVI.

Responsio contra sextum.

Sexti dicunt, quod ex ista pugna non sequitur fructus spiritualis, quia Saraceni magis convertuntur ad blasphemiam, quam ad fidem: occisi autem ad infernum mittuntur; nec etiam fructus temporalis, quia terras acquisitas non possumus retinere. Quibus respondendum est: in hoc est fructus triplex. Primus spiritualis, quia propter indulgentias, et alia bona annexa plures Christiani citius salvantur. Secundus corporalis, quia per hoc a Saracenorum invasione Christiani corporaliter defenduntur. Tertius temporalis, quia spolia adquiruntur, et ipsi tributis subduntur, et licet temporaliter ad Dei cultum reducuntur.

1. [This text was not included in the material that was compiled by Solomon Grayzel.—KS]

2. [Those who would argue a Dominican conspiracy against the Jews, based on the premise of an aggressive, anti-Christian Judaism, should contend with explicitly contradictory statements like Humbert's here. In the same way that all Dominicans were not inquisitors, nor did they identify with the Inquisition (on this see M.-H. Vicaire, "La prédication nouvelle des prêcheurs méridionaux au XIIIe siècle. In *Le crédo, la morale et l'Inquisition*, ed. M.-H. Vicaire. *Cahiers de Fanjeaux* 6 [Toulouse, 1971]: 39), so too, it is obvious that not all Dominicans perceived a Jewish conspiracy to undermine Christendom.—KS]

3. [This conspectus thus reiterates the principles underlying the canon *Dispar nimirum est (Gratian:* C.23,q.8,c.1), drawn from the letter of Alexander II (1063). The programmatic setting at Lyons is especially noteworthy. It argues that despite the clashes over the Talmud and the luring of converts back to Judaism,

the latter thirteenth century popes still subscribed to the traditional policies and attitudes toward Jews enunciated by their predecessors. To be sure, this text is not, precisely speaking, a direct papal expression. However, as Mansi notes, it was composed by a direct papal order, and so reflects papal feelings accurately.—KS]

37   Second Council of Lyons,[1] May 7–July 17, 1274

> Canons 26 and 27. On usury: There is no mention of Jews,[2] but there is a call for severe control and punishment of usurers: No one seeking to establish himself as a usurer may be permitted to remain in any locality longer than three months;[3] native usurers are to be excommunicated; a usurer may not receive Christian burial. Clergy or communities acting contrary to this edict are subject to suspension, excommunication, and even an interdict.

Alberigo, *Conciliorum Oecumenicorum Decreta*, pp. 304–305.
Mansi, 24:115.

De usuris

26. Usurarum voraginem, quae animas devorat et facultates exhaurit, compescere cupientes, constitutionem Lateranensis concilii contra usurarios editam, sub divinae maledictionis interminatione, praecipimus inviolabiliter observari. Et quia quo minor feneratoribus aderit fenerandi commoditas, eo magis adimetur fenus exercendi libertas, hac generali constitutione sancimus, ut nec collegium nec alia universitas vel singularis persona, cuiuscunque sit dignitatis, conditionis aut status, alienigenas et alios non oriundos de terris ipsorum, publice pecuniam fenebrem exercentes aut exercere volentes, ad hoc domos in terris suis conducere vel conductas habere aut alias habitare permittat, sed huiusmodi usurarios manifestos omnes infra tres menses de terris suis expellant, numquam aliquos tales de cetero admissuri. Nemo illis ad fenus exercendum domos locet vel sub alio titulo quocunque concedat. Qui vero contrarium fecerint, si personae fuerint ecclesiasticae, patriarchae, archiepiscopi, episcopi, suspensionis; minores vero personae singulares, excommunicationis; collegium autem seu alia universitas, interdicti sententiam ipso facto se noverint incursuros. Quam si per mensem animo sustinuerint indurato, terrae ipsorum, quandiu in eis iidem usurarii commorantur, extunc ecclesiastico subiaceant interdicto. Ceterum si laici fuerint, per suos ordinarios ab huiusmodi excessu, omni privilegio cessante, per censuram ecclesiasticam compescantur.

27. Quamquam usurarii manifesti de usuris quas receperant, satisfieri expressa quantitate vel indistincte in ultima voluntate mandaverint, nihilominus tamen eis sepultura ecclesiastica denegetur, donec vel de usuris ipsis fuerit, prout patiuntur facultates eorum, plenarie satisfactum vel illis quibus est facienda restitutio, si praesto sint ipsi aut alii qui eis possint acquirere vel, eis absentibus, loci ordinario aut eius vices gerenti sive rectori parochiae in qua testator habitat, coram aliquibus fidedignis de ipsa parochia (quibus quidem ordinario, vicario et rectori, praedicto modo, cautionem huiusmodi, eorum nomine liceat praesentis constitutionis auctoritate recipere, ita quod illis proinde actio acquiratur), aut servo publico de ipsius ordinarii mandato, idonee de restitutione facienda sit cautum. Ceterum si receptarum usurarum sit quantitas manifesta, illam semper in cautione praedicta exprimi volumus; alioquin aliam recipientis cautionem huiusmodi arbitrio moderandam. Ipse tamen scienter non minorem quam verisimiliter creditur, moderetur et si secus fecerit, ad satisfactionem residui teneatur. Omnes autem religiosos et alios, qui manifestos usurarios contra praesentis sanctionis formam ad ecclesiasticam admittere ausi fuerint sepulturam, poenae in Lateranensi concilio contra usurarios promulgatae, statuimus subiacere. Nullus manifestorum usurariorum testamentis intersit aut eos ad confessionem admittat sive ipsos absolvat, nisi de usuris satisfecerint vel de satisfaciendo pro suarum viribus facultatum praestent, ut praemittitur, idoneam cautionem. Testamenta quoque manifestorum usurariorum aliter facta non valeant, sed sint irrita ipso iure.

1. The reasons behind the council are discussed in the tenth volume of A. Fliche and V. Martin's *Histoire de l'Église, La Chrétienté romaine (1198-1274)*, by Augustin Fliche, Christine Thouzelier, and Yvonne Azais (Paris, n.d.), pp. 487–503.

2. In preparing for the council, the pope solicited information from various parts of Christendom on the state of beliefs and practices. The bishop of Olmutz, in his answer, reported that there were no heretics in his province, but he did complain that Jews openly practiced usury, had Christian domestics, and enjoyed public office; moreover, royal officials failed to enforce canonical regulations respecting these matters (Raynaldus, *Annales Ecclesiastici*, XIV, *a.a.* 1273, par. 18). For the situation in Hungary, see bull no. 14, above. Cf. Bondy and Dworský, *Zur Geschichte*, vol. 1, p. 37, no. 30.

3. [Cf. *Sext.* 5,5,1 (*de usuris, usurarum*), where this decree is incorporated into the canons. Its edicts likely added fuel to the animus of those fifteenth-century Franciscan preachers, like Bernardino da Feltre, who called for the expulsion of those Jews who had settled in Italian cities for the express purpose of loan-banking—even if they had done so according to a contractual arrangement (*condotta*).—KS]

38   September 10, 1274

To all the Christian faithful:

SICUT JUDAEIS[1] . . . Pope Gregory repeats the Bull of Protection issued by his predecessors. His model text was that of Innocent IV (22 October 1246) in *ChJ*, no. 111, pp. 261–262.

Potthast, no. 20915.
Ennen and Eckertz, *Quellen*, vol. 3, p. 64, no. 90.

Gregorius episcopus servus servorum dei, dilectis in Christo filiis fidelibus christianis salutem et apostolicam benedictionem.

Sicut iudeis . . .

Sanctus Petrus. Sanctus Paulus. Gregorius papa X^{mus}; . . . perfice gressus meos in semitis tuis.

Ego Gregorius catholice ecclesie episcopus.
Ego frater Johannes Portuensis et sancte Rufine episcopus.
Ego Petrus Tusculanus epis.
Ego Vicedominus Penestrinus epis.
Ego Simon tit. sancti Martini presbiter card.
Ego Ancherus tit. sancte Praxedis presb. card.
Ego Symon tit. sancte Cecilie presb. card.
Ego Ottolunus sancti Adriani diaconus card.
Ego Jacobus sancte Marie in Cosmydin. diac. card.
Ego Gotofridus sancti Georgii ad velum aur. diac. card.
Ego Ubertus sancti Eustachii diac. card.

> Datum Lugduni per manum magistri Lafranci archidiaconi sancte Romane ecclesie vicecancellarii, IIII. idus Septemb., indictione III., incarnationis dominice anno MCCLXXIIII, pontificatus vero domini Gregorii pape X. anno tertio.

1. The bull appears without the long insertion on ritual murder found in the first issue of the bull by Gregory X in October 1272 (no. 31, above). What prompted a second issuance of the document? Although the extant copy is housed in the archives in Cologne, it may have been solicited by the Jewish delegation which Zadoc Kahn mentions in his article "Étude sur le livre de Joseph le Zélateur," in *REJ* 1 (1880): 223 ff. and 3 (1881): 1 ff. Purportedly, "Because of a certain event, my father and teacher, Nathan—may he have rest in paradise—met with Pope Gregory" (*REJ* 1 [1880]: 230), and the two discussed such matters as Numbers

24:17 ("A star arose from Jacob") and the efficacy of auricular confession (*REJ* 3 [1881]: 11). Did this meeting take place in connection with Pope Gregory's repetition of *Lachrymabilem* (bull no. 34, above) as Rabbi Kahn seems to have thought? If so, it would have been a demonstration of solidarity with their fellow Jews across the border in Cologne. Since the Council of Lyons was meeting on French soil, perhaps a French-Jewish delegation had easier access to the pope. However, it is also possible that the delegation came on business of its own that had to do with the Inquisition's hunt for relapsed converts and was connected with the bull *Turbato corde* (no. 33, above). The Jews may have sought to convince the pope that *Turbato corde* placed an unusually cruel weapon into the hands of the local inquisitors. [Or, more adroitly, the Jews—if indeed a meeting took place—may have asked that *Turbato corde* not be exploited beyond its specific definitions, an exploitation which did occur on a number of occasions, as papal letters to be seen below reveal.—KS]

John XXI

Peter Julian Rebulo, a Portuguese physician who became cardinal-bishop of Frascati, was elected pope on September 8, 1276, following the death—within a few months of one another—of his immediate predecessors, Innocent V and Adrian V. He himself served only nine months, dying on May 20, 1277.

39   December 8, 1276

Ad perpetuam rei memoriam:[1]

LICET FELICIS RECORDATIONIS[2] . . . Pope John reserves for the direct use of the Apostolic See the income from the benefices Gregory X had bestowed upon his personal chaplain, Raymond de Peralta, including a tithe paid by the Jews and the transit tax at Calatayud.

Reg. Vat. 45, fol. 119v, c. 594.
E. Langlois, ed., *Les registres de Nicolas IV* (Paris, 1886), p. 578, no. 3837.

Universis Christi fidelibus presentes litteras inspecturis. Johannes episcopus servus servorum Dei. Ad perpetuam rei memoriam.

LICET FELICIS RECORDATIONIS Gregorius papa, predecessor noster. . . . Cupientes tamen ut archidiaconatus Toletanus, decanatus Tirasonensis, ecclesia de Rubiolis Cesaraugustana et canonia ecclesie Tutelane, Tirasonensis diocesis, decima judeorum et pedagi Calatarubensis, pertinens ad mensam Tirasonensis episcopi, tertie pontificales, archipresbyteratus de Ylliescas, de Benquerenza, de Caravanna, de Perales, de Tielmes et de Embric, Toletane diocesis, et alia beneficia ecclesiastica, que quondam Raymundus de Peralta, capellanus noster, qui nuper apud sedem apostolicam diem clausit extremum, tam in predictis quam in aliis quibuscumque ecclesiis obtinuit, per ejus obitum ad presens vacantia, illis personis, per prudentie nostre studium, sive infra sive post mensem, hujusmodi committantur per quas eisdem ecclesiis honor et comodum valeant provenire, archidiaconatum, decanatum, ecclesiam, canoniam, decimam, tertias et beneficia supradicta ex nunc donationi apostolice reservamus . . .

Datum Viterbii, vii id. Decembris, anno primo.

1. This introductory phrase, characteristic of a *breve* did not come into frequent use for at least another century. It was equivalent to what we would now express by a phrase like "for the (permanent) record."

2. The document was repeated verbatim by Nicholas IV, on November 27, 1290 (see bull no. 63, below).

Nicholas III

John Gaetan Orsini, of the influential Roman family, was elected on November 25, 1277. He was an energetic and gifted statesman.

40   1277–1278

The following bulls are mentioned in the records of the papal chancery. Pope Nicholas III ordered that certain forms (and formulae) be observed, but no record shows that bulls on the following subjects were actually issued.[1]

A. In his first year, Nicholas instructed his chancellor to prepare a bull on the subject of Jews paying tithes on property that had once belonged to Christians.[2]

Bibliothèque Nationale, Fond Latin 4169, fol. LXXII.
M. Tangl, *Die Päpstlichen Kanzleiordnungen von 1250–1500* (Innsbruck, 1894; reprint 1959), p. 75, item 25 (12).

B. Similarly: an order to diocesans (bishops) to compel Jews to wear garments distinguishing them from Christians.[3]

Tangl, *Päpstlichen Kanzleiordnungen*, item 26.

C. Similarly: instructions to bishops to have the Jews tear down a (new) synagogue built taller than the original (it replaced).[4]

Tangl, *Päpstlichen Kanzleiordnungen*, p. 80, item 70 (73).

Anno domini MCCLXXVIII, XII. die februarii, pontificatus domini Nicolai pape III. anno primo, cum quedam cedula continens formas litterarum apostolicarum infrascriptas oblata esset eidem domino per vicecancellarium: idem dominus papa dictis formis inspectis et discussis presentibus eodem vicecancellario et quibusdam notariis dedit certum modum, quem circa easdem formas vult observari, quousque aliud duxerit ordinandum:

1. (1) "Ea que de bonis" in maiori forma, ubi continetur, quod non obstantibus iuramentis renuntiationibus instrumentis et confirmationibus in forma communi ab apostolica sede obtentis bona ecclesiarum alienata illicite vel distracta ad ius et proprietatem ecclesiarum legitime revocentur.—Dentur.

2. (2) Item "Ea que de bonis" in minori forma, ubi non est aliquid non obstante.—Dentur.

3. (43) Item dispensationes super defectu natalium, que mittebantur sub sigillo cardinalis penitentiarii, tam pro presentibus quam pro absentibus expediebantur usque ad tempus domini Gregorii pape X., qui restrinxit eas ad presentes tantum; quarum nulla legebatur, nisi fuisset pro natis de adulterio vel regularibus aut incestu procreatis—Dentur presentibus sine lectione.

25. (12) Item contra Judeos super decimis de possessionibus et domibus, que a Christianis devenerunt ad illos.—Dentur.

26. Item solet scribi diocesano, quod Judeos compellat ferre habitum, quo distinguantur a Christianis.—Dentur.

70. (73) Item scribitur diocesanis, quod compellant Judeos ad demoliendum sinagogam plus quam veterem exaltatam.—Legatur.

1. The texts comprise notes and instructions given by the pope to his chancellor, but there is no way of knowing if they were ever translated into actual letters, i.e., drafted and sent to specific recipients. If the letters were drafted, no copies have been preserved either in the papal archives or by the recipients themselves. Still, all three items do reflect common canon law concerns and prohibitions. It may be that the instructions were merely formulaic, for the purpose of fixing formulae, should real letters ever have been necessary.

2. On the matter of tithes, cf. above, Clement IV, bull no. 23, n. 8; X.3,30,16.

3. On the badge, cf. Fourth Lateran Council, cap. x; ChJ, pp. 308–309.

4. On the rebuilding of synagogues, cf. Clement IV, bull no. 28, n. 4; X.5,6,3. Since no full document on these subjects has been found, it is tempting to connect one or another of the instructions, especially that concerning the synagogues, with an incident mentioned by I. Loeb in "Les négociants Juifs à Marseille au milieu du XIIIe siecle," REJ, 16 (1888): 76 (cf. VR, vol. 1, pp. 246 and 247, n. 1). A Jew of Montpellier named Bonjoudas, had been sent to Rome by the Jews of Montpellier in 1278 for the purpose of acquiring a privilege whose nature is not specified. He ran out of money and had to borrow some from a Christian named Ferrier Liautaud, a resident of Marseilles. Bonjoudas promised to repay the loan on his return to Montpellier. The assumption has been that the Jews of Montpellier were seeking a general grant of privileges. But they may equally have been seeking to prevent the curtailment of some privilege, in this instance, a

permit to enlarge their existing synagogue. Indeed, the Jews had managed shortly before to purchase a house in Montpellier adjacent to their synagogue. To halt the publication of a bull like that foreseen in this instruction would have been considered a victory. Interestingly, Fond Latin of Bibliothèque Nationale, 4169, fol. 75, also refers to instructions given to the papal vice chancellor to demolish a synagogue built higher than the one it replaced.

41   August 2, 1278

To all the Christian faithful:

SICUT JUDAEIS . . . Pope Nicholas repeats the Bull of Protection[1] as given by his predecessors from Calixtus II to Innocent IV.

G. and B. Lagumina, eds., *Codice diplomatico dei Giudei di Sicilia* (Palermo, 1884–1895), vol. 1, pp. 119 f., no. 82.

Nos Martinus et Maria etc. et Infans Martinus etc. pro parte universitatis Iudeorum felicis nostre urbis panormi camere nostre servorum fuit nostris culminibus exibitum et presentatum quoddam privilegium bulla plumbea munitum olim Iudeis concessum per dive memorie santissimum dominum dominum Nicolaum sacrosante romane ecclesie summum pontificem super certis gracijs et constitucionibus per ipsum summum pontificem ad supplicacionem Iudeorum editis atque factis continencie subsequentis. Nicolaus episcopus servus servorum Dei dilectis in christo filiis fidelibus christianis salutem et apostolicam benedictionem.

SICUT IUDEIS non debet esse licencia in sinagogiis suis ultra quam permissum est lege presumere ita in hiis que eis concessa sunt nullum debent prejudicium sustinere. Nos ergo licet in sua magis velint duricia perdurare quam prophetarum verba et suarum scripturarum archana cognoscere atque ad christiane fidei et salutis noticiam pervenire quia tamen deffencionem nostram et auxilium postulant et christiane pietatis mansuetudinem predecessorum nostrorum felicis memorie calixti eugenii alexandri clementis celestini innocencii honorij gregorii innocencii quarti romanorum pontificum vestigiis inherentes ipsorum peticionem admittimus eisque proteccionis nostre clipeum indulgemus statuimus eciam ut nullus christianus invitos vel nolentes eos ad baptismum per violenciam venire compellant set si eorum quilibet sponte ad christianos fidei causa confugerit postquam voluntas eius fuerit patefacta christianus absque aliqua efficiatur calumpnia veram quippe

christianitatis fidem habere non creditur qui ad christianorum baptismum non spontaneus sed invitus cognoscitur pervenire nullus eciam
christianus eorum personas sine iudicio potestatis terre vulnerare aut
occidere vel suas illis pecunias auferre presumat aut bonas quas actenus
in ea in qua habitant regione habuerint consuetudines immutare preterea
in festivitatum suarum celebracione quisquam fustibus vel lapidibus eos
ullatenus non perturbet neque aliquis ab eis coacta servicia exigat nisi ea
que ipsi pre ceteris facere temporibus consueverint ad hec malorum
hominum pravitati ac avaricie obviantes decrevimus ut nemo cymiterium
Iudeorum mutilare vel minuere audeat sive obtentu pecunie corpora
humata effodere si quis autem decreti huius tenore cognito temere quod
absit contraire temptaverit honoris et officii sui periculum paciatur aut
excommunicacionis ulcione plectatur nisi presumpcionem suam digna
satisfaccione correxerit eos autem dumtaxat huius proteccionis presidio
volumus communiri qui nichil machinari presumpserint in subvercionem fidei christiane. Ego nicolaus catholice ecclesie episcopus. Ego
ancherius tituli santi praxedis presbiter cardinalis subscripsi. Ego
guillermus tituli santi marci presbiter cardinalis subscripsi. Ego gerardus
basilice XII apostolorum presbiter cardinalis subscripsi. Ego ordonius
tusculanus episcopus subscripsi. Ego frater bentavenga albanensis episcopus subscripsi. Ego frater latinus (ostiensis) et velletrensis episcopus
subscripsi. Ego Iacobus sante marie in cosmedin diaconus cardinalis
subscripsi. Ego Goteofridus santi georgii ad velum aureum diaconus
cardinalis subscripsi. Ego matheus sante marie in porticu diaconus
cardinalis subscripsi. Ego Iordanus santi eustachii diaconus cardinalis
subscripsi. Datum viterbi per manum magistri petri de mediolano sante
romane ecclesie vicecancelarii IIII nonas augusti indictione VI incarnacionis dominici anno MCCLXXVIII pontificatus vero domini Nycolay
pape III anno primo. Et humiliter extitit nostris culminibus supplicatum
ut ipsum privilegium et omnia et singula in eo contenta de speciali gratia
et favore regio acceptare et confirmare de benignitate solita dignaremur
quorum Iudeorum supplicacionibus benigniter inclinati attendentes
presertim quod ipsis Iudeis favores debemus nostros porrigere speciales
ipsum privilegium et omnia et singula in eo contenta approbamus
laudamus et pleno favore regio confirmamus omnibus et singulis
officialibus dicti Regni nostri et potissime dicte urbis panormi tam
presentibus quam futuris huius rescripti serie iniungentes quatenus
dictam nostram confirmacionem et omnia et singula in dicto privilegio
contenta iuxta ipsius privilegii seriem et tenorem teneant firmiter et
observent et in nullo contraveniant seu aliquem contravenire permittant
aliqua racione vel causa si iram et indignacionem nostram cupiunt

evitare. In cuius rei testimonium presens fieri et sigillo nostri dicti ducis cum sigilla regia nondum sint facta impendenti iussimus communiri

Datum Viterbii, iiii non. August, anno primo.[2]

1. The bull was quoted in full in a confirmation (*vidimus*) by King Martin, Queen Maria, and the Infante Martin of Sicily, on June 28, 1392. It had been presented to them by the Jews of Palermo, who were threatened by the anti-Jewish riots that had spread from Spain to Sicily. The Nicholas III copy of the bull may have been the only one the Jewish community of Palermo had in its archives. Its reissuance in 1278 may have been a result of the Jews' concern that every new pope reaffirm its principles. The popes may have seen the reissue as a normal procedure (cf. Grayzel, "*Sicut Judeis*," pp. 242 ff.). It is, nevertheless, interesting that the bull was put to practical use very soon after the 1278 reissue. In "Bulles inédites," pp. 115 f., Loeb notes that a copy of the bull was addressed to Pamplona (Archives Nationales, J. 427, no. 12), with a *vidimus* by the local bishop (possibly the one listed by Robert in "Catalogue," p. 217, no. 51). It also bears a notation of the Pamplona Jewish community that explains their solicitation of the bull sometime between 1278 and 1286, namely: "*Hoc est translatum littere que (quam) habuimus a domino papa, ratione fratrum minorum qui impediebant orationes nostras ratione sermonis.*" The community was clearly suffering from the excessive zeal of the Franciscans. Loeb thought that the problem was a synagogue so close to a church that the loud praying of the Jews interfered with the preaching of the monks, whence the latter threatened to close down the synagogue. More likely, the Jews of Pamplona objected to the friars' forcing conversionist sermons upon them. [If Grayzel is correct, and he appears to be, we have a fascinating juxtaposition of texts, for the following letter, *Vineam sorec*, prescribes sermons to the Jews. However, the note *hoc est translatum . . .* , argues that the pope did not intend these sermons to be delivered to a coerced audience—contrary to the usual explanation for *Vineam sorec*. And, indeed, one must note the failure of *Vineam sorec* to call for indirect excommunication or for the aid of the secular arm, so readily invoked on other occasions when force was intended. The doctrine of *Sicut Judaeis* thus appears to have carried no little weight, at least with the popes themselves. Since forced sermons would violate the doctrine, there could be no forced sermons; the mendicant preachers obviously disagreed and did their best to circumvent the issue. But one must also wonder if the popes would not have recommended force—*were* it a legitimate option. They were most likely caught between their personal will and legal boundaries. Yet, their ambivalence was probably genuine, and it may explain why there are so few records of forced sermons being delivered and so few papal letters dealing with sermons, whether forced or otherwise.—KS]

2. [A question arises whether this *Sicut Judaeis*, as well as that of Martin IV (bull no. 45, below), is an authentic document. Both are preserved only in the archives of King Martin of Sicily—and both bear the same date, June 28, 1392. In fact, since the *Sicut Judaeis* bulls issued by both Nicholas IV and Eugenius IV mention a *Sicut Judaeis* of Nicholas III, there may be no doubt about this present letter. But there are problems with the letter of Martin IV. It contains clauses which, while plausible—even if phrased in inelegant and unusual syntax—

represent new ideas about procedures involving Jews and the Inquisition (on which, see nn. 3 and 4 there); and there is also a dating problem (again, see n. 5 there). Still, there is little reason why Jews should forge a text like *Sicut Judaeis*, present and permanently valid in Gregory IX's legally binding *Decretals.*—KS]

42   August 4, 1278

To the Prior of the Dominican Order in Lombardy:[1]

VINEAM SOREC . . . Taking up the parable of the House of Israel as the Lord's disappointing vineyard (cf. Isaiah 5:1–7), Pope Nicholas continues by eloquently describing the Jews as stubborn and hard-hearted in their refusal to accept God's repeated offers of grace. Their punishment has therefore been thorough and deserved. But since God wants no one to perish, the pope, as God's vicar, readily undertakes the great labor of making the Jews see the light of truth. Scattered as they are over the Earth, however, the Jews cannot be gathered into one place, and the pope must therefore find many sowers of God's word. Consequently he turns to the Dominican prior in the hope and with instructions that he find men in his order endowed with the spirit, the knowledge and the zeal to convoke the Jews, singly or in groups, and to preach the evangelical teachings in the desire that the Jews be reborn through baptism.[2] In addition, the addressees are to approach the secular rulers and the prelates of the territories where they preach and insure that converts be generously treated, like prodigal sons who have returned. Favors are to be heaped upon the converts; and their persons and property are not to suffer harm at the hands of Jews or others.[3] Moreover, should it happen that, persisting in their obstinacy, the Jews, like deaf adders, turn away from those deputized to perform this task and contemptuously flee from the call of the friars, it must be reported to the pope—no matter who they are or where they are to be found or under whose dominion they live—and the pope will ponder ways of dealing with the obstinate (*ut . . . de remedio . . . cogitemus*). The pope is to be informed frequently of the progress made in this matter.

Potthast, nos. 21382, 21383, 221504.
Ripoll, *Bull. Ord.*, vol. 1, pp. 558–559.
Sbaralea, *Bull. Francisc.*, vol. 3, p. 331, no. 50; p. 371, no. 92.
J. Gay, ed., *Les registres de Nicolas III* (Paris, 1898–1938), p. 408, nos. 965–966; p. 411, no. 1004.

Nicolaus Episcopus, Servus Servorum Dei, dilecto filio Priori Provinciali Fratrum Ordinis Predicatorum in Lombardia, Salutem, et Apostolicam Benedictionem.

VINEAM SOREC velut electam plantavit dextera Dei Patris, et omne semen verum seminavit in ipsa, Angelica custodia sepivit illam, lapides nocivos abjecit ex ea. Hanc de Aegypto in luto, et latere sub jugo Pharaonis oppressam, in signis, et prodigiis transferens, dux itineris ejus existens in Terram promissionis adduxit. Vinea enim Domini exercituum Domus Israel est, viri juda delectabile germen ejus. Hanc sic mire translatam, quasi adhuc rudem campum vomere legali proscindens, prophetali doctrina sulcavit, ut et ipsam ad maturam frugem, idest ad regenerationis gratiam prepararet. Sed proh dolor, peccatorum spinis obsita nullum imbrem gratie spiritualis excipiens, que sperabatur, ut uvas educeret, labruscas eduxit: unde sperabatur judicium, processit iniquitas: unde justitia, inde clamor. Hec est vinea, in qua fici arbor, scilicet synagoga judeorum, plantata Evangelica veritate describitur, cujus plantator Christus, cetus Apostolicus cultor existit. Hec triplici tempore, quasi tribus annis, ut fructum produceret, expectata, infructuosa reperta, cultori succidenda predicitur. Nam nec tempore circumcisionis ad perfectum deducta est, quia circumcisionem anime non querebat, nec sanctificata per legem, quia per eam tantum carnalia sequebatur, nec tandem justificata per Evangelii gratiam, quia gratiam recipere noluit, quin potius latorem Gratie justum injuste peremit, et quodammodo indurationem Pharaonis excedens, omne curantis, et cure refutavit antidotum, adeout nec verbis, nec signis, nec Sacramentis, quinimmo nec ipsa Christi, et Dei corporali presentia molliretur. Multifarie enim, multisque modis, olim Deus loquens antiquis ipsius synagoge Patribus in Prophetis, novissime in fine temporis locutus est ipsis, et nobis in Filio, quem constituit heredem universorum, per quem fecit et secula. Sed omnem escam abominata est anima ejus, et idcirco juste, justo Dei judicio reprobatam, exterminavit eam aper de silva, et singularis ferus depastus est eam, ablata est sepes ejus, prosternata maceries, et in direptionem posita, ut deferta, nec inventus est in terris amplius locus ejus. Verum quia miserationes Dei super omnia sua opera predicantur, qui omnes salvos fieri, et neminem vult perire, qui se ipsum pro nobis,et ipsis hostiam salutis exhibuit Deo Patri, qui exaltatus a terra, expansis in Cruce manibus, ad se cuncta trahere, evangelica voce predixit. Nos licet immeriti, vicem ejus tenentes in terris, qui etiam judaicam perfidiam a sua misericordia non repellit, libenter pro illius Populi obcecatione labores appetimus, ut, affectum nostrum divina prosequente clementia, cognita veritatis luce, que Christus est, a suis tenebris eruantur. Porro quia judeorum ipsorum, quasi per universum mundum divino judicio previsa dispersio, ipsos ad recipiendum Sacramenta fidei, ac doctrinam, commode in unum convenire non patitur, necessitate nos voluntarios urgente, compellimur, per diversas mundi partes, diversos seminatores eligere, per quos semen verbi Dei, prout possibile est, spargamus in singulos, quorum salutem universaliter, et singulariter affectamus. Ad te igitur inter alios, sub spe divine gratie, mentis nostre oculos convertentes, cum tui Ordinis claritate reluceas, et credaris ubilibet per opera utilia, et exempla laudabilia fructuosus, et ex data tibi divinitus gratia scire te confidamus, et posse, fructus uberes in domo Domini germinare, discretioni tue per Apostolica scripta mandamus, quatenus confidens in illo, cui proprium est spirituales gratias elargiri, tales umbrarum tenebris obcecatos in commissa tibi Provincia, per te, ac alios Fratres tui Ordinis, quos ad hoc honestate morum, experta scientia, probitatis virtutibus, circumspectione provida, et experientia comprobata, idoneos esse cognoveris, et quorum industria, atque doctrina divinis donis a Domino fecundata, intrepide pro catholica fide reluceat, et in sui claritate non titubet, sed tenebrosas mentes radiorum repercussione clarificet et obstinatas cervices reprimat perversorum, judeos eosdem in terris, et locis, in quibus habitant, generaliter, et singulariter convocando, semel, et pluries, ac toties repetitis instantiis, quoties proficere posse putaveris, prout melius fieri poterit, predicationibus, salutaribus monitis, et discretis inductionibus, evangelicis doctrinis, informans ipsos, studeas juxta datam tibi a Domino gratiam, fugatis tenebrarum nubibus, ad viam reducere claritatis, ut renati fonte Baptismatis, reluceant in lumine vultus Christi, et exinde chorus Angelicus delectetur. Tu quoque, ac alii quos ad prosecutionem tanti negotii duxeris eligendos, perennis boni premium, nostramque benedictionem, et gratiam vobis, de bono in melius vendicetis. Et ut affectum, quem ad salutem status ipsorum gerit Mater Ecclesia, percipiant per effectum, tu illos, ex eis, quos ad susceptionem sacri Baptismatis gratia divina perduxerit, Prelatis, ac Dominis locorum, in quibus tales habitare contigerit, ex parte nostra affectuosissime recommendes, ut Deo gratias in recuperata ove deperdita, et filio prodigo redeunti, vitulum exultationis, et gaudii exhibentes, eos caritative foveant, favoribus muniant, benigne pertractent, nec ipsos in personis, aut rebus per judeos, vel alios, indebite molestari, permittant, quin potius in omnibus favorabiliter ipsis assistant auxiliis opportunis. Sed si forte, quod absit, aliqui ex ipsis in eorum obstinata perfidia perdurantes, et, veluti aspis surda, suas aures incredulas obturantes, ne tui, et illorum, quos ad hec salutis opera deputabis, vocem audiant, ut de tenebris ad lucem exeant incantantium sapienter, tuas, et per te ad hec deputandorum Fratrum salutares convocationes aspernantes refugerent, de istis, si tales inveneris, qui sint, in quibus locis, et sub quorum Dominio commorentur, nobis rescribere non omittas, ut circa pertinaces hujusmodi de salutari eorum remedio, sicut expedire videbimus, cogitemus. Ut autem de premissis avidis nostris conceptibus, juxta nostra desideria, satisfiat, frequenter nobis intimare studeas, qualiter commissum tibi negotium prosperetur, et qualem fructum seminata semina repromittant.

Datum Viterbii, ii non. Augusti, anno primo.

1. The same bull was addressed to the heads of the Franciscans and Dominicans in various parts of Europe; Sicily and Austria are specifically recorded in Potthast.

2. A review of the efforts to convert the Jews by compelling them to listen to conversionary sermons is found in Browe, *Judenmission*, pp. 14–54, with *Vineam sorec* discussed on pp. 21 and 30. See above, under Clement IV, bull no. 24, n. 5, for the attempt of the Dominicans, in particular, to introduce sermons into Aragon. [See the discussion in bull no. 41, n. 1, above, on the implications of *Vineam sorec* for general policy toward the Jews.—KS]

3. For the protection of converts to Christianity against insults leveled by their former coreligionists, see the quotation of the order issued by James I of Aragon, quoted by Pope Innocent IV (*Ea que*), in *ChJ*, no. 105, pp. 256–257. The efforts to protect the property of converts against confiscation by the state are also referred to in the same bull, as well as in the canons of the Third Lateran Council (*ChJ*, pp. 296–297) and on many other occasions.

43   March 23, 1279

To the Bishop of Rieti:

Istud est memoriale secretum[1] . . . The pope lists a number of complaints against the king[2] of Castile and Leon which the bishop is to investigate. Among them are the following: the king permits the practice of usury from which he derives some advantages (though Jews are not mentioned in this connection); he appoints Jews to public office.[3]

Reg. Vat. 40, fol. 56, no. 10.
Gay, *Registres*, vol. 3, no. 743, p. 342.

Istud est memoriale secretum . . . episcopi Reatini. Non ostendendum set secreto tenendum, ut ex contentis in ipso idem episcopus se informet et adjuvet in commissis. Portavit nichilominus quosdam alios articulos prolixiores ad suam instructionem ex quibus sub brevitate fuerunt presentes eliciti, set illi non sunt registrati.

Articuli principales super quibus mittitur venerabilis pater . . . episcopus Reatinus sunt septem.

1. Primus est de tertiis ecclesiarum quas rex occupavit pluribus jam annis elapsis et detinet occupatas.

2. Secundus est de custodiis ecclesiarum cathedralium vacantium et monasteriorum seu de occupatis in eis quando vacant.

3. Tertius est de gravaminibus illatis archiepiscopo et ecclesie Compostellane, terris et vassallis eorum, sub quo sunt gravamina infrascripta.

Contra clericos et laicos super crimine usurarum sibi congnitionem usurpans, hujusmodi occasione multos gravat.

Item Judaeos Christianis preponit multipliciter, unde multa mala proveniunt.

Datum Romae, apud S. Petrum, x. kal. Aprilis, anno secundo.

---

1. The situation which occasioned this investigation by the bishop of Rieti is referred to in the document marked Potthast, no. 21556; cf. Raynaldus, *Annales Ecclesiastici*, a. a. 1279, par. 27. See also Graetz, *Geschichte*, vol. 7, p. 127. Cf. Peter Linehan, *The Spanish Church and the Papacy in the 13th Century* (Cambridge U. Press, 1971), pp. 175 f., to explain why the complaints about these matters had been made secretly.

2. Alfonso X, the Wise, King of Castile and Leon, 1252-1284.

3. For the Church's problem of office-holding by Jews in the Iberian peninsula and elsewhere, see *ChJ, passim*. In the second half of the thirteenth century, the question was raised with the king of Portugal (bull no. 23, above), and before that with the king of Hungary (bull no. 17, above). After that, it was again raised by Clement IV, who urged the exclusion of Jews from public office in Poland (bull no. 29, n. 4, above). One of the curious elements of the charge against the government of Alfonso X is the fact that his legal code, *Las siete partidas*, contains a clear statement against the use of Jews in capacities that might enable them to oppress Christians, in other words, public offices (p. 7, tit. 24, ley 3).

Martin IV

Simon de Brie, formerly chancellor of France, was elected pope on February 22, 1281.

44   March 1, 1281

To the friars of the Dominican and Franciscan Orders who are or will be deputized by the Holy See as inquisitors of heresy:

TURBATO CORDE . . . Pope Martin reissues the bull, as given in no. 33, above.

Bibliothèque Nationale, Fond Doat 37, fols. 193r–194r.[1]

TURBATO CORDE . . . [same as bull no. 33].

Datum kal. Martii, 1281.

1. There is no reason to doubt that Pope Martin, sometime during his reign, reissued the bull *Turbato corde* in language identical to that of Pope Gregory X in 1274. But there is a difficulty about the date. The Fond Doat text gives the year as 1281, which presupposes the issuance of the letter within a week after Martin's election and before his coronation. It also appears strange that the bulls of both Gregory X and Martin IV should each have been issued on March 1st. Cf. Robert, "Catalogue," p. 218, no. 53.

45   August 2, 1281

To all the Christian faithful:

SICUT JUDAEIS[1] . . . Pope Martin follows the example of his predecessors from Calixtus to Honorius[2] and reissues the Bull of Protection. He adds the following: No inquisitor, nor anyone else, whatever his office, may at the request of a third party use force against the Jews [to produce a confession—KS]. The accuser shall give proper assurance and a bond; and if he does not prove the accusation, he shall suffer the penalty that would have been inflicted on the accused.[3] If a "baptized Jew" maintains close relations with a Jew but does not recognize him as such, the Jew shall not be punished.[4]

Lagumina, *Codici diplomatici,* vol. 1, p. 117, no. 81.

Nos Martinus et Maria etc. et infans Martinus etc. pro parte universitatis Iudeorum felicis nostre urbis panormi camere nostre servorum fuit nostris culminibus exibitum et presentatum quoddam privilegium bulla plumbea munitum olim Iudeis concessum per dive memorie sanctissimum dominum dominum Martinum sacrosante Romane ecclesie summum pontificem super certis gracijs et constitucionibus per ipsum summum pontificem ad supplicacionem Iudeorum editis atque factis continencie subsequentis. Martinus Episcopus servus servorum dei dilectis in christo filijs fidelibus christianis salutem et apostolicam benedictionem.

Sicut Iudeis non debet esse licencia in sinagogijs suis ultra quam permissum est lege presumere ita in hijs que concessa sunt nullum debent preiudicium sustinere. Nos ergo licet in sua magis velint duricia perdurare quam prophetarum verba et suarum scripturarum archana cognoscere atque ad christiane fidei et salutis noticiam pervenire quia tamen defencionem nostram et auxilium postulant et christiane pietatis mansuetudinem predecessorum nostrorum felicis memorie Calixti Eugenij Alexandri Clementis Celestini Innocencij et Honorij romanorum pontificum vestigijs inherentes ipsorum peticionem admictimus eisque protectionis nostre clipeum indulgemus statuimus eciam ut nullus christianus invitos vel nolentes eos ad baptismum per violenciam venire compellat set si eorum quilibet ad christianos fidei causa confugerit postquam voluntas eius fuerit patefacta christianus efficiatur absque aliqua calumpnia veram quippe christianitatis fidem habere non creditur qui ad christianorum baptisma non spontaneus set invitus cognoscitur pervenire nullus eciam christianus eorum personas sine iudicio potestatis terre vulnerare aut occidere vel suas illis pecunias auferre presumat aut bonas quas actenus in ea in qua habitant regione habuerint consuetudines immutare preterea in festivitatum suarum celebracione quisquam fustibus vel lapidibus eos nullatenus non perturbet nec ab eis coacta servicia exigat nisi ea que ipsi pre ceteris facere temporibus consueverint ad hec malorum hominum pravitati et avaricie obviantes decrevimus ut nemo cymiterium Iudeorum mutilare vel minuere audeat sive obtentu pecunie corpora humata effodere. Volumus eciam et mandamus quod nullus inquisitor heretice pravitatis nec aliquis alter cuiuscumque dignitatis existat ad peticionem alicuius non teneatur cogere predictos Iudeos vel eorum alterum sed ille qui eos accusaverit det et prestet ydoneam fidejussoriam causionem curie sed si legitime non probaverit delictum de quo accusatus est (*sic*) quod accusator teneatur ad illam penam sicut accusatus est teneretur et auferatur eidem et si aliquis Iudeus baptizatus haberet aliquam familiaritatem cum aliquo alio Iudeo et non cognosceretur (*sic*) quod non teneatur ad penam aliquam. Si quis autem decreti huius tenore cognito quod absit contraire temptaverit honoris et officij sui periculum paciatur aut excommunicacionis ulcione plectatur nisi presumpcionem digna satisfaccione correxerit. Eos autem dumtaxat Iudeos huius proteccionis presidio volumus communiri qui nichil machinari presumpserint in subvercionem fidei christiane. Ego Ancherius tituli praxedis presbiter cardinalis subscripsi. Ego Guillelmus tituli sancti marcij presbiter cardinalis subscripsi. Ego Gerardus basilice XII apostolorum presbiter cardinalis subscripsi. Ego Matheus sancte marie in porticu diaconus cardinalis subscripsi. Ego Iordanus sancti eustachij diaconus cardinalis subscripsi. Ego Martinus catholice ecclesie episcopus. Ego Ordonius tusculanus episcopus subscripsi. Ego frater Bentavenga albanensis episcopus subscripsi. Ego frater Latinus ostiensis et velletrensis episcopus subscripsi. Ego Iacobus sancte marie in cosmidin diaconus cardinalis subscripsi. Ego Goctifredus sancti georgij ad velum aureum diaconus cardinalis subscripsi. Datum viterbij per manus magistri petri de mediolano sancte Romane ecclesie vice cancellarij IIIJ nonas augusti indictionis VI. incarnacionis dominice anno MCCLXXV pontificatus nostri domini Martini pape IIII anno primo. Et humiliter extitit nostris culminibus supplicatum ut ipsum privilegium et omnia et singula in eo contenta de speciali gracia et favore regio acceptare et confirmare de benignitate solita dignaremur quorum Iudeorum supplicacionibus benigniter inclinati attendentes presertim quod ipsis Iudeis favores debemus nostros porrigere speciales. Ipsum privilegium et omnia et singula in eo contenta approbamus laudamus et pleno favore regio confirmamus omnibus et singulis officialibus dicti Regni nostri et potissime dicte urbis panormi tam presentibus quam futuris huius rescripti serie iniungentes quatenus dictam nostram confirmacionem et omnia et singula in dicto privilegio contenta iuxta ipsius privilegij seriem et tenorem teneant firmiter et observent et in nullo contraveniant seu aliquem contravenire permittant aliqua racione vel causa si iram et indignacionem nostram cupiunt evitare. In cuius rei testimonium presens fieri et sigillo nostri dicti ducis cum sigilla Regia nondum sint facta impendenti iussimus communiri.

Datum Viterbii, iv non. Augusti, anno primo.[5]

1. Like that of Nicholas III in August 1273, this *Sicut Judaeis* has survived in the confirmation given by King Martin of Sicily, issued in both cases on June 28, 1292. Since the basic *Sicut Judaeis* text of the two documents was identical, the Jews must have asked for the confirmation of this second text because of its additional material.

2. Omitted from the list of predecessors were Gregory IX (May 1235) and Innocent IV (October 1246 and July 1247), although both were noted in the Nicholas III text. Missing, too, were the names of Alexander IV (September 1255), Urban IV (April 1262), Gregory X (October 1272), and Nicholas III.

3. This part of the addition appears to be an effort to implement the warning issued by Gregory X in his *Sicut Judaeis* (see bull no. 31, above) that accusations of ritual murder must not be believed without definite proof. [Or it may have to do with the permissibility of torture at the instigation of a third party. Jews should, it appears, be convicted only on the basis of voluntary confessions when there is a third party accusation, the accuracy of the accusation itself must be scrupulously verified, and there must be witnesses, too.—KS]

4. The sentence must be read in connection with the issues of the bull *Turbato corde* and the efforts of the inquisitors to convict recent converts on suspicion of Judaizing and to punish Jews on the charge of luring converts and born Christians into Judaism. Cf. J. Starr, "The Mass Conversion of Jews in Southern Italy," *Speculum* 21 (1946): 205, on the activity of the inquisitors in Naples in the 1290s, where they apparently succeeded in all but destroying the Jewish population. See below, under Boniface VIII, the complaint of the archbishop of Capua.

5. [Lagumina's text says *anno primo;* it also says MCCLXXV (1275). Is this a scribal error, or does it compound the other problems noted in discussing the *Sicut Judaeis* of Nicholas III, above?—KS]

46   October 21, 1281

To the archbishops and bishops of France:

EX PARTE DILECTORUM[1] . . . The pope relates that the inquisitors of heresy in France had recently reported the following: Some who were suspect and accused of heresy, as well as baptized Jews who had subsequently apostatized, were taking refuge in churches. They were doing this not for the sake of salvation but to escape punishment for their crimes. Thus, the inquisitors had asked the pope to find a remedy. And he, recognizing that the enemies of the orthodox faith must be extirpated, had empowered the inquisitors to execute their duties freely against persons suspected of heresy and against converted Jews who had then openly or quite evidently apostatized— even if they had fled for sanctuary to church structures. In addition, the pope instructs the prelates of France not to stand in the way of the inquisitors, but to give them every possible aid.

Reg. Vat. 41, fols. 19v–20r.
Raynaldus, *Annales ecclesiastici, a.a.* 1281 (vol. 14), no. 18.
Ripoll, *Bull. Ord.*, vol. 2, p. 1.
F. Olivier-Martin, ed. *Les registres de Martin IV* (Paris, 1901–1935), p. 30, no. 77.

Martinus Episcopus, Servus Servorum Dei, venerabilibus Fratribus Archiepiscopis, et Episcopis, per Regnum Francie constitutis, Salutem, et Apostolicam Benedictionem.

Ex parte dilectorum filiorum Inquisitorum heretice pravitatis, per Regnum Francie constitutorum, fuit nuper propositum coram Nobis, quod nonnulli de heretica pravitate culpabiles, vel suspecti, aut accusati; seu conversi de judaica cecitate ad fidem catholicam, postmodum apostatantes ab ipsa, ad Ecclesias confugiunt, non ad salutis remedium, sed ut eorum manus effugiant, et suorum scelerum vitent judicium ultionis: super quo Apostolice Sedis providentiam humiliter imploravit. Nos igitur, ad extirpandos orthodoxe fidei inimicos, et herbam tam noxiam, tamque pestiferam de horto dominico radicitus evellendam solicitis studiis intendentes, eisdem Inquisitoribus nostris damus litteris in mandatis, ut illos, quos de hujusmodi heretica pravitate culpabiles, vel de illa notabiliter suspectos esse, ipsis constiterit, accusatos etiam de labe predicta, conversos quoque judeos, et postmodum patenter, vel verisimilibus indiciis apostatantes a fide, juxta qualitatem delicti, libere officii sui debitum exequantur, ac si ad Ecclesias, vel loca predicta minime confugissent. Quocirca fraternitati vestre per Apostolica scripta mandamus, quatenus eosdem Inquisitores non impediatis, quo minus hujusmodi mandatum nostrum implere valeant; Sed potius ad requisitionem ipsorum in iis assistatis eisdem, sicut extiterit opportunum.

Datum apud Urbem Veterem, xii kal. Novembris, anno primo.

1. This bull gained special importance since it was cited as the basis for the suspension of the right of asylum for heretics. Cf. Henry Charles Lea, *A History of the Inquisition* (New York, 1922), vol. 2, p. 121; J. M. Vidal, *Bullaire de l'Inquisition française* (Paris, 1913), p. lxvi.

47   October 21, 1281

To the inquisitors of heresy in France:

EX PARTE VESTRA[1] . . . The pope repeats (except for the change in personal address) the above letter to the prelates of France. He concludes by saying: "And so that no one may put obstacles in your way, we are enjoining our venerable brothers, the archbishops and bishops of France, not to impede your labors, but rather to assist you when you turn to them and whenever opportunity arises."

Potthast, no. 21806.
Reg. Vat. 41, fol. 20r, no. 78.
Olivier-Martin, *Registres*, no. 78.

Inquisitoribus heretice pravitatis per regnum Francie constitutis.

EX PARTE VESTRA . . . et ut nullum in hac parte vobis possit obstaculum interponi, venerabilis fratribus nostris archiepiscopis et episcopis per regnum francie constitutis per alias litteras nostras injungimus ut vos non impediant quominus huiusmodo mandatum vestrum implere libere valeatis, sed potius ad requisitionem vestram in hiis vobis assistant sicut extiterit opportunum.

Datum apud Urbem Veterem, xii kal. Novembris, anno primo.

1. On July 3, 1322, Pope John XXII repeated this bull in substantially the same words. Cf. Grayzel, "References to the Jews in the Correspondence of John XXII," p. 325, no. XXII.

48   April 1, 1284

To the Bishop of Leon and to the Dean and Archdeacon of Ledesma in Salamanca:

ISTI SUNT ARTICULI[1] . . . These are the charges and responses in the dispute between the prelates of the Kingdom of Portugal and King Dionysius. Among the charges are the following which mention the Jews: The king, it is said, sometimes threatens archbishops and bishops, keeps them confined within their churches and monasteries, and uses Muslims, Jews, and other retainers to kill these prelates.

While the king denies that he has ever done this, he still promises not to do so in the future.

Acting contrary to the decision of the general council, the king is said to prefer Jews to positions and offices with power over Christians. He also does not force Jews to wear clothes that distinguish them from Christians. Once again, the king promises to act correctly in the future.

Moreover, when Jews or Muslims accept baptism, the king confiscates their property; and when Muslim slaves of Jews accept baptism, they are forced back into their former state of servitude. The king denies having done this and promises not to do so in the future. He promises to make amends if by chance anything of the kind did happen in the past.

If a Jew or Muslim gains possession of a Christian's property by purchase or through default on a loan, the king flouts the decision of the council that tithes and first fruits from these lands must still be paid. In fact, he makes a point of canceling these taxes when the new owners work the lands themselves. The king replies that he never did anything of the kind and promises not to do so in the future. If his father issued an edict condoning such acts, he promises to revoke it.

The pope orders the addressees to make certain that the king lives up to his promises, and the addressees are to report to the pope any future infractions, etc.

Reg. Vat. 41, fols. 194–198.
Olivier-Martin, *Registres*, pp. 231–239, no. 502 (esp. pp. 233, 236, and 238).

Venerabili Fratri . . . episcopo Legionensi et dilectis filiis decano et . . . archidiacono de Ledesma Salamantinis.

ISTI SUNT ARTICULI et responsiones ad eos reformate de nostro mandato, de quibus fit mentio in aliis litteris nostris ad vos directis per quas vobis inter prelatos regni Portugalie ex parte una et Dyonisium regem Portugalie illustrem ex altera, quedam committuntur que ipsarum litterarum series manifestat.

Item, quod personas ad ecclesias fugientes in illis casibus in quibus debent per ecclesias defensari, violenter facit ipse ac sui per sarracenos aut judeos, vel per christianos, extrahi ab eisdem vel facit eos ibi custodiri et compediri quandoque per suos satellites et eis cibaria denegari, ut sic exire de ecclesiis compellantur. Respondet idem rex quod talia nunquam fecit hactenus et promittit non facere in futurum.

Item, quod sepe minatur archiepiscopo et episcopis et quandoque procurat et facit eos inclusos in ecclesiis, monasteriis et alibi detineri sarracenis, judeis ac aliis suis apparitoribus, pretoribus et meyrinis ad interficiendum eos adhibitis, circumquaque facit etiam amputari auriculas servientum episcoporum et quandoque alios capi et alios interfici coram eis. Respondet idem rex quod talia nunquam fecit hactenus et promittit non facere in futurum.

Preterea, si quando Judei vel Sarraceni liberi, divina inspiratione, veniunt ad baptismum, tu bona ipsorum facis protinus confiscari et eos in novam redigi servitutem. Et si Sarraceni servi Judeorum, per baptismum Christi fidem acceperint, eos reduci facis in servitutem pristinam Judeorum. Respondet idem rex quod ipse de hiis omnibus nichil fecit et promittit non facere in futurum. Et si qua talia facta inveniantur, promittit emendare, in servitutem redactos restituendo libertati et de confiscatis etiam satisfactionem debitam impendendo.

Si Judei quidem, vel Sarraceni, emptionis vel pignoris titulo, christianorum possessiones obtineant, vel acquirant, non permittis edicto generali super hoc edito, ut de hujusmodi possessionum fructibus quas dicti Judei vel Sarraceni propriis manibus vel sumptibus excolunt, ecclesiis in quarum parrochiis possessiones ipse consistunt, decime ac primitie persolvantur. Respondet idem rex quod ipse nichil horum fecit et promittit quod permittet et non impediet solvi decimas, de quibus in articulo continetur, et edictum, si quod in contrarium fuit editum tempore patris sui, quod non credit, ex nunc revocat et statuit pro revocato haberi.

Datum apud Urbem Veterem, kal. Aprilis, anno quarto.

---

1. For the antecedents of this letter, see *ChJ*, pp. 190–194, no. 64, as well as bulls no. 32 and 23, above, with their notes. For its continuation, see bull no. 55, below.

Honorius IV

Jacques Savelli was elected pope on April 2, 1285, and reigned for two years.

49   September 17, 1285

Constitutio super Ordinatione Regni Siciliae

A. JUSTITIA ET PAX . . . Pope Honorius ratifies a number of provisions and ordinances for the Kingdom of Sicily (all of which modify the 1231 Constitutions of Frederick II).

Article 10. In cases of unsolved homicide, no community shall be penalized by a fine exceeding one hundred *augustales* where the victim was a Christian, and fifty *augustales* where the victim was a Jew or Muslim.[1] Any increases said to have been imposed by the king are rescinded. These fines apply only to populous settlements; they shall be proportionately reduced for smaller ones.

Reg. Vat. 43, fol. 29v, no. 93.
Potthast, no. 22290.
M. Prou, ed., *Les registres d'Honorius IV* (Paris, 1888), p. 88, no. 97.

B. DILECTUS FILIUS . . . Pope Honorius ratifies the regulations that Charles,[2] Prince of Salerno, son of the late King Charles of Sicily, proclaimed for the good of the Church in his kingdom:

Article 16. That the Jews, "who are the vassals of the churches,"[3] shall not be entrusted with public office; but neither shall they be made to suffer oppressive burdens or the curtailment of their rights.[4]

Reg. Vat. 43. fol. 25v, no. 92.
Potthast, no. 22291.
Prou, *Registres*, p. 72, no. 96.

Constitutio Super Ordinatione Regni Sicilie.

A. *Ad perpetuam rei memoriam.* JUSTITIA ET PAX complexe sunt se ita societate indissolubili sociate, sic se comitatu individuo comitantes ut una sine altera plene non possit haberi, et qui ledit alterutram pariter offendat utramque. Hinc complexus earum graviter impeditur injuriis per eas etenim lesa justitia pax turbatur, ipsaque turbata facile in guerrarum discrimina labitur, quibus invalescentibus justitia inefficax redditur, dum debitum sortiri nequit effectum. Sicque, ipsa sublata, nimirum pax tollitur, opus ejus et ipsius fructus subducitur seminandus in pace ac proinde complexis deficientibus necessario deficit et complexus. In horum vero defectu, licentia laxata dissidiis, multiplicantur bella, pericula subeunt animarum et corporum crimina frequentantur, nec rerum vastitas preteritur. Hec in presidentium injuriosis processibus et inductarum in subditos oppressionum excessibus patent apertius et evidentius ostenduntur. In quorum multiplicatione sauciantur corda lesorum et quanto minus datur oportunitas licite propulsandi que illicite inferuntur, tanto rancor altius radicatur interius et periculosius prorumpit exterius oportunitate concessa. Fiunt enim plerumque hostes ex subditis, transeunt auxilia securitatis in metum, munitiones in formidinem convertuntur; nutant regnantium solia, redundant regna periculis intestinis, quatiuntur insidiis, extrinsecis insultibus impetuntur audacius et regnantes in eis qui operantes justitiam exaltationis gloriam mererentur, humiliati propter injustitias frequenter opprobrium dejectionis incurrunt.

10. In homicidiis clandestinis providendo precipimus nihil ultra penam inferius annotatam ab universitatibus exigendum; videlicet ut pro Christiano quem clandestine occisum inveniri continget, ultra centum augustales, pro judeo vero vel Sarraceno ultra quinquaginta nichil penitus exigatur, augmento, quod circa eandem penam idem rex dicitur induxisse, omnino sublato, presertim cum memorati rex et primogenitus dicantur idem per suas constitutiones noviter statuisse, quas quoad hoc decernimus inviolabiliter observandas, et hec intelligi tantum in homicidiis vere clandestinis in quibus ignoratur maleficus nec aliquis accusator apparet, adicientes quod non nisi tantum in locis magnis et populosis exigi possit quantitas supradicta. In aliis vero infra quantitatem eandem pro qualitate locorum exactio temperetur.

B. *Ad perpetuam rei memoriam.* DILECTUS FILIUS nobilis vir, clare memorie C. regis Sicilie primogenitus, tunc princeps Salernitanus et ejusdem regis in regno Sicilie vicarius generalis, tanquam vir catholicus de genere ortus christianissimo devotam ad Deum et ipsius ecclesias mentem gerens ejusdem generis vestigia imitatus pro bono statu ecclesiarum regni predicti et ad conservationem jurium earundem inter cetera, licet sub alio forsan verborum scemate, dicitur statuisse et mandasse inviolabiliter observari.

16. Item, quod Judeis qui sunt ecclesiarum vassalli nulla committantur officia nec eis alie oppressiones vel gravamina inferantur.

Datum Tibure, xv kal. Octobris, anno primo.

1. [This clause closely follows the 1231 Constitutions of Melfi.—KS]

2. The pope, as suzerain of the Kingdom of the Two Sicilies, found it necessary to ratify and promulgate these constitutional provisions because Charles of Anjou had died in January 1284 and that his son, later Charles II, was at this time a prisoner of war in the hands of the Aragonese.

3. For a discussion of Jewish serfdom, whether to the Church or to the secular powers, see *SRH*, Vol. 9, esp. pp. 41 ff., and Kisch, *The Jews in Medieval Germany*, pp. 147 ff., but cf. G. Langmuir, "Tanquam servi," in M. Yardeni, ed., *Les juifs dans l'histoire de France* (Leiden, 1980). [In this specific instance, the vassalage may be a result of papal suzerainty over Sicily, thus accounting for the unusual expression "who are vassals of the churches," which, to my knowledge, appears nowhere else. On the other hand, "of the churches" may refer only to a simple relationship between certain Jews and specific church foundations, thus having no general application whatsoever.—KS]

4. An echo of the *Sicut Judaeis* Bull of Protection.

50 November 30, 1286

To the Archbishop of Canterbury and his suffragans:[1]

NIMIS IN PARTIBUS . . . Too freely has the damnable Jewish distortion of faith loosed its reins in English lands—as we have heard[2]—by outrageous actions and horrible works insulting to our Creator and detrimental to the Catholic faith. Jews are said to possess a certain book, composed with malicious deceit, which they commonly refer to as Thalmud,[3] and which contains abominations, falsifications, faithless and abusive matter of all sorts. They study this book constantly, devoting themselves with depraved solicitude to this nefarious document, and they condemn their own sons, from a tender age, to this death-dealing study. They stuff them with this poisonous diet, never fearing to inform and instruct them that the contents of this book are more to be believed than that which is set forth in the Law of Moses, in order that their sons might turn their backs on the Son of God, fleeing him through the byways of faithlessness and never approaching the path of truth.

Moreover, the Jews try to attract to their sect, not only faithful Christians, but, by means of inducements, they even approach those who have become converts to Christianity.[4] Indeed, they dwell with them obscenely and publicly in the very parishes where they have been baptized, thus scandalizing the faithful and bringing contumely on the Christian faith. These people are then sent to other places, where they are unknown, and there they openly revert to Judaism.

The Jews also criminally invite the orthodox to worship with them on Sabbaths and holidays in the synagogues. There, these Christians show reverence to the parchment scrolls of the Jews; and thus many of them Judaize no less than the Jews themselves.[5]

The Jews employ Christian domestics, upon whom they impose on Sundays and holidays the very servile labors from which they should abstain on those days.[6] The Jews also employ Christians in their homes as nurses and governesses for their children, and as a result opportunities arise for sexual intermingling.[7] There are also Christians and Jews who frequent one another's homes, eating and drinking together, thus preparing the soil for error.[8]

In their daily prayers, the Jews curse[9] Christians and commit other evils which are an offense to God and result in injury to Christian souls.

Although the English clergy had frequently been urged to take steps to remedy these matters it had not done so. A dangerous sickness like this, however, must not be neglected,[10] for it will only grow worse. The use of spiritual and temporal penalties to bring a halt to these excesses is ordered, as well as other methods, including fit and proper verbal exhortations.[11] Finally, the pope requests a report on the progress being made in fighting these excesses.

Reg. Vat. 43, fol. 208v, no. 42.
Potthast, no. 22541.
Prou, *Registres*, no. 809.
Calendar of Papal Registers, vol. 1, p. 491.
Raynaldus, *Annales Ecclesiastici, a.a.* 1286, nos. 25–27.
Sbaralea, *Bull. Francisc.*, vol. 3, p. 590, no. 71.

Venerabili Fratri . . . Archiepiscopo Cantuarien., et ejus Suffraganeis Sal., et Apost. Bened.

NIMIS IN PARTIBUS Anglicanis, prout accepimus Judaeorum damnata perfidia in nostri contumeliam Creatoris, et detrimentum Catholicae Fidei nefandis actibus, et horrendis operibus relaxavit habenas. Ipsi enim librum quemdam maligna fraude compositum habere dicuntur quem

Thalmud vulgariter nuncupant, abominationes, falsitates, infidelitates, et abusiones multimodas continentem: in hoc quippe libro damnabili suum continuant studium, et circa ipsius nefaria documenta ipsorum prava solicitudo versatur. Illius insuper doctrinae lethiferae proprios ab annis teneris filios deputant, ut ejus venenosis pabulis imbuantur; eosque instruere, ac informare non metuunt, quod magis in libro contentis eodem, quam expressis in lege Mosaica credi debet, ut iidem Filii Dei Filium fugientes per devia infidelitatis exorbitent; et ad veritatis semitam non accedant. Praefati quoque Judaei non solum mentes Fidelium ad eorum sectam pestiferam allicere moliuntur; verum etiam illos, qui salubri ducti consilio infidelitatis abjurantes errorem ad lucem Catholicae Fidei convolarunt, donis multimodis ad apostatandum inducere non verentur, quorum aliqui dolosa Judaeorum ipsorum seducti malitia publice illis cohabitant; et juxta ritum et legem ipsorum in Parochiis, in quarum Ecclesiis renati sacro fonte Baptismatis extiterunt, obscenam immo nequissimam vitam ducunt in nostri Redemptoris injuriam, Fidelium scandalum, et derogationem Fidei Christianae: ac etiam nonnullos ex talibus iidem Judaei ad alia loca nequiter destinant, ut ibi tamquam incogniti ad suam perfidiam revertantur. Non omittit Judaeorum ipsorum nequitia, quin Fidei orthodoxae cultores quolibet die Sabbati, ac aliis solemnitatibus eorumdem invitet, ac instanter inducat, ut in Synagogis suis ipsorum officium audiant, illudque juxta sui ritus consuetudinem solemnizent rotulo involuto membranis, seu libro, in quibus lex eorum conscripta consistit, reverentiam exhibentes: quamobrem plerique Christicolae cum Judaeis pariter judaizant. Praesumunt quoque praefati Judaei Christianos in sua familia retinere, quos in Divinae Majestatis opprobrium diebus Dominicis, et Festivis operibus occupari servilibus, a quibus est potius abstinendum, nefaria jussione compellunt. Admittunt etiam in suis domibus Christianas ad ipsorum infantes seu pueros educandos; et tam iidem Christiani, quam Christianae Judaeis ipsis cohabitant, eisque convivunt: sicque dum opportunitas suggerit, et pravis actibus tempus favet, Judaeorum mulieribus Christiani, et Judaei Christianorum Foeminis frequenter infausto commercio commiscentur. Alii nihilominus Christiani et Judaei vicissim in domibus propriis saepe conveniunt; et dum simul commessationibus, et potationibus vacant, erroris materia praeparatur. Singulis quoque diebus in orationibus, vel verius execrationibus suis in maledictionem Christianorum damnabili praesumptione prorumpunt, alia nonnulla committendo nequissima, quae noscuntur in offensam Dei, et animarum Christianorum dispendium redundare. Verum etsi nonnulli ex vobis saepe saepius fuerint, prout asseritur requisiti, ut super iis opportunum curarent remedium adhibere; id tamen efficere neglexerunt; de quo tanto propensius admirari compellimur, quanto ex debito pastoralis officii se promptiores et efficatiores exhibere tenentur ad ulciscendas nostri Salvatoris injurias, et hostium Fidei Christianae conatus nefarios reprimendum. Cum itaque non sit tam pestilens, et periculosus morbus aliquatenus contemnendus, ne, quod absit, relictus neglectui tractu temporis invalescat; et adversus tantae tamque damnabilis temeritatis audaciam promptis teneamini consurgere animis, et ad ejus repressionem, et confusionem omnimodam efficax studium, operamque solicitam impertiri, ut fraenatis hujusmodi perversis ausibus Catholicae Fidei dignitas gloriosis proficiat incrementis: Fraternitati vestrae per Apostolica scripta districte praecipiendo mandamus, quatenus per vos super praemissis et singulis praemissorum per inhibitiones, et poenas spirituales et temporales, aliosque modos, de quibus expedire videritis, in praedicationibus vestris, et aliis ad hoc temporibus congruis per vos, et alios exprimendos studeatis juxta officii vestri debitum sic efficaciter et solicite providere, ut morbus hujusmodi per adhibendae medicinae remedium amputetur; vosque proinde apud aeterni Regis Clementiam praemium consequi valeatis; ac Nos vestram curiosam solertiam, et diligentem vigilantiam dignis in Domino laudibus attollamus. Quod autem in hac parte feceritis, Nobis per vestras litteras plenius intimetis.

Datum Romae, ii kal. Decembris, anno secundo.

1. John Peckham, archbishop of Canterbury (1279-1292), was a Franciscan noted for his zeal in matters of ecclesiastical discipline. A similar letter, dated November 18, had been sent to the Archbishop of York and his suffragans. A copy of the bull, found in the archives of the bishop of Hereford, was dated November 19 (W. W. Capes, ed., *Registrum Ricardi de Swinfield* [London, 1909], pp. 139 f.).

2. From whom had the pope heard about the situation which he goes on to describe? A Church council was scheduled to meet at Exeter in a few months—it closed on April 18, 1287 (cf. D. Wilkins, *Concilia Magnae Britanniae et Hiberniae* [London, 1737], vol. 2, 155; and also no. XVI, below)—and certainly preparations for it were already being made, although cf. nn. 3 and 10 here. The greatest influence at the council would naturally be wielded by the primate of England, the archbishop of Canterbury. John Peckham had always resented the privileges enjoyed by the Jews of England, and he had tried to place them under severe restrictions. It is likely, therefore, that in preparation for the forthcoming council Peckham wrote to the pope asking for a policy statement on Jews to guide the council, especially since the archbishop felt that some of the English prelates (the bishop of London, for example) were not as zealous as they should have been.

3. The formulation of the attack on the Talmud is reminiscent of the bull of Gregory IX in 1239 (*ChJ*, pp. 240-241, nos. 96 ff.). It, too, linked the persistence of Judaism to talmudic study. Significantly, however, the question of the Talmud does not figure in the decisions of the council of Exeter. See n. 10, below.

4. The problem is that which had led to the bull *Turbato corde,* reissued as recently as March 1, 1281 (see bull no. 44, above). Archbishop Peckham himself had addressed King Edward I on the subject on November 2, 1281, in words that appear to have derived from that document: *Non sine dolore cordis et angustia est nostris auribus inculcatum quod nonnulli, sexus utriusque, tam in civitate London quam alibi, qui a Judaica perfidia ad Christianam religionem conversi fuerant, ad vomitum redierunt, superstitionem Judaicam. . . .* He asked the king to take active measures against such criminals (*Registrum epistolarum Fratris Johannis Peckham Archiepiscopi Cantuariensis,* ed. by Ch. T. Martin, [London, 1908-1912], p. 230). Cecil Roth's *History of the Jews in England* (Oxford, 1941), p. 83, discusses this issue with some particulars. The Council of Exeter approached the problem indirectly, by imposing a badge on Jewish men and women and by forbidding any social contacts between Jews and Christians: *ut Judaei utriusque sexus super vestes exteriores duas tabulas laneas habeant alterius coloris ad pectus consutas, quarum latitudo digitorum duorum et longitudo quatuor sit ad minus* (Wilkins, *Concilia,* vol. 2, p. 155). The Council of Oxford (*ChJ,* no. XVI, pp. 314-315), had passed the same resolution. See below, Appendix B.

5. Objections to Christians visiting synagogues go back to Chrysostom (cf. *SRH,* vol. 7, p. 84, and W. Meeks and R. Wilken, *Jews and Christians in Antioch* [Missoula, Montana, 1978], including a translation of two of the homilies against Jews). It may be that such visits were the motive behind Peckham's attempt to deprive the Jews of their synagogues in London, although he did not oppose the one synagogue to which they were canonically entitled (cf. Martin, *Registrum,* pp. 212 f., 407; H. G. Richardson, *The English Jewry under Angevin Kings* [London, 1960], p. 197). The permission to maintain one synagogue, provided it was neither new nor imposing, was also conceded by the Council of Exeter: *prohibemus ne novas erigant synagogas; sed si veteres corruerint vel ruinam minentur, ipsas reaedificare, ita quod ampliores vel pretiosiores non faciant, ipsis satis novimus esse permissum.* Wilkins, *Concilia,* vol. 2, p. 155). Cf. also the Council of Oxford in 1222, *ChJ,* no. XVI, pp. 314-315.

6. The complaint about servile labor imposed on Christians on Sundays perhaps goes back to Charlemagne (*MGH,* Capitul., I, 152, a text of doubtful origins). It was easily derived from the old prohibition originally applied to slaves and *colonii* (cf. X.5,6,2).

7. The prohibition against Jews employing Christian nursemaids and governesses—it would be interesting to know the duties of these women and the ages of the children under their care—goes back to more recent canonical legislation, principally that of the Third Lateran Council (*ChJ,* p. 297). The council of Exeter gives the reason for the prohibition by quoting from another canonical dictum (Gratian, C.28,q.1, col. 12), namely that familiarity might turn the simpleminded to Judaizing: *ne forte per assiduam familiaritatem ad eorum perfidiam simplicium animos valeant inclinare* (Wilkins, *Concilia,* vol. 2, p. 155). Cf. Council of Oxford, in *ChJ,* no. XVI.

8. An incident of this sort caused a furor in Church circles in August of the same year. A wealthy Jew had invited his Christian friends to the wedding of his daughter. Richard of Swinfield, Bishop of Hereford, was so outraged that he threatened and then actually imposed excommunication on any Christian who

attended (Capes, *Registrum*, pp. 120-122). The prohibition of common festivities was an old one, dating back to the Council of Vannes in Brittany, in 465 (Hefele, *Histoire des Conciles*, vol. 2, p. 905, c. 12), and the council of Macon, in 583 (Hefele, *Histoire des Conciles*, vol. 3, p. 204, c. 15); other councils are listed in Blumenkranz, *Juifs et Chrétiens*, 171-173. At Exeter such fraternization was prohibited in strong terms: *Et quoniam cum eis sumere cibum non licet, inhibemus ne Judaei christianorum vel Christiani ad Judaeorum accedant convivia.*

9. That the Jews cursed Christianity during their synagogue services was a comparatively new charge, dating from the 1240s (cf. no. 25, above, and especially see J. Rosenthal "The Talmud on Trial," *JQR* 47 [1956]: 162). The "other" offensive acts were not specified. Yet the clergy still apparently recognized that tradition (as in the bull *Sicut Judaeis*) did not permit interference in Jewish ritual. No action on this subject was taken at the Council of Exeter.

10. This and what follows is an open invitation for the forthcoming council to take strong action. And if, on the other hand, the English clergy at Exeter did nothing about the Talmud, they did go beyond the pope's counsel by reminding the king that he must not appoint Jews to any public office, by forbidding Christians to use Jewish physicians, by repeating the canonical regulation that Jews must keep doors and windows closed during Easter week, and by reaffirming the demand that Jews pay tithes on agricultural land in their possession and on the homes in which they dwelled. Cf. Wilkins, *Concilia*, vol. 2, p. 155; and the council of Oxford, *ChJ*, no. XVI.

11. In 1280, King Edward I had issued an order for all English Jews to attend the sermons of the Dominican preachers during the approaching Lenten period, see Roth, *Jews in England*, pp. 78-79. The pope's recommendation here, however, refers to preaching to Christians, whose attention was to be drawn to the evils in the bull. There is no hint of preaching directly to Jews.

51   1285-1286

To all the Christian faithful:

SICUT JUDAEIS . . . Pope Honorius reissues the Bull of Protection.[1]

[No extant text.]

Datum . . .

1. Although no text has yet been discovered, the issuance of this bull by Pope Honorius IV may be assumed. In the *Sicut Judaeis* issued by Nicholas IV, Honorius's name appears last in the list of predecessors. (See Grayzel,

"Thirteenth-Century Formulary," p. 65, referring to ASV, Armarium 31, tome 72, fol. 307, no. 3578.) In the copy of the bull issued by Pope Eugenius IV, in 1432, the name Honorius also appears between the names of Nicholas III and Nicholas IV (*Reg. Vat.* 372, fol. 136r; cf. M. Stern, *Urkundliche Beiträge*, p. 43, no. 34). For the most recent prior issuance of *Sicut Judaeis*, see bull no. 45, above.

Nicholas IV

After an interregnum of eleven months, caused principally by differences on Angevin policy among the cardinals, a neutral, Girolamo Masci, was elected. Of humble origins, Masci had risen to become Minister-General of the Franciscan Order and, then, the first of the order to be elected pope. His reign began on February 22, 1288; he died April 4, 1292.

52   March 5, 1288

To Franciscus Dominicus, scholar at Lisbon:

CONSTITUTUS IN PRESENTIA . . . The pope grants Dominicus's application for a legitimization of his birth, so that he would be eligible for ecclesiastical promotion. Dominicus was the child of a married Jew and an unmarried Muslim woman who had subsequently become a Christian.[1]

Reg. Vat. 44, fol. 2v, no. 4.
Langlois, *Registres*, p. 4, no. 7.

Dilecto filio Francisco Dominici, scolari Ulixbonensi . . .

CONSTITUTUS IN PRESENTIA . . . nobis humiliter supplicasti ut, cum ascribi desideres militie clericali, super defectu natalium quem de Judeo conjugato et soluta tunc Sarracena nunc christiana genitus pateris, quod huiusmodi non obstante defectu ad omnes ordines promoveri et ecclesiasticum beneficium, etiam si curam habeat animarum, obtinere possis, dispensare tecum misericorditer curaremus. Nos itaque tuum in hac parte propositum pia benevolentia persequentes tecum quod defectu non obstante predicto possis ab huiusmodi ordine promoveri et ecclesiasticarum beneficium etiam si curam animarum habet obtinere auctoritate apostolica dispensamus. Ita tamen quod sicut requiret onus beneficii quod te post dispensationes huiusmodi obtinere contingerit statutis temporibus ad ordines promoveri te facias et personaliter resideas in eodem. Alioquin huiusmodi gratia quo ad beneficium ipsum nullius penitus sit momenti. Nulli ergo, etc.

Datum Laterani, iii non. Martii, anno primo.

1. Such requests for the removal of the stain of illegitimacy begin to occur fairly frequently from this time on. Though Jewish involvement in the parentage was rare, it gave credence to the charge of sexual transgression used to justify the imposition of the badge [although occurances as arabesque in their complexity as this one must have been rare.—KS]

53   May 7, 1288[1]

SICUT NOBIS SIGNIFICARE . . . The pope replies to a question addressed to him by the inquisitors. In the course of a riot[2] against the Jews in the County of La Marche, a number of Jews, in fear for their lives, were baptized. Their baptism could not be considered "precisely forced,"[3] for, under the influence of the same terror, these Jews had *consented* to the baptism of their infant children. Consequently, when these converts returned to Judaism, the papal inquisitors seized and imprisoned them. Despite a warning that they were courting excommunication and despite imprisonment for more than a year, they persisted in their refusal to return to Christianity. To the inquisitors' question of how the apostates are to be dealt with, the pope replies that they must be treated as heretics.[4]

Bibliothèque Nationale, Fond Doat, 37, fols. 191r–192r; 206r–208r.
Robert, "Catalogue," p. 217, no. 50; p. 219, no. 62.

SICUT NOBIS SIGNIFICARE curastis dudum in Comitatu Marchiae contra [Judaeos] inibi commorantes per Christianos illarum partium persecutionis insurgente procella, plures ex dictis Judaeis, metu mortis qui eis per prefatos Christianos inserebatur, non tamen absolute seu precise coacti, se baptisari fecerunt, aliqui vero ipsorum quibusdam infantibus lactentibus filis suis et consanguineis baptismum conferri per huius metum illatum ipsis modo simili permiserunt, de quo vobis per ipsorum confessiones facta extitit plena fides. Postmodum vero predicti taliter baptisati, sacramentum baptismatis quod sic recepterunt damnabiliter contempnentes nec notari apostasiae crimine formidantes, ad caecitatem iudaicam redierant, propter quod inquisitores haereticae pravitatis tunc in regno Franciae auctoritate apostolica deputati eos capi fecerunt et carcerali custodiae mancipari; ac nihilominus ipsos quia moniti diligenter ab eis ad Catholicam fidem redire derelicto praedictae citationis errore contumaciter non curarunt excommunicationis sententiam exigente iusticia promulgantes ipsos fecerunt eorum excrescente pertinacia excommunicatos publice nunciari, sed sibi predictam excommunicationis sententiam et squalores carceris per annum et amplius contemptibiliter sustinuerunt animis induratis ad Christianam fidem redire penitus denegantes. Quia vero edoceri postulastis a nobis qualiter circa tales apostatas ulterius sit agendum, nos super hoc taliter respondemus quod veris existentibus supradictis contra dictos apostatas tamquam contra hereticos potestis commissum vobis ab apostolica sede officium exercere.

Datum Romae, apud Sanctum Petrum, non. Maii, anno primo.

1. The scribe of the Fond Doat, 37, text gives the identical bull for both Nicholas III and Nicholas IV (iiii[!]), both dated on the nones of May in their first year. But May 7 of Nicholas III's first year would make it 1278, rather than 1277 as given in Fond Doat. Further, the occasional content of the bull argues against its repetition by a second pope. The text ascribed to 1288 also provides the names of the inquisitors. It therefore seems reasonable to place it among the texts of Nicholas IV. Robert, in "Catalogue," nos. 50 and 62, lists the bull under both popes. See Starr, in "Mass Conversion," p. 205, n. 15.

2. Local riots of this nature were so frequent that most of them left no record. The riot in La Marche (central France) and its vicinity must have occurred between 1280 and 1286. It, and others like it, may account in part for Martin IV's *Turbato corde, Ex parte dilectorum,* and *Ex parte vestra* (nos. 44, 46, and 47, above).

3. The meaning of *coacti,* conversion by force, had to be more closely defined as the Church grew in power. The reversion of Jews to their former religion from the Christianity forced upon them by the crusaders in 1095-1096 roused protest from the antipope Clement III in 1099 (Jaffe, ed., *Monumenta Moguntina,* p. 378, no. 32; Aronius, no. 207), but apparently not from Pope Urban II. The basic definition, ultimately going back to the Fourth Council of Toledo in 633 and beyond that to King Sisebut (Mansi, 10:633), [and to be later repeated by Gregory IV and cited by Gratian, *Decretum,* D.45,c.5.—KS] was given by Pope Innocent III in 1201 (*ChJ,* pp. 100-103, no. 12, and X.3,42,3). He argued that even if sufficient force was applied to reveal the relative unwillingness of the person to accept Christianity, that person, nevertheless, had to remain a Christian, because his reversion to his original faith would be an insulting negation of the sacrament of baptism. The result, of course, was the practical [after the fact; cf. above, bull no. 31, n. 5—KS] nullification of the principle asserted in the bull *Sicut Judaeis* that conversion by force was not acceptable to God. Pope Nicholas IV here followed the example of Innocent III, adding that the converts at La Marche had not been *precise coacti.* The willingness of the Jews to save the lives of their infant children could just as easily have served as proof that the parents did not expect to survive the ordeal they were undergoing; but the pope chose to make his own interpretation or follow that of the inquisitors. Canon law (*Sext.,* 5,2,13) quotes Boniface VIII (see below) as fully accepting the interpretation of Nicholas IV.

[One might wonder, in addition to the reasons set out here by Grayzel and in the earlier discussion of this problem (just noted), whether Nicholas IV's Franciscan membership affected his attitudes: Did he feel specially pressured by the Inquisition? The answer is probably negative—if only because of the precedent and tradition on this specific subject, a precedent accepted (cf. the reference to Gratian) even before the *Sicut Judaeis* doctrine itself had first matured. The specifics of the immediate circumstance or the personal identity of the pope, that is, were of secondary importance.—KS]

4. [Was there not perhaps a cruel parody at work here? Rather than sacrifice themselves and their children for Kiddush ha-Shem, these Jews had allowed their children to be baptized. Thus, the pope—if he knew of this practice, which is not improbable—may have concluded: Any act less than Kiddush ha-Shem is an act of assent to baptism, whence these Jews should not be considered *precise coacti*. But this is pure speculation, and, in any case, it would not have affected the decision, based squarely on canonical precedent, to insist on the irreversibility of the baptisms.—KS]

54   August 29, 1288

To my dearest son in Christ, Rudolph,[1] illustrious King of the Romans:

ACTUS TUOS . . . The pope praises Rudolph for his love of truth and fear of God, which leads him to believe and hope that where justice and equity are involved, the king will give the matter a ready hearing. Certain Jews had pointed out to the pope that Master Meir of Rothenburg, who lives under Rudolph's jurisdiction, had done nothing offensive to Christianity or the Royal Majesty and was guilty of no crime, yet had been taken prisoner at the king's command and kept in prison without cause.[2] The Jews had therefore humbly implored the pope to intervene to obtain Meir's release. This the pope is prepared to do, because humanity dictates that it is proper to act generously toward Jews; indeed, Jesus himself chose to assume human form among them. Moreover, there should be no punishment where there was no crime. The king will acquire merit by heeding this appeal from the Apostolic Throne.[3]

Reg. Vat. 44, fol. 45r, no. 185.
Langlois, *Registres*, p. 58, no. 313.

ACTUS TUOS credimus et speramus quod ad ea que iustitiam sapiunt et continent equitatem libenter praestas auditum. Nuper siquidem ex parte quorundam Judaeorum fuit expositum coram nobis quod, licet Magister Mehir de Ruthenburth, Judaeus tuae jurisdictioni subditus, nihil in offensam Christiane Religionis vel Majestati Regie commisisset neque de aliquo crimine culpabilis fuerit vel devictus, nihilominus tamen de mandato regio captus extitit et carcerali custodiae detinetur absque causa rationabili mancipatus. Quare pro parte ipsius Judaei fuit humiliter supplicatum ut pro libertatem ipsius apud serenitatem regiam interponere preces nostras de benignitate apostolica dignaremur. Nos itaque attentes quod ex eo Judaeos humanitatis causa fovere nos convenit quod Dominus noster Ihesus ex stirpe ipsorum carnem voluit assumere temporalem, quodque nulli pena debetur ubi delictum aliquod non processit, moti erga ipsum paterne compassionis affectu, Serenitatem Regiam rogamus et hortamur attente quatenus eundem Judaeum, si aliquid in subversionem Christianae fidei non commisit nec offendit Majestatem Regiam, et alias culpabilis non existat, ob reverentiam Apostolice Sedis et nostram restitui facias pristine libertati, ita quod ex hoc Deo reddaris receptior, Apostolice Sedi complaceas, et mereatur extolli dignis laudibus et mansuetudine nomen tuum.

Datum Reate, iv kal. Septembris, anno primo.

1. Rudolph I, the first Hapsburg to rule in Germany, 1273–1291. He never came to Rome to be crowned emperor.

2. Cf. Irving A. Agus, *Rabbi Meir of Rothenburg* (Philadelphia, 1947), vol. 1, pp. 125–153, for a discussion of the background of this plea. At the time, Rabbi Meir ben Baruch of Rothenburg, the foremost Jewish teacher of his day, had already been in prison for three years. Agus interprets the incident as part of Rudolph of Hapsburg's effort to regain the royal prerogatives lost during the long and disastrous interregnum. The Jews, it seems, had little faith in the ability or the readiness of the Hapsburgs to give them adequate protection and had preferred to rely on special arrangements, making themselves into quasi *servi camerae* of the local town or ecclesiastical governments under which they lived. Meir's arrest was thus a means of asserting the Jews' legal dependence (*servi camerae*) on the emperor alone. The Jew in their representations to Nicholas IV made use of the argument that Rabbi Meir was guilty of no crime against Church or State. But they may also have relayed to the pope a further fact, of which he made no use, namely, that a number of Jewish communities had already paid a substantial ransom for the rabbi, but that Rudolph had gone back on his promise to release Meir, presumably because he wanted the Jews to yield on the larger issue of their belonging to him as *servi* (cf. Agus, *Rabbi Meir*, pp. 131, 150). On this issue Rabbi Meir refused to have the Jews yield. [One wonders to what extent the Jews themselves could determine whose *servi* they were.—KS] What efforts the Jews made to obtain this highly unusual papal intervention is not known. It must have been considerable, it achieved nothing. Rabbi Meir died, still in captivity, on April 27, 1293. Fourteen years later, a certain Alexander Wimpfen paid a large sum to Albert, Rudolph's son, to permit Meir's remains to be brought to Jewish burial. It was a personal arrangement and did not go against the rabbi's instructions.

3. [The juxtaposition of this text and *Sicut nobis* (no. 53, above) should be noted. Such juxtapositions reveal that papal policy had not changed disastrously as some might argue. As always, the issue was a matter of principles; in these two cases, they were (1) the sanctity of baptism and (2) the obligation to protect Jews who merited protection (the due process prescribed by *Sicut Judaeis*). The popes saw no contradiction in their activities, and neither should we (irrespective of our personal feelings of censure for the overall repressiveness of papal policy). Nevertheless, there were conflicts of interest and clashes of principle, because Church needs often precluded sustaining the entirety of Jewish rights. Here, the Jews had to be on guard. See K. R. Stow, *The "1007 Anonymous" and Papal Sovereignty: Jewish Perceptions of the Papacy and Papal Policy in the High Middle Ages* (Cincinnati, 1984).—KS]

55   August 8, 1288

To the King of Hungary:[1]

SI SPARSA SEMINA . . . The pope addresses the king in angry terms, urging him to return to the Church by giving up his association with Muslims, pagans, and other nonbelievers, whose practices and norms he follows,[2] and by taking back his queen, whom he has imprisoned. Should he refuse, the archbishop of Gran is empowered to excommunicate him.

Reg. Vat. 44, fol. 25v, c. 106.
Potthast, no. 22764.
Langlois, *Registres*, p. 32, nos. 194–201.
A. Theiner, *Monumenta Historica Hungariae*, vol. 1, pp. 357 f., no. 577.

Carissimo in Christo filio L. regi Ungarie illustri.

SI SPARSA SEMINA . . . . Religione christiana postposita, vel potius abjecta, in contemptu divini nominis, te cum Tartaris, Sarracenis, Neugeriis et Paganis conversatione dampnata confederare (te) diceris, specialiter vivendi cum eisdem Neugeriis norma sumpta et abjecta immo potius carceri tradita immaniter uxore propria, videlicet carissima in Christo filia nostra E. regina Ungarie illustri, deseviens in te ipsum et regiam domum Ungarie. . . . Unde . . . celsitudinem regiam monemus, rogamus et hortamur attente, per apostolica tibi scripta mandantes, quatenus eorumdem Tartarorum, Sarracenorum, Neugeriorum et Paganorum ac aliorum infidelium dimissis erroribus . . . que docet et servat universalis ecclesia, velut plantatus in domo Domini devote conversionis studiis amplectaris, et eandem reginam resumens et in securo statu conservans, eam, ut teneris, maritali affectione pertractes . . . Et ne videatur correctio paterna tepescere circa filium delinquentem, venerabili fratri nostro . . . archiepiscopo Strigoniensi, de cujus circumspectione ac examinata probitate confidimus, per alias diversas litteras nostras injungimus, ut in hac parte datas sibi a domino virtutes exercens te a sic nephandis erroribus retrahat. . . . Et si dicti Tartari, Sarraceni, Neugerii et Pagani dampnatos suos conatus contra catholicos fidei professores exercitare voluerint, ne ipsorum invalescat severitas in dispendium fidei christiane, contra predictos Tartaros, Sarracenos, Neugerios et Paganos ac alios adherentes eisdem, vel eos in hiis quomodo libet confoventes . . . studeat sollicite proponere verbum crucis et contra te specialiter, nisi predictam reginam resumpseris, et eam ut predicitur tute tractaveris, exerceat censuram ecclesiasticam auctoritate nostra munitus. Et nichilominus certis regibus, ducibus, comitibus et baronibus ac populo illarum partium scribimus, ut super hiis archiepiscopo assistant eidem, nec cessabimus quantumcumque invite, si oportuerit, quod non credimus, ad tuam correctionem partes apostolice sollicitudinis, sicut expediet, adhibere. Per hoc autem quod te in presenti littera cum solite benedictionis eloquio salutamus, quia nondum de hujusmodi tuis actibus patet nobis veritas narratorum, scutum alicujus confidentie non assumas, quominus hominis et canonis sententiis, si eas forsan incurreris, sis ligatus . . . . Dat. Reate, vi idus augusti, anno primo.

In e. m. . . . archiepiscopo Strigoniensi mandat quatenus, si praedictus rex reginam resumere ac tute tractare noluerit, eum ad id per censuram ecclesiasticam compellat. Dat. ut supra.

In e. m. Lodomerio archiepiscopo Strigoniensi mandat quatenus si praedicti Tartari, Sarraceni, Neugerii et Pagani suos conatus contra catholicos exercere voluerint, contra eos et adherentes eisdem omnibus Christi fidelibus per regnum Ungariae ac per Poloniam, Boemiam, Austriam, Stiriam, Carinthiam, Sclavoniam et Ystriam verbum crucis proponat. Eique concedit potestatem largiendi omnibus sic crucis signaculum assumentibus eandem indulgentiam quam in Terrae Sanctae subsidium proficiscentibus concedit apostolica sedes. Dat. ut supra.

In e. m. archiepiscopis et episcopis ac electis, abbatibus, prioribus, decanis, archidiaconis, praepositis, plebanis et aliis ecclesiarum praelatis ac ministris, guardianis et custodibus, ac capitulis et conventibus Cisterciensis, S. Benedicti, Praemonstratensis, praedicatorum et minorum fratrum aliorumque ordinum et universo clero Hospitalique S. Johannis Jerosolimitani, militiae Templi et Sanctae Mariae Theotonicorum magistris, praeceptoribus et fratribus per regnum Ungariae ac circumpositas provintias constitutis. Eos hortatur quatenus contra Tartaros, Sarracenos, Neugerios, Paganos et alios praedictos eidem archiepiscopo ad requisitionem ejus assistant. Dat. ut supra.

In e. m. . . . Poloniae ac . . . Sclavoniae aliisque ducibus, marchionibus, comitibus et baronibus, ac universo populo Christi fidelibus per regnum Ungariae ac alias circumpositas provintias constitutis.

In e. m. . . . regi Romanorum.

In e. m. . . . regi Boemiae.

In e. m. . . . duci Austriae.

1. Ladislas IV had a brief but stormy career. Born in 1262, he was king of Hungary from 1272 to 1290, in a poorly organized kingdom that was dominated by an unruly nobility. Pope Urban IV, on July 19, 1262, had recognized that conditions in Hungary called for special consideration (cf. bull no. 17, above). But Ladislas's way of life stirred Pope Nicholas to action. He sent copies of this bull to the prelates and ruler of neighboring states.

2. The term "nonbelievers" refers to and probably includes Jews, who are not mentioned specifically in the bull. Theiner (*Monumenta*, vol. 1, pp. 357 ff.) refers to this bull in the index under the rubric "Judaei." [However, the matter is perplexing. The 1262 letter of Urban IV did refer to office-holding by non-Christians, yet this was not an offense that would be described, as here, in terms of *"religione . . . abjecta"* and requiring *"dimissis erroribus."* Further, if Judaizing were involved, the pope would have said so explicitly. Moreover, apart from the issue of the queen, the text is vague and it may not involve Jews at all. Its interpretive history, however, justifies its inclusion in this collection.—KS]

56 September 5, 1288

To the Dominican and Franciscan friars deputized as inquisitors of heresy:

TURBATO CORDE[1] . . . The pope reissues this important bull, using the version of Gregory X.

Reg. Vat. 44, fol. 47r, c. 194.

Bibliothèque Nationale, Fond Doat 37, fol. 209r.

Potthast, no. 22795.

Langlois, *Registres*, p. 62, no. 322.

A. Bzovius, *Annalium Ecclesiasticorum* (Cologne, 1616), a.a. 1288, no. 9.

Ripoll, *Bull. Ord.*, vol. 2, p. 22.

Bullarium Romanum, vol. 3, pt. 2, p. 52, II.

Dilectis filiis fratribus predicatorum et minorum ordinum, inquisitoribus heretice pravitatis auctoritate sedis apostolice deputatis et in posterum deputandis.

TURBATO CORDE audivimus et narramus . . . quod quamplurimi christiani, veritatem catholice fidei abnegantes, se dampnabiliter ad ritum judaicum transtulerunt, quod tanto magis reprobum fore cognoscitur, quanto ex hoc nomen sanctissimum Christi quadam familiari obstilitate securius blasphematur . . . . Universitati vestre per apostolica scripta mandamus quatenus infra terminos vobis ad inquirendum contra hereticos auctoritate sedis apostolice designatos, super premissis tam per christianos quam etiam per judeos inquisita diligenter et sollicite veritate, contra omnes quos talia inveneritis hactenus commisisse ac committere etiam in futurum tanquam contra hereticos . . . procedere studeatis. Judeos autem qui christianos utriusque sexus ad eorum ritum execrabilem induxerunt aut inveneritis de cetero inducentes pena debita puniatis . . .

Datum Reate, non. Septembris, anno primo.[2]

1. It was first issued by Clement IV on July 27, 1267, then by Gregory X on March 1, 1274, and again by Martin IV, perhaps on March 1, 1281 (see under the relevant dates, above). It should be noted, however, that the bull recorded here adheres more closely to the latter two texts than to that of Clement IV. Like them, it begins with a statement about baptized Jews who have reverted to Judaism. For a second issue of the bull by Nicholas IV, see below, September 9, 1290. Cf. also Robert "Catalogue," p. 220, no. 66.

2. There may be a connection between this letter and the December 8, 1288, expulsion of the Jews from Maine and Anjou by Charles II of Sicily and Anjou. See L. Lazard "Les Juifs du Touraine," *REJ* 17 (1888): 225 f., no. 6.

57   March 7, 1289

To the Archbishop of Braga,[1] and the Bishops of Portugal:

CUM OLIM INTER . . . The pope confirms a document enumerating forty points on which the king of Portugal[2] and the Church had reached an understanding.[3] No. 15 deals with the employment of Jews and Muslims to the detriment of the Church, especially as police and executioners, even in matters involving the clerical hierarchy; no. 27 deals with the appointment of Jews to public office and the failure to enforce the wearing of a badge; no. 36 deals with the confiscation of the property of Jewish and Muslim converts to Christianity; and no. 37 deals with the failure to compel Jews to pay tithes to local churches.

Reg. Vat. 44, fol. 117r, c. 50.
Langlois, *Registres*, no. 716, pp. 151 ff. Cf. nos. 717–719.
Raynaldus, *Annales Ecclesiastici, a.a.* 1289, pp. 412 ff.
Potthast, no. 22899.

Ad certitudinem presentium et memoriam futurorum.

CUM OLIM INTER . . . . Tenor autem instrumenti et articulorum . . . talis est.

Tenor vero articulorum predictorum et responsionum, ut predicitur, subsecutarum ad ipsas de verbo ad verbum talis est.

Hii sunt articuli qui pro parte prelatorum regni Portugalie et Algarbii coram felicis recordationis predicto domino Clemente papa IIII fuerunt oblati:

Quintus decimus articulus est: Item quod sepe minatur archiepiscopo et episcopis mortem, et quandoque procurat et facit eos inclusos in ecclesiis, monasteriis et alibi detineri, Sarracenis, judeis et aliis suis apparitoribus, pretoribus et meyrinis ad interficiendum eos adhibitis circumquaque; facit etiam amputari auriculas servientum episcoporum, et quandoque alios capi et alios interfici coram eis. Respondent procuratores sepedicti quod idem rex talia nunquam fecit, et promittunt quod ipse non faciet in futurum.

Vicesimus septimus articulus est: Item quod preficit judeos indifferenter, contra generalis statuta concilii legemque paternam, in officiis christianis, quos ad deferendum signum, quo a christianis qualitate habitus distinguantur, compellere deberet, prout in generali concilio est statutum; propter quod dampnate comixtionis excessus sub erroris potest velamento presumi; nec ipsos judeos ad debitas decimas persolvendas compelli permittit. Respondent supradicti procuratores quod idem rex, quantum est ad judeos, quod non preferantur christianis in officiis publicis, servabit quod super hoc statutum est in concilio generali; quantum est de signis, quod distinguet judeos a christianis per aliquod signum; quantum est de decimis judeorum, respondent quod ipse permittet eos compelli; et promittunt ipsum regem ita perpetuo servaturum.

Tricesimus sextus articulus est: Preterea, si quando judei vel Sarraceni liberi divina inspiratione veniunt ad baptismum, tu bona ipsorum facis protinus confiscari, et eos in novam redigi servitutem, et si Sarraceni servi judeorum per baptismum Christi fidem acceperint, eos reduci facis in servitutem pristinam judeorum. Respondent procuratores prefati quod idem rex de hiis omnibus hactenus nichil fecit, et promittunt quod non faciet in futurum, et si qua talia facta inveniantur, promittunt quod ipse emendabit, in servitutem redactos restituendo libertati, de confiscatis etiam satisfactionem debitam impendendo.

Tricesimus septimus articulus est: Si judei vel Sarraceni emptionis vel pignoris titulo christianorum possessiones obtinent vel acquirant, non permittis, edicto generali super hoc edito, ut de hujusmodi possessionum fructibus, quas dicti judei vel Sarraceni propriis manibus vel sumptibus excolunt, ecclesiis in quarum parrochiis possessiones ipse consistunt decime ac primitie persolvantur. Respondent procuratores predicti quod idem rex nichil horum fecit, et promittunt quod ipse permittet et non impediet solvi decimas de quibus in articulo continetur, et quod edictum, si quod in contrarium fuit editum tempore patris sui, quod non credit, revocabit et statuet pro revocato haberi.

Datum Romae, apud S. Mariam Majorem, non. Martii, anno secundo.

1. Tellius, 1278–1292.

2. Dionysius (Diniz), king of Portugal from 1279 to 1325.

3. The quarrel had been raging for a long time. See above, bulls no. 23 (c. 1266), 2 (May 28, 1273), and 48 (April 1, 1284), where the same points are outlined. The bulls are nearly identical to the present text. For the background, see J. Amador de los Rios, *Historia social*, vol. 1, pp. 379–381 ff. Cf. also Raynaldus, *Annales Ecclesiastici*, a.a. 1289, nos. 32–37; Sbaralea, *Bull. Francisc.*, vol. 4, pp. 55–60, no. 85.

58   January 28, 1290

To the Archbishops, Bishops, Abbots, and other Prelates in the provinces of Aix, Arles, and Embrun:[1]

ATTENDITE FRATRES . . . The pope urges these churchmen to listen carefully to his words. Pointing to the danger that heresy constitutes to the unity of Christendom, he insists that the duty of churchmen, for both their own sake and that of the purity of the Faith, is to counteract this poisonous spiritual ailment. Distressing information has reached us, he continues, that in your provinces, and in places nearby, the crime of heresy has infected many. A considerable number have, through vicious apostasy, damnably divested themselves of the shield of eternal salvation which their rebirth through sacred baptism conferred upon them and girt themselves with darkness and the shadow of death. The Jews, corrupters of our faith, daily foment apostasy.[2] They do so not only among those of their own who have been baptized in our faith, but, in contempt of our faith, they infect born Christians too. The prelates must, therefore, not erringly hesitate, lest the purity of devotion become beclouded in their provinces and the worship of the Divine Name be scoffed at lamentably.

The pope begs and commands the prelates to extend their aid and counsel to the inquisitors now, or soon to be, appointed in their provinces, enabling the inquisitors to fullfil their duties for the glory of the Divine Name. The prelates must respond whenever their aid is requested in order to extirpate the poisonous plant. The inquisitors must not be hindered in their efforts to cleanse the provinces of the pollution now afflicting them and to restore the people to sincere devotion.

The pope ends on an urgent note of warning: if the contrary to that herein mandated occurs, he will be deeply distressed and he will punish those delinquent in their tasks.[3]

Reg. Vat. 44, fols. 284r–v, no. 783.
Potthast, no. 23170.
Sbaralea, *Bull Francisc.*, vol. 4, p. 131, no. 209.
Langlois, *Registres*, no. 2028.

Venerabilibus Fratribus Archiepiscopis, et Episcopis, ac dilectis filiis universis Abbatibus, ac aliis Ecclesiarum Praelatis per Aquen. Arelaten., et Ebrodunen. Provincias constitutis Salutem, et Apostolicam Benedictionem.

ATTENDITE FRATRES, et Filii attentis auribus, et devotis mentibus verba Patris, pensate consultius, quod vere ipsa honoris vestri commoda exhortatio paterna prosequitur, etsi Fidei orthodoxae fulcimenta prosequi videatur. Nostis, quod inconsutilem tunicam Dei nostri dissuere conantur Haeretici, contra quos professionis Christianae Catholici

Praesules praelucent nitore sydereo in orthodoxae Fidei firmamento, et sunt nihilominus ipsius veluti columnarum stabilium fortitudo: nam in virtutem, et decorem Fidei constitutae censentur a Domino personae dignitate Pontificia praepollentes, quae sicut, dum illam fulciunt, et se operosos exhibent in illius dilatatione ministros, fama crescunt, et meritis, sicque ipsis deperit, et ponitur in eorum gloria macula, cum eadem Fides vim patitur, et haeresis lacessitur morsibus venenosis. Numquid frequenter errore membrorum caput affligitur, et nonnumquam Principibus poena propter peccata plebis infertur? Inter alios equidem, quos nexu paternae dilectionis astringimus, et vos in arce nostrae mentis sincera dilectione portamus, cupientes eo potius vos pollere virtutibus, quo estis, et esse debetis ad dilatandos praedictae Fidei palmites, ut acceptum reddatis commissum vobis a Domino populum, promptiores. Verum ad nostrum non sine mentis turbatione pervenit auditum, quod in Provinciis vobis subjectis, et locis ipsis adjacentibus multos crimen haereticae pravitatis infecit; plerique per apostasiae vitium salutis aeternae loricam, quam eis sacri baptismatis regeneratio contulit, damnabiliter exuentes, tamquam in tenebris, et in umbra mortis positi corruptam tunicam induunt Judaicae caecitatis; ac ipsi Judaei nostrae fidei corruptores conversos, et baptizatos de ipsis ad fidem nostram, immo ipsos etiam Christianos inficere, et apostatare pro posse nituntur quotidie in contumeliam fidei Christianae; propter quod est non immerito haesitandum, ne in illis partibus devotionis obnubiletur claritas, et Divini nominis cultui miserabiliter illudatur. Quocirca Universitatem vestram rogamus, et hortamur attente, per Apostolica vobis scripta districte praecipiendo mandantes, quatenus Christi operariis dilectis filiis hujusmodi pravitatis Inquisitoribus in illis partibus per Sedem Apostolicam deputatis, et in posterum deputandis opportunum favoris, et auxilii praesidium impendentes, ut melius proficere valeant, et commissum eis officium ad laudem Divini nominis efficacius exequantur, tam ipsis, et eorum alteri, quam Nuntiis eorumdem, quoties per eos fueritis requisiti, ad extirpandam herbam mortiferam, quae messem benedictionis extenuat, opportuna studia, et efficaces auxilii, favoris, et consilii vestri operas liberaliter impendatis, nec permittatis eos aliquatenus ab aliquo in eorum processibus impediri, ut eaedem Provinciae coinquinatorum labe purgatae, populi earumdem raddantur devotione sincera Deo placibiles, et accepti, vosque per hoc digne valeatis divinae retributionis praemium promereri. Nam si contrarium audiremus, quod absit, turbaremur ab intimis, et contra delinquentes procedere poena debita curaremus.

Datum Romae apud Sanctam Mariam Majorem V. Kal. Februarii, Pont. nostri Anno II.

1. All the provinces in southeastern France. See also the next item.

2. Obviously, the pope is repeating what he heard from his appointed inquisitors. Nor is this the first time that Jews were accused of luring Christians to observe their rites; see, for example, Honorius IV's bull *Nimis in partibus* (November, 1286; bull no. 50, above) to the archbishop of Canterbury. Two cases of outright conversion did occur in thirteenth-century England (cf. Roth, *Jews in England*, p. 53). No convincing evidence, however, has been uncovered to prove the existence of Jewish missionizing activity this late in the Middle Ages. There was, of course, the kabbalist Abraham Abulafia, who, when in Rome in 1280, sought to convert Pope Nicholas III. Fortunately for him, he timed his efforts badly. The pope had died a few days before, and Abulafia, declared insane, was permitted to go on his way (VR, vol. 1, pp. 247 ff.). That Jews and Christians visited one another is likely. That Jews actively sympathized with fellow Jews who had been forced into baptism and then sought ways of reverting to their Jewish faith is certain. Still, thirteenth-century Jews had learned to avoid the dangers of active missionary activity. Inquisitorial logic, nevertheless, thrives on conspiracy; and in the popular mind Judaism itself was considered a conspiracy (Joshua Trachtenberg, *The Devil and the Jews* [New Haven, 1943], passim). The charge that Jews were active missionaries remained part of the inquisitors' stock in trade; and when Bernard Gui, around 1322, compiled his inquisitors' manual, he included the following oath to be taken by a Jew charged with the "crime" of missionizing: "I swear and promise—by the Law of Moses which is now before me, which I have kissed and which I now touch—never from now on to invite or induce a Christian to Judaize, that is, to observe Jewish rites. I shall not in any way invite or induce a baptized convert to re-Judaize, that is, to return to Judaism or to deny the faith into which he had been baptized." The Jew is made to go on and promise never knowingly to harbor or aid a Christian heretic or a reverting convert. Cf. Bernard Gui, *Manuel de l'Inquisiteur*, ed. G. Mollat (Paris, 1927), pp. 46–47.

3. The tone and content of this bull suggest that the bishops were not eager to aid the inquisitional courts, which competed with their own. [Indeed, one must ask about tension within and between various Church bodies on matters concerning Jews. Who initiated and who was zealous to prosecute these charges of Jews "corrupting" Christianity; and how far back do the charges go? The answer seems to be that the charges begin, explicitly, with John Chrysostom, lurk behind the cries of Agobard of Lyons that the Jews are an *impedimentum* to the *ratio fidei*, and reemerge, in direct terms, in the letters of Peter the Venerable and, ominously, a few decades before Peter, in the pornographic accusations of Guibert de Nogent. Indeed, this line of thinking is implicit already in the remarks of Paul in Galatians that a little leaven acts on the whole dough (Galatians 4:21–5:12, esp. 5:9). The discovery of truly suspect—from a Christian point of view—passages in the Aggadah brought matters to a head in the mid-thirteenth century, with the attacks on the Talmud and its blasphemies. To this were then added the inquisitional claims about apostasy and the role played in it by the Jews.

Still, those who thought in terms of a constant and overwhelming Jewish threat were not a majority. And, on the question of how to perceive and deal with the Jews, a tension is manifest between elements within the Church itself. The papal—and, as in this specific case, the episcopal—response to charges of a "corrupting" Jewish influence was almost always carefully circumscribed, and often, as with the Talmud, it revealed sincere ambivalences and pulls. The popes, especially, were never willing to generalize as did many inquisitors. They were not prepared to leap from a specific charge of misconduct to a condemnation of Jewish existence as a whole, or to a prohibition of Jewish observance in its totality. Indeed, for all that they were aghast at Jewish meddling with converts— which did occur—and although they did seem to believe in the existence of outright Jewish proselytizing, the popes never called for anything that went beyond the correction of the violations themselves. Their policy rested on two fundamentals: the due process guaranteed by *Sicut Judaeis* and the need—and papally claimed right—to police the purity of Jewish observance and action, a right which Innocent IV, more explicitly than anyone else, insisted upon. (See on this, B. Z. Kedar, "Canon Law and the Burning of the Talmud," *Bulletin of Medieval Canon Law* 9 (1979): 79–82, for both the text and the important interpretation presented there; cf. J. Cohen, *The Friars*, for a different assessment of these events.)

Thus were created the striking juxtapositions involving force and baptism, noted above in bull no. 53, n. 3, and, equally striking, the proximity (in time) of this letter to *Orat mater ecclesia* (below, bull no. 64), which demands that Jews must not be subject to violence. Most of all, there is the simultaneous existence of texts like *Attendite fratres* and those grouped together in bull no. 62, below, which insist that jurisdictional bodies, including possibly the Inquisition, not overstep their limits. Moreover, the Inquisition itself was not always monomaniacal, as may be seen in the texts of acquittals published by J. Shatzmiller, "L'Inquisition et les Juifs," *passim*. It was with the papal stance and the "rational" Inquisition that the bishops tended most to identify. Sometimes, however, as here, the bishops actually ignored the canons and papal letters (*Turbato corde*), and then the tensions between prelates, inquisitors and popes required defusing. In the present letter, the papal warning to the bishops insisting they aid the Inquisition was made in unusual and especially punitive terms, although the strident tone may also reflect in part the Franciscan background of Nicholas IV himself.—KS]

59   January 28, 1290

To the Rector, Barons, Officials, and Nobles of the Comtat Venaissin:[1]

INTER INNUMERABILES SOLLICITUDINES . . . Among the cares imposed upon the Apostolic Office the foremost is to preserve the Christian people from evil and to drive the destructive little foxes from the vineyard of the Lord. The pope has been informed that in the Comtat and its neighboring territories the crime of heresy . . . [continue as in the preceding document].

The pope therefore urges and commands that the inquisitors of heresy now in these lands receive every aid and counsel so that they may achieve their aims more effectively . . .

Reg. Vat. 44. fol. 284v.
Langlois, *Registres,* no. 2029.

INTER INNUMERABILES SOLLICITUDINES . . . [Text identical to that of bull no. 58 after the address and introductory paragraph.]

Datum ut supra.[2]

1. The Comtat, a papal possession, lies to the east of the provinces named in the previous bull, *Attendite fratres.*

2. The date in full is *v. kal. Februarii, anno secundo.*

60 February 20, 1290

To the Franciscans who serve as inquisitors in Arles, Aix, and Embrun:[1]

AD AUGMENTUM . . . The pope maintains that the polluting presence of heresy must be removed if the Catholic Faith is to grow in effectiveness. He has been told that in some places under the jurisdiction of the addressees, there are men and women who, though they had been reborn through baptism, have since fallen into evil ways. Whenever they are visited by some misfortune, they hold lighted lamps and candles in the synagogue and make offerings there, and hold vigils especially on the Sabbath, that the sick may regain their health, that the shipwrecked may reach a safe port, that women may survive childbirth without danger, and that the sterile be blessed with children. For these and other matters they implore aid by means of the said rites, showing wicked devotion and every sign of reverence to the Scroll as though serving an idol.[2] All this is highly injurious to the Faith and insulting to the Creator.

Since he wants to remove this type of evil, the pope requests that the inquisitors look into the entire matter most carefully. If they find Christians of the sort described, and others, whether they be Jews or Christians, who mislead them,[3] the inquisitors are to disregard any papal privileges or indulgences these people may claim[4] and proceed against them as idolators and heretics, denying them any right of appeal, and omitting no canonical punishment, so that the guilty may feel the severity of justice.[5]

Reg. Vat. 44, fol. 294v, no. 848.
Potthast, no. 23185.
Langlois, *Registres*, nos. 2124-2125.
Raynaldus, *Annales Ecclesiastici* vol. 14, *a.a.* 1290, no. 49.

Dilectis filiis inquisitoribus ordinis fratrum minorum.

AD AUGMENTUM. . . . Ad nostrum pervenit auditum, quod in nonnullis locis, vestrae jurisdictioni subjectis, quamplures sacri renati fonte baptismatis utriusque sexus, per erroris invium incedentes, dum languorum afflictionibus, et tribulationum periculis a Domino visitantur, ad Judaici ritus vanum auxilium errando recurrunt, in synagoga Judaeorum lampades et candelas tenentes accensas, et oblationes inibi facientes, vigilias quoque die praecipue sabbati protrahunt, ut infirmi recuperent sanitatem, naufragantes ad portum salutis perveniant, existentes in partu absque periculo pariant, et steriles prolis foecunditate laetentur; ibi pro his et aliis suffragia implorantes dicti ritus, rotulo quasi per idololatriae modum nefarium devotionis et reverentiae signa patentia exhibendo, non absque multa fidei orthodoxae injuria, nostri non modica contumelia Creatoris, ac universalis Ecclesiae gravi opprobrio et contemptu. Volentes igitur hujusmodi tam funestis abusibus manifestis remediis obviare, discretioni vestrae, per apostolica scripta districte praecipiendo mandamus, quatenus de praemissis, et quolibet praemissorum, ac etiam aliis hujusmodi erroribus diligenter et solicite inquiratis; et si quos tales inveneritis Christianos cujuscumque conditionis aut status existant, tam contra eos quam alios, etiam si Judaei vel Christiani esse noscuntur, qui eis talia suadeant; Et infra: procedere tanquam contra idololatras seu haereticos poena canonica nullatenus omittatis, ut severitate justitiae cognoscant quantum Christum humani generis Redemptorem offendant taliter deviando.

Datum Romae apud S. Mariam Majorem, x. kal. Martii, anno secundo.

[A copy of this letter was sent on the same date to the inquisitors in the Comtat Venaissin.]

1. There must have been a reason why it was considered necessary to send a second papal communication, in addition to *Turbato corde* (bull no. 56, above, sent in September 1288), on the subject of Jews and heresy, and one addressed to the Franciscan inquisitors only. Does one assume there were no Dominican

inquisitors active at the moment in those parts of France, although they are mentioned in the *Turbato corde* of 1288? Perhaps the letter is simply a response by a Franciscan pope to a specific Franciscan request?

2. The synagogue always afforded opportunities for personal prayer, and sometimes oil and candles for lighting the synagogue were offered as individual gifts. Some of the procedures described here, however, are reminiscent of church practices rather than synagogue practices. The carrying of lighted candles and lamps, or holding vigils, could hardly have been practiced in the synagogue on the Sabbath. The Scroll of the Torah is the only synagogue article treated with reverence; it is not worshiped. Still, Jews would adopt such customs, as seen in Elliot Horowitz, *Jewish Confraternities in Seventeenth Century Verona: A Study in the Social History of Piety*, Ph.D. diss., Yale University, 1982.

3. On the relationship between Jews and converts from Judaism, see above, *Attendite fratres* (bull no. 58, n. 2).

4. The reference may be to *Sicut Judaeis*, which promises not to disturb the Jews in their ritual observances, or, more probably, to texts like bull no. 61, below.

5. On the Church's right to compel neophytes to stay within the Christian fold, see bull no. 30, above.

61   September 9, 1290

To the Franciscan friars deputized, or to be deputized in the future, as Inquisitors in the province of Romagna:[1]

TURBATO CORDE . . . Pope Nicholas reissues the bull which several of his predecessors had issued and which he himself had addressed to all inquisitors two years earlier.[2]

Potthast, no. 23391.
Reg. Vat. 45, fol. 75r, c. 379.
Langlois, *Registres*, p. 511, no. 3186.
J. Sbaralea, ed., *Annales Minorum* (Rome, 1650; reprint Rome, 1906), vol. 5, p. 234.

Fratribus minoribus inquisitoribus heretice pravitatis in Romana provintia per sedem apostolicam deputatis et in posterum deputandis.

TURBATO CORDE audivimus . . .

Datum apud Urbem Veterem, v id. Septembris, anno tertio.

1. Again, as in the previous bull (no. 60, above), only the Franciscan inquisitors are addressed. The Romagna, in the northeastern part of Italy, included Ravenna, where there had always been a small Jewish community.

2. Cf. bull no. 56, above.

62   A   November 5, 1290

To the Inhabitants of the Comtat Venaissin:

SICUT AD NOSTRUM . . . The pope has been informed that certain clergy and laymen[1] exploit the powers conferred upon them by the Apostolic See and cause much trouble and expense for the inhabitants of the Comtat by hailing them before other judicial bodies (in another venue) even though they properly belong to the jurisdiction of the local bishop and the rector appointed by the pope for such purposes. The pope, therefore, grants the inhabitants of the Comtat the privilege that as long as they are prepared to appear before local courts, they may not be dragged before another jurisdiction, unless the accusers produce proof that this present privilege is specifically abrogated. Jews, as inhabitants of the Comtat, now or in the future, are to be included in this privilege.

Reg. Vat. 45, fol. 102v, c. 505.
Langlois, *Registres*, p. 552, no. 3574.

Eisdem episcopis, etc.

SICUT AD NOSTRUM pervenit auditum, nonnulli clerici et laici vos coram diversis judicibus per litteras apostolicas faciunt ad judicium evocari et fatigant plerumque laboribus et expensis, quanquam ordinarii vestri super causis ad eorum forum spectantibus, ac rector dicte terre per sedem apostolicam deputatus, super hiis que ad jurisdictionem suam pertinent, de vobis parati existant cuilibet conquerenti exhibere justitie complementum. Nos igitur quieti vestre, ne taliter impetamini, providere volentes, vobis auctoritate presentium indulgemus ut, quandiu coram dictis ordinariis et rectore ac suis officialibus parati fueritis, ut premittitur, stare juri, per hujusmodi litteras impetratas, quarum auctoritate nullus habitus est processus, et etiam impetrandas, que de presentibus non fecerint mentionem, super premissis molestari ab aliquibus nullatenus valeatis. Volumus etiam ut judei habitatores dicti comitatus quique in posterum ibidem perpetuum elegerint incolatum hujusmodi indulto gaudeant, sicut alii supradicti . . .

Datum apud Urbem Veterem, non. Novembris, anno tertio.

B November 6, 1290

To the Bishop of Carpentras:

INTELLECTO DUDUM . . . Identical to the above, this letter (addressed to the pope's administrator in the Comtat) specifies that the privilege of local trial is to extend to bishops, clerics, monks and nuns, nobles, barons, communities, and other persons, including Jews.

Langlois, *Registres,* p. 552, no. 3575.

In e.m. . . . episcopo Carpentoratensi.

INTELLECTO DUDUM quod . . . . Fraternitati tue per apostolica scripta mandamus quatinus eosdem episcopos, clericos, religiosos, nobiles, barones, communitates ac homines et etiam judeos non permittas per te vel alium seu alios contra indulti nostri tenorem ab aliquibus molestari.

Dat. apud Urbem Veterem, viii idus Novembris, anno tertio.

C November 9, 1290

To the Bishops, Clerics, Members of the religious orders, Noblemen, Barons, Communities, as well as all Inhabitants of the Comtat:

UT EX GRATIA . . . The pope informs the addressees that the bishop of Carpentras, currently in charge of upholding their liberties, immunities, and privileges, and whoever may be appointed in his place in the future, shall not be impeded in the execution of his task, unless those who seek to do so can produce a papal document specifically authorizing such interference. This edict applies to all inhabitants of the Comtat, Jews included.

Langlois, *Registres,* p. 552 , no. 3573.

Nicolaus, etc. Venerabilibus fratribus episcopis et dilectis filiis clericis et religiosis, nobilibus viris, baronibus, communitatibus quoque ac hominibus universis habitatoribus comitatus Venaysini, ad romanam ecclesiam pleno jure spectantis, salutem, etc.

UT EX GRATIA . . . Vobis auctoritate presentium indulgemus ut venerabilis frater noster . . . episcopus Carpentoratensis, seu quilibet alius conservator seu conservatores, super libertatibus, immunitatibus, indulgentiis et gratiis vobis ab eadem sede concessis deputatus seu deputati ab ea, aut etiam in posterum deputandi, ne commissa sibi executio in hiis que statum, personas ac bona vestra et etiam judeorum inibi habitantium contingunt quomodolibet valeat impediri, excommunicari, interdici aut suspendi non possint auctoritate litterarum sedis apostolice vel delegatorum aut conservatorum seu executorum ipsius quibuscumque personis concessarum, que plenam et expressam de indulto hujusmodi ac nominibus propriis eorumdem conservatorum vobis deputatorum vel deputandorum et comitatu Venaysino non fecerint mentionem . . .

Datum apud Urbem Veterem, v. id. Novembris, anno tertio.

1. [Who are these people, and what kind of jurisdiction did they possess? Even though these texts do apply to papal territories, meaning, in other words, that they may in part concern purely secular matters—and there *is* mention of lay interference here, it seems clear that the vague references must largely be to inquisitorial jurisdiction, especially because of the pointed singling out of Jews; Vidal, in *Bullaire*, cites texts like these that explicitly refer to the Inquisition, especially no. 318, April 15, 1383. Here, as in Vidal, the problem is with juridical excesses—the very thing with which Philip IV charged the Inquisition in 1293 (Saige, *Juifs de Languedoc*, pp. 235-236). Grayzel, in a note omitted from his last draft, felt the texts meant only inquisitors and their lay familiars and lawyers. However, by definition, the Inquisition was a special jurisdiction. It never served as an alternative to the ordinary court system. Furthermore, inquisitional courts did not include bishop ordinaries among their members as a standard procedure until after 1312. Thus it is hard to understand why, as it seemingly does, the bull opposes local episcopal to some other jurisdiction, if that other jurisdiction was indeed that of the Inquisition. There is a note of unclarity in the picture, and it suggests a need for a thorough examination of late thirteenth century courts in southern France in order to understand these bulls completely.—KS]

63   November 27, 1290

To all Christians:

TENOREM QUARUNDAM . . . The pope repeats a bull issued by Pope John XXI reserving all the benefices enjoyed during his lifetime by

Raymond de Peralta for the Apostolic See.[1] Raymond had been chaplain to Pope Gregory X. Part of the income he enjoyed had come from tithes paid by the Jews of Calatayud.

Reg. Vat. 45, fol. 119v, no. 594.
Langlois, *Registres*, p. 578, no. 3837.

[Text identical to no. 39 above.]

Datum apud Urbem Veterem, v kal. Decembris, anno tertio.

1. The bull of John XXI, *Ad perpetuam rei memoriam: Licet felicis recordationis*, was issued on December 8, 1276. Apparently someone in the church of Calatayud was claiming that the reservation had lapsed.

64   January 30, 1291

To the papal Vicar in Rome:

ORAT MATER ECCLESIA . . . The pope argues that since the Church hopes to draw the Jews to Christ by removing the veil from their hearts and the scales from their eyes, it cannot patiently tolerate their injury and abuse by those who profess the Christian faith. Recently, however, the Jews of Rome had informed him rather tearfully that some clerics of the city had treated them violently, visiting them with oppressive exactions and injuries and constantly molesting their property. Humbly they pleaded for papal aid in their plight.

Convinced that it is not proper for Christian generosity to molest the Jews or blaze against them insolently, the pope desires that the Jews be protected by apostolic favor, and he orders that his vicar not permit the Jews to be molested in the future.[1]

Reg. Vat. 45, fol. 147r, no. 724.
Potthast, no. 23541.
Langlois, *Registres*, p. 612, no. 4184.
Theiner, *Codex Diplomaticus*, vol. 1, p. 315, no. 486.

Nicolaus Episcopus etc. Dilecto filio . . . Vicario nostro in Urbe, salutem etc.

ORAT MATER ECCLESIA pro subducendo velamine de cordibus Iudeorum, ut de ipsorum oculis squamis cecitatis eductis Christum illuminati agnoscant, candorem lucis eterne, propter quod ipsa ecclesia non tolerat patienter, ut Iudeos iniuriis vel iacturis indebite afficiant Christiani nominis professores. Nuper siquidem Sinagoga Iudeorum de Urbe nobis insinuatione admodum flebili patefecit, quod nonnulli clerici de predicta Urbe manus infestationis extendentes pontice in eos, ipsos gravare exactionibus gravibus, afficere iniuriis, et in bonis suis graviter molestare non cessant: quare ipsi pressi tam infestis angustiis humiliter implorarunt super hoc presidium apostolice pietatis. Nos itaque attendentes, quod mansuetudinem christianam non decet in Iudeos molestiis et insolentiis excandere, ac propterea volentes, ut ipsi apostolice clementie favore protecti contra iustitiam non vexentur, discretioni tue per apostolica scripta mandamus, quatenus prefatos Iudeos non permittas super hiis a talibus indebite molestari, Molestatores huiusmodi per censuram ecclesiasticam, appellatione postposita, compescendo.

Datum apud Urbem Veterem, iii kal. Februarii, anno tertio.

1. This was not a case where the Inquisition was acting arbitrarily. Rather, some of the clergy in Rome were taking advantage of the turbulent state of affairs in the city (cf. Ferdinand Gregorovius, *History of the City of Rome in the Middle Ages*, trans. Annie Hamilton [N.Y., 1967], vol. 5, pt. 2, pp. 514 f.; VR, vol. 1, p. 252). Quite possibly, moreover, they had before them the example of the unhindered persecution of the Jews in the Kingdom of Naples (see below, bull no. 66, n. 2). The effect of this bull is not clear. In view of the continuing political dissention in Rome, despite the forceful rule of Pope Boniface VIII, serious difficulties for the Jews continued, as will be seen below. Cf. VR, vol. 1, pp. 254-257. [It should be noted that the terms of this bull are essentially those of *Sicut Judaeis*, especially with reference to improper expropriations, etc.—KS]

65   March 28, 1291

To the Archbishop of Trier:[1]

ACCEDENS AD PRESENTIAM[2] . . . Enfridus of Boppard, an acolyte of the archdiocese of Treves, personally petitioned the pope for the legitimization of his birth. Thus he would be eligible for ecclesiastical promotion, although he was born out of wedlock. His father had been a Jew, and his mother a Christian, both unmarried. The pope orders this case investigated and, if Enfridus himself has not indulged in the incontinence of his father[3] and is otherwise of good character, his petition may be granted.

Reg. Vat. 46, fol. 26v, no. 136.
Langlois, *Registres*, p. 685, no. 4798.

Venerabili fratri . . . archiepiscopo Treverensi.

ACCEDENS AD PRESENTIAM . . . [The text is regular for this kind of petition, except for the following:] si paterne non est incontinentie imitator atque bone conversationis et vite . . . super premissis auctoritate nostra dispenses.

Datum apud Urbem Veterem, v. kal. Aprilis, anno quarto.

1. Boemund of Warnesberg, 1289–1299.

2. This is the second bull on the same subject involving a Jew (cf. bull no. 52, above, esp. n. 1).

3. [Is this a not so subtle way of saying: if he is not guilty of Judaizing and apostasy?—KS]

66 A May 23, 1291

To the Archbishop of Capua:[1]

CUM A NOBIS . . . The pope confirms for the newly elected archbishop the grant made (almost a century before) by the Empress (and queen of Sicily) Constance, to the church of Capua. The grant included the *Judaicam* (the Jewish district and/or its revenues).

Reg. Vat. 46, fol. 45r, c. 224.
Langlois, *Registres*, p. 717, no. 5165.

CUM A NOBIS petitur . . . Nos itaque tue supplicationi inclinati . . . tenores praedictarum litterarum de verbo ad verbum presentibus inferri facientes quod talis est.

Constantia, Dei gratia romana imperatrix semper augusta et regina Sicilie, una cum carissimo filio suo Frederico, eadem gratia rege Sicilie, ducatus Apulie et principatus Capue. Notum facimus universis regni nostri fidelibus tam presentibus quam futuris, presentem paginam intuentibus, quod nos, de solita gratia et liberalitate nostra, pro remedio quoque anime domini regis Rogerii, bone memorie, necnon et domini imperatoris, inclite recordationis, attendentes quoque puram fidem et grata servitia que Matheus, venerabilis Capuanus archiepiscopus, dilectus fidelis et familiaris noster, ipsi domino imperatori et nobis diligenter exhibuit et cotidie exhibet, concedimus ei et ecclesie Capuane ac successoribus suis in perpetuum judaicam civitatis Capue libere et sine alicujus exactione servitii. Volumus etiam ut terram que fuerat Pandulphi Compalatii, quam prenominatus dominus imperator bone memorie ipsi archiepiscopo et ecclesie Capuane concessit et ad presens idem archiepiscopus, permissione nostra, Ricie, filie ipsius Pandulphi, in baroniam tribuit, quocumque tempore ipsa filia Pandulphi vel heredes ejus sine herede decesserint, ad demanium ipsius ecclesie Capuane deveniat. Ad hujus autem nostre donationis et concessionis memoriam et perpetuam firmitatem, presentem scribi paginam et majestatis nostre sigillo jussimus communiri.

Datum apud Urbem Veterem, x kal. Junii, anno quarto.

B May 23, 1291

AD TUE SUPPLICATIONIS . . . The pope confirms and transcribes for the newly elected archbishop[2] the grant made by Charles I, King of Sicily, on January 25, 1275, and June 8, 1279, namely, thirty ounces of gold in compensation for the income from the Jewish district and the dyeing establishment of Capua.[3]

Reg. Vat. 46, fol. 46r, c. 227.
Langlois, *Registres,* p. 718, no. 5168.

Venerabili fratri Salimbene, archiepiscopo Capuano.

AD TUE SUPPLICATIONIS instantiam . . . Caroli Regis Siciliae patentes . . . tenores de verbo ad verbum fecimus presentibus annotari qui per omnia talis est.

Carolus, Dei gratia rex Sicilie, ducatus Apulie . . . tam presentibus quam futuris fidelibus suis gratiam suam et bonam voluntatem. Cum in signum universalis domini qui dat omnibus omnia ex divina institutione noscantur decretis constitute, horrendum profecto et multa videtur animadversione plectendum, si per humanam fraudem vel malitiam in reddendis eisdem cuiusquam subtractionis vel dilationis dispendium ingeritur, supplicante igitur nobis venerabili patre Capuano Archiepiscopo ut super exhibendis etiam singulis annis de proventibus bajulatoris Capue pro decima ipsorum proventuum unciis auri viginti sex et in recompensationem Judaice et tintorie Capue unciis auri triginta et in festo purificationis beatae Mariae de cera decenas octo et totidem pro cereo paschali in festo resurrectionis dominice de proventibus supradictis ponderis generalis in quorum exhibitione per officiales curie nostre fraudari diversisque calumpniis fatigari se quaeritur opportunum adhibendum remedium dignaremur. . . . Dat. Neapoli, per magistrum Guillelmum de Farunvilla, decanum Sancti Petri virorum Aurelianensis, regni Sicilie vicecancellarium, anno Domini MCCLXXV, die XXV januarii, tertie indictionis, regni nostri anno decimo.

Carolus, Dei gratia rex Sicilie, ducatus Apulie . . . tam presentibus quam futuris fidelibus suis gratiam suam et bonam voluntatem. Dudum ad petitionem . . . —Dat. Neapoli, anno Domini MCCLXXVIIII, mense junii, octavo ejusdem, septime indictionis, regnorum nostrorum Jerosolimitani anno tertio, Sicilie vero quarto decimo.

Dat. apud Urbem Veterem, kalendas junii, anno quarto.

1. Not Salimbene of Parma, author of the famous *Chronicon,* who died c. 1290 and was never an archbishop.

2. Soon after his assumption of office, Archbishop Salimbene submitted a number of documents for ratification by the Pope. Cf. Langlois, *Registres,* nos. 5162–5166.

3. On the tragic fate which had befallen the Jews of the Kingdom of Naples in 1290, see J. Starr, "Mass Conversion," pp. 203–211; see also D. A. Cassuto, "The Destruction of the Yeshivot in Southern Italy in the Thirteenth Century," in *Studies in Memory of Asher Gulak and Samuel Klein* (Jerusalem, 1942), pp. 139–152. On the continuing activity of the local inquisitors, see Ferorelli, *Gli Ebrei,* pp. 54 ff. and for the results of this activity, see the letter which Pope John XXII sent to the inquisitors in Apulia in response to a complaint by the Bishop of Trani in 1328: *Verum vos tot gravissima retroacto tempore intulistis et continue infertis eisdem quod valde pauci inibi remanserunt.* Cf. Grayzel, "References to the Jews," no. XXXIII, pp. 334–335, below. [Does not this last, together with the two papal letters (A & B, here), suggest that the mass conversions were not as total and rapid as assumed, or was Capua too far north to be affected? More hard evidence is needed. The inquisitors obviously did something, but what and how—and why did some Jews (*pauci*) survive?—KS]

67   December 13, 1291

To Marguerite, Queen of France:[1]

BENIGNO SUNT TIBI . . . The pope is glad to promote the spiritual welfare of the queen. Her conscience troubles her about money she acquired from Jews, both men and women, and she has doubts about the identity of those from whom the money had originally been taken (usuriously).[2] In view of her uncertainty about the people to whom this money should be returned, the pope allows her to keep the money, provided she donates a third of it toward the support of the Holy Land.[3]

Reg. Vat. 46, fol. 125r, c. 623.
Langlois, *Registres*, p. 849, no. 6318.

Carissime in Christo filie Margarete, regine Francie illustri.

BENIGNO SUNT TIBI illa concedenda favore per que saluti tue salubriter consulatur. Cum itaque, sicut ex parte tua fuit expositum coram nobis, a nonnullis judeis terre tue utriusque sexus diversis temporibus diversas receperis pecuniarum summas et quibus dictarum pecuniarum sit restitutio facienda prorsus ignores, provideri conscientie tue super hoc per sedem apostolicam suppliciter postulasti. Nos itaque, petitionibus tuis benignius annuentes, devotioni [tue] presentium tenore concedimus ut, si ignoretur quibus de predictis pecuniis sit restitutio facienda, ad restitutionem pecuniarum ipsarum, dummodo tertiam partem earumdem pecuniarum convertas suo loco et tempore in subsidium Terre Sancte, minime tenearis. Nulli ergo, etc., nostre concessionis, etc.

Datum Rome, idibus Decembris, anno quarto.

1. Marguerite de Provence, 1221–1295, married Louis IX in 1234 and greatly admired her saintly husband. Her sister Eleanore, younger by a year, married Henry III of England; another sister, Cincia, married Richard, Earl of Cornwall, Henry's brother; and her youngest sister, Beatrice, was the first wife of Charles I of Naples.

2. Nothing is said about how the money was acquired. She may have held lands in her own right, so that the money had come from imposts, regularly or irregularly levied upon her Jews. The same is true of another Marguerite, second wife and widow of Charles I of Naples, who received from Pope Boniface VIII a similar release from the burden upon her conscience on September 3, 1297 (see below), where the phrase used is *de quacumque illicita extorsione*. Other women whose consciences bothered them about money derived from Jews were Alice, Duchess of Brabant (see bull no. 15, above) and Mary, Queen of France, on two occasions (see bulls no. 81 and 91, below). Two queens of England were less conscience-stricken: Eleanore, wife of Henry III, mentioned above, surrounded herself with money-hungry relatives and thus aroused some hostility among the English. She at one time used the excuse of a ritual murder accusation to extort a huge sum from Aaron of York (cf. M. Adler, *Jews of Medieval England* [London,

1939], p. 136). Despite her reputation for piety and virtue, she did not apply to the pope to ease her conscience over her personal use of money gained through usury. Her daughter-in-law, wife of Edward I and likewise named Eleanore, sister of Alfonso X of Castile, aroused the ire of Archbishop John Peckham of Canterbury. The queen had made a practice of borrowing money from Jews and using it to buy up noble estates. The archbishop first wrote to her about the matter (cf. Martin, *Registrum*, vol. 2, pp. 619 f.), and, then, in a letter to the queen's confessor, December 13, 1286, he insisted that the queen's business dealings had created a scandal all over England (Martin, *Registrum*, vol. 3, p. 937). Cf. H. P. Stokes, "The Relationship between the Jews and the Royal Family of England in the 13th Century," *Transactions of JHSE* 8 (1918): 153–170, esp. 164 ff.

3. Since the crusade which Nicholas IV tried to organize after the fall of Acre in 1290 never materialized, Queen Marguerite may have kept the entire sum. [The first letter on the pious use of confiscated usuries may be that of Gregory IX to Louis IX in 1237; see *ChJ*, nos. 90–93.—KS]

68   1291

To the Bishop of Beauvais:

Nicholas IV instructs the Bishop of Beauvais to provide for Jewish converts to Christianity.

Bibliothèque Nationale, Fond Moreau 1233, fol. 90, no. 381.[1]

Ut Judaeis conversis faciat episcopus ac monasterium in vitae necessariis provideri.

Datum . . . anno quarto.

1. Only a brief description of this letter survives; but there is no reason to doubt its authenticity. A number of similar documents are given below in Grayzel, "Jewish References," pp. 315 f.; cf. above, under Urban IV, bull no. 20.

69   no date

To all the Christian faithful:

SICUT JUDAEIS . . . Following the example of his predecessors: Calixtus, Eusebius,[1] Alexander, Clement, Coelestine, Innocent,

Gregory, Nicholas, and Honorius,[2] the pope renews the Bull of Protection.

———

ASV, Armarium 31, 72, fol. 307v.
Grayzel, "Thirteenth Century Formulary," p. 65.[3]

Privilegium generale Judaeis ad instar predecessores concessum.

Dilectis in Christo filiis . . . fidelibus Christianis, etc.

SICUT JUDAEIS non debet esse . . .

Datum . . . ?

1. Eusebius is a copyist's error for Eugenius.

2. One must assume that, as usual, the names are given in chronological order, although several are omitted from the list. On this assumption, the last one would be Honorius IV, so that the one issuing this *Sicut* would be Nicholas IV; see bull no. 51, above, for other corroborating evidence.

3. The collections in the Armarium were evidently kept for future reference, probably to serve as models for bulls and letters by other popes; they therefore did not indicate the date when the original (exemplary) document was dispatched.

Boniface VIII

Benedict Gaetani, of a knightly family of Anagni and a nephew on the maternal side of Pope Alexander IV, took the name of Boniface VIII. He was not the immediate successor of Nicholas IV. Two years of wrangling among the cardinals had followed the death of Nicholas IV, and the delay scandalized all Christendom. In desperation, the cardinals went outside their own number and elected Peter the Anchorite, despite his reluctance to give up his hermit's life. He ascended the papal throne under the name of Celestine V, but on December 13, 1294, after six painful months, he took the unprecedented step of resigning. The next day, the cardinals elected Gaetani, the most able of their number, who was also the most contentious. Boniface VIII was handsome and intellectually gifted, but he was also haughty and quarrelsome (cf. Gregorovius, *City of Rome,* vol. 5, pt. 2, pp. 516–597, especially 596 f.). His attempt to restore the papacy to the status it had enjoyed at the beginning of the century ended in the tragedy of Anagni, where he was insulted and humiliated by the emissary of Philip the Fair of France. Boniface died soon thereafter, on October 11, 1303. (See B. Tierney, *The Crisis of Church and State* [Englewood Cliffs, N.J., 1964], pp. 172–192.)

70   no date

Boniface's official entrance into Rome was magnificently celebrated on January 23, 1295. It was later described in verse by Cardinal Jacobus, namely, Thomasius Gaietanus of Anagni, a member of the Pope's family (L. A. Muratori, *Rerum Italicarum scriptores* [Milan, 1723–1751], vol. 3, pt. 1, pp. 650 ff.). Stanza XII of this adulatory description portrays the first official meeting between the new pope and a delegation of Roman Jews. A note by Muratori quotes an older book of papal ceremonies which describes the scene in less flowery language (Muratori, *Scriptores,* p. 653, n. 15): When the pope reached Mons Jordanus [a square not far from the streets inhabited by the Jews of Rome], the Jews came to meet him. Kneeling, they extended a Law [that is, a scroll of the Torah] to the pope, while chanting its praise in Hebrew and urging the pope to revere it. Having heard them, the pope responded with the following sentiment: "The Holy Law, O Hebrew men, we praise and revere, since it was given to your fathers by Almighty God, by the hand of Moses. Your observance [of it], however, and foolish interpretation we condemn and reject (*damnamus atque improbamus*). For the Apostolic Faith teaches and preaches that the Savior, whom you vainly still expect, our Lord Jesus Christ, has already come and, with the Father and the Holy Ghost, lives and reigns as God everywhere and forever and ever."

Muratori and his source say nothing about how this scroll was returned to the Jews or even whether it was returned. He does say that others like it may still be seen in the Vatican Library.

CAPUT III.

Reliquae dictae Processionis et solennitatis ceremoniae.

CAP. X.

Sic igitur vadens, redimitus tempora Regno,
Summus Apex, propriam signabat acumine dextrae
Devotamque sibi cupidamque invisere plebem;
Quae laudes exclamat Hero, quae et vivere longum
245. Optat. At incluso sibimet condicere Praesul
Posset, dum metuit summae fastigia molis,
Causa laboris honos, timor intus, gloria pulsans
Deforis: ac thalamo sublimis in aethera Petri
Quisque preest, paveat; vix tam sub turbine vita
250. Expedit. O quam orbis durum est disponere habenas!
Haec dum Pastor agit; Senior Levita Priorque,
[Et conjunctus ei Proto camerarius, istic]
Effigies ubi sacra manet, protractaque tandem
Cernitur, aspectu rutilans a numine divo
255. Effigies; vacuas gestantes pollice ferlas,
Diffusas repetunt acies, illasque recursant
Saepius; et legem statuunt, ne forte vagentur
Immemores, redeuntque sua consistere scala.

CAP. XI.

Hoc illi: verum populus lustraverat Urbem
260. Arcubus, in morem veterem, qua tendere mos est,
Atque frequens Patrem currens stipabat euntem:
In quem jactus erat validae per cuncta monetae.
Sive auri, seu forte nitens argentea stridat,
Consulibus quondam licuit dispergere passim

265. Quodque genus nummi, vetitum nunc temporis aurum
Jactari in vulgus: tenet haec insignia Princeps.
Instaurat populus varios ad lucida ludos,
Atque secans animos studia in contraria plebes
Pascitur obtutu. Juvenum pars pascitur amplas
270. Excerpsisse manu faleras, pars altera pubes
Infremit alispedum nudari vestibus ancas,
Purpureasque dolet fronti decedere vittas:
Pars laudes, pars gliscit opes, pars ludere campo
Certat, et obliquas effringere cursibus hastas.
275. Pars stupet insuetas senii succrescere pompas
Spem praeter: sic fracta dies, mirata vetustum
Tempus, ut extollat compellitur invida praesens.
Occurrunt ad festa viri, vexilla ferentes
Ecclesiae, de sorte Dei qui nomine Clerus
Dicitur, in partes varias redolentia thura
280. Obtulit: oblata suscepit, sumptaque in ignes
Intulit, atque focis signatis pectore fumum
Accepit; psallente choro, dum flexilis unda
Arrigitur fumi, spiratque vaporibus ignis.

CAP. XII.

285. Ecce super Tibrim positum de marmore Pontem
Transierat, provectus equo; turrique relicta
De Campo, Judaea canens, quae caecula corda est,
Occurrit vaesana Duci, Parione sub ipso
Quae Christo gravidam legem plenamque sub umbra
290. Exhibuit Moysi. Veneratus et ille figuram,
Hanc post terga dedit, cauto sermone locutus:
Ignotus Judaea Deus, tibi cognitus olim;
Qui quondam populus, nunc hostis; qui Deus et Rex
Obnubi patitur, praesentem temnere mavis,
295. Quem fragilem reputas hominem sperasque futurum;
Et latet ipse Deus. Gentes accedere norunt,
Tu fugis: in propria venientem pellere faeva
Non metuis: roseum pro te pius ecce cruorem
Fudit humi, quem dira necas, et credere stulta
300. Detrectas: moritura ruis, quia nescia sensus:
Sed redeas, miserante Deo, dum Christus in ara,
Filius et Verbum Patris, de Lumine Lumen,
Nostra salus, tensis manibus sub stipite pendet:
Tempus erit quo justa dabit, meritumque laboris
305. Judicio reddet, Judex super aethera vivus.

CAP. XIII.

Hos linquens, qua et Sacra via est, qua templa coluntur
Marci, quaque ferox juvenisque Adrianus in armis,
Romulei qua templa jacent, celsusque Colossus,
Quaque pius colitur Clemens, qui dexter eunti est,
310. Progrediens Princeps, Lateranum Summus in Orbe
Appulit; haud frigium, Mitram sed vertice gestans,
Pondere confectus nimio. Tunc Coetus ovantum
Ac si sesta Patris caperent exordia, pompas
Ostentant, ludosque novant, clanguntque tubarum
315. Aera, repercusso laterum per concava flatu.
At litui stridere vices, et cymbala strident:
Tympana congeminant sonitum, nec verbere tunsa
Discunt ferre gradum, tibi sed cornubia substant

MURATORI'S NOTE:

Rem totam sic notat vetus Pontificale, Cum Pontifex venerit at Montem
Jordani, Judaei illi obviam veniunt, genuflexi Legem Pontifici offerunt,
lingua Haebraica legem laudant, et hortantur Pontificem ut illam
veneretur. Pontifex vero illis auditis in hanc sententiam respondet:
Sanctam Legem, viri Hebraei, et laudamus et veneramur, utpote quae ab
omnipotenti Deo per manus Moysi patribus vestris tradita est: observantiam vero vestram, et vanam interpretationem damnamus atque
improbamus, quia Salvatorem, quem adhuc frustra expectatis, Apostolica fides jam pridem advenisse docet et praedicat, D. N. Jesum
Christum, qui cum Patre et Spiritu Sancto vivit et regnat Deus, per
omnia saecula saeculorum. Sed quia non numquam accidit ut Judaei
populi multitudine opprimantur, solent aliquando obtinere pro eorum
securitate, ut id faciant super antemurale arcis S. Angeli, in angulo, ad
viam, qua itur ad Palatium. Dicunt autem qui viderunt offerre ipsos
Legem, non descriptam in libris foliatim percurrendis, sed in continuis
unius membranae voluminibus, antiquo veterum more, qualia etiam
nonnulla videre est in Bibliotheca Vaticana.

71   July 17, 1295

To the Bishop of Paris:[1]

PETITIO DILECTI FILII . . . Pope Boniface tells of a petition submitted
to him by Raynerius Flamingus, a citizen of Paris, which tells the

story of a miracle involving a holy wafer.[2] Some Jews had pierced the wafer with a knife and then put it in furiously boiling water, whereupon the water miraculously turned into blood. The petitioner would like to build a chapel on the spot where the miracle occurred and support it out of his own funds; he and his heirs should then be permitted to exercise the right of patronage[3] over it. The pope praises Raynerius for his zeal and orders the bishop of Paris to let him establish the chapel, if the property where the miracle occurred belongs to him, or as soon as he acquires it. He and his heirs may then enjoy the right of patronage in perpetuity.

Reg. Vat. 47, fols. 102v–103r, no. 441.

Potthast, no. 24139.

D. Michel Felibien, *Histoire de la Ville de Paris* (Paris, 1725), vol. 3, pp. 296 f.

G. Digard et al., eds., *Les registres de Boniface VIII* (Paris, 1904–1939), col. 156, no. 441.

Venerabili fratri . . . episcopo Parisiensi salutem, etc.

PETITIO DILECTI FILII Raynerii Flamingi civis Parisiensis nobis exhibita continebat, quod ipse in illo loco civitatis Parisiensis in quo quidam Judaei inventam venerandam Eucharistiam cultello pungentes eam in ferventi aqua calidariae igni superpositae immiserunt, quae quidem aqua divino miraculo in sanguinem noscitur fuisse conversa quandam capellam affectat honorem Domini nostri Jesu Christi construere, ac ei de bonis propriis sufficientes redditus assignare, de quibus capellanus in ea perpetuo serviturus commode valeat sustentari, jure patronatus sibi et suis haeredibus in capella ipsa retento. Quare idem civis nobis humiliter supplicavit ut apostolici favoris sibi praesidium impertire, per quod huiusmodi suum votum adimplere valeat, dignaremur. Nos igitur ipsius civis laudabile in hoc parte propositum commendantes, ac de tua circumspectione plenam in Domino fiduciam obtinentes, fraternitati tuae per apostolica scripta mandamus quatenus praefato civi capellam ipsam in loco praedicto construendi, si locus ipse ad eum civem pertineat, alioquin postquam illum juste acquisierit dummodo quod offert haeredibus ac successoribus in perpetuo reservato.

Datum Anagnie, xvi kal. Augusti, anno primo.

---

1. The bishop of Paris in 1295 was Simon Matifas de Bucy (1290–1304), a Doctor of Laws.

2. Reports of the miracle differ. Raynaldus (Annales Ecclesiastici, *a.a.* 1290, no. 54) tells of a Christian woman who had pawned some of her clothing with a

Jew. He offered to return the pledge to her if she would bring him a consecrated wafer. At communion on Easter Sunday, the woman took the wafer in her mouth, but did not swallow it. When the Jew received it, he put it in boiling water, pierced it with a sword, and then put it into icy water, where it turned red. Christians entering the house saw what was going on. The *Recueil des Historiens des Gaules et de la France,* ed. M. Bouquet et al. (Paris, 1737-1904), contains a number of accounts. The "Chronique de St. Denis," (Bouquet, *Historiens,* vol. 20, p. 658) gives the date of the miracle as 1291; two anonymous chronicles (Bouquet, *Historiens,* vol. 21, pp. 127 and 132) give it as 1289 and 1291; while a fourth, (Bouquet, *Historiens,* vol. 22, pp. 32-33) gives it as 1290. Each one of them adds details that enhance the miracle. The fourth chronicle speaks of bystanders, including the Jew's wife and child, who promptly converted to Christianity. *MGH, Scriptores* (vol. 25, p. 578), offers a document solicited by a Jew named John from the administrator of the Paris diocese in which the story is told; John claims to have been an eyewitness to the miracle, whereupon he became a convert.

The chapel built by Raynerius soon became famous and popular for pilgrimages under the name of *Chapelle des Bilettes.* A few years later even Philip IV contributed to its upkeep (for his attitude to the Host desecration itself, see Saige, *Languedoc,* 235-236). At its dedication, a procession took place in which the wafer was carried through the streets of Paris. At first this was an annual event, although evidence from the fifteenth century shows the procession had gradually come to take place less frequently. By then, of course, there were no Jews in Paris.

The late Father Peter Browe discussed the subject of Host Desecration by Jews in two highly informative essays: "Die Eucharistenwunder des Mittelalters," in *Breslauer Studien zur historischen Theologie,* n.s., 4 (1938): 128-139, 162-165; and at greater length in "Die Hostienschändungen der Juden im Mittelalter," in *Römische Quartalschrift* 34 (1926): 167-197. He points out that, until this accusation of 1290, the references to such events were few and led to no anti-Jewish outbursts among the Christians. After 1290, however, the accusations became numerous and often led to widespread rioting and forced conversions. In the latter article (pp. 173-175) Browe lists about fifty such accusations between 1230 and 1566. There were thirty incidents between 1290 and the end of the fourteenth century, of which fifteen ended in the death of many more than those presumed guilty; in the fifteenth century there were ten incidents, six of which ended in rioting. Browe concludes that the accusation was false; and yet, great scholar that he was, he could not believe that so many accusations could have all been unfounded: *Unmöglich können all diese Vorwürfe nur hasserfüllte Verleumdungen sein.*

Father Browe's discussion in *Römische Quartalschrift* lists five occurrences of charges of Host desecration by Jews which antedated the one in Paris. He himself indicates doubt about the first one, that in Trani in southern Italy in 1220. The one in Santarem, Portugal, in 1266, mentioned by Brandão, *Monarchia Lusytana,* vol. 4, p. 226, is too vague to be accepted without further investigation. The remaining incidents are supposed to have taken place in Germany. They are discussed by Hans Lichtenstein, "Der Vorwurf der Hostienschändung und das erste Auftreten der Juden in der Mark Brandenburg," in *Zeitschrift für die Geschichte der Juden in Deutschland* 4 (1932): 189-197. He finds that each incident is dated before the moment when Jews first settled in the place where it reputedly occurred. The desecration reports, too, with all their lurid details, date from at least a century after the presumed events. Thus, the report from Brandenburg of 1287, accompanied by fourteen woodcuts, dates from the sixteenth century (cf. Lichtenstein, "Hostienschändung," p. 192, n. 17).

After the 1290 accusation in Paris, Browe points out, the charge of Host desecration became as frequent as the blood accusation and stories about Jews desecrating images of the Madonna. As for the miraculous blood, this present letter of Pope Boniface expresses no doubts about that. Pope Clement V, in a letter of June 1, 1310 (*Licet eis; Regestum Clementis Papae V*, no. 6046), granting an indulgence to visitors of St. Basil's church in Bruges, spoke of a quantity of the Savior's blood guarded in that church which remained as hard as a rock all week but became fluid on Friday afternoons: *in ecclesia s. Basilii de Brugis, Tornacen. diocesis . . . existit non modica quantitas sacratissimi sanguinis pretiosissimi Corporis humani generis Redemptoris . . . qui per omnes dies ebdogmade, die veneris dumtaxat excepta, quasi quandam in modum lapidis duritie (sic) representat, die vero predicto ut plurimum hora sexta liquiescit, guttatimque distilllat.* The idea of miracle-working blood was thus accepted without question, [as it still is today in connection with the congealed blood of St. Gennaro in Naples, which melts yearly on his feast day.—KS]

[The only question remaining unanswered here is why Boniface VIII accepted the Paris Host story as true. Or did he? The letter contains none of the boiling anger that marks those papal texts that charge Jews with offending Christianity. Its tone is matter of fact, and there is no hint that another letter exists castigating the Jews, etc. Did Boniface know that people simply believed in the miracle? If so, he might as well make the most of it and allow a new chapel to be built. There is, furthermore, no report of an attack on the Jews in the wake of the alleged desecration. Such an attack might have made the pope hesitate before effectively certifying that the miracle took place. In the absence of an attack, Boniface presumably had no need for restraint. Still, none of this is terribly convincing, and we must, for the moment, simply raise questions with no satisfactory answers. Boniface's other letters concerning Jews supply no clues either.—KS]

3. The right of patronage involved the privilege of having a say in the appointment of the chaplain.

72   August 31, 1295

To Magister Pavlinus of Aspalt, Canon of St. Paul of Treves:

CONQUESTI SUNT NOBIS . . . The heads of the Convent of the Holy Virgin Mary in Aldenburg, of the Premonstratensian Order, informed the pope that the Jewish inhabitants of Wetzlar, of the Diocese of Treves, had erected a new synagogue within the parish of the convent, despite the fact that this is prejudicial to the interests of the prior . . . and the convent, and contrary to canon law.[1] If this is so, the pope concludes, the said Jews must be compelled, on pain of a boycott by the faithful, to make amends for this injury. Witnesses must not be permitted to refuse testimony because of gratitude or fear or hate. But no one may, by authority of this letter, be dragged before a judge outside his city or diocese, nor may any other proceedings be undertaken against him.[2]

Potthast, no. 24175.

V. F. de Gudenus, ed., *Codex diplomaticus . . . res Moguntinas* (Frankfort, 1747), vol. 2, pp. 286 f., no. 232.

Bonifatius Episcopus Servus servorum Dei. Dilecto filio Magistro Pavlino de Aspalt. Canonico ecclesie Sci Paulini Treverensis, salutem et Apostolicam benedictionem.

CONQUESTI SUNT NOBIS . . . Prior . . . Magistra et Conventus Monasterii Sce Marie Virginis in Aldenburg, per Priorem et Magistram soliti gubernari, Premonstrat. Ordinis, quod Iudei habitantes in Wetflaria, Trever. dioc. quandam Sinagogam in Parochia dicti monasterii edificaverunt de novo, contra canonicas Sanctiones, in dictorum Prioris . . . ac Conventus preiudicium et gravamen. Ideoque Discretioni tue per apostolica scripta mandamus, quatinus, si est ita, dictos Iudeos, quod ab huiusmodi iniuriis penitus conquiescant, monicione premissa per subtractionem communionis Fidelium, appellatione remota compellas. Testes autem qui fuerint nominati, si se gratia, odio vel timore subtraxerint, per Censuram ecclesiasticam, appellatione cessante, compellas veritati testimonium perhibere. Proviso, ne aliquis extra suam Civitatem et Diocesim, auctoritate presencium ad Iudicium evocetur, vel procedatur in aliquo contra cum.

Datum Anagnie, ii kal. Septembris, anno primo.

1. The canons referred to are X.5,6,3 and X.5,6,7. A parallel to this bull is that of Gregory IX to the Abbot of St. Emmeran in Regensburg, on March 31, 1227 (*ChJ*, pp. 178–179, no. 57). One must assume that in Wetzlar, as was probably the case in Regensburg, the synagogue was erected with the consent of the local authorities. If so, it is strange that the convent had not protested earlier. Nor is it clear how the existence of the synagogue injured the convent, since it was not built on land belonging to the convent, but only in its diocese. It is noteworthy that the pope did not suggest the confiscation of the land, as at Regensburg, or the destruction of the synagogue, [unless, of course, the complaint was against excessive noise only. Necessity demanded the concession of the new synagogue itself. Such excessive noise was, indeed, prohibited by long use; cf., the 1299 letter of Philip IV (Saige, "Languedoc," p. 295, no. 20) where the king links new synagogues and excessive noise in one complaint.—KS]

2. The warning against dragging witnesses before distant jurisdictions or making other difficulties for them should be borne in mind in connection with the bull *Exhibita nobis,* no. 75, below, as well as the text of Nicholas IV, no. 62, above. [It does not, however, seem to concern Jews here, whether they were witnesses or defendants; nor does it refer to the Inquisition.—KS]

73 September 3, 1297

To Marguerite,[1] widow of King Charles of Sicily:

PIUM ARBITRAMUR . . . Boniface VIII grants the queen permission to choose a confessor who will absolve her from the sin of having extorted money from the Jews of her territory[2] and from other people whom she can no longer identify—provided that, under the advice and guidance of this confessor, she uses the money for sustaining the feeble and the poor.[3] The pope further absolves her from any decree of excommunication imposed upon her by the late bishop of Le Mans[4] or by any other ecclesiastical judge.

Reg. Vat. 48, fol. 314r, no. 452a.
Digard, *Registres,* no. 2120.

Carissime in Christo filie Margarete regine Sicilie illustri vidue relicte clare memorie C. regis Sicilie.

PIUM ARBITRAMUR et congruum ut in hiis prompti simus ad gratiam que salutem respiciunt animarum presertim circa sublimes personas que pura fide conspicue deo et ecclesie sunt devote. Tuis itaque supplicationibus favorabiliter annuentes auctoritate tibi presentium indulgemus ut liceat tibi aliquem idoneum presbyterum in tuum eligere confessorem qui audita confessione tua de quacumque illicita extorsione pecunias a iudaeis terrarum tuarum vel quibuscumque aliis personis de quibus memoriam non habueris dummodo huiusmodi extortas pecunias in refectionem et sustentionem infirmorum et pauperum iuxta consilium et mandatum confessoris electi converti feceris, etiam juxta formam ecclesie ab omnibus excommunicationum in te sententiis sique per bone memorie cenomanensem episcopum vel quemlibet alium iudicem ordinarium in te fuerit promulgate . . . salutarem penitentiam et absolutionis beneficium a culpa et pena auctoritate nostra impendere valeat in te . . .

Datum . . . iii non. Septembris, anno tertio.[5]

1. Marguerite of Burgundy (1248-1308) was the daughter of Odo, count of Nevers, and therefore granddaughter of Hugh IV, duke of Burgundy. She was the second wife of Charles I of Sicily, whom she married in 1268.

2. Since it was the bishop of Le Mans (*Cunomanum*) who had excommunicated her, the money in question must have been extorted from Jews living in France. Money of Jewish origin was always suspect of having been gained through usury, and it had to be returned to the original borrowers, if they could be found, or put to "pious uses" (cf. "De Regimine Judaeorum," in *Thomas Aquinas, Writings*, ed. d'Entrèves, p. 87). Perhaps the more immediate cause of the need for absolution was the other extortionist activity of the queen, in this case from "other persons," presumably Christians. For similar instances of noble ladies seeking relief from the popes in money matters, see, e.g., above, bull no. 67, n. 2.

3. The very next letter in Reg. Vat. 48 is also addressed to Marguerite. Boniface expresses his pleasure over a hospital and chapel that she was building at her own expense. For her other queenly benefactions, all in France, also aimed at softening the decree against her, cf. *Registres*, nos. 2121-2123.

4. The bishop of Le Mans from 1279 to 1293 was Johannes de Chanlaio.

5. The year is missing. The document immediately preceeding in the Reg. Vat. is dated *apud Urbem Veterem, iii non. Septembris, anno tertio (1297)*.

74   February 17, 1299

To the Bishop[1] and Chapter of Pamiers[2] and to Roger, Count of Foix:

EA QUE JUDICIO . . . Pope Boniface confirms an agreement between the ecclesiastical and secular rulers of Pamiers. One of its sections stipulated an equal division of income derived from ovens, mills, banks, Jews, markets, and courts.

Reg. Vat. 49, fol. 140.
Potthast, no. 24786.
Digard, *Registres*, col. 331, no. 2907.
Gallia Christiana, (Nova), ed. D. de Sainte-Marthe et al., (Paris, 1715-1865), vol. 13, *Instrumenta*, cols. 103-106.

Venerabili fratri . . . episcopo et dilectis filiis capitulo Appamiarum, ac nobili viro Rogerio, comiti Fuxi, Appamiarum diocesis.

EA QUE JUDICIO vel concordia terminantur firma debent et illibata persistere et, ne in recidive contentionis scrupulum relabantur, Apostolico convenit presidio communiri. Sane petitio vestra nobis exhibita continebat quod, cum olim inter vos, frater episcope et filii capitulum, ex parte una, et te, fili comes, ex altera, super temporali jurisdictione civitatis Appamiarum, et civitate ipsa ejusque pertinentiis, et quibusdam aliis diversis articulis orta fuisset materia questionis, demum, mediante dilecto filio nobili viro Guidone de Levis, domino de Mirapesce, talis inter vos amicabilis compositio, si ad id nostrum beneplacitum et assensus accederent, intervenit, videlicet quod tu, predicte comes, tuique successores et posteri castrum civitatis ejusdem habeatis et teneatis, quod cum munitionibus dicte civitatis expensis propriis teneamini fideliter custodire, tuque, prefate episcope, habeas et teneas quandam turrim imperpetuum magnam et fortissimam cum suis edificiis et pertinentiis, ibidem de novo constructam per te, comes memorate; et quod merum et mixtum imperium, et omnimoda ordinaria jurisdictio, et eorum exercitium, ac omnes proventus et redditus civitatis ejusdem, provenientes ratione furnorum, molendinorum, bancorum, judeorum, leude, curie, omnes incursus rerum mobilium et immobilium, temporalium tamen, et bona vacantia dicte civitatis et ejus territorii quoquomodo evenientia, et omnes justitie pecuniarie sexaginta solidorum Tholosanorum et septem solidorum et quecumque alie, sive majores fuerint sive minores.

Datum Laterani, xiii kal. Martii, anno quinto.

1. Bernardus; he was the first bishop of the newly constituted diocese. The monastery of St. Anthony became the first cathedral. In a real sense, therefore, the bishop now took over the negotiations referred to in bull no. 14, above, dated Nov. 24, 1262.

2. An active Jewish community existed in Pamiers throughout the thirteenth century. Its continuous relations with other communities in the Provence and the interest in the local Jews on the part of the inquisitor of the district are evident from several references in Richard W. Emery, *The Jews of Perpignan* (New York, 1959), *passim;* in a document given by J. Blanchet in "Les Juifs à Pamiers en 1256," in *REJ* 18 (1889): 139–141; and in a number of documents listed by Robert in "Catalogue," p. 223, nos. 87 and 88, which date from about the time of this bull. Cf. also *ChJ*, p. 77, n. 6, where an excerpt is given from a document issued by the inquisitor of Pamiers, Arnold Dejean, promising that *non enim intendimus vobis facere aliquas graves et insolitas novitates.* This text is cited in full in Grayzel, "Popes, Jews and the Inquisition," p. 43, above, n. 129. Pope Clement V reaffirmed this principle, although not with reference to Jews, on November 23, 1308 (cf. *Regestum Clementis Papae V,* anno IV, no. 5021).

75   June 13, 1299

To the Jews in the City of Rome:[1] may they recognize the truth of the Catholic Faith.[2]

EXHIBITA PRO PARTE . . . The attention of Boniface VIII had been called to a serious complaint made by the Jews.[3] The pope had recently ordered that, in cases involving heresy, the names of the accusers and the witnesses be made known, as in a normal trial, unless the investigation involved persons of great power. Nevertheless, when inquisitors were authorized to proceed against Jews, they regularly denominated Jewish defendants as powerful persons and refused to make public the names of the witnesses against them. Thus they stripped these Jews of their proper rights of protection and made it possible to unjustly harm Jews obedient to the popes. The pope, however, recognizing the weakness of the Jews and numbering them among the powerless, even if they sometimes possess great wealth, indicates that the inquisitors are henceforth to consider Jews weak (*tanquam impotentibus*). In those cases in which the Inquisition may legitimately act against them, Jews are to be informed of the names of those who accuse them or testify against them, except in such instances where the power of the Jew concerned is common knowledge. If doubt exists, and the names are not made public, the inquisitorial proceeding must halt pending the findings of the Apostolic See.

Reg. Vat. 49, fol. 175v.

Digard, *Registres*, vol. 2, col. 412, no. 3063.

Vidal, *Bullaire*, nos. 269–270 (which preserves the text as reissued by Gregory XI on June 1, 1372, and is the document reproduced below from Reg. Aven. 185, fol. 431).

Universis et singulis Iudeis in civitate nostra Avenionen. constitutis, catholice fidei cognoscere veritatem.—Dudum fel. rec. Bonifacius papa VIII predecessor noster ex certis causis motus universis et singulis Iudeis in comitatu Venayssini constitutis quoddam privilegium per suas certi tenoris litteras concessit, cuius privilegii tenor sequitur in hec verba:

Bonifacius episcopus, servus servorum Dei, universis et singulis Iudeis de comitatu Venayssini ubilibet constitutis, catholice fidei cognoscere veritatem.

EXHIBITA PRO PARTE vestra non sine gravi querela petitio continebat, quod licet nos nuper inter cetera statuerimus ut, cessante periculo quod propter potentiam personarum contra quas inquiritur super heretica pravitate, testibus in inquisitionis huiusmodi causa receptis et accusatoribus etiam imminere posset, eisdem personis eorumdem testium et accusatorum nomina, prout in aliis fit iudiciis, publicentur, inquisitores tamen pravitatis eiusdem in casibus in quibus contra vos auctoritate apostolice Sedis ad inquirendum descendunt, vos asserentes potentes, publicationem huiusmodi vobis aliquando facere denegant; sicque vobis ex hoc debite deffensionis facultas subtrahitur et vos odientibus iniuste nocendi materia preparatur. Nos autem considerantes imbecillitatem vestram et propterea vos etiam si divitiis habundetis impotentum numero ascribentes, volumus ut tanquam impotentibus predicti inquisitores in casibus in quibus contra vos possunt eadem auctoritate inquirere vobis predictam publicationem faciant nec potentiam ad eam denegandam pretendant nisi adeo de potentia illius contra quem in dictis casibus inquiretur esset notorium quod non posset quin esset potens aliqua tergiversatione celari vel per negationem in dubium revocari. Quod si super huiusmodi potentia dubietas oriatur, precipimus ut per inquisitores non facta vobis publicatione iamdicta, ad ulteriora minime procedatur antequam id dicte Sedi refferant et responsionem obtineant ab eadem; decernentes irritum et inane si secus super hiis contigerit attemptari. Nulli ergo [etc.].

Datum Anagnie, nonis iulii, pontificatus nostri anno quinto.

Nos igitur ex similibus causis moti pariter et inducti privilegium ipsum ad vos et vestrum singulos auctoritate apostolica extendimus, vobisque nichilominus concedimus per presentes quod privilegio ipso perinde a data presentium gaudere et uti possitis ac si vobis universis et singulis per dictum Bonifacium, predecessorem, specialiter et expresse concessum extitisset. Nulli ergo [etc.].

Datum Anagnie, id. Junii, anno quinto.

1. The same bull was extended to the Jews of the Comtat Venaissin on July 7, 1299: cf. Digard, *Registres*, no. 3215; Reg. Vat. 49, fol. 212r; see Laborde, *Layettes*, vol. 3, nos. 4112 and 4221, for earlier legislation concerning the Inquisition and powerful persons.

2. *Catholice fidei agnoscere veritatem* was used when Jews were addressed directly, in place of the usual *salutem et apostolicam benedictionem* for Christians. Honorius III employed a somewhat different wording when addressing Isaac Beneveniste, on August 26, 1220 (cf. *ChJ*, pp. 152–155, no. 41). There may also be a connection between this brief salutation and the longer statement made by Nicholas IV at the beginning of the bull *Orat mater*, of January 30, 1291, addressing the Papal Vicar of Rome regarding the troubles the Jews of the city were then experiencing: *pro subducendo velamine de cordibus Judaeorum ut de ipsorum oculis squamis cecitatis eductis Christum illuminati agnoscant.* [Still, in this period the phrase is formulaic, not programmatic, as it became later.—KS]

3. VR, vol. 1, pp. 255–257, makes the plausible connection between this bull and the martyrdom of Elia de Pomis, which they date in July 1298. The inquisitors

had apparently leveled a charge against the entire Jewish community; they may have accused its Jews of blasphemy, or, perhaps, of siding with the Colonna family, with whom the pope was then at war. Declaring the Jews "powerful persons," the inquisitors withheld the names of the accusers. Elia de Pomis, foremost religious personality among the Roman Jews, took all the blame upon himself and died at the stake (cf. *Kobez al Yad,* vol. 4, pp. 30–33). So VR.

76   June 5, 1300

To the Bishops, Clerics, Nobility and all Inhabitants of the Comtat Venaissin:

SICUT AD NOSTRUM . . . Boniface VIII reassures the inhabitants of the Comtat Venaissin that as long as they are ready to answer a lawsuit before the local authorities, they cannot be dragged before distant courts by persons who have no specific authorization to do so.[1] He does not, however, (if the version we have is correct[2]), want to extend the same privilege to the Jewish inhabitants of the Comtat.[3]

Reg. Vat. 49, fols. 309v–310.
Digard, *Registres,* no. 3618.

Venerabilibus fratribus episcopis et dilectis filiis clericis et religiosis, nobilibus viris, baronibus, comunitatibus quoque, ac hominibus universis habitatoribus comitatus Venaysini, ad Romanam Ecclesiam pleno jure spectantis.

SICUT AD NOSTRUM pervenit auditum, nonnulli clerici et laici vos coram diversis judicibus per litteras Apostolicas faciunt ad judicium evocari, et fatigant plerisque laboribus et expensis, quanquam ordinarii vestri super causis ad eorum forum spectantibus, ac rector comitatus Venaysini per Sedem Apostolicam deputatus, super hiis que ad jurisdictionem suam pertinent, de vobis parati existant cuilibet conquerenti exhibere justitie complementum. Nos igitur, quieti vestre ne taliter impetamini providere volentes, vobis auctoritate presentium indulgemus ut, quamdiu coram dictis ordinariis et rectore ac suis officialibus parati fueritis, ut premittitur, stare juri, per hujusmodi litteras impetratas, quarum auctoritate nullus habitus est processus, et etiam impetrandas, que de presentibus non fecerint mentionem, super premissis molestari ab aliquibus nullatenus valeatis. Nos enim excommunicationis, suspensionis et interdicti sententias, ac quicquid contra hujusmodi indulti nostri tenorem, in vos

comuniter, seu aliquos vel aliquem vestrum, ab aliquo contigerit pro-
mulgari decernimus non tenere. Ad Judeos autem, habitatores ipsius
comitatus, quique in posterum ibi elegerint incolatum, nolumus quod
indultum hujusmodi aliquatenus extendatur. Nulli ergo, et cetera. Nostri
indulti, et cetera.

Datum Anagnie, non. Julii, anno sexto.

1. Cf. the bull on the same subject by Nicholas IV on November 5, 1290, (no. 62,
above). There the Jews are specifically protected.

2. The bull *Cum sicut,* which follows here and which was issued on the same
day, may shed some light on this change of papal policy toward the Jews of the
Comtat. It seems clear that the exclusion of the Jews stemmed from an anti-
Jewish ferment in the Christian population. [In fact, after comparing this clause
with its counterpart in bull no. 62, above, as well as with the text of John XXII
(no. II, p. 303, below), suspicion about its accuracy must arise. The wording in all
three cases is nearly identical. If *"nolumus"* here were read as *"volumus,"* it
would be thoroughly identical. Given papal policy as a whole and especially as in
bull no. 75, above, there is every reason to assume that *"volumus"* is correct. The
error is a simple scribal one. Moreover, "aliquatenus" does not make sense with
"nolumus." There is no need to explain a sudden reversal of policy; it did not
occur.—KS]

3. The question naturally arises as to what an oppressive change of venue is. It
was eventually decided that there must be no more than a single day's journey. An
application, specifically mentioning a one-day journey appears in a letter of
Nicholas V (26 June, in year 2) to French inquisitors—*ultra unam dietam extra
civitatum seu diocesium.*

77   June 5, 1300

To the Rector of the Comtat Venaissin:

CUM SICUT . . . The communities of the Comtat had complained to
the pope that Christian[1] aliens newly settled in the Comtat, as well as
many Jews, were taking usury, which was harmful to the old
residents of the province. The pope therefore orders the rector to
expel these recently arrived usurers, Jews included, and prohibits
him from admitting usurers in the future.[2]

Reg. Vat. 49, fol. 310.
Digard, *Registres,* no. 3621.

. . . Rectori comitatus Venaysini, ad Romanam Ecclesiam pleno jure spectantis.

CUM SICUT ex parte dilectorum filiorum comunitatum terrarum comitatus Venaysini, ad Romanam Ecclesiam pleno jure spectantis, fuit expositum coram nobis quod multi Christiani in eodem comitatu sint alienigene, usurarii manifesti, multique Judei, exercentes usuras, ex quibus comitatus ejusdem incolis multa dampna et rerum dispendia provenire noscuntur, nos, qui comitatum eundem affectione paterna prosequimur, nolentes ut incole prelibati, propter moram quam iidem usurarii et Judei contrahunt, supradicta dampna hujusmodi et dispendia patiantur, discretioni tue per Apostolica scripta mandamus quatinus hujusmodi alienigenas, et alios non oriundos de comitatu predicto, ac Judeos, pecuniam fenebrem exercentes publice aut exercere volentes, de predicto comitatu expellas, numquam aliquos tales in comitatu predicto de cetero admissurus.

Datum Anagnie, non. Junii, anno sexto.

1. The problem for the Church of Christians practicing usury was widespread. In 1296, Boniface VIII had written on the subject to the Province of Autun, in France (Digard, *Registres*, no. 937), and in April of the same year to Utrecht, in Holland. In the latter case he ordered that usurers be denied Christian burial (Digard, *Registres*, no. 1043). On June 20, 1303, he again addressed the problem in Avignon. *Not mentioning Jews*, he repeated his order to expel known usurers, especially those who were of foreign birth (*Circa statum*, June 20, 1303, Digard, *Registres*, no. 5246). The first order had apparently done little good.

2. The proposed expulsion of Jews did not apply to all Jews, but only to those who practiced usury. It is doubtful that even they were expelled. [In fact, the text may apply only to Jews newly arrived in the Comtat. Thus, Boniface was putting into practice the dictum first enunciated by Gregory X at the II Lyons Council of 1274 and just recently (1298) inserted into the *Liber Sextus* of the Canon Law by Boniface himself (*Sext.* 5,5,1 *usurarum*) prohibiting individuals from relocating for the express purpose of usury. The canon does not refer to Jews explicitly, but it was interpreted on occasion to apply to them. This interpretation of the present text resolves the problem of what otherwise would appear to be a large-scale papal expulsion. Nothing of the sort was intended. Rather, we have here an extension of the concept of "not immoderate usury." Just as there was to be a control on amounts, so there was to be a control on the number of lenders. This interpretation also makes the emendation suggested for bull no. 76 (above) more acceptable.—KS]

78   Before 1298

From the *Decretals* of Boniface VIII:[1]

"One must proceed against Christians who adopt or revert to the rites of the Jews, even if they were originally baptized as infants[2] or under fear of death—although they were not absolutely or precisely compelled to baptism[3]—as one would proceed against heretics who had confessed or been convicted on the testimony of Christians or Jews. One should proceed against abettors, receivers, and defenders of these people as one proceeds against abettors, receivers, and defenders of heretics."

Potthast, no. 25097.
Digard, *Registres*, no. 4424.
Sext. 5,2,13.

Contra Christianos, qui ad ritum transierint vel redierint Iudaeorum, etiamsi huiusmodi redeuntes, dum erant infantes, aut mortis metu, non tamen absolute aut praecise coacti, baptizati fuerunt, erit tanquam contra haereticos, si fuerint de hoc confessi, aut per Christianos seu Iudaeos convicti, et, sicut contra fautores, receptatores et defensores haereticorum, sic contra fautores, receptatores et defensores talium est procedendum.

1. This decretal in its original form (May 7, 1288)—cited here from the *Liber Sextus*, title *De hereticis*—is an instruction to inquisitors.

2. On the question of infant baptism, see bull no. 30, above.

3. On the meaning of compulsion in connection with baptism, cf. *ChJ*, pp. 13-15, and pp. 100-103, no. 12. Similarly, the *Turbato corde* bull, repeated five times in the course of this half century, was clearly premised on the definition made explicit in the present decretal. For further discussion, see Browe, *Judenmission*, pp. 258-260. [But especially see above, bull no. 30, n. 5, discussing this issue. The *Liber Sextus* was, then, merely formalizing in law the desire first expressed at the Fourth Toledan Council never to allow a baptism to be invalidated; it was too great an insult for the Church to bear. Still, cases of force continued to be treated on an individual basis, and not summarily either; cf. Grayzel, "The Confession of a Medieval Jewish Convert," *Historia Judaica* 17 (1955): 105-106 on one Solomon of Ondes in the 1320s, as well as the case of Baruch itself (Grayzel, "Confession," pp. 105-106). Jacques Fournier, the inquisitor, went to great pains to ascertain the circumstances of Baruch's baptism.

Clement V

Bertrand de Got, an influential figure at the French court, was elected pope on June 5, 1305, and was crowned at Lyons on November 14. He was not the immediate successor of Boniface VIII, who had died on October 11, 1303. In the interim, Benedict XI reigned from October 22, 1303, until his death shortly thereafter, on July 7, 1304. The length of the interregnum which followed and the ultimate choice of a Frenchman have been attributed to the political maneuvering of Philip the Fair (cf. G. Mollat, *The Popes at Avignon* [New York, 1963-1965], pp. 3-8). With Clement began the period popularly known as "The Babylonian Captivity of the Church." From 1305-1378, the popes resided outside Italy (from 1309 in Avignon), with the result that not only did the Church become temporarily subservient to the French, but also that further claims by the Church to supremacy over the medieval State would hold little weight.

79   July–August, 1305

To Philip, King of France:

[SANE NOBIS][1] . . . In response to the king's plea, Pope Clement excuses him for having forced financial contributions from the French Church, as well as from the Jews and the Lombards.[2] In explaining his actions, the king pointed to his dire need to bolster the falling value of the royal coinage. His defense requirements had compelled him to decrease the weight of his coins, which hurt both his own, as well as neighboring, peoples.

A. Grunzweig, "Les incidences internationales des mutations monetaires de Philippe le Bel," *Le Moyen Age* 59 (1953): 141 f.

SANE NOBIS exponere curasti quod dudum—expediens, immo necessarium visum fuit antiquas regias et predecessorum tuorum pro hujusmodi defensione intrinseca regni tui mutare monetas, quibus ex consilii tui deliberatione mutatis, alias diversis successive temporibus cudi fecisti, legitimis lege et pondere diminutis; e qua quidem diminutione non solum subditi tui, verum etiam circumadjacentium et aliarum undique populi regionum damna et deperdita gravia sunt perpessi.

Datum . . .[3]

1. This could not have been the incipit of the bull; it must have been the beginning of the exposé of Philip's plea. The actual bull is no longer extant. Grunzweig, "Incidences Internationales," reproduces an excerpt of a few lines which he found in Le Blanc, *Traité historique des monnoyes de France* (Amsterdam, 1690), pp. 212 f.

2. Cf. Siméon Luce, "Catalogue des documents du Trésor des Chartes relatifs aux Juifs sous le règne de Philippe le Bel," *REJ* 2 (1881): 31, no. XVIII, lists a royal order to the bailiffs to impose as high a contribution as possible on all known usurers. The order is dated Paris, August 19, 1303. This may have been what King Philip had in mind. If so, he was not asking, and the pope was not granting, absolution for his seizure of the money, but rather for his use of it. Broadly speaking, its use to alleviate the difficulties resulting from the devaluation could be interpreted as a "pious purpose." There was no connection between *this* extraordinary seizure of money from Jews and Lombards and the expulsion of the Jews from France in 1306. On the contrary, the documents collected by Luce indicate that until just prior to the expulsion, King Philip had nothing of the sort in mind. The decision to expel was made in haste and in light of the continuing precipitous fall in money values. Total seizure of Jewish-owned property was then decided upon. When that, too, proved insufficient to shore up royal coinage, the Templars were the next victims and their wealth was confiscated. See *SRH*, vol. 11, p. 217. See too, S. Schwarzfuchs, "The Expulsion of the Jews from France, 1306," *JQR Seventy-Fifth Anniversary Volume*, ed. A. Neuman (Philadelphia, 1967) pp. 482–490.

[Others have tried to explain the 1306 expulsion in terms of broader political and ideological issues. Kings had discovered a conflict of interests between their needs and the traditional privileges of Jews and others. Thus, the seizure of 1305 went beyond Jewish monies gained through usury. The king had also badgered the pope into validating a special tax on clergy, a matter which had once caused an explosion between Philip and Boniface VIII. The present tax on the Jews was also extraordinary, a break in their "good custom." It was the kind of tax which Thomas Aquinas had specifically argued against in *de regimine Judaeorum* (Aquinas, *Writings*, ed. d'Entrèves, p. 87). Bull no. 80, below, reflects a similar situation; and see the citation of Aquinas in n. 3 there.—KS]

3. Grunzweig, "Incidences Internationales," argues for a date between the latter part of July and early August, when the pope met the first embassy of the king at Bordeaux.

80   January 2, 1306

Addressee unknown:[1]

GRATA DEVOTIONIS OBSEQUIA . . . A noble landowner asked permission to retain money and property which he himself had unjustly[2] taken from the Jews who live on his lands. The pope grants the request; but he insists that this wealth be set aside for the needs of the poor.[3]

Bibl. Vaticana, *Ottobon. 2546*, fol. 12a.
Regestum Clementis Papae V, vol. 1, p. 205, no. 1139.

GRATA DEVOTIONIS OBSEQUIA . . . Hinc est quod Nos, tuis supplicationibus inclinati, auctoritate presentium tibi indulgemus ut, si minus juste a Judaeis in terra tua commorantibus aliqua hactenus exegeris bona et pecunie quantitates, ad earundem quantitatum et bonorum restitutionem cuiquam faciendam nullatenus tenearis dummodo bona et quantitates eadem in usu eriges pauperum.

Datum Lugduni, iv. non. Januarii, [anno primo].

1. The name is not given; he was clearly not royalty.

2. The money and property were apparently extorted over and above the customary taxes and imposts, perhaps on the excuse that it had been acquired through usury.

3. The poor here may, on a technicality, include those who had paid the Jews interest on loans. See the advice which Thomas Aquinas gave the Duchess of Brabant on this subject: "although the Jews have no right to retain the money they have extorted from others by usury, neither have you any right to retain it if you take it back from the Jews . . . . If they possess goods which they have extorted from others, it is your duty to restore them to those persons to whom the Jews are obliged to make restitution. So if you can find with certainty those of whom usury was extorted, you must make restitution to them . . ." *Aquinas, Writings*, ed. d'Entrèves, pp. 86–87; cf. the other texts of this nature, above and below.

81   January 3, 1306

To Mary, Queen of France:[1]

DEVOTIONIS TUAE . . . To ease the queen's conscience, the pope grants her the right to retain money taken[2] from the Jews of her territory, provided she assigns some[3] of that money for the support of the Holy Land.

Reg. Vat. 52, fol. 84r.
Regestum Clementis Papae V, vol. 1, no. 491.

Carissime in Christo filie Marie regine Francorum illustri.

DEVOTIONIS TUAE promeretur affectus ut que predepossis a nobis favorabiliter consequaris. Cum itaque ex parte tua fuit expositam coram nobis, tu ex eo habens conscientiam remordentem quod a nonnullis iudaeis de terris tuis quasdam pecuniarum summas tamquam de tuis propriis redditibus exegisti, Nos tuis supplicationibus inclinati summas huiusmodi sic exactas dummodo huiusmodi pecuniarum convertas in subsidium terre sancte prout conscientia tibi dictaverit portionem apostolica tibi auctoritate remittimus ad eandem conscientiam frenandam . . .

Datum Lugduni, iii non. Januarii, anno primo.

1. Mary of Brabant (1254-1321), widow of Philip III, whom she married as his second wife in 1275 (cf. *Biographie nationale . . . de Belgique* vol. 13, pp. 704-710). On December 5, 1308—after the expulsion from France—she presented a house and garden at Mantes, which used to belong to a Jew, to a valet of the king (cf. Siméon Luce, "Catalogue," p. 58, no. 72).

2. Whether the money was over and above the taxes agreed upon, it was still considered to have been gained originally by usury, so that her conscience troubled her. For similar instances of conscience-stricken ladies, see above, bull no. 67, n. 2, and bull no. 73.

3. Note that the size of the portion is not stipulated.

82   1306-1307

[To the Dean and Chapter of Toledo]:

The pope urges the enforcement of the canons prohibiting usury.[1]

Baer, *Die Juden*, vol. 1, pp. 110-114, n. 121.

Datum[2] . . .

1. The actual bull is not extant. That there was such a communication is evident from its mention in a warning issued by King Ferdinand IV of Castile and Leon.

He forbade the use of the bull by the Church authorities in Castile to prosecute Jews for taking usury. The Jews had complained to him on this score: *Sepades que el aljama de los judios de Toledo se me embiaron querellar por si e por las aljamas del arcobispado que algunos omes, clerigos e legos, ganaron cartas del papa para el dean de Toledo et para el cabildo . . . que costrengan a algunos judios que les tornen el logro que han levado dellos, et otrossi que non les den logro ninguno de las cartas que les deven, et que por esta razon que algunos arcidianos e canonigos pusieron en sentencia a algunos judios.* Now, it may be that the bull in question did not even mention the Jews explicitly, but was directed against the practice of usury generally. The clergy themselves then broadened the scope of their mandate. The argument of the king is interesting. He did not claim that Jews were exempt from Church law; he argued rather that the Jews in his realm were his property (*mios judios*) and that interference with them without explicit royal permission was the same as interference with the king. Cf. Amador de los Rios, *Historia social* (1943), vol. 1, pp. 424 f. [One wonders if the Toledan clergy was applying to the Jews dicta drawn from papal letters, or whether it was relying on a more rigid interpretation than that normally subscribed to by the popes. The latter allowed "not immoderate interest"; the clergy was often in favor of allowing no interest whatsoever.—KS]

2. Since the order of King Ferdinand IV (see above, n. 1) was sent in February 1307, the bull in question, if there was one, must have been dated several months earlier. It could have had no connection to a proposed crusade, as Baer suggests, since Clement V called for a crusade only in 1308 (see bull no. 83, below).

83   August 11, 1308

To the Knights Hospitallers:[1]

EXURGAT DEUS . . . Pope Clement makes an impassioned appeal to all Christendom to organize another crusade[2] for the redemption of the Holy Land. Among the privileges granted to crusaders[3] is freedom from the payment of interest on debts to Jews. If the Jews fail to remit usury already collected, the secular authorities must cooperate in establishing a boycott against them.

Reg. Vat. 52, fol. 124r, c. 626.
Regestum Clementis Papae V, vol. 2, 154–165, nos. 2988–2990.
J. Delaville le Roulx, *Cartulaire Generale de l'Ordre des Hospitaliers de St. Jean de Jerusalem 1100–1310* (Paris, 1906), vol. 4, pp. 181 f., no. 4807.

EXURGAT DEUS et inimici dissipentur ipsius, exurgant cum eo fidei zelatores, apprehendant arma timoris Domini, induant se fidei ortodosse lorica divini amoris, scutum assumant et sub potentia virtutis Altissimi roborentur. Obprobriorum etenim Crucifixi, que fiunt ei ab inspicientibus tota die, vindices eius sint memores et erga statum miserabilem Terre sancte plenitudinem miserationum exerceant, compassionis fluenta derivent et misericordis aperiant viscera pietatis, quia venerunt gentes in hereditatem Domini et sanctum eius tabernaculum polluerunt. Accendantur quidem ut ignis corda fidelium ad ipsius Terre necessitatibus succurrendum et affectus auctis pie considerationis ardoribus inflammentur; prebeant quoque promptas manus ad opera et sub spe celestis auxilii prelium Domini preliantes ad iuvandum illius causam ferventi magnanimitate consurgant, . . .

Si qui vero ipsorum ad prestandum usuras iuramento teneantur astricti, creditores per diocesanos ipsorum censura simili compellantur, ut iuramentum huiusmodi penitus relaxantes ab usurarum ulterius exactione desistant. Si autem aliqui creditorum eos ex tunc ad solutionem coegerint usurarum, ipsos ad restitutionem ipsarum per eosdem diocesanos simili volumus districtione compelli. Iudeos quoque ad remittendas ipsis usuras per secularem compelli precipimus potestatem, et donec eas remiserint, ab omnibus Christi fidelibus, quibus hoc per suos diocesanos denuntiatum extiterit, tam in mercimoniis quam in aliis sub excomunicationis pena iubemus eis comunionem omnimodam denegari. etc.

Datum Pictavis, iii Id. Augusti, anno tertio.

1. The prelates of all Catholic Europe received the call; cf. *Regestum Clementis Papae V*, vol. 2, pp. 154–165. nos. 2988–2990. Earlier that year, the grandmaster of the Hospitallers had advised the pope on the organization of the planned crusade. As a final item on the subject, the grandmaster suggested that it was reasonable to compel the Jews to contribute substantially to the redemption of Jerusalem (*erit bonum quod dominus papa ordinet aliquam talliam et contributionem super omnes Judaeos in terris habitantes Christianorum*), to the extent of at least a tenth of their property, although it might be proper to confiscate all their property. It would moreover be wrong for kings and lords to object to such a tax on their Jews. cf. Delaville le Roulx, *Cartulaire*, p. 110, no. 4681.

2. Jean Stengers (*Les Juifs dans les Pays-Bas au Moyen Age* [Brussels, 1950], pp. 16 ff. and the notes on pp. 104–108) describes the tragic effects of the crusade on the Jews. In 1309, bands of unorganized crusaders drawn from the lowest elements of the population began arriving in the cities along the Rhine and the Lowlands. They wandered in the general direction of Avignon, which had been fixed as the crusaders' meeting place. In the meantime, they attacked the relatively defenseless Jews they found there (Ullmann, *Juifs en Belgique*, pp. 17 f., plausibly suggests that many of these Jews were exiles from England and France; Stengers, *Juifs dans les Pays-Bas*, thinks most were of German origin), especially those of Duke Jean II of Brabant, who had welcomed the Jews into his lands because he expected much from them financially, since he had just gotten rid of the Lombard moneylenders (cf. *Regestum Clementis Papae V*, vol. 2, p. 102,

no. 1967). Many Jews were killed; others were besieged in the fortress of Genappe, until Duke Jean hurried to their aid and drove the crusaders off. In the end, in 1310, when the crusaders gathered in Avignon, Pope Clement V found their presence so troublesome that he ordered them back to their homes. The crusading project was postponed to a more propitious time. On this attack see Z. Baras, "Persecution of Jews in Brabant in 1309," *Zion* 34 (1969): 111–116.

3. For similar privileges of crusaders, see *ChJ*, nos. 1, 9, 10, 28, 58, 77, 80, 121, and 129.

84   May 27, 1309

To the Noblewoman Blanche of Brittany:[1]

DEVOTIONIS TUE . . . The pope accords her the right of establishing four chapels or a hospital in the diocese of Paris, for which purpose she may use half the monies she had acquired from the Jews of her territory.[2] She is also to enjoy the rights of patronage over these chapels or the hospital.[3] The other half of the money she may turn over to the Knights Hospitallers to support their planned invasion of the Holy Land.[4]

Reg. Vat. 52, fol. 90v, c. 415.
Regestum Clementis Papae V, vol. 4, p. 144, no. 4109.

Dilecte in Christo filie nobili mulieri Blance de Britania.

DEVOTIONIS TUE promeretur affectus . . . [ut valeat quatuor capellanias sive unum hospitale . . . construere et in ipsorum constructione expendere et convertere medietatem bonorum] quae ad te de Judaeis terre tue pervenisse noscuntur.

Datum Avinioni, vi kal. Junii, anno quarto.

1. Obviously a woman of wealth, perhaps attached to the royal court.

2. No doubt the money fell into her hands after the expulsion of the Jews in 1306, and she was now using this money for "pious ends."

3. The right of patronage involved the right to nominate the incumbent clerics. Nepotism may have been involved, but not necessarily profit.

4. [All these letters concerning the restitution of usury suggest a true wave of piety among the nobility on this issue. Usury was not solely an ecclesiastical concern. See Stow, "Papal and Royal Attitudes," pp. 161–184.—KS]

85 July 1, 1309

To the Bishop of Barcelona:

OBLATA NOBIS . . . Pope Clement agrees to overlook the sin of Bernard Cardona, now a subdeacon of the church of Barcelona. While he was still in lower orders, Cardona had been called to testify in a criminal case involving a Jew. He withheld the truth and, as a result, the Jew was hanged. Cardona, not thinking that he had committed a serious offense, had forgotten the entire matter, and, meanwhile, had accepted ecclesiastical promotion. Now that Cardona has asked for forgiveness, the pope desires to be merciful and suggests that an appropriate penance be imposed on the subdeacon. Afterward, he may join one of the orders, where he may become a deacon but not be promoted to an administrative post, or he may stay a secular, rising in grade only with special license.[1]

Reg. Vat. 52, fol. 123v, c. 590.
Regestum Clementis Papae V, vol. 4, p. 192, no. 4329.

Venerabili fratri . . . episcopo Barchinonen.

OBLATA NOBIS ex parte dilecti filii Bernardi Cardona subdiaconi tue diocesis petitio continebat, quod cum olim quidam iudex secularis quemdam iudeum occasione quorundam excessuum ab eo commissorum capi fecisset, prefatus subdiaconus tunc tantum in minoribus consistens ordinibus a iudice predicto vocatus super eisdem excessibus tanquam iuris ignarus perhibuit coram eodem iudice testimonium veritati idemque iudeus propter excessus predictos fuit postmodum per eundem iudicem ad suspendium condempnatus. Dictus vero subdiaconatus non credens circa hoc in aliquo deliquisse nec habens memoriam predictorum quoddam simplex beneficium sine cura sibi alias canonice collatum, cuius proventus decem librarum Turonen. parvorum valorem annuum non excedunt, recepit, ad cuius titulum ad subdiaconatus ordinem est promotus et in illo frequenter etiam ministravit. Cum autem huiusmodi excessus dicti subdiaconi dicatur esse occultus nullaque super hoc laboret infamia contra eum, ac idem subdiaconus super hiis nostram gratiam suppliciter implorarit, nos volentes secum benigne agere in hac parte, ac ad te remittentes eundem fraternitati tue mandamus, quatinus imposita sibi super hoc pro modo culpe penitentia salutari, si tandem ad aliquam de religionibus approbatis transire voluerit, cum ipso, quod in susceptis ministrare possit ordinibus et ad ordinem diaconatus dumtaxat ascendere ac administrationes illius ordinis, ad quem transiverit, non curatas, sine dignitate et personatu etiam obtinere; si autem in seculo potius remanere voluerit, secum, quod huiusmodi beneficium simplex, quod ut premittitur obtinet, et preter illud adhuc unicum aliud beneficium ecclesiasticum sine cura, cuius fructus, redditus et proventus viginti librarum Turonen. parvorum secundum taxationem decime valorem annuum non excedant, si alias ei cum dispensatione tua canonice offeratur, libere recipere et una cum predicto obtento retinere licite valeat premissis nequaquam obstantibus, auctoritate nostra dispenses, prout secundum Deum anime sue saluti videris expedire, ita tamen quod idem subdiaconus, etiam si ad religionem transiverit, ad sacerdotium non ascendat, et si remanserit in seculo, nequaquam in susceptis ministret ordinibus, nec superiores recipiat absque sedis apostolice licentia speciali.

Datum Avinioni, kal. Iulii, anno quarto.

1. For a similar instance of participation in the death of a Jew as a cause for denial of ecclesiastical preferment, see Grayzel, "References to the Jews," p. 333, below, no. XXXI [There were many reasons for denial of promotion; see those discussed in various locations in Raymond de Peñaforte's *Summa de poenitentia et matrimonia* (Rome, 1603), for instance, p. 328.—KS]

86   September 8, 1309

To the Faculty of Medicine at Montpellier:[1]

AD PASCENDUM OVES . . . The pope responds to a request made by the medical faculty in the University of Montpellier for a syllabus of medical studies. Among those the pope mentions as deserving of the highest attention—including Galen, Hippocrates, Constantine,[2] Rhazes, and Hohannitius—is a certain Isaac, and in particular his work on fevers (*aut febrium ipsius Isaac*).[3]

Reg. Vat. 52, fol. 269, c. 1085.
Regestum Clementis Papae V, vol. 4, p. 382, no. 6273.

Dil. filiis universis magistris facultatis medicine in Montepesulano, Magalonensis diocesis, commorantibus.

AD PASCENDUM OVES dominicas cure nostre, divina dispositione, commissis in sana prudentia et doctrina, montes excelsos, pinguis et virentis pascue, perscrutamur, ut ipsis in eisdem montibus nostro ministerio collocatis, reficiantur, per huiusmodi pascua, salutaribus documentis. Rivos etiam aquas dulcedinis proferentes ad potandum illas perquirimus, ut in saturitate potus aquarum ipsarum, variam ex eis cum gaudio, sicut de fontibus Salvatoris, scientiarum auriant ubertatem. Sed in facultate laudabili medicine, eo potiores in sinu matris ecclesie aggregare filios cupimus, et agregatos amplioris honoris favoribus prevenire, quo frequentius mortalitatis humane corporibus ipsorum exercitium salutare, necessarium et utile comprobatur. Sane oblata nobis vestra petitio continebat quod ad hoc precipue dirigitis desideria mentis vestre, quod Baccalarii, quos in facultate ipsa in studio, quod in Montepesulano Magalonensis diocesis haberi dinoscitur, sufficientes et ydoneos pro tempore contigerit repperiri, et non alii ad statum magisterii in facultate predicta pro bono comuni, et ut ipsi premia reportent de meritis, assumantur. Nos igitur, vestris in hac parte iustis desideriis, benivolentie paterne favoribus annuentes, ac volentes quod de Baccalariorum ipsorum ydoneitate et sufficienti peritia plene constet, apostolica auctoritate, de consilio, et ad instantiam dil. filiorum magistrorum Guillelmi de Brixia, et Iohannis de Alesto phisicorum et capellanorum nostrorum, necnon et magistri Arnaldi de Villanova phisici, eiusdem utilitate studii suadente, statuimus quod singuli Baccalarii in facultate ipsa in eodem studio ad statum huiusmodi promovendi, medicinales scilicet, Commentatos et Galieni de complexionibus, de malitia complexionis diverse de simplici medicina, de morbo et accidenti, de crisi, et creticis diebus, de ingenio sanitatis, et Avicenne vel, eius loco, Rasis ac Constantini et Isaac libros habere, huiusmodi promotionis tempore, teneantur. Et insuper duos Commentatos, et unum non Commentatum videlicet Tegne et pronosticorum vel amphorismorum Ipocratis quo ad ipsorum quinque particulas, ac regimenti, et Iohannitii, aut febrium ipsius Isaac, vel antidotarii, seu de morbo et accidenti et de ingenio sanitatis, libros quo ad eius octo particulas legerint, et ad questiones faciendas eisdem per quemlibet vestrum legentium publice in scolis facultatis eiusdem, ad minus semel respondeant, ipsarum repetendo rationes et nodos communiter dissolvendo, in locis famosis, quinque annis, si in artibus magistri existant ydonei, alioquin per sex annos, et quolibet anno, octo dumtaxat mensibus computatis, eiusdem facultatem audiverint medicine, ac in similibus locis per octo menses aut duas estates, ad minus, eiusdem medicine praticam duxerint exercendam. Et nichilominus tempore promotionis eiusdem, ad statum magisterii memoratum, legant duas, videlicet in theorica, reliqua vero in pratica coram vobis ad vocationem cancellarii studii supradicti, vel vices gerentis ipsius, in s. Marie de Tabulis, vel s. Firmini ecclesiis predicti loci de

Montepesulano, hora vesperarum congregatis more solito lectiones et ad singulas per vos faciendas eis super lectionibus ipsis, modestia tamen in illis et ordine debitis observatis, respondeant questiones, ut vos per lectionem, responsionem, et solutionem huiusmodi, eorum possitis scientiam experiri, et demum, Baccalariis ipsis recedentibus a presentia vestra seorsum, vobisque sub debito prestiti iuramenti, de sufficientia vel insufficientia Baccalariorum ipsorum, referentibus veritatem, si iidem Baccalarii promovendi per vos, ac relationem huiusmodi, ad honorem ipsum habeantur et reperiantur ydonei, prius de observandis statutis universitatis eiusdem corporali per ipsos prestito iuramento, per illum vel illos ad prefati magisterii promoveantur honorem, ad quem vel quos promotio talium dinoscitur pertinere. Nos enim ex nunc decernimus irritum et inane quicquid, circa concessionem magisterii supradicti, contra huiusmodi statuti nostri tenorem, privilegiis seu consuetudine quibuscumque contrariis nequaquam obstantibus, contigerit attemptari. Nulli etc. nostrorum statuti et constitutionis etc.

Datum Avinioni, vi kal. Septembris, anno quarto.

1. The University of Montpellier, incorporated in 1220, was already famous as a school for medicine. It was first established in 1137.

2. Constantine (died in 1087) may have been of Jewish origin. He migrated to southern Italy and there converted to Christianity. He specialized in translations from Arabic into Latin. Cf. E. R. Bevan and Charles Singer, eds., *The Legacy of Israel* (Oxford, 1927), p. 208.

3. For Isaac Israeli (fl. 900) see Harry Friedenwald, *The Jews and Medicine* (Baltimore, 1944), vol. 1, pp. 185-190. Isaac Israeli's *Book on Fevers* enjoyed the highest reputation all through the Middle Ages. Friedenwald calls attention to the fact that Petrus Hispanus (Peter Julian Rebulo), who was a physician and became Pope John XXI (1276-1277), wrote a commentary on Isaac's work. [See, too, Luke Demaitre's *Doctor Bernard de Gordon: Professor and Practitioner* (Toronto, 1980), for a further discussion of contacts between Jewish and Christian physicians.—KS]

87   October 11, 1311

To the Dean of the Church of Zeitz, in the Diocese of Naumberg:

CONQUESTI SUNT . . . The pope was concerned by the complaint of the abbot and chapter of the Benedictine monastery of Paulinzelle. A number of Jews, all brothers and resident in Querfurt, were charging the monks high rates of interest.[1] The dean is ordered to look into the matter and, if the charge is proved, to compel the Jews, by means of a boycott, to have everything above the principal[2] restored to the monks.

Ernst Anemüller, *Urkundebuch des Klosters Paulinzelle,* 1068–1534, vol. 7 of *Thuringische Geschichtsquellen* (Jena, 1905), p. 151, no. 149.

Clemens episcopus servus servorum dei dilecto filio decano ecclesie Cycensis, Nuenburgensis dyoceseos, salutem et apostolicam benedictionem.

CONQUESTI SUNT [coram] nobis . . . abbas et conventus monasterii de Cella domine Pauline, ordinis sancti Benedicti, Moguntine dyoceseos, quod Brendeke, Abraham, Scauedei et Matheus fratres de Quernvurte Iudei Halberstadensis dyoceseos multa extorserunt ab eis per usurariam pravitatem, ideoque discretioni tue per apostolica scripta mandamus, quatinus, si est ita, dictos Iudeos, ut sua sorte contenti sic extorta restituant conquerentibus, monicione premissa per subtractionem communionis fidelium appellatione remota compellas. Testes autem, qui fuerunt nominati, si se gratia, odio vel timore subtraxerint, per censuram ecclesiasticam appellatione cessante compellas veritati testimonium perhibere.

Datum Vyenne, v. id. Octobris, anno sexto.

1. On the efforts of Clement V to eliminate at least immoderate usury, see bull no. 82, above.

2. A final report on the investigation was rendered in November 1316. The Jews were condemned to pay a total of eighty marks for debt, penalties, and expenses incurred by the monastery in its suit. Should they refuse to pay, a boycott is declared against them, to be observed by all Christians. Cf. Anemueller, *Urkundenbuch,* vol. 7, pp. 174 f., no. 172; and *Germania Judaica,* vol. 2, pt. 2, p. 67 f. [This condemnation does not signal a change in the papal policy of allowing "not immoderate interest." First, the Jews took *multa* in interest, i.e., immoderate interest, that forbidden by the popes; and, in this instance, the penalty was the loss of all their profits. Second, the text just cited (Anemueller, *Urkundenbuch,* vol. 7, pp. 174 f., no. 172) makes it clear that Jews in the Naumberg region regularly *did* make loans, obviously interest-bearing; and this practice there was not condemned.—KS]

88   March 14, 1312

To the *Scholasticus* of the Church of St. Maria ad Gradus, Mainz:

SUA NOBIS . . . The pope had received a petition from the rector of the Frankfurt church that the Jews of that parish were not paying tithes and other dues on property which had once belonged to Christians and had now fallen into Jewish hands.[1] The *Scholasticus* is to look into the matter and, if the complaint is justified to compel the Jews to pay the taxes in question, even by means of a boycott. Witnesses, too, must be forced to testify.[2]

J. F. Böhmer, ed., *Codex diplomaticus Moenofrancfurtanus* (Frankfurt, 1901), vol. 1, p. 492, no. 949.

Clemens episcopus, servus servorum dei. Dilecto filio . . . scolastico ecclesie sancte Marie ad Gradus Maguntine, salutem et apostolicam benedictionem.

SUA NOBIS Siffridus, rector ecclesie Frankenvordensis, Maguntine diocesis, petitione monstravit, quod nonnulli iudei et iudee, in parrochia sua ipsius ecclesie habitantes, decimas sive census et res alias de proventibus domorum et possessionum ac aliarum rerum, que a christianis in eadem parrochia devenerunt ad ipsos, prout a christianis ipsis antea solvebantur predicte ecclesie, solvere indebite contradicunt, in eorundem ecclesie et rectoris preiuditium non modicum et gravamen. Quare idem rector nobis humiliter supplicavit, ut providere sibi super hoc paterna sollicitudine curaremus. Quocirca discretioni tue per apostolica scripta mandamus, quatinus, si est ita, dictos iudeos et iudeas ad debitam satisfactionem predictorum eidem ecclesie exhibendam, vel domos, vineas et possessiones dimittendas eisdem, monitione premissa, per subtractionem comunionis fidelium, appellatione remota, compellas. Testes autem, qui fuerint nominati, si se gratia, odio, vel timore subtraxerint, per censuram ecclesiasticam, appellatione cessante, compellas veritati testimonium perhibere.

Datum Vienne, ii id. Martii, anno septimo.

---

1. For the beginning and development of the claim that Jews must pay tithes on property that once belonged to Christians, cf. Blumenkranz, *Juifs et Chrétiens*, p. 349, who also notes that secular authorities were not always eager to enforce this Church rule. For tithes in the first half of the thirteenth century, see *ChJ*,

passim; the regulation concerning their payment became a fixed part of canon law with its inclusion in the *Decretals* of Gregory IX (X.3,30,16). In the second half of the thirteenth century, the question of tithes figured in a bull of Alexander IV (Sept. 17, 1259) and in Clement IV's complaint against the king of Portugal (Jordan, *Registres Clem. IV*, p. 236, no. 669). It surfaced again in a text of Gregory X (May 28, 1273) and in the draft of a bull for Nicholas III recorded by M. Tangl in *Päpstlichen Kanzleiordnungen*, p. 75, item 25/12. It appeared once more in the final settlement of the disputes between the king of Portugal and, first, Martin IV, on April 1, 1284 (Olivier-Martin, *Registres Mart. IV*, no. 502, esp. p. 238), and, then, Nicholas IV, on March 7, 1289 (Langlois, *Registres Nic. IV*, no. 716). By this time, early in the fourteenth century, the requirement that Jews pay the same tithes as Christians was extended to include town dwellings and not just landed property.

2. I. Kracauer, *Geschichte der Juden in Frankfurt a. M.* (Frankfurt, 1925), vol. 1, p. 14, asserts that the Jews of Frankfurt were then so powerful that they were able to stand in the way of such an investigation. The assertion is based on the final sentence of the bull, that witnesses may be afraid to testify, and, if so, should be compelled to do so (*Testes autem . . .*). This phrase, however, was a standard formula used whenever an investigation took place (e.g., bull no. 89, below). Besides, it is probable that any real fear would have been inspired by civil authorities who did not want the money to go to the Church. King Diniz of Portugal, referred to in the note above, admitted discouraging Jews and Saracens from paying tithes.

The bull also shows that Jews could still own property in German lands, a point seconded by Guido Kisch in *The Jews in Medieval Germany*.

89 July 1, 1312

To the Archbishop of Bremen and to the Bishops of Hildesheim and Brandenburg:

SI EX INIUNCTI . . . The pope acknowledges his obligation to aid Archbishop Burchard of Magdeburg[1] escape his financial plight. The archbishop's predecessors had alienated a considerable amount of property and rights, including those over certain Jews, to various persons and communities, with the result that the churches in his province had fallen into serious debt. The pope requests the addressees to help the archbishop of Magdeburg and his church regain their property and rights,[2] but this is to be done quietly, without scandal or resort to judicial procedures. Nobles, churchmen, and Christian laymen are to be threatened with ecclesiastical punishment; Jews are to be threatened with a boycott. Witnesses who refuse to testify out of hatred or fear should be compelled to speak out.

Reg. Vat. 59, fol. 126r, no. 598.
Regestum Clementis Papae V, no. 8283.

Venerabilibus fratribus . . . archiepiscopo Bremen. et . . . Hildensemen. ac Brandeburgen. episcopis.

SI EX INIUNCTI . . . nobis pastoralis officii debito singularum . . . ecclesiarum commoda gerimus, dignum est ut earum dispendiis promptis affectibus occurramus. Oblata siquidem nobis venerabilis fratris nostri Porchardi Archiepiscopi Magdeburgensis petitio continebat quod nonnulli predecessores sui Magdeburgensis archiepiscopi qui fuerunt pro tempore manus interdum ad alienationem rerum et iniuriam Magdeburgensis ecclesie sacris interdictam canonibus extendentes quasdam villas possessiones terras munitiones castra iurisdictiones et iura ad archiepiscopalem mensam seu ecclesiam predictam spectantia nonnullis religiosis ecclesiasticisve personis exemptis et non exemptis, nobilibus, comitibus, communitatibus ac aliis clericis et laicis, necnon aliquibus Judaeis, diocesium diversarum pro certis pecuniarum quantitatibus absque sedis apostolice licentia et alias illicite alienaverunt seu etiam distraxerunt in eius mense ac ecclesie gravem preiudicium et non modicam lesionem. . . . [Whence, the archbishop is to aid in regaining the property. He should attempt to do this] summarie de plano sine strepitu et figura iudicii . . . iudaeos vero per subtractionem communionis fidelium. Testes,[3] etc.

Datum in Prioratu de Grausello, kal. Julii, anno septimo.

---

1. Burchard of Schraplau became archbishop of Magdeburg in 1307; he died in 1325.

2. Moritz Güdemann, "Zur Geschichte der Juden in Magdeburg," in *MGWJ* 14 (1865; reprinted Breslau, 1866): 14 and 36 f., contains a document showing that the archbishop's problem was moving to a resolution. In November 1312, Abbot Arnold and the convent of Magdeburg presented the archbishop with a piece of land near the convent—it may have been land alienated by Burchard's predecessors; this he promptly sold to the Jews for the purpose of enlarging their cemetery. The 100 marks which the Jews paid were used to reduce the Church's debt.

3. On the *testes* formula, see bull no. 88, n. 2, above.

90   1311–1312

The Ecumenical Council of Vienne:[1]

A

QUUM JUDAEI . . . Since Jews and Muslims who are protected (against Christian testimony) by privileges specially granted by kings and princes cannot be convicted in civil and criminal cases through the testimony of Christians alone—an arrangement which is not only unjust, but even insulting to the Christian religion—the pope exhorts kings and princes not to grant such privileges in the future nor to allow those already granted to be observed. If Jews continue to enjoy these privileges, they must be deprived of all contact with Christians.[2]

Clem. 2,8,1.

Clemens V. in concilio Viennensi.

QUUM IUDAEI quidam et Sarraceni, sicut accepimus, quod super civilibus aut criminalibus convinci per Christianos non possint, se privilegiis regum et principum tueantur; quia id nedum iuri contrarium, sed et Christianae religioni opprobriosum est quamplurimum et adversum, reges eosdem et principes in Domino exhortamur, ne concedant huiusmodi de cetero privilegia, vel servent aut servare permittant etiam iam concessa. Quodsi Iudaei aut Sarraceni privilegiis talibus uti praesumpserint: Christianorum communio eis subtrahatur sic, quod Christiani ab eorum abstinere communione censura ecclesiastica, si opus fuerit, compellantur.

B

INTER SOLLICITUDINES . . . The pope expresses his belief that the conversion of non-Catholics depends on the proper exposition of the word of God. But this cannot be accomplished if the preachers of the word are ignorant of the languages understood by the diverse peoples they address.[3] He therefore makes provision that Hebrew, Arabic, and

Chaldean be taught wherever the curia resides, as well as at the universities of Paris, Oxford, Bologna, and Salamanca. Each university is to have two experts in these languages who will teach and translate books into Latin. Royal and ecclesiastical authorities are to provide these teachers with salaries.[4]

Clem. 5,1,1. 1179.

H. Denifle, *Chartularium Universitatis Parisiensis*, (Paris, 1889–1897), vol. 2, p. 154, no. 695.

Clemens V. in concilio Viennensi.

INTER SOLLICITUDINES nostris humeris incumbentes perpeti cura revolvimus, ut errantes in viam veritatis inducere, ipsosque lucrifacere Deo sua nobis cooperante gratia valeamus, hoc est, quod profecto desideranter exquirimus, ad id nostrae mentis sedulo destinamus affectum, ac circa illud diligenti studio et studiosa diligentia vigilamus. Non ambigimus autem, quin ad huiusmodi nostrum desiderium assequendum divinorum eloquiorum sit expositio congrua, ipsorumque fidelis praedicatio admodum opportuna. Sed nec ignoramus, quin et haec promi noscantur inaniter vacuaque redire, si auribus linguam loquentis ignorantium proferantur. Ideoque illius, cuius vicem in terris, licet immeriti, gerimus, imitantes exemplum, qui ituros per universum mundum ad evangelizandum Apostolos in omni linguarum genere fore voluit eruditos, viris catholicis notitiam linguarum habentibus, quibus utuntur infideles praecipue, abundare sanctam affectamus ecclesiam, qui infideles ipsos sciant et valeant sacris institutis instruere, Christicolarumque collegio per doctrinam Christianae fidei ac susceptionem sacri baptismatis aggregare. Ut igitur peritia linguarum huiusmodi possit habiliter per instructionis efficaciam obtineri: hoc sacro approbante concilio scholas in subscriptarum linguarum generibus, ubicunque Romanam curiam residere contigerit, nec non in Parisiensi et Oxoniensi, Bononiensi et Salamantino studiis providimus erigendas, statuentes, ut in quolibet locorum ipsorum teneantur viri catholici, sufficientem habentes hebraicae, arabicae et chaldaeae linguarum notitiam, duo videlicet uniuscuiusque linguae periti, qui scholas regant inibi, et libros de linguis ipsis in latinum fideliter transferentes, alios linguas ipsas sollicite doceant, earumque peritiam studiosa in illos instructione transfundant, ut instructi et edocti sufficienter in linguis huiusmodi fructum speratum possint Deo auctore producere, fidem propagaturi salubriter in ipsos populos infideles. Quibus equidem in Romana curia legentibus per sedem apostolicam, in studiis vero Parisiensi per regem Franciae, in Oxoniensi Angliae, Scotiae, Hiberniae ac Waliae, in Bononiensi per Italiae, in Salamantino per Hispaniae praelatos, monasteria, capitula, conventus, collegia exempta et non exempta, et ecclesiarum rectores in stipendiis competentibus et sumptibus volumus provideri, contributionis onere singulis iuxta facultatum exigentiam imponendo, privilegiis et exemptionibus quibuscunque contrariis nequaquam obstantibus, quibus tamen nolumus quoad alia praeiudicium generari.

C

EX GRAVI . . . The pope had heard that certain communities approve the taking of usury, although the practice is contrary to divine and human law. Their statutes *even enforce the payment* of usury, sometimes by means of subterfuges. The pope, with the approval of the council, decrees that every civil and judicial officer who issues or consents to legislation explicitly approving and defending usury shall be subject to excommunication; present legislation to this effect must be rescinded within three months. Moreover, anyone asserting that the practice of usury is not sinful shall be open to the charge of heresy and subject to punishment by the local bishop or inquisitor.[5]

Clem. 5,5,1.
Alberigo, *Conciliorum*, pp. 360 f.

Clemens V. in concilio Viennensi

EX GRAVI ad nos insinuatione pervenit, quod quorundam communitates locorum in offensam Dei et proximi, ac contra iura divina pariter et humana usurariam approbantes quodammodo pravitatem, per statuta sua iuramento quandoque firmata usuras exigi et solvi nedum concedunt, sed ad solvendas eas debitores scienter compellunt, ac iuxta ipsorum continentiam statutorum gravia imponendo, plerumque usuras repetentibus onera, aliisque utendo super his diversis coloribus et fraudibus exquisitis, repetitionem impediunt earundem. Nos igitur, perniciosis his ausibus obviare volentes, sacro approbante concilio statuimus, ut, quicunque communitatum ipsarum potestates, capitanei, rectores, consules, iudices, consiliarii ut alii quivis officiales statuta huiusmodi de cetero facere, scribere vel dictare, aut quod solvantur

usurae, vel quod solutae, quum repetuntur, non restituantur plene
ac libere, scienter iudicare praesumpserint, sententiam excommunicationis incurrant, eandem etiam sententiam incursuri, nisi statuta huiusmodi hactenus edita de libris communitatum ipsarum, (si super hoc
potestatem habuerint,) infra tres menses deleverint, aut si ipsa statuta
sive consuetudines, effectum eorum habentes, quoquo modo praesumpserint observare. §. 1. Ceterum, quia foeneratores sic ut plurimum
contractus usurarios occulte ineunt et dolose, quod vix convinci possunt
de usuraria pravitate: ad exhibendum, quum de usuris agetur, suarum
codices rationum censura ipsos decernimus ecclesiastica compellendos.
§. 2. Sane, si quis in illum errorem inciderit, ut pertinaciter affirmare
praesumat, exercere usuras non esse peccatum: decernimus, eum velut
haereticum puniendum, locorum nihilominus ordinariis et haereticae
pravitatis inquisitoribus districtius iniungentes, ut contra eos, quos de
errore huiusmodi diffamatos invenerint aut suspectos, tanquam contra
diffamatos vel suspectos de haeresi procedere non omittant.

1. The Ecumenical Council of Vienne was held between October 16, 1311, and
May 6, 1312. Its decisions were incorporated in papal pronouncements at its
conclusion. The decisions of the council are found in Alberigo, *Conciliorum*,
pp. 312-377.

2. This canon was included in the Clementine Constitutions, although the same
view had been expressed somewhat less forcefully by a canon of the Third
Lateran Council of 1179 (*ChJ*, no. I, pp. 296-297) that was eventually incorporated into the *Decretals* (X.2,20,21). Nevertheless, Martin IV recognized the
injustices which could occur if Jews were arbitrarily accused of crimes before the
Inquisition. He thus tried to guard against perjured or hastily given testimony by
adding a threat against perjurers to the Bull of Protection issued to the Jews on
August 2, 1281 (cf. Grayzel, "*Sicut Judeis*," pp. 243-280, esp. p. 261; and bull
no. 45, above. See also bull no. 31, above, where Gregory X in 1272, forbade
convicting Jews by Christian testimony alone in cases such as blood libels. In
short, the popes realized that exceptions to the general rule were needed as much
as was the rule in favor of Christian testimony itself. For the general situation
with regard to Jewish and non-Jewish testimony, see the references in *ChJ*,
p. 56; Kisch, *Jews in Medieval Germany*, pp. 250 ff. and 269 ff.; J. E. Scherer,
Rechtsverhältnisse der Juden (Leipzig, 1901), pp. 164-172, and K. Stow, *Catholic
Thought and Papal Jewry Policy, 1555-1593* (New York, 1977), pp. 109 and
382-385.
　　The provincial Council of Zamora (in Spain), held in 1313, the year after
Vienne, repeated and strengthened the present canon (Baer, *Die Juden*, vol. 2,
pp. 118 ff.; Amador de los Rios, *Historia Social*, vol. 2, p. 439.

3. For a discussion of the subject, cf. Browe, *Judenmission*, pp. 272 ff. Raymond
de Peñaforte had urged linguistic instruction for this purpose almost a century
earlier, and, more recently, Raymond Lull had called for such a decision by the
pope and council at Vienne (Denifle, *Chartularium*, no. 611).

4. Implementation was long in coming, if ever. In 1326, Pope John XXII was still asking the bishop of Paris for a report on the situation (Denifle, *Chartularium*, p. 293, no. 857). In this period, Christian scholars of Hebrew were most frequently converts from Judaism (cf. Browe, *Judenmission*, pp. 274 ff.); this was no longer so in the fifteenth and sixteenth centuries.

[Given the terms of the canon, moreover, one must wonder if it was ever intended seriously to apply to Jews. The preachers were to learn the languages understood and *spoken* by their prospective audiences. In the case of European Jews, those would have been primarily *European* languages. Hebrew was certainly not their everyday tongue. On the other hand, this canon made perfect sense in terms of the large missionary effort to infidels other than Jews then being carried on in the East.—KS]

5. Jews are not mentioned in this conciliar resolution; it was meant [primarily, at least—KS] to apply to the widespread practice of usury among Christians. So, too, the bull sent by Pope Clement to Ferdinand of Castile, on April 28, 1309 (*Serenitati tue, Regestum*, vol. 4, nos. 4048 and 4051), empowering him to make use of monies which were the fruit of usury to aid in his struggle against the Muslims, makes no mention of Jews. None of this, however, kept the Council of Zamora (par. xii; cf. no. XXIV, below) from trying to apply *ex gravi* to the Jews: *quod non exerceant usuras cum Christianis . . . cum hoc sit prohibitum per constitutionem domini Clementis Pape V edictam in dicto concilio Viennensi* (cf. Baer, *Die Juden*, vol. 2, pp. 188 f.; cf. p. 309, below, for Grayzel's first thoughts on *ex gravi.*). [In fact, given the tacit and consistent papal acceptance of moderate Jewish interest rates (see Stow, "Papal and Royal Attitudes"), it appears that the Zamora canon was not consistent with papal intentions. This is obviously so in general, but it is so with respect to Vienne as well. The intention of *Ex gravi* was to prevent the legislation of an explicitly pro-usury statute, for such a statute would topple the delicate papally constructed balance that purposefully allowed moderate usury in practice, while, in theory, permitting complete Church control over lending, including the right to cancel interest when circumstances required. On the other hand, to prohibit Jewish usury outright would have had the same effect as a statute enforcing the observance of loan contracts: namely, it would result in either secular interference or clandestine loan operations and thus thwart the thoroughgoing ecclesiastical control the popes were seeking to maintain.—KS]

91 December 29, 1312

To Mary, Queen of France:

CONSUEVIT INTERDUM . . . From the Jews who lived in her territory before their recent expulsion from France,[1] the queen[2] had acquired a sum of about ten thousand pounds. The pope grants her the right to retain half of this sum (goods), provided she uses the other half for the support of the crusade in the Holy Land. She shall not be compelled to make any further restitution, since she cannot identify the Jews[3] who owned the money or those from whom the Jews had usuriously taken it.

Reg. Vat. 60. fol. 72v.
Regestum Clementis Papae V, no. 9134.

Carissime in Christo filie Marie regine Francie illustri.

CONSUEVIT INTERDUM sedes apostolica personis generositate sublimibus postulata concedere, ut ex hoc Deo et ipsi sedi se reddere gaudeant plus devotas. Cum itaque, sicut asseris, de bonis, que erant apud Iudeos in tua terra morantes, tempore generalis et novissime expulsionis ipsorum et aliorum Iudeorum de regno Francie ad te usque ad summam decem millium librarum Turonen. parvorum pervenisse noscatur, nos tuis supplicationibus inclinati, ut medietatem huiusmodi bonorum, que ad te, ut premittitur, devenerunt, retinere tibi et de illis disponere, prout expedire videris, libere ac licite valeas, reliquam vero medietatem convertere in Terre sancte subsidium tenearis, ita quod alia restitutio de tota huiusmodi quantitate vel aliqua eius parte tibi aliquatenus non incumbat nec ad id a quoquam possis quomodolibet coartari; dummodo illi Iudei, quorum huiusmodi bona fuerunt, seu alii, a quibus ipsi Iudei bona eadem illicite habuerunt, omnino a te sciri vel inveniri non possint, auctoritate tibi presentium indulgemus. Nulli etc.

Datum Avinioni, iv kal. Januarii, anno octavo.

1. See bull no. 80, above.

2. For Queen Mary, see bull no. 81, above. For a similar grant, see bull no. 84, above.

3. Is it conceivable that by 1312 the possibility of readmitting the Jews was already being considered? Otherwise, why even weigh the question of returning the property to Jews?

92   no date[1]

To the Bishop of Lucca:

QUAMVIS REPROBANDA . . . The pope urges the bishop to use ecclesiastical powers against the civic authorities of Lucca who *encourage Jews*[2] in their usurious activities.[3]

Moritz Stern, "Papsturkunden: Ein Beitrag zur Geschichte der Juden, aus Archiven mitgeteilt." *Beilage zum Berichte der israelitischen Religionsschule zu Kiel über das Schuljahr 1892/3*, p. 16, no. 4.

Nicholaus episcopus servus servorum Dei dilectis filiis antianis, communi, universitati et singularibus personis civitatis Lucane salutem et apostolicam benedictionem.

QUAMVIS REPROBANDA sit Judeorum perfidia, utilis tamen est illorum conversatio Christianis, prout hoc tempore experientia teste comprobatur, unde cum sint ab omnium creatore creati non debent a Christi fidelibus evitari. Nuper siquidem pro parte vestra nobis expositum fuit, quod vos pro rei publice utilitate Judeos feneratores, prout hactenus fecistis, libenter teneretis, si id absque alicuius pene incursu aut conscientie scrupulo facere possetis. Qua propter pro parte vestra nobis fuit humiliter supplicatum, ut vobis in eadem civitate unum vel plures Judeum seu Judeos feneratores cum eorum familiis tenendi ac eis domos pro eorum usu et habitatione impune locandi et cum eis, quantum necessitas exigit, conservandi licentiam concedere aliasque vobis et statui vestro in premissis oportune providere de benignitate apostolica dignaremur. Nos igitur cupientes vestris ac eiusdem rei publice, quam carissimam habemus, indemnitati ac commodo providere, huiusmodi supplicationibus inclinati vos ac omnes et singulos cives vestre civitatis utriusque sexus ab excommunicationis ac aliis ecclesiasticis sententiis, censuris et penis, si quas pro eo, quod huiusmodi Judeos tenuistis et eis domos locastis seu locari tacite vel expresse consensistis aut cum ipsis estis quomodocunque conversati incurrisse censemini, presentium tenore absolventes et absolutos fore decernentes vobis, ut in eadem civitate unum vel plures Judeum sive Judeos feneratores, quotiens vobis placuerit, tenere eisque domos et habitationes pro eorum usu locare et cum eis necessitate postulante conversari absque alicuius pene incursu, libere et licite valeatis, auctoritate apostolica tenore presentium indulgemus; proviso quod propter hoc Judei ipsi novis exactionibus non graventur et usuras, quanto mitiores seu minori pretio fieri potest, exercere aut committere teneantur, non obstantibus felicis recordationis Clementis pape V. predecessoris nostri et statutis curie episcopalis Lucane de Judeis loquentibus, quibus, quantum contra predicta disponant, expresse derogamus illis alias in suo pleno robore permansuris et aliis constitutionibus et ordinationibus apostolicis ceterisque contrariis quibuscunque. Nulli ergo omnino hominum liceat hanc paginam nostre absolutionis, constitutionis et concessionis infingere vel ei ausu temerario contraire; si quis autem hoc attemptare presumpserit, indignationem omnipotentis Dei et beatorum Petri et Pauli apostolorum eius se noverit incursurum.

> Datum Rome apud sanctum Petrum anno incarnationis dominice millesimo quadringentesimo quinquagesimo secundo duodecimo kalendas Septembris pontificatus nostri anno sexto.

Petrus de Noxeto.

1. The date could have been before 1310, in connection with the quarrel between the bishop on the one side and the administration of the city on the other. The nature of the quarrel is recorded in the *Regestum Clementis Papae V*, vol. 4, nos. 4735, 4736, 4847, and 4952, for September 11, 1309. The present text may also reflect the antiusury decision of the Council of Vienne and, therefore, date from after 1312.

2. There was an active Jewish community in Lucca as early as the tenth century. Cf. Attilio Milano, *Storia degli Ebrei in Italia* (Turin, 1963), pp. 58 and 63.

3. The text of this letter has not yet been found, but its existence is mentioned in a bull issued by Nicholas V at Rome on August 21, 1452, which Stern found in the State Archive of Lucca. The letter was addressed to the civic authorities of Lucca and permits them to employ Jews as moneylenders, despite the prohibition issued by Clement V and the contemporary bishop of Lucca in their day: *non obstantibus felicis recordationis Clementis Papae V, predecessoris nostri, et statutis curie episcopalis Lucane de Judaeis loquentibus*. It seems unlikely that a letter of Clement V would have been so specifically mentioned had no document existed. One must keep in mind that the Benedictines who compiled the *Regestum* of Pope Clement V drew only on materials present in the Vatican Archives and in the Apostolic Library. Moreover, the Avignon archives have suffered a good many misfortunes (*Regestum Clementis Papae V*, p. xxx of the Introduction to vol. 1). It is therefore not surprising that some of Pope Clement's correspondence is no longer extant.

Legislation from Provincial and Local Councils Concerning the Jews

The Later Thirteenth Century

Legislation from Provincial and Local Councils Concerning the Jews
The Later Thirteenth Century

THE POLICY OF THE POPES theoretically determined that of the Church as a whole. This was not always so in fact. As was seen in the register of papal letters (e.g., bull no. 62), the popes had to restrain the radicalism of the mendicant inquisitors more than once. The secular prelates too were not always willing followers of the papal lead. They especially fought the pope over his claim that tradition in the Church was to be synonymous with papal policy irrespective of the possible contradiction between that policy and previously accepted theological positions, including those held by the Fathers of the Church.[1] Some of the clergy were even ready to do battle with the pope over his support of the mendicants in their mid-1250s struggle with the seculars over the proper distribution of the chairs in theology at the University of Paris.[2] The rigid usury doctrines of the Parisian school of Peter the Chanter also gave more than one pope no little uneasiness.[3]

Still, the extent of opposition to the papacy must not be exaggerated. This point is brought home by examining the actions of local and regional, mostly episcopal, councils in matters concerning Jews. The legislation of these councils, which reflects the attitudes of the broadest possible segment of the clergy, again and again reaffirms the basic stance of the (papally approved) canons toward the Jews. The exceptions are rare and, most noticeably, there is no reference whatsoever to the questions of the Talmud, forced sermons, or the Inquisition,[4] the matters which particularly exercised clerical radicals. Similarly, calls for a total ban on interest, in opposition to the papal acceptance of "not immoderate interest," are few. The two references to apostasy following conversion from Judaism to Christianity conform to or explicitly confirm the papally sanctioned position on the subject. In short, conciliar decrees in

235

the late thirteenth and early fourteenth centuries basically conformed to the lines of papal policy.

Primarily because of this conformity, as well as the apodictic, laconic, and repetitious language of the conciliar texts, which often repeat the edicts of papal letters verbatim, there seemed little purpose in continuing the detailed and expansive format used above in presenting the papal letters. Rather, following a brief overall discussion—based on the decisions of forty-five councils held in England, France, Spain, Germany, Italy, and Poland[5]—the texts are divided and presented according to six categories, each introduced by an analytical table, with summaries of their contents preceding individual texts. For the sake of integrity, the decrees of each council have been presented as a unit; this has necessitated some repetition in categories Four through Six. The majority of the texts were collected by Solomon Grayzel; I assume responsibility for the order of presentation, the introduction, and the tables of legislation.[6]

The legislation of the councils falls into six general categories that almost invariably follow the lead of earlier canons, ecumenical councils, and, most consciously, the *Decretals* of Gregory IX. The largest number of later thirteenth century conciliar edicts (Category One) reiterate, and often cite by name, the decrees of the Fourth Lateran Council (themselves assumed into the *Decretals*) concerning Jewish dress, behavior at the Easter season and the use of Christian servants. This legislation is highly restrictive, but it also recognizes limits which are not to be surpassed. Regional synods and episcopal councils thus accepted the pope as the unqualified arbiter in matters of Jewry policy.

Category Two deals with forbidden sexual contact, a concern of centuries' standing that was discussed in ecumenical as well as local councils. More properly, regulation of sexual mores should have been classed as a subdivision of Category One. However, the legislation deals not so much with the nature of the delict as with the question of the correct authority for meting out punishments when infractions occurred. That authority is declared to be the bishop, and him alone; this explains why the legislation classifies forbidden sexual contact between male Christians and Jewish or Muslim women together with true sodomy and sexual intercourse with animals. There is no suggestion here or elsewhere in canonical literature that sex with a Jewess is itself sodomy.

Category Three is lending at interest. Surprisingly, only two texts argue against all interest. Others suggest loopholes enabling lending activity to go on; they even allow the pledging of church vessels, an action normally prohibited vociferously. The majority of the councils, as noted above, accept unquestioningly the papal practice of beneficently ignoring the taking of "not immoderate interest."

Category Four must be understood within a special context. The issue is regulation not of the Jews but of *the English king:* when ought he to allow Jews to appear before "courts Christian" and ecclesiastical judges. The Church, it is claimed, is entitled to exercise jurisdiction in *"rebus ecclesiasticis,"* specifically, sacrilege, striking a cleric, and sexual relations between Jews and Christian women; the king thought otherwise. As texts brought forth in Addendum B show, the English king did not quibble about the need to punish Jews for these offenses, but he was not prepared to limit his exclusive jurisdiction over Jews. Interestingly, these clerical demands on the royal prerogative were made in the late 1250s, at the time of the baronial revolt that resulted in the controls on the king enunciated by the Provisions of Oxford and Westminister. "Sacrilege," it should be noted, is a general term and refers to no particular offense in the present context. It is used only to establish a principle.

Category Five is noteworthy, since it expands the bounds of canonically defined limits, but not enormously. The long-established concept of social segregation had, in the past, raised questions of condominium. Thus Christian servants could not reside under the roofs of Jewish masters, nor could Christians and Jews dwell in a single structure on a permanent basis. But now, for the first time, four councils sought to limit Jewish settlement itself to those specific localities which were either "designated" as permitted or where "synagogues [already] existed." The probable intention of these decrees was that no new areas of Jewish settlement should be established. One synod, Wratislava (1266) went further. To protect the young shoot of Christendom in Poland, it declared, a moat or wall should be constructed between the Jewish and Christian sections of the city. However, a glimmer of the ghetto to come is not an actual ghetto, and such residential legislation did not begin to proliferate until the fifteenth century. Whether its thirteenth-century version, as propounded by local church councils, had any relation to the royally sponsored expulsions of 1290 and 1306 is a purely speculative question; the response is probably a negative one. Indeed, it should be remembered that as early as 1253, Henry III of England had anticipated the councils and decreed that Jews might dwell only in specified localities. Philip III of France issued a similar decree in 1283.

Category Six, the final one, deals with conversion. Once more, the legislation adheres firmly to established papal policy: Before the fact, no force may be applied to promote conversion; after the fact, there was no way to invalidate baptism yet preserve the honor of the Christian faith intact. From the Jewish point of view, this was a threatening policy; still, contemporary Jews did not believe its second part nullified the first. Rather, as texts like the thirteenth-century narrative of the so-called

"Terrible Events of 1007" and the record of the 1354 convocation at Barcelona indicate, Jews learned how to work around the problems and potential contradictions and to insist on their rights whenever they had the chance. The pope, the Jews were convinced, obeyed his own laws assiduously.

The section on councils concludes with two brief addenda.[7] The first is a report, albeit considerably after the fact, of a synod held at London in 1290, following the royally edicted expulsion of that year. Because of the *Dunstable Annals,* it has always been said that the English clergy voted a tax in thanks for the expulsion. The report indicates that the clergy, as distinct from Parliament, acted no earlier than three months after the expulsion.

The second addendum must be read in the light of the 1286 bull of Honorius IV *Nimis in partibus* (no. 50) and of the 1287 Council of Exeter (no. XVI). This is a rare opportunity to reconstruct the interplay between popes, kings, radical prelates, and clergy of more conservative leanings. The texts in the addenda are inquiries composed in 1285 by clergy of the Province of Canterbury in England and addressed to the king, Edward I. They are followed by royal responses and then further clerical rebuttal. Sir Maurice Powicke believed that the Franciscan, sometime Parisian professor of theology, and now archbishop of Canterbury, John Peckham, was not directly involved in this interchange of views and that, for that matter, neither was the king. The tenor of the inquiries argues differently; their preoccupation with serious offenses like apostasy and usury was shared by Peckham himself. The king's response, that there was little more he could do, has an authentic ring. The *Statutum de Judaismo* of 1275, devoted to resolving precisely the issues now raised by the clergy ten years later, had failed. Still, Peckham was dissatisfied with the royal position, and he said so in the rebuttal to the royal response. He also went further and solicited a bull from the pope, Honorius IV. That bull was *Nimis in partibus,* with its strongly worded demands and its attack, the first in nearly twenty years, on the Talmud and its blasphemies. Nevertheless, Peckham did not win over the body of even his own clergy, which in fact constantly resisted his overzealous meddling and reforms. The 1287 Council of Exeter (within the province of Canterbury) thus passed a long list of restrictive legislation touching the Jews, but it was drawn exclusively from standard canonical or Fourth Lateran texts and did not refer to the questions of apostasy or the Talmud. As for the king, Edward I's radical solution to the problem of the Jews was something not even Peckham had suggested. The archbishop's surprising 1270s defense of the canonical right of London Jewry to rebuild freely its one synagogue indicates he had not contemplated this solution either, namely, the royally ordered expulsion of 1290.[8]

This scenario has been necessarily condensed. The point, however, should be clear: Radicalism, even in the thirteenth century, could come from surprising quarters when the Jews were involved. But radicalism was not the dominant viewpoint, and certainly not the dominant viewpoint of contemporary Church councils. In those councils, the majority of the clergy assiduously followed the papal lead: prescribing strict regulation, but always according to legally (canonically) predetermined and carefully defined lines. The real question then was whether legal theory, with its fine, and sometimes overfine, distinctions could be turned into an everyday working reality. All too often, it could not be.

NOTES

1. See K. F. Morrison, *Tradition and Authority in the Western Church, 300–1140* (Princeton, 1969), *passim.*

2. The struggle is summed up and put into full perspective by M.-M. Dufeil, *Guillaume de Saint-Amour et la polémique universitaire parisienne, 1250–1259* (Paris, 1972).

3. See K. R. Stow, "Papal and Royal Attitudes Toward Jewish Lending in the Thirteenth Century," *AJS Review* (1981): 161–184.

4. The texts in Addendum B, which do refer to the Talmud and the Inquisition, are not conciliar legislation.

5. The legislation of the papally ordained Ecumenical Councils of Lyons (1274) and Vienne (1311) was dealt with above in the register of papal letters (nos. 36–37 and 90).

6. The best edition for the overwhelming majority of conciliar texts is still that of J. D. Mansi, *Sacrorum Conciliorum Collectio* (Venice, 1779–1782), 59 vols.; although, where appropriate, alternate editions, besides that of Mansi, will be cited together with the texts themselves below. Other parallel editions, as well as pertinent articles and additional bibliography, may be located by consulting J. T. Sawicki, *Bibliographia synodorum particularium, Monumenta Iuris Canonici,* Series C: Subsidia, vol. 2. (Vatican City, 1967). For Ecumenical Councils, the edition of J. Alberigo (Basel/Bologna, 1962) is now standard.

7. The texts are taken from F. M. Powicke and C. R. Cheney, *Councils and Synods with Other Documents Relating to the English Church, A.D. 1205–1313* (Oxford, 1964).

8. On Peckham, see Decima Douie, *Archbishop Pecham* (Oxford, 1952), esp. p. 325; although note should be made that Douie would disagree with other parts of my reconstruction. See the additional references concerning these events found together with the texts themselves in the addenda.

1. Traditional Legislation and Restrictions

The following conciliar legislation and restrictions repeat in the main decrees of the canons and the Fourth Lateran Ecumenical Council prescribing appropriate Jewish dress, public appearance by Jews during the Easter season, Jewish behavior in the presence of a consecrated host, and social contacts between Jews and Christians. They prohibit Christians from serving Jews, dining at a common table, and Jews from holding public office of any description, including financial posts. Many of the councils edicted a comprehensive list of this legislation. The Latin texts appear in the following order.

I   1257

Constitutiones Aegidii Saresbiriensis Episcopi (in synodo latae)

Following decrees of the Fourth Lateran Council and the Council of
Oxford (ChJ. p. 315), Christian women acting as wetnurses, mid-
wives, and in other servile occupations for Jews are threatened with
excommunication. They are also admonished against committing
the dire offense of having sexual relations with a Jewish man.

Mansi, 23:912.
Powicke and Cheney, *Councils and Synods,* p. 560.

De mancipiis Judaeorum.

Licet in concilio Lateranensi et Oxoniensi prohibitum sit expresse, ne
Judaei mancipia habeant christiana, plerique tamen Judaei nostrae
dioecesis, ut dicitur, hujusmodi prohibitione contempta, nutrices, obste-
trices, et alia mancipia christiana damnabiliter praesumunt retinere; et
hujusmodi transgressione contenti, in graviorem prorumpunt audaciam,
ut non solum cum christianis solutis, sed in nostrae fidei scandalum; et in
suae legis contemptum, et cum mulieribus se commisceant conjugatis.
Unde praesentis synodi approbatione statuimus, ut mulieres tam solutae
quam conjungatae, super hujusmodi crimen confessae vel convictae,
nominatim excommunicationis sententia percellantur; et donec ad arbitrium nostrum vel officialium nostrorum satisfecerint, arctius evitentur.
Judaeis vero super hoc convictis vel confessis, donec hoc competenter
emendaverint, omnis christiana communio per censuram ecclesiasticam
denegetur. Quod vero circa distinctionem habitus dictum est, propter
pericula, quae ex habitus confusione contingunt, omni diligentia statuimus observandum.

II   1259

Concilium Provinciale Moguntinum

> Jews are ordered to wear a badge. They are not to hold public office
> or retain female Christian servants. The secular powers are called
> upon to enforce these edicts under threat of excommunication.
> During the Easter season, Jews must remain within their homes.
> Violations will be punished by "indirect excommunication," pro-
> hibiting Christians from all contact with Jews.

Mansi, 23:1000.

De Judaeis.

Statuimus, ut in universis civitatibus, oppidis, castris, et villis civitatis,
dioecesis et provinciae Moguntinae, gens Judaeorum utriusque sexus
infra duos menses post publicationem hujusmodi statuti, talia signa et
habitum, quibus, seu per quem sine ambiguitate a christiano populo
distinguatur, sibi eligat et deferat manifeste; dignitates quoque seculares
et officia publica; scilicet in quibus de gente praefata aliquis praeest, et
mancipia christiana prorsus dimittat. Alioquin in omnibus locis, ubi
Judaei dicto statuto obedire nolentes habitare vel domicilia obtinere
noscuntur, in poenam Christianorum potentum, tamdiu cessetur ab
officio divinorum, donec per praefatos Principes et nobiles Christianos, in
quorum territoriis praedicta gens perfida et misera conversatur, ad
observationem praemissorum omnium compellatur. Ipsi autem Judaei
per locorum dioecesanos indirecte per subtractionem communionis
fidelium excommunicationis sententia percellantur. Si quis vero de gente
praefata in die parasceve visus fuerit in platea vel per ostium domus suae
prospicere, vel fenestras, ad quod probandum duorum Christianorum
stabitur juramento, is loci dioecesano in marca argenti, poenae nomine
teneatur, ad cujus solutionem etiam omnes defendentes eum, per excommunicationis sententiam compellantur, et ne quis christianus hujusmodi
statuti ignorantiam valeat allegare, universis ecclesiarum rectoribus per
Mogunt. civitatem et provinciam constitutis, in quorum Parochiis Judaei
morantur, sub poena excommunicationis dicti concilii latae sententiae
praecipimus firmiter et districte, ut quilibet in sua parochia singulis
diebus dominicis, singula quatuor tempora immediate sequentibus, infra
missarum solemnia publice praefatum statutum lingua materna non
obmittat exponere.

III   1260

Concilium Arelatense (a Florentino archiepiscopo cum suffraganeis)

Jews are to wear a special habit which must be distinguishable from the round capes of clerics.

———————
Mansi, 23:1007.

Ne Judaei ferant habitum sacerdotalem: immo signo aliquo distinguantur a fidelibus.

Item quia ridiculosum est et turpe, quod habitus sacerdotales, ut sunt capae rotundae clausae, quibus ambulando per vias et plateas ministri ecclesiastici a cunctis popularibus discernuntur, perfidis Judaeis et infidelibus cum eisdem Christi sacerdotibus sint communes: districtius inhibemus, ne de cetero ab infidelibus habitus hujusmodi deportentur; sed rotis, aut signis aliis in exteriori eorum habitu patentibus utantur, quibus infideles a fidelibus distinguantur. Si quis autem laicus, aut saecularis potestas, Judaeum aliquem, aut infidelem alium, habitum hujusmodi sacerdotalem deferre compulerit, excommunicetur, et a sanctae matris ecclesiae liminibus arceatur: maxime cum a sanctis patribus praedecessoribus nostris, et sanctae sedis Apostolicae legatis, fuerit hoc idem alias solemniter promulgatum.

IV   1260

Statuta Domini Guidonis (archiepiscopi Narbonensis)

Markets may not be held on Sundays. If Jews presume to hold them, they will be denounced publicly by a sentence of excommunication, as if they were rebels.[1]

———————
Mansi, 23:1032.

V. Mercata etiam in diebus Dominicis inhibemus, nisi in nundinas solemnes inciderint. Et qui trina monitione praemissa non cessaverint ab eisdem, simili per omnia coerceantur censura.

VI. Si vero Judaei illud praesumpserint, postquam hoc mandatum nostrum fuerit publicatum, denuncientur ballivo loci. Et nisi ter monitus eosdem Judaeos cessare compulerit, excommunicationis sententia, quam nunc ferimus in rebelles, denuncietur publice innodatus.

1. The use of the term is figurative. Strictly speaking, no Jew could be "excommunicated." On this problem, see both J. Shatzmiller, "Jews 'Separated from the Communion of the Faithful in Christ,'" in *Studies in Medieval Jewish History and Literature*, ed. I. Twersky (Cambridge, 1979), pp. 307–314, and W. C. Jordan, "Christian Excommunication of Jews in the Middle Ages," *Jewish History* 1 (1986): 31–38.

V 1261

Constitutiones Synodales (Episcopi Valentini)

> Clerics drinking the wine of Jews in the homes of Jews are to be excommunicated. They should also refrain from the purchase of Jewish wine, except in cases of necessity.

Mansi, 23:1052.

De vino Judaeorum non bibendo.

Item statuimus, quod si quis clericus bibit vinum Judaeorum in domibus ipsorum (quod omnino fieri prohibemus) ipso facto sit excommunicatus, si hanc praesentem constitutionem sciverit, vel recoluerit. Item qui eorum vinum scienter emerit, nisi tempore necessitatis, nostrae subjaceat ultioni.

VI 1266

Synodus Wratislaviensis (Breslau)

> par. 12. To protect the tender Christian shoot of Poland, Jews should be made to dwell in one contiguous area, separated by a wall, or even a moat, from the dwellings of Christians. Diocesan bishops should make efforts to have all other Jewish homes sold. Jews must remain closed within their homes when a procession bearing the Sacrament

passes through their streets. Jews may have only one synagogue in any town.

par. 13. Jews must wear a pointed hat.

par. 14. Parish priests are to prevent Christians from mixing with Jews in baths, taverns, and public drinking places. No Christian woman may serve in the home of a Jew. Jews may not hold public office. If a Jew has sexual relations with a Christian woman, he is to pay a fine and she is to be publicly whipped.[1]

Hube, *Antiquissimae Constitutiones Synodales Provinciae Gneznensis*, p. 69.

par. 12. Item cum adhuc terra Polonica sit in corpore Christianitatis nova plantatio, ne forte eo facilius populus Christianus a cohabitantium Judeorum superstitionibus et pravis moribus inficiatur quo levius atque citius Christiana religio in fidelium cordibus in his partibus est plantata, districte praecipimus: ut Judei in hac provincia Gneznensi commorantes inter Christianos permixti non habitent; sed in aliquo sequestri loco civitatis vel villae domos suas sibi contiguas sive conjunctas habeant; ita quod a communi habitatione Christianorum sepe, muro, vel fossato Judeorum habitatio separetur. Praecipimus autem: ut per episcopum dioecesanum et per dominum temporalem tam Christiani quam Judei, quorum domus intermixtae sunt, ut ad venditionem seu permutationem earum ad arbitrium bonorum virorum, censura qua convenit, compellantur. Quod si haec separatio infra proximum festum natale sancti Johannis Baptistae non fuerit adimpleta, tam dioecesanus loci, quam dominus temporalis ingressum ecclesiae extunc noverint sibi interdictum, si jurisdictionis seu interdictionis officium exercere distulerint in rebelles. Interim autem, si sacramentum altaris ante domos Judeorum deferri contingat, ipsi Judei, audito sonitu primo, intra domos suas se recipiant et fenestras et ostia sua claudant. Postquam autem haec separatio facta fuerit, decrevimus, ut Judei in una civitate vel villa unicam tantum habeant synagogam.

par. 13. Item statuimus atque ordinavimus: ut Judei cornutum pileum, quem quondam in istis partibus consueverunt deferre, et sua temeritate deponere praesumpserunt, resumerent, ut a Christianis discerni valeant evidenter sicut olim in generali concilio fuit definitum. Quicumque autem Judeus sine tali signo deprehensus fuerit incedere, ad morem terrae poena pecuniaria puniatur.

par. 14. Item praecipimus: ut Judei sacerdoti parochiali, infra cujus parochiae terminos manserint, pro eo, quod loca in quibus Christiani habitare deberent occupant, juxta quantitatem damni, quod ei ex hoc inferunt, ad arbitrium dioecesani loci, omnes proventus refundere compellantur. Prohibemus etiam: ne stubas et balnea seu tabernas Christianorum frequentent, nec servos aut anchillas aut nutrices seu quaecumque mancipia die noctuque in suis domibus retinere praesumant, nec ad recipiendum theloneum seu aliud publicum officium aliquatenus assumantur. Si quis vero Judeus cum aliqua Christiana fornicationis vitium deprehensus fuerit commisisse quoadusque decem marcas ad minus pro emendatione solverit, districto carceri mancipetur, et mulier Christiana quae tam damnatum coitum peregerit per civitatem fustigata, de ipsa civitate sine spe redeundi penitus expellatur.

1. The Fourth Lateran Council decreed that such relations were punishable irrespective of the sex of the Jewish partner. So far, these conciliar texts have emphasized offenses committed only by Jewish men. See below, nos. XXVII–XXX, on Christian men having sexual relations with Jewesses.

VII 1267

Concilium Viennense (Auctoritate Guidonis Sedis Apostolicae Legati)

XV. To restrain Jewish insolence, Jews must wear a pointed hat, as the (Fourth Lateran) Council ordered. Local priests are to calculate the losses suffered by the Church when Christians sell their homes to Jews and then make efforts to have the Jews pay the tithes the former Christian owners would have paid.

XVI. Jews may not appear in taverns or baths frequented by Christians, nor are they to have female Christian servants within their homes.

XVII. Sexual relations between Jews and Christian women are prohibited. Jews will be jailed and Christian women flogged out of town for violations.

XVIII. Christians should not dine together with Jews, nor should they attend Jewish weddings or join in their games and entertainments. Christians are not to buy meat from Jews.

XIX. Under pain of "indirect excommunication," no immoderate usury is to be taken, and any *immoderate usury* that has been taken must be restored.[1] Jews must close their windows when a consecrated wafer is carried through the streets in a procession. There are to be no disputes between Jews and Christians. Christians may not be enticed into Judaism, nor may they be circumcised for any reason. Jews may not visit sick Christians or provide them with medication. There are to be no new synagogues. Jews may not consume meat in public during Lent.

Mansi, 23:1174.

XV. *De habitu Judaeorum*

Item, cum in tantum insolentiae Judaeorum excreverint, ut per eos in quampluribus Christianis jam dicatur infici puritas catholicae sanctitatis, non tam nova cudentes, quam summorum pontificum statuta vetera renovantes, districte praecipimus, ut Judaei, qui discerni debent in habitu a Christianis, cornutum pileum, quem quidam in istis partibus consueverunt deferre, et sua tenuitate deponere praesumpserunt, resumantur, ut a Christianis evidenter discerni valeant, sicut olim in generali concilio extitit definitum. Quicumque autem Judaeus sine tali signo deprehensus fuerit incedere, a domino terrae poena pecuniaria puniatur. Adjicientes, ut Judaei sacerdoti parochiali, infra cujus parochiae terminos manserint, pro eo quod loca in quibus Christiani habitare deberent, occupant, juxta quantitatem damni, quod ei ex hoc inferunt, ad arbitrium dioecesani loci omnes proventus quos ex Christianis, si ibidem manerent, sacerdos perciperet, refundere compellantur. Decimas etiam praediales cum omni integritate persolvant.

XVI. *De mancipiis Judaeorum*

Prohibemus insuper ne stubas et balnea seu tabernas Christianorum frequentare, seu intrare praesumant, nec servos, vel ancillas, aut nutrices, seu quaecumque Christiana mancipia die noctuve in domibus suis retinere praesumant, nec ad recipiendum telonium seu ad alia publica officia aliquatenus assumantur.

XVII. *De coitu Judaei cum Christiana*

Se quis vero Judaeus cum aliqua Christiana fornicationis vitium deprehensus fuerit commisisse, quoadusque decem marcas argenti ad minus pro emendatione solverit, districto carceri mancipetur: et mulier Christiana, quae tam damnosum coitum elegerit, per civitatem fustigata, de ipsa civitate sine spe redeundi penitus expellatur.

XVIII. *De conviviis eorumdem*

Item omnibus Christianis istius provinciae et civitatis et dioecesis Pragensis sub poena excommunicationis districtius inhibemus, ne Judaeos vel Judaeas secum ad convivandum recipiant, vel cum eis bibere vel manducare audeant, aut etiam cum ipsis in suis nuptiis, vel neomeniis, vel ludis saltare vel tripudiare praesumant: nec Christiani carnes venales, seu alia cibaria a Judaeis emant, ne forte Judaei per hoc Christianos, quos hostes reputant, fraudulenta machinatione venenent.

XIX. *De synagogis Judaeorum*

Adjicientes, ut si de cetero quocumque praetextu Judaei a Christianis graves seu immoderatas usuras extorserint, Christianorum eis participationem subtrahatur, donec de immoderato gravamine satisfecerint competenter. Unde Christiani, si opus fuerit, per censuram ecclesiasticam compellantur ab eorum commerciis abstinere. Principibus autem injungimus, ut propter hoc non sint Christianis infesti, sed potius a tanto gravamine Judaeos studeant cohibere. Si vero sacramentum altaris ante domos eorum deferri contigerit: ipsi Judaei, audito sonitu praevio, intra domos suas se recipiant, et fenestras ac ostia sua claudant. Hoc etiam in quolibet die parasceves per praelatos ecclesiae facere compellantur. Nec praesumant de fide catholica cum simplicibus disputare, nec filios et uxores Judaeorum ad fidem Christianam venientes, invitos audeant detinere. Nec Christianos ad Judaismum alliciant, aut aliquo ausu temerario circumcidant. Nec Christianos infirmos visitent, vel circa ipsos exerceant opera medicinae. Synagogas novas non erigant: et si quas erexerint, eas removeant aut deponant. Vetustam, si opus fuerit, reficiant, non ampliorem, pretiosiorem faciant, seu etiam altiorem. Carnes in Quadragesima, quando Christiani a carnibus abstinent et jejunant, aperte vel publice non deportent. Praecipimus autem episcopis, ut ad haec omnia observanda in singulis articulis Judaeos per abstractionem communionis Christianorum compellant. Ipsos quoque principes ac judices eorumdem districtius admonemus, ne Judaeis statuta nostra servare nolentibus alicujus protectionis seu defensionis fervorem impendant: sed si aliqua eis a praelatis ecclesiasticis injungantur, ea fideliter exequantur, alioquin introitum ecclesiae et communionem Divinorum officiorum sibi noverint interdicta. Volumus etiam, et sub poena excommunicationis praecipimus, ut dominus electus Saltzburgensis ejusque suffraganei, nec non et episcopus Pragensis, has constitutiones nostras sigillo nostro sigillatas habeant, easque singulis annis in synodis episcopalibus et in provinciali concilio faciant recitari, et diligentius observari; et ea quae tangunt laicos, faciant per parochiales ecclesias suarum dioecesum publicare.

Acta sunt haec Viennae in Austria anno Dom. MCCLXVII. IV. Idus Maii, pont. domini Clementis PP. IV. anno III.

1. There obviously was some rate of interest that was considered *moderate,* probably 20 percent; see Stow, "Papal and Royal Attitudes," p. 165.

VIII   1268

Statuta Synodalia Claromontensis Ecclesia

> Priests are to see to it that their parishioners do not live in the homes of Jews, dine at their tables, or accept their medicines. No one may entrust Jews with offices or magistracies.

Mansi, 23:1205.

Et inhibeant sacerdotes parochianis suis, ne cum Judaeis in eisdem domibus habitent, vel cum eis commaneant; nec eos ad convivia sua recipiant; . . . medicinam; nec eisdem judiciis praeposituras aut ballias committere praesumant.

IX   1279

Concilium Apud Pontem Andomari

> Christians may not dwell in the homes of Jews or serve them domestically. Jews must wear some insignia distinguishing them from Christians.

Mansi, 24:223.

IX. *Ut Christiani Judaeis non serviant, aut cohabitent: et ut Judaei signo aliquo discernantur.*

Inhibemus, ne aliqui Christiani, seu aliquae Christianae, Judaeis servire in hospitiis suis, seu cum ipsis habitare praesumant: et praecipimus, quod Judaei signa patentia deferre cogantur, per quae a catholicis discernantur.

X   1279

Synod of Buda, Philippus Firmanus Episcopus Legatus

> par. 125. Jews must wear a circle of red cloth on the left breast of their outer garments to avoid possible dangers to Christians. Muslims are to wear saffron.
>
> par. 126. Jews may not hold public office or be entrusted with the collection of tolls, etc.

Hube, *Ant. Const.,* p. 159.

par. 125. Quia valde periculosum est et sacris canonibus inimicum, quod Judei, quos pietas Christiana receptat et sustinet cohabitationes eorum, a Christianis per aliqua non distinguantur et cognoscantur insignia et signa, quod cum Christianis in familia habitent, vel morentur, vel in curiis ac domibus conversentur, aut Christiani habitent cum eis; praesenti constitutione statuimus: quod omnes et singuli Judei utriusque sexus, in terris nostrae legationis, portent unum circulum de panno rubeo, pro signo, assutum sive consutum ante pectus, in parte sinistra, in veste superiori, quam communiter et regulariter portant de super vestes suas alias, cum extra domos sive habitationes exeant, vel incedant, vel publice quocumque modo appareant, aut se exhibeant, vel ostendant et hujusmodi signum infra. . . . Quod si in hujusmodi signo assumendo infra terminum supradictum, aut etiam de cetero deferendo, prout superius est expressum, Judei prefati vel eorum aliqui contumaces fuerunt rebelles, extunc Christianorum commercium, nec non ignem et aquam sibi noverint interdictam. Christiani vero qui contra constitutionem hujusmodi praefatis Judeis in merciis commutare aut eis ignem vel aquam dare, aut aliquos Judeos in familia retinere, aut ipsis Judeis familiariter adhaerere, aut cum eis in familia, curia sive domo stare praesumpserint, ipso facto sciant sibi ingressum ecclesiae interdictum: nec prius eis in ecclesiam pateat ingressus, quam ad mandatum episcopi, abbatis, praepositi; archidiaconi seu cujuslibet alterius praelati in cujus dioecesi, dominio vel jurisdictione Christiani hujusmodi commorantur, sufficienti, sub certa poena, cautione praestita, quod ulterius in talibus non excedant, ad ingressum ecclesiae fuerint restituti. Quod autem constitutum est de Judeis, hoc de Saracenis, Ismaelitis, et quibuscumque aliis non colentibus baptismatis sacramentum statuimus inviolabiliter

observandum; hoc excepto: quod ubi Judei portant circulum pro signo rubeum, alii supradicti signum croceum teneantur deferre.

par. 126. Praeterea statuimus: quod tributa, vectigalia, telonea, seu pedagia vel quaevis alia publica officia Judeis, Sarracenis, Ismaelitis, Scismaticis seu quibuscumque aliis, ab unione fidei Catholicae alienis, nullatenus committantur; et specialiter praelati ecclesiarum suarum redditus seu proventus eis vendere non audeant, vel locare. Quod si quis contra hoc venire praesumpserit, si episcopus fuerit, ab executione pontificalium, inferiores vero praelati seu clerici, cujuscumque sint ordinis, dignitatis ac status, ab executione suorum ordinum per tres menses ipso facto noverint se suspensos. Vel si infra tres menses ipsos non expulerint vel expulsos reassumpserint, excommunicationis sententiam ipso facto incurrant. Laicos autem cuiuscumque honoris, conditionis, dignitatis, praeeminentiae, sive status, qui in derogationem constitutionis praesentis huiusmodi officia Judeis vel prohibitis supradictis tam diu volumus excommunicationis sententiae manere subjectos, donec Judeis et aliis infidelibus praefatis ab officiis amotis et ejectis supradictis, et praestita sufficienti cautione dioecesanis suis, quod nullos ex praedictis de cetero in aliquo recipient, retinebunt aut habebunt officio, juxta formam ecclesiae fuerint absoluti.

XI　1279

Concilium Avenionense ab Arelatensis Provinciae episcopis, XVI kal. Jun. anno MCCLXXIX celebratum

> Jews must wear a prominent sign on their garments. They may have no Christian wet nurses or maidservants, nor may they sell their meats to Christians. During Lent, they are not to consume meat publicly. They are to avoid religious processions. Disobedience will be punished by indirect excommunication.

Mansi, 24:237.

VI. *Ut serventur jura edita de Judaeis.*

Insuper etiam statuimus, ut jura edita de Judaeis serventur: videlicet in pectoribus appendentia vestimentis exterioribus dissimilia signa portent; talia siquidem, per quae faciliter et distincte valeant a Christianis agnosci pariter et discerni. Sed neque teneant Christianos nutricios aut nutrices: carnes autem per eos occisas nullus vendat fidelibus Christianis. Ipsi quoque Judaei dies excolant manifeste. In Quadragesima carnes publice non manducent. Obviantes autem cruci, sive Christi corpori, vel penitus se recludant, aut cito recedant, vel reverentiam exhibeant, ut Christiani. Alioquin Judaei quilibet contra facientes, per subtractionem communionis fidelium, et Christiani per excommunicationis sententiam, per ordinarios, vel officiales, seu loca tenentes eorum, solicite compellantur.

XII   1280

Synodis Pictavensis, Constitutiones factae per fratrem Cualterum tunc episcopum Pictavensem.

> No Christian nurses may serve within the homes of Jews on pain of a fine of 50 solidi, three-quarters of which is to be donated to the poor. To make it more difficult to lend at usury, no cleric may write or seal loan contracts for Jews. Christians are not to lend to Jews at interest. Christians are not to partake of Jewish foods or medicines, nor are they to take money at usury from Jews, *except in cases of necessity,* and in the presence of witnesses. Otherwise, they will pay a fine of 50 solidi, three-quarters of which will be donated to the poor.

Mansi, 24:384.

VI. *De servientibus Judaeis et usurariis.*

Cum Judaeis, ne sub pretextu alendorum puerorum, vel pro servitio, vel alia qualibet causa, nutrices vel servientes cujuscumque sexus fidem tenentes catholicam, in domibus secum habere praesumant, canonica inhibeant instituta; nos volentes inhibitionem hujusmodi, quam multorum fertur temeritas praeterire, poenae adjectione innovare: statuimus, quod quicumque Judaeus contra praemissa fecerit, pro quolibet excessu in quinquaginta solidos puniatur secundum jura: Judaei possint ab illicitis per ecclesiam, etiam pecuniariter coerceri: quarta parte illius poenae detegenti promissa, et deferenti in publicam notitiam, et residuo pauperibus parochiae in qua delinquens Judaeus morabitur, applicando. Christianus vero vel Christiana, qui contra inhibitionem nostram et monitionem praedictam, quam super hoc in generali facimus, servitio institerit Judaeorum, excommunicationis ipso facto incurrat sententiam.

Ceterum cum fere omnes Judaei, in civitate et dioecesi Pictavensi, usuras utriusque testamenti pagina detestatas non vereantur publice exercere: nos considerantes quod eo magis adimetur Judaeis libertas vel opportunitas foenebrem pecuniam exercendi, cum minor sibi aderit commoditas foenerandi: districtius inhibemus, ne decani rurales, archipresbyteri, et alii subditi nostri, super contractibus Judaeorum, obligationibus, seu conventionibus, ad commodum eorum initis, litteras sigillare, vel eas scribere, vel auctoritatem impertiri praesumant. Item ne aliquis Christianus audeat Judaeis mutuo dare pecuniam, vel rem aliam consistentem pondere, numero, vel mensura, nec cum ipsis Judaeis, alium contractum in fraudem mutui celebrare, nec ipsos Christianos a Judaeis, vel Judaeos a Christianis delegatos suscipere debitores, nec cum ipsis potu, vel cibo, vel medicamento participare. Item inhibemus, ne aliquis Christianus, extra casum necessitatis, a Judaeis voluntariam pecuniam accipiat sub usuris, vel cum eis contractum ineat sapientem usurariam pravitatem. Si vero necessitas ipsum Christianum compulerit recipere a Judaeis pecuniam, sub usuris eam non accipiat, nec super hoc se obliget, nisi sub duarum vel trium testimonium personarum: poenam quinquaginta solidorum pro quolibet actu imponentes cuilibet contrarium facienti: quarta parte deducenti praedicta in plenam notitiam, et aliis partibus, pauperibus parochiae ubi delinquens morabitur, juxta nostrum arbitrium applicandis. Praedictum vero statutum de non sigillandis litteris super contractibus Judaeorum, vel obligationibus ad eorum commodum initis, volumus ad officialem nostrum, et ad auditorem nostri capituli Pictavensis, qui in hoc consenserint, extendi.

XIII   1282

Concilium Terraconense

> Any Christian woman who lives in the home of a Jew or serves as a
> nurse will be excommunicated.

Mansi, 24:490.

V. *Quod Christianae non habitent cum Judaeis, et eorum filios non nutriant.*

Statuimus etiam, sacro approbante concilio, quod nulla mulier alicujus loci provinciae Terraconensis audeat habitare cum Judaeis, aut filios eorum nutrire seu lactare; et quaecumque contra hujusmodi inhibitionem nostram, postquam monita super hoc fuerit, praesumserit supradicta, decernimus eam ex tunc excommunicationis sententiae sub-jacere: ita videlicet, quod cum illud dioecesano, aut rectori loci illius ubi mulieres super hoc culpabiles inventae fuerint, extiterit nuntiatum, per jam dictum dioecesanum aut rectorem ipsae mulieres excommunicatae nuntientur, et tanquam excommunicatas ab omnibus faciant evitari; et ne ipsae mulieres de facili in excommunicationis laqueum incidere valeant, ipso facto, volumus et mandamus, quod praesens constitutio per dioecesanum, aut rectorem locorum, in quibus Judaei morantur, semel annis singulis publicetur.

XIV   1284

Synodus Apud Sanctum Hippolytum Godefrido Pataviensi Episcopo

> All Christian servants and female nurses of Jews will be excommuni-cated. Christians who give Jews money at interest or receive from Jews at usury are to be denounced in the churches.

Mansi, 24:510.

Quod Christiani servientes Judaeis excommunicentur.

Item cum dudum Judaeis prohibita et interdicta sint mancipia Chris-tiana, volumus et praecipimus, ut plebani et alii Rectores Ecclesiarum, ubi sunt domicilia Judaeorum, diebus Dominicis omnes de fide Catholica Judaeorum nutrices, et servientes denuncient excommunicatos: etiam denuncient omnes alios Christianos, qui apud Judaeos pecuniam suam locant, aut a Judaeis usuram recipiunt, vel ut Judaei eamdem pecuniam mutuent ad usuram.

XV   1284

Synodus Nemausensis

> Only bishops may ordain penances for forbidden acts of sexual intercourse, including that with nuns, virgins, Jewesses, Muslim

women, or brute animals. Furthermore, Jews must wear a rose on their breasts. They may not appear in public during the Easter season, nor are they to consume meat in public during Lent. Christians must refrain from eating unleavened bread at Passover, living in Jewish homes, frequenting public baths in Jewish company, or receiving medicines from Jewish physicians.

No one may be forced to the baptismal font against his will. If he comes on his own accord, the matter is to be properly ascertained. Following baptism, his lord may not distrain the property of the new convert.

Mansi, 24:528, 533–534, 561–562.

Item interroget quemlibet confitentem prout secundum conditionem personae viderit faciendum. Scilicet de perjurio, invidia, odio, detractione, de superbia, et utrum injuste habeat, vel detineat alienum. Item de fornicatione, adulterio, et incestu. Et si dixerit, se peccatum incontinentiae commisisse, quaeratur utrum peccaverit cum monacha consecrata, vel non consecrata, vidua, virgine, seu corrupta, Christiana, Judaea, vel Saracena, et utrum in loco sacro, vel non sacro, et an in diebus Dominicis, vel festivis, et temporibus jejuniorum, et utrum unam cognoverit, vel plures, et quoties, et an in aliis peccatis alios invitaverit, vel induxerit ad peccandum:

Isti sunt casus in quibus poenitentes ad episcopum sunt mittendi.

Si quis confitebitur se credere aliquam haereticam pravitatem. Item simoniacus quocumque modo commiserit simoniam. Item clerici excommunicati majori excommunicatione, vel interdicti, aut suspensi, qui ante absolutionem Divina officia celebrarunt, scilicet Missam cantando, evangelium, epistolam, vel alias horas canonicas dicendo, faciendo principaliter officium suum in ecclesia. Item clerici per saltum promoti aliquo ordine praetermisso. Item clerici, qui ab alieno episcopo se fecerunt ordinare, nostra licentia non obtenta. Item incendiarii. Item illi qui suos filios occiderunt studiose, vel etiam negligenter. Item illi, qui tractaverunt in malos usus Eucharistiam, seu chrisma. Item illi, qui tractaverunt facto, verbo, consensu, vel alio modo, homicidium. Item sacrilegi, et violatores ecclesiarum. Item illi, qui luxuriam expleverunt cum matre, sorore, vel aliqua consanguinea sua, vel uxore fratris, vel cum sanctimoniali consecrata, vel non consecrata. Item illi, qui in ecclesia luxuriam commiserunt. Item illi, qui cum Judaea, vel Saracena, vel bruto animali coire ausu nefario praesumpserunt. Item mulier quae de adulterio concepit infantem quem maritus credit esse suum, propter quem legitimi liberi fraudantur haereditate paterna.

De perfidis Judaeis.

Praecipimus ut Judaei in Nemausensi dioecesi commorantes, omni tempore in medio pectoris rosam portent, ut per hanc a Christianis discernantur: et in diebus lamentationum, et Dominicae passionis, in publicum non procedant: nec occasione puerorum suorum nutriendorum, vel alia qualibet causa, nutrices, seu servientes teneant in domibus suis Christianas: et si contra praesumpserint, omnibus Christianis inhibeatur districte, ne cum eis audeant aliquod commercium exercere. Interdicimus quoque, ne Judaei ipsi in diebus Dominicis et festivis, praesumant publice operari; et ne carnes suas vendant, vel eas comedant publice in Quadragesima, seu aliis diebus, in quibus ab esu carnium abstinent Christiani. Quod si contra praedicta fecerint, Christianorum participatio, seu comunio, usque ad satisfactionem condignam, eis in commerciis et omnibus aliis denegetur. Sub poena excommunicationis inhibemus, ne quis Christianorum, carnes refutatas a Judaeis in macello Christianorum praesumat vendere, vel alibi infra villam, praecipientes, ut omnes Christiani vitent convivia Judaeorum, nec eos ad convivium recipiant: quia cum ipsi apud Christianos cibis communibus non utantur, indignum, atque sacrilegum est eorum cibos a Christianis sumi, cum ea quae Domino Jesu permittente nos sumimus, ab illis judicentur immunda. Nullus etiam Christianus, vel Christiana, azyma Judaeorum manducet, aut cum eis in eadem domo habitet, nec aliquem eorum pro medico in infirmitatibus vocet, aut aliquam medicinam recipiat, aut cum eis balneo se lavet: nec eis supra Christianos bailiviae, aut aliqua publica officia committantur, ne in Christianos occasionem habeant saeviendi. Christiani vero qui non servaverint praedicta, monitione praemissa, excommunicationis sententiae supponantur. Item volumus, et districte praecipimus, ut nullus invitos vel nolentes paganos, Judaeos, seu quoscumque alios infideles, ad baptismum venire compellat. Si quis autem eorum ad Christianos causa suscipiendae fidei confugerit: postquam voluntas ejus fuerit ecclesiae patefacta, Christianus efficiatur, absque contradictione et calumnia aliquorum, et etiam dominorum: nec a possessionibus, seu aliis bonis suis, propter hoc ullatenus excludatur. Baptizati tamen servitia debita et consueta non minus debent propriis dominis exhibere: si tamen eorum domini fuerint Christiani, quia in hoc casu servi remanent post baptismum. Tamen si eorum domini Judaei fuerint, vel alii infideles; baptismus a talium dominorum servitio ipsos penitus liberavit.

XVI 1287

Synodus Exoniensis, A Petro Quivil episcopo, Exonii congregata finita XVI. Calend. Maii, anno Domini MCCLXXXVII

Christians are free men while Jews live in a state of perpetual servitude. Hence, it is wrong for Christian maids to serve the sons of the servant woman (Hagar). As the Fourth Lateran decreed, Christian women are not to serve in the homes of Jews: "Consorting with evil corrupts the good." Jews are to hold no public office, build no new synagogues, share no food in common with Christians, provide them with no medicines, nor are they to appear in public at Eastertime. They are furthermore to wear two woolen tablets of another color (than that of their clothing) sewn on their breasts, which are minimally to be two digits wide and four long. Jews are also to pay the tithes on their homes, which Christian owners would otherwise be paying.

Mansi, 24:830.
Powicke and Cheney (1964), 1045.

XLIX. *De Judaeis et eorum mancipiis.*

A Judaeis regimen Dei ablatum, et datum genti justitiam facienti, scriptum in canonibus reperitur. Per quod liquet Christicolas libertate donatos, Judaeosque subactos eorum perpetuae servituti. Cum igitur scriptum sit: Ejice ancillam et filium ejus, non enim erit haeres filius ancillae cum filio liberae; nimis reputamus absurdum, ut filii liberae, ancillae filiis famulentur.

Quapropter Lateranensis concilii statuta sequentes, districte prohibemus ne Judaei sub obtentu alendorum puerorum suorum, neque pro servitio vel qualibet alia causa, in domibus suis mancipia habeant Christiana: ne forte per assiduam familiaritatem, ad eorum perfidiam simplicium animos valeant inclinare. Saepe enim malorum consortia, bonos corrumpunt. Christiani qui contra hanc prohibitionem venire praesumpserint, excommunicentur: Judaei gravi subjaceant ultioni.

Prohibemus insuper, ne Judaei publicis fungantur officiis, quorum praetextu Christianis nimium sint molesti. Et quoniam cum eis sumere cibum non licet: inhibemus, ne Judaei ad Christianorum, vel Christiani ad Judaeorum accedant convivia. Item si quis Christianus infirmatus fuerit, a Judaeo non accipiat medicinam. Item die parasceves, ostia et fenestras habeant clausas, quia Christianis afflictis consueverant illudere illo die. Item prohibemus ne novas fabricent synagogas. Sed si erigant veteres quae corruerint, vel ruinam minentur: si ipsas reaedificare permittantur, ita quod ampliores vel pretiosiores non faciant, ipsis satis novimus esse permissum.

Ad haec, districte praecipimus, ut Judaei utriusque sexus, super vestes exteriores, duas tabulas laneas habeant alterius coloris, ad pectus consutas: quarum latitudo digitorum duorum, et longitudo quatuor sit ad minus: ut sic per diversitatem habitus a catholicis discernantur; et damnatae commixtionis excessus inter hos et illos valeant evitari.

Ne autem ecclesiae parochiales per ipsos suis juribus defraudentur: praecipimus, quod Judaei de terris quas colunt, decimas solvere, vel possessionibus ipsis renunciare; et pro domibus quas inhabitant, parochialia jura ecclesiae parochiali debita tribuere, arctius compellantur.

XVII   1288

Concilium Insulanum, A Praesulibus Arelaterisis provinciae

> Jews are to wear "unlike signs" on their breasts.[1] They are not to have Christian nurses, partake of foods in common with Christians or appear in public at Eastertime.

Mansi, 24:960.

XII. *Ut serventur jura edita de Judaeis.*

Item VI. caput ejusdem concilii innovamus, et praesenti concilio approbante praecipimus observari omnia in eo contenta, quod incipit. "Insuper etiam statuimus, ut jura edita de Judaeis serventur: videlicet, in pectoribus appendentia vestimentis exterioribus dissimilia signa portent: talia siquidem, per quae faciliter et districte valeant a Christianis agnosci pariter et discerni. Sed neque teneant Christianos nutricios aut nutrices: carnes autem per eos occisas nullus vendat fidelibus Christianis. Ipsi quoque Judaei dies excolant manifeste. In quadragesima carnes publice non manducent. Obviantes autem cruci, sive Christi corpori, vel penitus se recludant, aut cito recedant, vel reverentiam exhibeant ut Christiani. Alioquin Judaei quilibet contra facientes, per subtractionem communionis fidelium, et Christiani per excommunicationis sententiam, per ordinarios, vel officiales, seu loca tenentes eorum, sollicite compellantur.

1. One is struck by the dissimilarity in legislation concerning the special habit or badge worn by Jews. The Fourth Lateran Council had indeed decreed only a special habit, and the first papal reference specifically to a "sign" was made by Honorius III as late as 1219 (*ChJ*, no. 38). Yet during the next seventy years no one "badge" became standard; see, too, *Encyclopaedia Judaica*, s.v., "Badge, Jewish." This inconsistency seems to indicate that the spread of the badge was slow and fitful.

XVIII   1292

Concilium Aschaffenburgense

> Although the General Council (Fourth Lateran) had issued decrees about Jewish clothing, Christian maidservants, the holding of public office, and the appearance of the Jews in public at Eastertime, appropriate statutes to enforce these decrees (on the local level) had yet to be enacted. The council now issued such statutes, along with penalties, including fines against violators.

Mansi, 24:109.

XVIII. *De Judaeis.*

Licet olim in generali concilio provide fuerit institutum, ut uterque sexus de gente Judaeorum in omni Christianorum provincia signum vel habitum publice deferre debeat, quo a populo Christiano manifeste distingui valeat et discerni, fueritque adjectum et salubriter provisum in concilio memorato, ut in diebus Dominicae passionis in publicum prodire non debeat gens praedicta sed in suis se domibus continere clausis domorum ostiis et fenestris; ut sicut in eodem concilio tangitur, christianis qui sacratissimae passionis memoriam exhibentes lamentationis signa protendunt, illis diebus ab eodem Judaeorum populo non illudatur, licet etiam alias in sacris canonibus prohibeatur expresse, ut Judaei nec publica officia, nec aliquas seculares habeant dignitates, aut in suis domibus aut servitiis mancipia teneant christiana. Quia tamen nec contra Judaeos in praedictis praehabitis casibus contrarium facientes, nec contra Christianos potentes, ipsos sine distinctionis signo vel habitu in suis terminis tollerantes aut publicis officiis aut secularibus dignitatibus praeficientes eosdem, certa et sufficiens poena in canonibus reperitur: considerantes quod facilitas veniae incentivum tribuit delinquendi, et plus solet timeri quod specialiter praecipitur, quam quod generaliter imperatur, de multa deliberatione, et unanimi approbatione hujus sacri concilii irrefragabiliter duximus statuendum, ut in universis civitatibus, oppidis, castris et villis civitatis, dioecesis et provinciae Moguntinae gens Judaeorum utriusque sexus infra duos menses post publicationem hujus statuti talia signa et habitum, quibus sine qualibet ambiguitate a Christiano populo distinguatur, sibi eligat et deferat manifeste, dignitatesque seculares et officia publica, quibus de gente praefata aliquis forte praeest, et mancipia Christiana prorsus dimittat, alioquin in omnibus locis ubi Judaei huic sacro et salubri concilio in hac parte obedire nolentes, habitare vel domicilia obtinere noscuntur, in poenam Christianorum potentum tamdiu cessetur ab officiis divinorum, donec.per principes, potestates, nobiles Christianos in quorum territoriis praedicta gens misera conversatur, ad observationem praemissorum omnium compellantur. Ipsi autem Judaei per locorum Dioecesanos indirecte per subtractionem communionis Christi fidelium excommunicationis sententia percellantur. Si quis vero de gente praefata in die Parasceve visus fuerit in platea vel per hostium suae domus aut fenestram prospicere, ad quod probandum duorum Christianorum stabitur juramento, is loci Dioecesano in marca argenti poenae nomine teneatur, ad cujus solutionem reus et omnes defendentes eumdem per excommunicationis sententiam compellantur, et ne quis Christianus aut Judaeus hujus statuti ignorantiam valeat allegare, universis parochiarum rectoribus per Moguntin. civit. dioeces. et provinciam constitutis, in quorum parochiis Judaei morantur, sub poena excommunicationis in quoslibet transgressores auctoritate praesentis concilii ex nunc latae praecipimus firmiter et districte, ut quilibet in sua parochia in singulis dominicis diebus, singula quatuor tempora immediate sequentibus infra missarum solemnia publice praefatum statutum lingua materna exponere non omittant.

XIX   ca. 1295

Bishop Wm. Durand's Instructions to his clergy

> If Jews and Christians have been warned three times about providing domestic service to Jews, yet persist in their actions, then the Christian will be excommunicated and the Jew denied the communion of the faithful. Christians are also prohibited from grinding the Jews' wheat, baking their bread, and providing them services of any

kind. No notary may write an act providing for either manifest or hidden usury. Jews are to wear a round badge on their breast of a color different from that of their clothing. Jews may not dine with Christians, share meat with them, hold office, or appear in public at Eastertime. No one is to be forced into baptism, but any one coming willingly is to be received, and his lord is not to distrain his property.

Jos. Berthelé. "Les instructions et constitutions de Guillaume Durand." *Academie des sciences et lettres de Montpellier, Memoires de la Section des Lettres,* 2nd series, 3 (1900): 93–94.

De Judeis

Judei nutrices, ancillas et alia mancipia christiana in domibus propriis tenere non presumant. Christiani vero qui contra hoc fecerint, moneantur ter ut a judeorum servicio recedant. Quod si facere noluerint, excommunicentur, et tamdiu excommunicati publice nuncientur, donec ab illorum servicio recesserint et de tanta offensa satisfecerint competenter. Judei vero tercio moneantur ut tales a se abjiciant. Quod si facere noluerint, eis christianorum participatio subtrahatur, ita videlicet quod mercatores et alii christiani tercio moneantur ut nullos contractus aut aliqua commercia cum eis faciant, nec ad molendum bladum suum vel ad coquendum panem sive quecumque alia christianorum subsidia admittantur.

Nullus tabellio instrumenta judeis faciat in quibus sciverit vel crediderit esse usuras occultas vel manifestas; qui vero moniti contra fecerint, excommunicentur et excommunicati publice nuncientur.

Judei in diebus lamentationum et dominice Passionis in publicum non appareant, vel procedant, nec in diebus dominicis et sollempnibus publice operari presumant.

Nullus christianus carnes judeorum refutatas ab eis presumat vendere in macello christianorum vel alibi infra villam.

Sed nec judei carnes publice vendant vel comedant in diebus [in] quibus ab esu carnium se abstinent christiani.

Omnis quoque christianus judeorum convivia vitet, nec eos quiusquam ad convivia recipiat, quia, cum ipsi cibaria nostra vitent, sacrilegium est a christianis eorum nefandissimos cibos sumi.

Nullus quoque christianus azima judeorum manducet.

Nullus judeum medicum in sua egritudine advocet, aut ab eo recipiat medicinam, vel cum eis in balneo se lavet.

Judei quoque, ut a christianis discernantur, in superiori veste, in medio pectoris, rotam bene apparentem et coloris alterius quam sit vestis ipsa, publice portent.

Nemo eis aut aliis infidelibus bajulias seu alia publica officia super christianos committat, ne ex hoc occasionem in christianos habeant seviendi.

Nullus judeos aut alios infideles ad baptismum venire absolute compellat; verumptamen si aliquis eorum, causa fidei suscipiende, ad christianos confugerit, postquam de hoc constiterit, christianus efficiatur, non obstante domini sui, patris vel matris seu cujuslibet alterius contradictione, nec a possessionibus seu bonis suis propterhoc excludatur. Baptizatus tamen servicia debita et consueta non minus debet proprio domino exhibere, et hoc si dominus christianus sit, quia in hoc casu servus remanet post baptismum. Si vero dominus judeus vel infidelis sit, baptismus a talis domini servicio liberat baptizatum.

XX   1299

Concilium Ansanum

> Jews are to wear a badge of a distinct color, not have Christian domestics, not share meat with Christians, be present at processions, hold back tithes, or enjoy public office of any nature.

Mansi, 24:1219.

De Judaeis quod aliquod signum portent, per quod possint a Christianis discerni.

Cum ex eo quod Judaei aliquod signum patenter non portant, per quod Judaei sunt, a Christianis valeant reprehendi, quam plura possint, prout pro certo comperimus, inimica Christianae fidei perpetrari; ideoque provide atque consulte statuimus, ut Judaei in quocunque loco nostrae dioecesis et provinciae commorantes in superiori veste quam gestant et gestabunt in antea, aliquod signum portent de panno vel tela consutum ita magnum et coloris dissimilis in veste superiori in qua debeat consui, ut possint videri et cognosci. Prohibemus insuper ne teneant christianos nutricios et nutrices: carnes autem pro Judaeis occisas nullus vendat fidelibus christianis.

Obviantes autem Judaei Cruci, sive corpori Christi, vel penitus se recludant, vel cum festinantia recedant, aut reverentiam cum humilitate exhibeant Salvatori.

Praeterea ecclesiis in quarum parochiis Judaei commorantur, satisfaciant pro decimis et oblationibus de domibus et possessionibus quas noscuntur in ipsis parochiis possidere.

Si vero Judaei contra praemissa fecerint vel aliquod eorumdem, eis christianorum participatio denegetur, et christiani ab eorum participatione abstinere nolentes, per censuram ecclesiasticam compellantur, donec satisfecerint de praemissis.

Insuper juxta statuta generalis concilii monemus et moneri praecipimus omnes principes, barones Castellanos, et alios Dominos seculares, et quorumlibet eorum vices gerentes existentes in dioecesi et provincia Lugduni, ne Judaeos praeferant in quibuscumque publicis officiis Christianis; et si qui jam sunt praepositi, locorum domini eos studeant removere, alioquin contra eos per dioecesanum, in cujus dioecesi haec contingent, auctoritate praesentis concilii per excommunicationis sententiam procedatur, et alias prout providendum noverit expedire.

XXI   1303

Concilium Nugaroliense, ab auscitanae provinciae episcopis praeside Amaneo archiepiscopo celebratum IV Non. Decemb. anno MCCCIII

> An unconsecrated church that has been polluted by the spilling of seed or blood, or by the burial within it of those under interdict, heretics, schismatics, pagans, or Jews—whose bones cannot for some reason be identified or exhumed—may be blessed through the sprinkling of water performed by a bishop alone.

Mansi, 25:114.

XII. *De ecclesia nondum consecrata, si polluatur.*

Ecclesia nondum consecrata, attamen Divino cultui dedicata, si polluatur seminis aut sanguinis effusione hominis violenta, vel sepultura excommunicatorum, interdictorum, haereticorum, schismaticorum, paganorum seu Judaeorum, nec ossa discerni et exhumari possint: per episcopum tantum aspersione aquae benedicatur: si vero inferior ipso ecclesiam aut coemeterium hujusmodi, vel etiam consecratam, reconciliare praesumpserit, eo ipso ecclesiastico supponatur interdicto.

XXII   1310

Concilium Moguntinum

> The decrees of the council of 1292 (no. XVIII, above) are reiterated
> verbatim. In addition, the decree of another Mainz council, concerning servants of Jews is repeated, as is also the decree of Boniface VIII
> (*Sext.* 5,2,13) ordering that those baptized (without their consent) as
> infants or in fear of death, yet not by true force, must be dealt with as
> heretics if they return to Judaism.

Mansi, 25:333.

De Judaeis: ex eodem concilio.

Licet olim in generali concilio provide fuerit institutum, ut uterque sexus
de gente Judaeorum in omni christianorum provincia signum, vel
habitum publice deferre debeant, et frequenter, quo a populo christiano
manifeste distingui valeat, et discerni, fuitque adjectum, et salubriter
provisum in concilio memorato, ut in diebus dominicae passionis in
publicum prodire non debeat gens praedicta, sed in suis se continere
domibus, clausis domorum ostiis, et fenestris, ne sicut in eodem concilio
tangitur christiani, qui sacratissimae passionis memoriam exhibentes
lamentationis signa praetendant illis diebus ab eodem Judaeorum populo
illudantur. Licet etiam in aliis sacris canonibus prohibitum inveniatur
expresse, ut Judaei, nec publica officia, nec aliquas saeculares dignitates
habeant, aut in suis domibus, et servitiis mancipia teneant christiana.
Quia tamen nec contra Judaeos in praedictis prohibitis casibus contrarium facientes, nec contra christianos potentes, ipsos sine districtionis
signo, vel habitu in suis terminis tolerantes, aut publicis officiis, vel
saecularibus dignitatibus praeficientes eosdem, certa, et sufficiens poena
in canonibus reperitur. Considerantes prout facilitas veniae incentivum
tribuat delinquendi, et plus solet timeri, quod generaliter imperatur,
de multa deliberatione, et unanimi approbatione hujus concilii irrefragabiliter duximus statuendum, ut in universis civitatibus, oppidis,
castris et villis civitatis, dioeces. et provinciae Moguntinen. gens Judaeorum utriusque sexus infra duos menses post publicationem hujus statuti

talia signa, et habitum, quibus sine qualibet ambiguitate a christiano populo distinguatur sibi eligat, et deferat manifeste, dignitatesque saeculares, et officia publica, si quibus de gente praefata forte aliquis praeest, et mancipia christiana prorsus dimittant. Alioquin in omnibus locis ubi Judaei huic sacro, et salubri concilio in hac parte obedire nolentes habitare, vel domicilia obtinere noscuntur, in poena christianorum potentum tamdiu cessetur ab officiis divinorum, donec per principes, et nobiles, ac potestates christianos, in quorum territorio praedicta gens misera conservatur, ad observationem praemissorum omnium compellatur, ipsi autem per locorum dioeces. indirecte per subtractionem communionis fidelium excommunicationis sententia percellantur. Si quis vero de gente praefata in die parasceves visus fuerit in plateis, vel per ostium suae domus prospicere, ad quod probandum duorum christianorum stabilitatem in juramento stabilitur, idem loci dioecesano in marca argenti poenae nomine teneatur ad ejus solutionem reus, et omnes defendentes eumdem per excommunicationis sententiam compellantur. Et ne quis christianus, aut Judaeus hujus statuti ignorantiam valeat allegare, universis parochiarum rectoribus per Moguntinen. civitatem, dioeces. et provinciam constitutis, in quorum parochiis Judaei morantur sub poena excommunicationis in quoslibet transgressores, auctoritate praesentis concilii ex nunc latae praecipimus firmiter, et districte, ut quilibet in sua parochia singulis dominicis diebus singula quatuor tempora ipsa immediate subsequentibus infra missarum solemnia praefatum statutum lingua materna exponere non obmittat.

De servitiis Judaeorum: ex concilio domini Petri Moguntinen.

Item cum in sacro concilio olim sacratissime sit statutum, ne Judaei sub alendo puerorum obtentu, nec pro servitio, nec pro qualibet alia causa christiana mancipia habere permittantur in domibus suis, et quod excommunicentur christiani, qui cum ipsis praesumpserint habitare, cum ipsi propter continuam conversationem, et assiduam familiaritatem ad suam superstitionem, et perfidiam execrabilem incontinentium possint simplicium christianorum animos de facili inclinare; nos qui Dei injurias graviter portamus, hujus canonis auctoritate statuimus, ut omnes christiani nostrae provinciae sub quocumque praetextu domibus Judaeorum inhabitantes infra duos menses post publicationem hujus statuti de Judaeorum domibus nunquam postmodum reversuri recedant. Alioquin christiani contrarium facientes, per sententiam excommunicationis percellantur. Et alii christiani tamdiu a Judaeorum familiaritate et commercio coerceantur, quamdiu Judaei hujusmodi christianos in domibus suis praesumpserint retinere.

De haereticis: ex concilio fritzlar.

Excommunicamus, et anathematizamus omnes haereticos quibuscumque nominibus censeantur, facies quidem habentes diversas, sed caudas ad invicem colligatas, quia de vanitate conveniunt in id ipsum. Damnati vero per ecclesiam saeculari judicio relinquantur, animadversione debite puniendi, clericis vero a suis ordinibus degradatis.

De redeuntibus ad ritum Judaeorum.

Statuimus, immo statutum Bonifacii publicamus, ut christianos, qui ad ritum transierint, vel redierint Judaeorum, etiam si hujusmodi redeuntes dum erant infantes, aut mortis metu, non tamen praecise, sed coacti baptizati fuerint, tamquam contra haereticos, si fuerint de hoc confessi, aut per christianos, vel Judaeos convicti: et sicut contra fautores, receptores, et defensores haereticorum, ita contra fautores, receptores, et defensores talium per locorum ordinarios procedatur.

XXIII 1311

Concilium Ravennate II, pro disciplina et moribus ecclesiae reformandis, celebratum anno MCCCXI

> Jewish men are to wear a round saffron badge on the breasts of their garments; women, the same, on their head (coverings).

Regestum Clementis Papae V.

De Judaeis. Rubrica XXIII.

Etsi Judaei, de misericordia, et ad testimonium incredulitatis eorum, debeant ab ecclesia et fidelibus in suis ritibus tolerari, quia tamen ex ipsorum conversatione permixta multa mala scandala provenisse noscuntur, statuimus, et perpetua stabilitate firmamus, quod Judaei portent in pannis superioribus certum signum, scilicet rotam panni crocei coloris: et mulieres eorum in capite, ut sic a Christianis possint discerni. Nec recipiantur alicubi ultra mensem ad habitandum, nisi in locis, in quibus habuerint synagogas.

XXIV   Dec. 18, 1312, to Jan. 1313

Concilium Ocelloduriense

Following the decree of the Council of Vienne (1311; *Clem.* 2,8,1), the council decrees that kings are not to give Jews privileges protecting them from Christian testimony. Repeating the terms of Innocent III (*Etsi Judaeos,* 1215), the council insists that Jews enjoy no privileges benefitting them at Christian expense. Christian testimony should, hence, be considered valid against Jews even in criminal cases, just as that of Jews is valid against Christian defendants. Jews are to hold no public office. Christians are to avoid the close company of Jews. Christians may not serve in Jewish homes. There is to be no dining in common, no new synagogues, no holding back on tithes, no public appearance by Jews at Eastertime, and, following the decree of the Council of Vienne (*Clem.* 5,2,1), no new Jewish settlements founded for the express purpose of lending at interest.

Y. F. Baer, *Die Juden im Christlichen Spanien,* vol. 2, pp. 118–120, n. 133.

1. Primera mient, como don Clemente quinto . . . entre las otras constituciones que fizo en el concilio general que fue celebrado por el en Viena ordeno, que los judios non usasen de previlegios que toviessen [gana]dos de reyes nin de principes seglares que non pudiesen ser vencidos en juyzio en ningun tienpo por testimonio de christia[nos], et amonesta a los dichos [reye]s e principes seglares que daqui adelante non otorguen tales privilegios nin guarden los otorgados, et manda a nos e a todos los otros prelados que se acertaron en aquel dicho concilio, que tan bien esta constitucion como las otras constituciones fechas contra los dichos judios para constrennir e vedar las sus malicias e la sus presunciones, con que se abuelven contra los christianos e contra la guarda del nonbre de dios, que en nuestras cibdades e en nuestros obispados e nuestras provincias las fiziesemos guardar e que las publicasemos con nuestros concilios provenciales nos e todos los otros arçobispos cada anno en nuestras provincias, segunt manda el derecho. Et nos queriendo, assi como somos tenudos, obedescer a los mandamientos apostolicales parando mientes, en que guisa estos dichos judios assi como desgradescidos dan por gracia denuesto por con[. . .] en menoprecio de los christianos, a qui conviene que sean subjudgados e daqui son mantenidos tan sola mient por que son omes, et dan les por galardon, segunt dize el proverbio seglar,

el que da a su huesped el mur en el esportiella e la serpiente en el regaço e el fuego en el seno, esforçandose contra ellos el ganar de los reyes e de los principes nuevos sin razon e non convenibles previlleios para asencion de su servimiento, por la qual cosa por la su culpa muy descumunal deven ser atados par sienpre e en servicio de los christianos et en onra del nonbre de dios por la offensa e el menosprecio tan grande que [fi]zieron: amonestamos primero, segundo e tercio, dando espacio de treynta dias por qualquier amonestacion a todos los judios que moran en nuestra provincia agora o moraran daqui adela[nt] que daqui adelant e agora para sienpre en los pleitos criminales e civiles e en otros pleitos qualesquier non osen contradecir nin aun deffender se con los dichos previlegios, diciendo que pues en testimonio non fue llamado judio contra ellos nin judios, que en tal pleito non deven ser vencidos, que non ussen de tales nin de o[tro]s qualesquier privillegios en prejuyzio de la fe de los christianos nin osen ganar tales privilegios nin semeiante destos. Et por esto ordenamos que en todos los pl[eitos] tan bien criminales vala e tenga el testimonio de los christianos, si este testimonio fuere suficiente en otro tienpo, contra lo[s] judios, e non la del judio contra los christianos, nin sean [oydo]s en testimonio, assi como se contiene en el derecho. Et el que en este logar quisiere proponer los judios a los christianos e las dichas constituciones e las otras so[bre e]sto fechas contra los judios non quisiere guardar, si quier sea clerigo, si quier lego, si quier religioso, si quier seglar, venga sobre el la maldicion de dios que es poderoso e de Sant Pedro e de Sant Pablo, cuyas constituciones sanctas se movio a quebrantar, e que venga sobre el la maldicion de Sant Iago. Et los prelados ordinarios constringan, que lo fagan gardar esto que dicho es, segunt fuere derecho, et a los que los fizieren lo contrario den les la pena segunt el pecado que fizieren por sentencia de sancta eglesia.

2. Lo segundo es que daqui adelant non tengan officios nin dignidades de reyes nin de otros principes seglares quales quier e dexen los que tienen fastal termino sobredicho.

3. El tercero es que se quiten de participar e de andar con los christianos a menudo, por que non tomen yerro aquellos que poco entendien contra fe con la su grant conpannia.

4. El quarto es que se guarden de dar testimonio contra los christianos nin usen de los actos legitimos de los christianos daqui adelant.

5. El quinto que es que non tengan ninguna christiana sennalada para collaça para tienpo nin para sienpre, e que non tengan amas christianas para criar sus fijos.

6. El sexto es que non parescan en publico en miercoles de las tiniebras fasta el sabbato, e el dia de viernes sancto que cierren sus puertas e sus finiestras todo el dia, por que non puedan fazer escarnio de los christianos que andan dloridos por la memoria de la passion de Jesu Christo.

7. El seteno es que todos tan bien judios como judias que trayan sennal descubierta, por que parescan que andan departidos de los christianos, segunt dize el derecho e se guarda en otras provincias.

8. El otavo es que non usen de fiseca con los christianos, por letrados nin provados que sean.

9. El nono es que non conviden a los christianos en sus comeres, nin los christianos non coman el comer de los judios, sennalada mient que non coman de su carne nin bevan de su vino.

10. El dezeno es que den diezmo de sus heredamientos, si los an, e que den aniversarios de las casas, en que moran, asi como los dav[an] los christianos, ante que fuessen de los judios.

11. El onzeno es que t[orne]n las sinagogas alçadas e ennoblecidas de nuevo al estado, en que fueron fechas primera mient, daqui fastal dia de pasqua mayor de resureccion primera que viene. Este espacio les sen-nalamos perenptorio, e si fastal dicho plazo los dichos judios non lo quisieren asi conplir, passado el plazo los juezes e los alcalles, com-unidades, universidades de las cibdades e de las villas e de los castillos, do quier que estas sinagogas fueren fechas de nuevo o alçadas, que lo conplan e lo fagan conplir en virtud de santa obediencia so la pena sobre dicha.

12. El dozeno es que non usen de usuras con los christianos nin ge las demanden nin otra cosa por ellas, ca esto es vedado por la constitucion de don Clemente papa quinto que fue fecha en el dicho concilio de Viana. Et qui quisiere contra esto e lo presumiere provar, caya en las penas que son ordenadas sobresto en el dicho concilio de Viana.

13. El trezeno es que en los domingos e en las otras fiestas que guardan los christianos, que non fagan obra en publico, quier sea agena.[1]

---

1. A.H.N. Toledo, Cat., Pap. leg. 634. (Übersetzung des lateinischen Orig-inalaktes, verfertigt vom Notar von Medina del Campo für diese Ortschaft; zeitgenössische Schrift.)—Cop. Burriel B.N. ms. 13078 f.84. Ed. Amador de los Rios II, 561 f. nach Cop. Burriel. [Baer's source note.]

XXV   1277

Trevirense Concilium

> Priests are not to display sacred objects before Jews. Uneducated priests may not hold discussions with Jews in the presence of laity. No medicine may be received from Jews.

Mansi, 24:200.

71. Item sacerdotes numquam exponant aliquid de ornamentis ecclesiasticis, nec aliquid religiosi audeant exponere Judaeis sine licentia nostra speciali.
79. Item, praecipimus quod sacerdotes illitterati non conferant cum Judaeis coram laicis, et sacerdotes praecipiant omnibus subditis suis, ne aliquam potionem, vel medicinam ab eis sumant.

XXVI   no date, 13th or 14th century

Statuta Ecclesie Ruthenensis

> Apart from rules governing a badge, appearance in public at Easter, domestics, consumption of meat during Lent, selling ritually slaughtered Jewish meat to Christians, dining and bathing in common, Christian consumption of unleavened bread, resort to the services of a Jewish physician, and the holding by Jews of public office, the council decrees concerning baptism that force may not be used and willing converts are not to lose their possessions. If they are bound in service, and the lord is a Christian, converts remain in service. If the lord is not a Christian, they are to go free.[1]

Martène and Durand, *Thesaurus Novus Anecdotorum*, vol. 4, p. 769.

XV. De Judaeis statuimus, ut in civitatibus et castris et aliis locis insignibus, et non in aliis habitare permittantur, et ut omni tempore in medio pectoris rotam portent, ut propter hoc a populo christiano discernantur, et in diebus lamentationis, et Dominicae passionis in publicum non procedant, nec occasione puerorum suorum vel alia qualibet causa in suis domibus nutrices aut servientes teneant Christianos, nec in diebus dominicis et festis praesumant publice operari, nec carnes suas vendant, vel eas comedant in quadragesima publice seu aliis diebus in quibus ab esu carnium abstinent Christiani; et si contra hoc fecerint, Christianorum participatio in commerciis et aliis, eis usque ad satisfactionem condignam denegetur. Illud quoque praecipimus, ne carnes refutatas a Judaeis vendat aliquis Christianus, et ut omnes Christiani vitent convivia Judaeorum, nec illos ad sua convivia Christiani admittant, nec Judaeorum azyma comedant nec cum eisdem in domibus habitent, aut in eorum balneo se lavent, nec tempore infirmitatis sub Judaeorum cura se ponant, nec ab eis recipiant medicinam, nec super Christianos bailiviam vel alia publica officia habere permittantur.

XVI. Item, volumus et districte praecipimus, quod nullus invitos Judaeos, vel paganos, vel alios infideles ad baptisma venire compellat: si vero volentes fuerint baptizati, non propter hoc eorum bona domini accipiant eorumdem, licet non obstante baptismo dominis suis Christianis facere teneantur servitia consueta. Si autem eorum domini sunt infideles, a servitute illorum per baptismum penitus liberantur.

1. This last probably did not apply to Jews. It is, in fact, not clear to whom it might have applied in southern France at this time.

2. Sexual Contact between Christian Men and Jewish Women

These decrees concern the right of bishops alone to mete out punishments for this offense, as for all other sexual offenses.

XXVII 1275

Concilium Arelatense, a Bertrando de sancto Martino, Arelatensi archiepiscopo, cum suffraganeis celebratum circa annum Dom. MCCLXXV

> Various offenses concerning matters of Christian belief or clerical promotions are reserved for bishops and the pope alone. In addition, they are to be the only competent judges for a number of sexual and marital transgressions, including sexual relations with a Jewess, a Muslim woman, or an animal. Abortion too falls under this heading.

Mansi, 24:150.

XII. *De casibus episcopo, vel papae reservatis.*

Item statuimus, quod si quis confitebitur se credere pravitatem haereticam: item si quocumque modo commiserit simoniam: item clerici excommunicati majori excommunicatione, vel interdicti aut suspensi, si ante absolutionem divina officia celebrarent, scilicet missam cantando, evangelium, epistolas, vel alias horas canonicas dicendo, et faciendo principaliter officium suum in ecclesia: item clerici per saltum promoti, aliquo ordine praetermisso: item clerici, qui ab aliquo episcopo se fecerunt ordinari, episcopi sui licentia non obtenta: item incendiarii: item illi, qui tractaverunt in malos usus Eucharistiam sive chrisma: item illi, qui suos filios occiderunt: item illi, qui facto, verbo, consensu, vel aliquo modo, homicidium perpetrarunt: item sacrilegi et violatores ecclesiarum: item illi, qui luxuriam expleverunt cum matre, vel sorore, vel cum alia consanguinea sua, vel uxore fratris, vel cum sanctimoniali consecrata, vel qui violenter virginem defloraverunt: item illi, qui in ecclesiis luxuriam commiserunt: item illi qui cum Judaea vel Saracena vel bruto animali coire ausu temerario, vel alias contra naturam, praesumpserunt: item mulier, quae de adulterio recepit infantem, quem maritus ejus credit esse suum, propter quem legitimi liberi fraudantur haereditate paterna: item qui mulieribus aliquid fecerunt, propter quod fecerunt abortivum, vel non concipiunt; mulier contra si hoc fecerit, vel sibi procuraverit fieri: transmittantur absolvendi per ipsos episcopos, si id eis de jure competit; alioquin, cum eorum litteris, ad sedem apostolicam transmittantur.

XXVIII 1284

Synodus Nemausensis

> Sexual relations with a Jewess, a Muslim woman, and a brute animal are forbidden.

[See no. XV, above.]

XXIX 1289

Statuta Synodalia Cadurcensis, Ruthenensis et Tutelensis

> Sexual relations with Jewesses, Muslim women, and beasts are forbidden; likewise, incest and the defloration of virgins. Church burial is denied to usurers, suicides, and predators, as it is to Jews, heretics, and Muslims.

Mansi, 24:984, 1026.

XIV. *Casus episcopales*

Casus vero episcopales in quibus poenitentes ad episcopum sunt remittendi, sunt isti. . . . Item, de sortilegiis, non tamen levibus, et maxime si cum Eucharistia vel chrismate, vel aliis rebus sacris committantur. Item, de vitio contra naturam enormi. Item, de his qui coeunt cum Judaea, vel Sarracena, vel cum bestiis. Item, de incestu, qui committi dicitur cum consanguinea seu fratris uxore, seu alia affini. Item, de defloratione virginum.

Sunt autem quidam quibus debet denegari ecclesiastica sepultura, scilicet Judaeis, haereticis, Sarracenis, excommunicatis majori excommunicatione et minori, et interdictis, et illis qui in torneamentis moriuntur, et illis qui se interfecerunt, et usurariis, et concubinariis, et praedonibus manifestis, et omnibus quos manifestum esse constiterit in peccato decessisse mortali. Haec autem intelligenda sunt et servanda, nisi in morte apparuerint signa poenitentiae manifesta . . .

XXX 1310

Concilium Trevirense

> Christians knowingly having intercourse with a Jewess, a Muslim woman, or a pagan, and vice versa, are to be dealt with by the bishop.

Mansi, 25:272.

XCIII. *Illi mittendi sunt ad dominum episcopum.*

Vicesimo-septimo, scienter cojens cum Judaea vel Saracena, vel pagana, et e converso.

3. Matters Involving Usury

The Church demanded jurisdictional rights over usury, which it considered an ecclesiastical crime irrespective of the religion of the lender. The statutes here concern (a) clerics acting as guarantors (*fideiussores*) for Jews or lawyers representing them against Christian borrowers, (b) the taking of immoderate usury and the question of paying anything beyond the amount of the principal, (c) secular courts forcing clerics to pay debts to Jews, (d) the nature of permitted pledges and (e) the problem of pledges that were really stolen goods, (f) the delict of Christians collecting usury from Jews or (g) involving themselves as partners in the usurious dealings of Jews, and, finally, (h) the matter of church burial for usurers. Most of the councils dealt with only one of these issues, and, in no case, did a council deal with more than two. With the exception of the two councils, XXXII and XLIV, which expressly prohibit it, all of the others effectively accept the legitimacy of moderate interest.

XXXI 1255

Constitutiones Synodales Valentinae Diocesis (sub episcopo Valentino)

Persons who are baptized and confirmed and who then become Muslims or Jews, but who, afterward wish to return to Christianity, do not require rebaptism or reconfirmation. Rather, the bishop is to reconcile them. No cleric should serve as a guarantor for a Jew or pledge sacred objects. There is to be no alienation of Church lands.

Mansi, 23:887, 893.

De Confirmatione.

Et est sciendum, quod soli episcopi possunt confirmare, consecrare virgines, ecclesias dedicare, clericos ordinare, cruces, vestimenta, calices, corporalia benedicere, et litteras ordinationis dare, indulgentias facere, secundum canonica instituta. Illud autem sciendum est, quod sacramenta Baptismi et Confirmationis nunquam iterantur. Etiam si baptizatus et confirmatus faceret se Judaeum vel Sarracenum, et postea vellet redire ad fidem catholicam, non baptizaretur nec confirmaretur; quia sufficit contritio in hac parte, cum reconciliatione episcopi.

Item moneant populum, quod illi qui veniunt ad vigilias ecclesiarum, caute et honeste se habeant, nec permittant choreas facere in ecclesiis vel coemeteriis. Nec in ecclesiis fiant conjurationes aquae ferventis, vel ferri candentis, vel aquae frigidae conjuratae, quia omnia ista superstitiosa sunt penitus, et contra Deum. Item nullus clericus fidejubeat Judaeo, vel faeneratori, vel obliget calicem, vel vestimenta, vel pallas altaris Judaeis, vel libros. Item mandamus clericis, quod immobilia non alienent aliquo casu episcopo inconsulto, et faciant inventarium de omnibus possessionibus ecclesiae, et scribant omnia in Missali; ut cum episcopus, vel Ordinarius, alias archidiaconus, videre voluerint, meliorata inveniant. Nec aliquis faciant mutuum super ecclesias episcopo inconsulto; quia satis est quod clerici habeant reditus ecclesiarum, et non obligent sine caussa, quam episcopus debet scire.

XXXII 1258

Concilia Monspeliense (per Archiepiscopum Narbonensem et suffraganeis)

> To restrain unbridled Jewish avarice, it is ordered that Jews may be permitted to take back from borrowers only the principal with no interest. No one is to aid Jews in the collection of debts unless they go into court and swear the loans bear no interest.

Mansi, 23:992.

V. *Ut Judaei usuras non exigant, sed tantum sortem.*

Ceterum Judaeorum avaritiam exitiabilem, quantum cum justitia possumus, refraenantes, statuimus, ut nullus de cetero Judaeum aliquem contra Christianum super exactione debitorum audiat, nec ei audaciam aliquam praebeat: nisi prius sacra lege Mosaica coram posita, Judaeus ipse, qui justitiam postulat sibi exhiberi, per suum declaraverit advocatum, quid et quantum de ipso debito quod exigit, usura vel sors fuerit: ut ex tunc super forte solummodo audiatur, usurarum petitione penitus submota: salva tamen nihilominus defensione qualibet Christiano, si velit et postulet se ad probandum admitti, quod totum fuerit usura quod Judaeus exigit, vel in majori quam declaraverit quantitate.

XXXIII 1267

Concilium Viennense

> No immoderate usury may be taken.

[See no. VII, above.]

XXXIV   1271

Concilium apud S. Quintinum, ab episcopis Remensis provinciae vacante sede Remensi, celebratum, anno MCCLXXI.

> To insure that Jews not be of "higher status"[1] than Christians, as well as to prevent offences against both canon and civil law, secular princes are threatened with excommunication if they aid Jews in collecting debts owed by clerics, and especially if they give this aid by distraining [church] property.[2]

Mansi, 24:19.

V. *Ut saeculares magistratus non cogant clericos ad debita Judeis persolvenda.*

Sacras constitutiones legentibus satis liquet, quod nullam habeant de rebus ecclesiasticis disponendi laici aliquo modo potestatem. Verum nobis multorum quaestio patefecit, quod in tantum quorumdam principum saecularium processit temeritas, ut si Judaei conquerantur de aliqua ecclesiastica persona, quod eis sit debitis obligata, statim irrequisito loci praelato, non convictos, nec confessos, per captionem bonorum eorumdem nituntur compellere ad ea debita persolvenda. Cum igitur istud manifeste sit contra omnia jura tam canonica quam civilia, et etiam a ratione discordet, ut injuria Crucifixi, melioris conditionis sint quam Christiani: praecipimus, ut praelati quando in eorum jurisdictione tale quid acciderit, in delinquentes hujusmodi poenam canonicam vigilanter exercere non relaxent, donec non solum de damnis, sed de injuria, satisfecerint competenter.

1. *Melior conditio* is a phrase used throughout the canons to indicate the relative status of Jews and Christians. Converts to Christianity, in particular, must enjoy this "better (or improved) station." See Stow, *Catholic Thought,* pp. 387–389, for the laws in question.

2. Is the greater concern here the question of usury or the violation of canon law by the princes acting against clerics?

XXXV   1280

Synodus Santonensis, ex codice Constitutionum ecclesiae Santonensis.

> Judges are not to issue letters bearing a seal ordering the distraint of property in disputes between Jewish (lenders) and Christian (borrowers). If such are issued, they are invalid and the issuing official excommunicate. Debtors may not be forced to pay their debts to Jews, even if the Jewish lender has an (official) letter to that effect.

Mansi, 24:378.

XIII. *Ne litterae concedantur Judaeis.*

Item inhibemus sub poena excommunicationis, ne aliqui judices ordinarii, vel eorum vicarii, civitatis et dioecesis Santonensis, aliquas litteras concedant sigillis suis sigillatas, seu confessiones audiant, super tractatibus Judaeorum contra Christianos, nec aliquas litteras executorias executioni demandent, seu faciant demandare. Et si aliquae litterae pro ipsis contra Christianos emanaverint, easdem decernimus non valere: inhibentes sub poena excommunicationis praedicta, ne aliquis judex ordinarius civitatis et dioecesis Santonensis, vel eorum vicarii, aliquos debitores compellant ad solutionem dictorum Judaeorum, etiamsi praedicti Judaei super hujusmodi debitis, litterarum testimonio sint muniti.

XXXVI   1280

Synodus Pictarensis

> Christians may not borrow at interest unless witnesses swear they have no choice but to borrow. Clerics are not to register Jewish loan contracts.

[See no. XII, above.]

XXXVII   1284

Synodus apud Sanctum Hyppolytum

Christians are not to take interest from Jews or become their partners as lenders.

[See no. XIV, above.]

XXXVIII   1285

Synodus Incerti Loci, Jacobus Archiepiscopus Gneznensis

To prevent Jews from achieving a "higher status" than Christians, it is decreed that just as Christians must return any stolen goods in their possession to the rightful owner, so too must Jews.[1] No sacred objects may be pledged with Jews.

_____

Hube, *Ant. Const.*, p. 165.

par. 32. Item cum Judei melioris conditionis non debeant esse Christianis, et Christiani res furtivas, quamvis emptas vero domino, absque solutione pretii, cogantur ad restitutionem ipsarum, statuimus: ut Judei, apud quos res furtivae inventae fuerint, absque solutioni pretii cogantur ad restitutionem ipsarum rerum. Si qui vero in hac abusione fuerint, ut res apud eos repertas, nisi data pecunia restituant, aut manutenuerint, aut etiam defensaverint per censuram ecclesiasticam compescantur.

par. 33. Item statuimus: ut nullus apud Judeos res sacras vel libros deponere praesumat, vel quomodolibet obligare nisi in gravi necessitate de licentia praelatorum.

_____

1. The Jews intended are lenders who had been given stolen goods as pledges.

XXXIX 1287

Statuta Synodalia Johannis Episcopi Leodiensis

> No advocate should offer his services to a usurer, heretic, or Jew, unless a judge so decrees for good cause. Advocates should make their services available to the poor free of charge. No advocate, notary, or judge should attempt to compromise the reputation of women litigants.

Mansi, 24:934.

VII. Nullus advocatus patrocinium suum praestet manifesto usurario, haeretico, vel Judaeo contra Christianum, nisi judex ex causa aliqua advocato hoc duxerit committendum, et assistant advocati pauperibus et miserabilibus personis gratis: et nullus advocatus, procurator seu notarius vel judex attentet pudicitiam mulierum litigantium.

XL 1287

Synoda Meldensis

> No cleric should serve as a (loan) guarantor for a Jew or other lender. Nor should he give in pledge any church objects or books.

Martène and Durand, *Thes. nov. anecd.* 4:898.

XXXVII. *Ne fide jubeat foeneratoribus.*

Nullus clericus fidejubeat Judaeo vel foeneratori, nec obliget pro pignore aliquo modo ornamenta ecclesiae vel libros.

XLI 1289

Statuta Synodalia Cadurcensis . . .

> As is the case for Jews, no usurers are to be buried in a church.

[See no. XXIX, above.]

XLII   1292

Cistercian . . . Chapter General, *Statuta*

> No abbot or other member of the (Cistercian) order should receive a
> deposit (i.e., a pledge for safekeeping) from a Jew. Should he do so, he
> must abstain from wine while the deposit remains in his monastery.

Martène and Durand, 4:1487.

7. Item, auctoritate capituli generalis inhibetur abbatibus et omnibus
personis ordinis, ne de cetero aliqua deposita recipiant a Judaeis.
Ubi contrarium fuerit attentatum, abbas, prior, cellerarius, et bur-
sarius tamdiu a vino abstineant, quamdiu deposita penes se habuerint
praedictorum.

XLIII   1298

Synodus Dioecesana Herbipolensis a Manegoldo Herbipol. Episcopo

> No church objects may be given as pledges to Jews: nor may holy
> objects be displayed before them or touched by them, lest disgrace be
> brought upon the Savior.

Mansi, 24:1191.

VII. Statuimus quod ornamenta ecclesiae non obligentur pignori, nisi
pro necessitate ecclesiae, et de consensu parochianorum: calices vero et
vestes sacrae Judaeis non exponantur nisi firmiter non obserentur, ne
ipsorum manibus valeant attrectari, quibus, ubi possunt, contumeliam
irrogant Salvatori.

XLIV   1312-1313

Concilium Ocelloduriense

No one may settle in a locality for the purpose of lending, as decreed by the Council of Vienne.

[See no. XXIV, above.]

4. Jews before Ecclesiastical Courts

The specific question of granting ecclesiastical courts direct jurisdiction over Jews was confronted only by three English councils and only in the four-year period 1257–1261. The councils demanded rights in cases of sacrilege, striking clerics, and adultery with a Christian woman. There was also a reference to *"rebus ecclesiasticis,"* referring, most likely, to usury and, perhaps, blasphemy.

XLV   1257

Londinense Concilium Provinciale (pro Ecclesiae Anglicanae negociis tractandis)

> Jews guilty of offences against Church property or clerics, as well as sacrilege, and, in particular, the use of violence against a cleric[1] are to be tried by Courts Christian. The same applies to the case of adultery with a Christian woman. The king has tried to prevent this by claiming the Jews have their own judge and justiciars. Yet, these judges have no cognizance in the above matters; furthermore, anyone convened by them may purge himself of wrongdoing without an oath.

Mansi, 23:959.
Powicke and Cheney, *Councils and Synods,* p. 545.

XXXII. Item cum Judaeus in ecclesiasticam personam delinquat, vel super rebus ecclesiasticis, aut super sacrilegio, aut etiam violenta manuum injectione in clericum, vel super adulterio cum Christiana conveniatur coram judice ecclesiastico; per regiam prohibitionem causae cognitio impeditur, quia allegavit, quod judicem habent proprium, vicecomitem locorum, et justiciarios proprios deputatos, qui super talibus cognoscere non possunt, nec debent. Et tamen, si a clerico et laico super hujusmodi conveniantur coram eis, persona solam negationem et alterius Judaei et unius Christiani simplicem assertionem absque omnis juramenti praestatione se purgant, probatione actoris penitus recusata.

1. Cf. *ChJ*, nos. 27 and 47 for similar claims in the case of violence by Innocent III, in 1212, and Honorius III, in 1221.

XLVI 1258

Mertonense Concilium

> Jews who commit offenses against Church property or ecclesiastical persons are to appear before ecclesiastical judges. All contact with Christians is denied them if they refuse to comply.

Mansi, 23:980.
Powicke and Cheney, *Councils and Synods,* 580.

Et quia modo consimili praelatorum officium impeditur, cum contingat, quod Judaeus delinquens in rebus ecclesiasticis et personis, super his conventus fuerit coram ipsis, et super aliis, quae ad forum ecclesiasticum pertinent mero iure; providemus, quod Judaeus per interdictum commercii, contractuum, et communionis fidelium ad respondendum in his casibus nihilominus compellatur. Inhibentes quoque impeditores et distringentes, penas interdicti et excommunicationis incurrant.

XLVII 1261

Concilium Lambethense (per Cantuariense archiepiscopum)

> Anyone who impedes Jews guilty of ecclesiastical crimes[1] from appearing in Courts Christian is to be excommunicated.

Mansi, 23:1067.
Powicke and Cheney, *Councils and Synods,* 679.

Quod Judaeus delinquens in rebus ecclesiasticis, respondeat coram judice ecclesiastico.

Et quia modo consimili ecclesiastica censura confunditur, et praelatorum officium impeditur, cum Judaeus delinquens in rebus ecclesiasticis et personis, super his vel super aliis, quae ad forum ecclesiasticum pertinent, mero jure coram ecclesiastico judice convenitur, et per regem, seu per vicecomites, aut ballivos super praemissis non permittitur coram ecclesiastico judice stare juri, sed potius declinare compellitur ad forum ejus: statuimus, ut hujusmodi Judaei per interdictum commercii, contractuum et conventionis fidelium, ad respondendum in his casibus coram ecclesiastico judice compellantur: et quod inhibentes et impedientes in hoc casu jurisdictionem ecclesiasticam, et hac de causa, judices vel alios distringentes et molestantes, per excommunicationis et interdicti sententias arceantur.

1. On the problem of direct jurisdiction by the Church over Jews and the resulting conflict with lay authorities, see K. Stow, *Catholic Thought*, pp. 115-116, and K. Stow, *The 1007 Anonymous and Papal Sovereignty: Jewish Perceptions of the Papacy and Papal Policy in the High Middle Ages* (Cincinnati, 1984), pp. 36-37.

5. Areas of Jewish Residence

These texts reflect early attempts at segregation.

XLVIII   1266

Synodus Wratislaviensis

Jews are to live in separate areas surrounded by a moat or wall.

[See no. VI, above.]

XLIX   1276

Concilium Bituricense, a Simone S. Caeciliae cardinale Apostol. sedis
legato celebratum, Id. Septembr., anno Domini MCCLXXVI

Lords are to specify those locations in which Jews may or may not
dwell, thus to prevent them from fraudulently deceiving Christians.

Mansi, 24:176.

XIV. *De Judaeis.*

De Judaeis, quorum perfidia plerumque simplices Christianos fraudulen-
ter decipit, et malitiose secum pertrahit in errorem, sacro approbante
concilio duximus ordinandum, ut non nisi in civitatibus, castris, et aliis

locis insignibus, habitare praesumant: temporalibus locorum dominis, et vices gerentibus, seu loca tenentibus eorumdem, districtius inhibentes, ne Judaeos ipsos permittant alibi, quam in locis expressis superius habitare: ipsis ad hoc, si res exegerit, a dioecesanis locorum, ejusdem authoritate concilii, per censuram ecclesiasticam compellendis.

L   1280

Synodis Pictavensis

> The poor of the parishes where Jewish lenders dwell are to benefit from fines levied for violations of the canons on usury and Christian servants.

[See no. XII, above.]

LI   1311

Concilium Ravennate II

> Jews may not remain in any location for longer than a month if there is no synagogue there.[1]

[See no. XXIII, above.]

1. As per the decree of the Council of Vienne (*Clem.* 5,2,1).

6. Problems Relating to Baptism

Problems relating to baptism: a number of specific problems, but all within the framework of force being prohibited *before* the fact and baptism being irreversible (it is not a question of force being justified) *after* the fact:

LII　1255

Constitutiones . . . Valentinae

> Should a baptized Christian leave the fold and then return, there is no need for rebaptism.

[See no. XXXI, above.]

LIII   1267

Concilium Viennense

> Jews are not to dissuade other Jews from embracing Christianity, nor are they to induce Christians into apostasy.

[See no. VII, above.]

LIV   1310

Concilium Moguntinum

> Any Christian reverting to Judaism, even if he was baptized as an infant or brought into the fold by (conditional) force, is a heretic.

[See no. XXII, above.]

LV   1257

Statuta Synodalia Ecclesiae Gerundensis

> Anyone desiring baptism is to receive it, but Jews and Muslims are to be delayed for a number of days until their will is known of a certainty.

Mansi, 23:930.

8. Quibus sit baptismus conferendus? dicimus quod omnibus indifferenter, quod nulli mater ecclesia claudit gremium suum, et Dominus Jesus Christus hoc ostendere voluit, cum dixit: Eum qui venit ad me, non ejiciam foras. Sed Sarracenus vel Judaeus cum venerit ad baptismum, est per aliquot dies retinendus, ut instruatur in fide, et probetur quo spiritu ducitur ad baptismum.

LVI   1284

Synodus Nemausensis

> No one is to be forcibly baptized, but all who desire the sacrament are to receive it. Lords are not to confiscate the property of former Jews.

[See no. XV, above.]

LVII   1295

Instructions of Bishop Wm. Durand

> No forced baptism. No confiscation of the property of new converts.

[See no. XIX, above.]

LVIII   1302

Concilium apud Pennam Fidelem, a Toletanae provinciae praesulibus celebratum

> Rulers are not to confiscate the property of converts to Christianity.

Mansi, 25:104.

X. *De Baptismo.*

Item quia nonnulli, tam judaei, quam Agareni, caecitatem sui erroris attendentes, ad fidem converti desiderant orthodoxam scilicet, mundus eos. . . . bona timentes quae habent perdere universa: ne propter hoc hostis antiquus animas perdere cupiens, bonum propositum revocet, quod Dei spiritus inspiravit: statuimus et mandamus, ut quicumque Judaeus, vel Agarenus, baptizari voluerit, propter baptismi sacramentum bona, quae ante habuit, ut jura praecipiunt, non amittat.

LIX   13th–14th Century

Statuta Ecclesie Ruthenensis

No forced baptism or the confiscation of the goods of a convert is permitted.

[See no. XXVI, above.]

Addenda

A   1290

Concilium Londinense. De ejectione Judaeorum, habitum anno Christi MCCXCI [sic]. tempore Nicolai papae IV

Although the apostolic legate had not arrived, the Council was convened. Much discussion took place about the expulsion of the Jews, of whom there had been a multitude in England. A public edict was issued,[1] and the Jews, that miserable people, were ordered to leave within a few days, taking their goods along with them, which they did.

In the same council, the king declared his intention of going on Crusade. Since the matter concerned *religio,* the king wanted a clerical contribution to aid in financing it. Finally, the king made laws concerning the disposition and sale of clerical property. When the legate then arrived, he, together with Archbishop Peckham, made much to do about the royal impiety in devising such laws.

Mansi, 24:1079, citing A. Bzovius, *Annalium Ecclesiasticorum* (Cologne, 1616).

Cf. F. M. Powicke and C. R. Cheney, *Councils and Synods, with Other Documents Relating to the English Church,* vol. II, pt. II (London, 1964), on the Council of the Province of Canterbury, 2 Oct. 1290, pp. 1091–1093.

De ejectione Judaeorum, habitum anno Christi MCCXCI. tempore Nicolai papae IV.

De rebus in hac synodo gestis ita Bzovius:

Bernhardo episcopo Grossetano, sedis apostolicae legato, in Anglia nondum praesente, Londini ad Westmonasterium celebratum est concilium. In hoc in primis agitatum est de ejectione Judaeorum, quorum erat

per omnem Angliam ingens multitudo: quo sic oves ab hoedis segre-
garentur. Itaque publico jussum est edicto, ut infra paucos dies omnes
abirent cum bonis. Illi jussis concilii parentes, alii alio discesserunt. Ita
profuga gens de Anglia in perpetuum exivit, misera semper alicubi
terrarum peritura, usque eo dum denique deleatur. Eodem in concilio
Eduardus exposuit se cupere ire auxilio Christianis in Asiam; et quia res
ad religionem pertinebat, voluit ut sacerdotes pecuniam suppeditarent.
Postremo placuit regi, similiter atque principibus, illud injurium jure
iterato statuere, ne cui hominum liceret dare praedia collegiis mon-
achorum: neve liceret monachis, aut aliis sacerdotibus, emere possessiones. Supervenit tandem legatus, et una cum Joanne Beccano archiepiscopo Cantuariensi sibi adjuncto, regem iniquitatis atque impietatis
redarguit, legemque abrogare, et ecclesiis, ecclesiasticisque rebus ac
personis, libertatem restituere coegit.

1. Edward I ordered the expulsion on or shortly after July 18, 1290. Bzovius here
gives the impression that it resulted from a conciliar debate in October 1290!
Iussum est should probably be read *iussum erat*, i.e., three months previously.

B   1285

Clerical complaints and royal responses, England[1]

May–July 1285. *Clerical complaints and royal responses*[2]

Soon after the Easter parliament of 1285 began, on 4 May, the prelates
of the province of Canterbury presented seventeen articles of griev-
ances against the lay power. Replies were given in the name of the
chancellor, Robert Burnell, bishop of Bath and Wells (no. I), and
further discussion on them followed (nos. II and III). Debates in this
parliament over the Statute of Westminster II (which was apparently
given public reading on 28 June) led to a second series of articles,
which criticized certain clauses of the statute and which again
produced discussion and replies (nos. IV and V). Finally, a writ issued
on 1 July, designed to restrict narrowly the jurisdiction of ecclesiastical judges (no. VI), brought forth a third series of sixteen articles, and
discussion upon them (nos. VII and VIII).

Documents I–II, IV, VI–VII, found in the register of the bishop of
Worcester, have a quasi-official character, but they are not a complete
record; documents III, V, and VIII are informal memoranda of some
of the debate and remind us how much may be missing. No exact

dates can be attached to the separate documents, but their order and setting have been roughly established by Richardson and Sayles, *EHR* lii. 220–34 (cf. Graves, ibid. xliii. 2–4).[3]

Powicke and Cheney, *Councils and Synods,* 955, 959, 961–962, 963.

Complaint and Response I

The king is petitioned that he observe the Great Charter, that he allow bishops to proceed against clerics forging papal letters, that he stop Jewish malice and fraud, and that he sanction the operations of the Inquisition against Jewish apostates. The king agrees in principal, but argues that the cleric-judges of the archbishop of Canterbury refuse to sit alongside his justiciars. As far as Jewish malice is concerned, he simply has lost all hope of coping with it.

[14] Item, quod magna carta de libertatibus ecclesie et foreste in singulis articulis observetur, presertim cum excommunicati sint transgressores eiusdem; que etiam sententia est per sedem apostolicam confirmata.

Responsio ad xiv: Rex credit quod observatur.

[15] Item, quod ordinarii possint libere capere, tenere, et procedere contra clericos falsarios bullarum apostolicarum vel sigillorum suorum, et falsos questores, laicos etiam falsarios capere et tenere saltem donec requirantur ipsi laici a vicecomitibus et ballivis domini regis.

Responsio: Habeant ordinarii potestatem arrestandi illos.

[16] Item, quod contra iudeos apostatas inquiratur rigide et procedatur.

Responsio: De iudeis effectis christianis et ad iudaicam pravitatem reversis, non remanet nisi in clericis domini archiepiscopi qui nolunt convenire cum iustitiariis ad hoc assignatis.

[17] Item, quod iudeoum fraudibus et malitiis salubriter obvietur.

Responsio: Quod nescitur qualiter, propter eorum nequitiam.[4]

Complaint and Response II

> Archbishop Peckham responds that if the royal justiciars are clerics, he will not oppose their sitting alongside purely ecclesiastical judges. Usury, however, must be stopped[5] if Jewish malice is to be restrained. Jews are to be made to work with their hands[6] and return the interest they have received. Otherwise, they should suffer awful punishments.

Item, circa responsionem ad xvi articulum, respondet archiepiscopus pro clericis suis quod libenter convenient cum iustitiariis assignatis ad inquirendum de apostatis iudeorum, dum tamen iustitiarii sint clerici et breve eis concedatur in forma efficaci, quod nunquam adhuc potuit optinere; immo semper per quasdam tergiversationes quorundam falsorum christianorum delusa fuerunt mandata regis ne effectum debitum sortirentur.

Item, circa responsionem ad xvii articulum, mirantur prelati quia nescit curia regia qualiter possit iudaica malitia refrenari; nec certe unquam sciet quamdiu permittat iudeos per contractus usurarios involvere christianos et nobilium maneria adquirere per voraginem usurarum; quia hoc est favere iudeis in suis criminibus contra christianos. Cogat igitur regia clementia iudeos, ut est possibile, restituere christianis omnia ab illis per pravitatem usurariam occupata que ab eis tenentur dampnabiliter et dampnabilius tenentur ab omnibus christianis. Cogat etiam eos vivere de labore manuum suarum vel industria mercature, et nullo modo communicare in contractibus vel colloquiis cum christicolis in secreto, set tantum in puplico coram testibus fidedignis; et sub pena horribili nec nostris labiis nominanda eos studeat ab omnibus mutuis usurariis cohercere, et signum ante et retro gerere manifestum. Et sic poterunt faciliter refrenari. . . .

Ad xiiii^m articulum bene concedit rex quod mangna carta servetur.

Ad xv^m articulum bene permittat rex quod laici falsarii coram iudicibus ecclesiasticis arrestentur, donec vicecomiti vel aliis quorum interest eosdem recipere liberentur.

Ad xvi^m articulum de iudeis apostaticis bene concedit rex quod fiat iustitia per archiepiscopum cum iustitiariis assingnatis in forma de qua alias est conventum.[7]

1. This group of texts, showing the interplay between royal and ecclesiastical forces, is best read together with no. XVI (the 1287 Council of Exeter) and no. 50 (the bull *Nimis in partibus*). The texts are reprinted by permission from F. M. Powicke and C. R. Cheney, *Councils and Synods, with Other Documents Relating to the English Church*, vol. II, pt. II (London: Oxford University Press, 1964), pp. 955, 959, 961–962, 963. Cf. also J. A. Watt, "The English Episcopate, the State and the Jews: The Evidence of the Thirteenth-Century Conciliar Decrees," in *Thirteenth Century England*, ed. P. R. Cross and S. D. Lloyd (Newcastle-upon-Tyne, 1988).

2. For the circumstances see Flahiff, *Mediaeval Studies*, vi. 305–7, Powicke, *Thirteenth Cent.*, pp. 480–1, and Douie, pp. 302–16, who describes the following documents in detail. [Powicke and Cheney, *Councils and Synods*, p. 955. Reprinted by permission.]

3. Powicke and Cheney, *Councils and Synods*, p. 955. Reprinted by permission.

4. Powicke and Cheney, *Councils and Synods*, p. 959. Reprinted by permission.

5. Edward I had prohibited the taking of interest in the 1275 Statute on the Jews. His intentions were serious; reality defeated them. See K. Stow. "Papal and Royal Attitudes," pp. 180–181.

6. Louis IX and Thomas of Aquinas had also suggested manual labor as an alternative to lending.

7. Powicke and Cheney, *Councils and Synods*, pp. 961–962 and p. 963. Reprinted by permission.

References to the Jews in the Correspondence of John XXII

References to the Jews in the Correspondence of John XXII

SOLOMON GRAYZEL
Philadelphia

JACQUES DUÈSE, cardinal-bishop of Porto and bishop of Avignon, was elected to the papacy on August 7, 1316, and took the name of John XXII.[1] He was seventy-two years old at the time, but, despite the hopes—and the plots—of his enemies, he reigned for eighteen years. He was the second in the line of Avignon popes;[2] it was he, however, rather than his predecessor, Clement V, who established the papal court in that city so firmly that it was to take almost half a century after his death to move it back to Rome.

John XXII was a man of energy, self-confidence and great organizing ability, but not of an original turn of mind. His attitude toward the Jews was therefore such as one would expect from a man of his day. Practicality, rather than either kindness or religious zeal,[3] can be glimpsed behind his actions for or against them. The initiative in Christian policy regarding the Jews was now in the hands of the Inquisition and the secular powers.[4]

The references to the Jews collected here touch upon almost every phase of Jewish life and destiny during this period which saw many expulsions and forced conversions.[5] The documents were gathered from various collections of source material[6] and were checked, wherever possible, against the papal registers at the Vatican Archive.[7] Consequently, it was often possible to give here more of the document than can be found in the collections consulted. Nevertheless, only a summary is given of most of the documents, although an effort was made to point out those portions which mention Jews or touch upon their fate.

301

NOTES

1. The best biography of John XXII is that by Noel Valois, *"Jacques Duèse,"* in *Histoire littéraire de la France,* vol. 34 (1914). G. Mollat, *Les Papes d'Avignon,* 7th edition, Paris, 1930, pp. 37–62, also contains an excellent biography, with a further bibliography on pp. 37–8.

2. Because of the popes' sojourn in Avignon, and because that city and its vicinity became papal property, the relationship between the Jewish communities of Avignon and the Comtat and the papacy assumed added significance. Armand Mossé, *Histoire des Juifs d'Avignon et du Comtat Venaissin,* Paris, 1934, offers a good summary of that relationship. He also offers a further bibliography at the end of his book.

3. L. Bardinet, "Condition civile des Juifs du Comtat Venaissin pendant le séjour des Papes à Avignon (1309–1376)," in *Revue historique,* XII (1880), implies (p. 17) that John XXII was moved by pity for the Jews. Noel Valois denies this (*loc. cit.,* p. 421).

4. Contrast the spirit of the documents given here with the papal utterances in Solomon Grayzel, *The Church and the Jews in the XIIIth Century,* Philadelphia, 1933 (hereinafter referred to as "Grayzel").

5. On conversion during the Middle Ages, see Peter Browe, *Die Judenmission im Mittelalter und die Päpste,* Rome, 1942 (*Miscellanea Historiae Pontificiae,* vol. VI). It is referred to below as "Browe, *Judenmission.*"

6. The following are the collections of source material which are cited below in abbreviated form: Fritz Baer, *Die Juden im Christlichen Spanien,* vol. I, *Aragonien und Navarra,* Berlin, 1929; vol. II, *Kastilien und Inquisitionsakten,* Berlin, 1936. L. Cherubinus, *Bullarium Romanum,* 4 vols., Rome, 1638. A. Coulon, *Lettres secrètes et curiales du pape (Jean XXII) relatives à la France,* Bibliothèque des Écoles Françaises d'Athènes et de Rome, series 3, no. 1. G. Mollat, *Lettres communes de Jean XXII,* Bibliothèque, ut supra, series 3, 1 bis, Paris, last fascicle in 1937. Th. Ripoll, *Bullarium Ordinis FF. Praedicatorum,* 8 vols., Rome, 1729–40. H. V. Sauerland, *Urkunden und Regesten zur Geschichte des Rheinlandes aus dem Vatikanisches Archiv* (Publikationen der Gesellschaft für Rhein. Geschichtskunde, no. XXIII), 1902. See also the discussion of the documents given in Sauerland by Adolf Kober, "Die rechtliche Lage der Juden im Rheinland während des 14. Jahrhundert etc." in *Westdeutsche Zeitschrift für Geschichte und Kunst,* 1909. J. M. Vidal, *Bullaire de l'inquisition française au XIVe siècle,* Paris, 1913.

7. I take this opportunity of thanking the Vatican Archive, and its gracious chief, Monsignor Angelo Mercati, for the many courtesies shown me during my stay in Rome in 1938.

I   December 10, 1316

To William Pascalis, a Cleric in the Royal Chapel at Majorca:

CLARA MERITA . . . At the request of Sancho, king of Majorca, the pope grants William a benefice in the diocese of Majorca, notwithstanding the fact that the king had already conferred on him a chaplaincy, without cure of souls, in a church recently converted from a synagogue[1] (. . . *quod capellaniam sine cura noviter per dictum regem in civitate Majoricarum in loco ubi synagoga Judeorum consueverat esse dotatam nosceris obtinere*).

Dat. Avin., iiii Idus Decembris, anno primo.

Mollat, no. 2216.
Reg. Vat. 64, fol. 235r.

1. For the events leading to the conversion of the synagogue see Baer, *History of the Jews in Christian Spain* (Hebrew), I, p. 258; also Fidel Fita, *España Ebrea*, Madrid, 1889, II, pp. 188 f. The cause for this and other severe penalties, including expulsion from Majorca, was the aid the Jews were alleged to have given to two Christian Germans who desired to become Jews. For the reduction of the penalties see below, no. III. The same case caused similar penalties to be imposed on the Jews of Tarragona (Baer, I, p. 204, no. 266) and Montblanch (*ibid.*, p. 207, no. 168).

II   May 26, 1317

To the Bishops, the Clergy, the Secular Princes and all other Inhabitants of the Comtat Venaissin:[1]

AD NOSTRI APOSTOLATUS . . . For a period of five years the pope grants that, as long as a person is willing to appear before the episcopal court or the rector of the Comtat and his officials, he may not be forced to appear before other judges unless the latter receive special papal authorization.[2] This is to apply to the Jewish inhabitants as well. (*Volumus etiam quod ad Judeos habitatores comitatus ipsius quique imposterum ibi elegerint incolatum indulgentum huiusmodi extendatur.*)

Dat. Avin., vii Kal. Junii, anno primo.

Mollat, no. 3907.
Reg. Vat. 65, fol. 314r, no. 2983.

1. Similar letters were sent to the Bishops of Avignon and Orange and to the Archdeacon of Cavaillon.

2. The reference is to the numerous conflicting jurisdictions—feudal, episcopal, rectoral, civic and papal—to which the population of the Comtat was subject (cf. Mossé, p. 76). John XXII was to deal with the subject again in 1320. The courts of the Inquisition no doubt further complicated the situation.

III   June 2, 1317

To the Bishop of Majorca:

PETITIO DILECTI FILII . . . The petition of William de Ortis, rector of the parish of Ste. Julalia of Majorca, relates that a chapel had been established there in the place of the synagogue when the Jews had been expelled (. . . *quibus postmodum ex quibus causis legitimis exinde repulsis per inquisitores heretice pravitatis in synagogam predictam quandam capellam . . . constructa extitit*). A chaplain conducted divine services there and the king aided in its endowment. Subsequently the Jews came to an agreement (*ex compositione quadam*) with the king and were permitted to return to their former homes. The Christian chapel was now within the enclosure of the Jews (*clausura*).[1] Consequently Christians refuse to attend services there[2] (*ita quod ibi propter hoc paucis vel nihil ad predictam capellam confluentibus orthodoxis in ea divina officia more solito minime celebrantur*). The pope therefore asks the bishop to help, if the above be true, in the transfer of the chapel[3] (*extra dictam clausuram in locum alium a fidelibus habitatum*).

Dat. Avin., iiii Non. Junii, anno primo.

Mollat, no. 3999.
Reg. Aven. 6, fol. 451r.

1. The situation thus changed radically since the dispatch of no. I, above.

2. See Paul Fournier in *Histoire littéraire de la France*, vol. 36, p. 439. He says that the Jews, finding the existence of the chapel in their midst offensive, paid a

substantial sum to have it removed. Judging from the above, the cause for the removal was quite different.

3. King Sancho forbade the return of the former synagogue to the Jews. The Jews were permitted to erect another synagogue (cf. Fidel Fita, *España Ebrea*, II, pp. 182, 190 f.).

IV   January 7, 1318

To Master Peter Textor, Prior of St. Anthony of La Rouergue, and Peter de Pres, Provost of Clairmont:

SUCCESSOR PETRI . . . The pope asks the two Churchmen to inquire into the rumors about the criminal activities of Robert, bishop of Aix.[1] The latter is accused of blasphemies and indecent activities, among them believing in and practicing magic and consorting with others, Jews[2] and Christians, who practiced magic. (*Nonnullos etiam alios sortilegos, mathematicos aut divinatores tam Judeos quam Christianos, quandoque consuluit, eorum consilio et ministerio in hiis utens.*)

Dat. Avin., viii Idus Januarii, anno secundo.

Coulon, no. 468.
Reg. Vat. 109, f. 114r–v.

1. The archbishop resigned his office without waiting for sentence to be pronounced (Coulon, *ibid.*, note).

2. On magic and superstition among the Jews see M. Güdemann, *Ha-Torah veha-Hayyim*, Warsaw, 1896, I, pp. 174 ff. On the presumed connection between magic and the Jews see Joshua Trachtenberg, *The Devil and the Jews*, New Haven, 1943, pp. 88 ff. The inquisition had jurisdiction over Jews when charged with practice of magic. See also below, no. XVI, where Jews are accused of the practice.

The belief in magic was almost universal. The trial of Hugh Géraud, bishop of Cahors, had shaken the Christian world only a few months before this letter was written. This bishop had tried to murder the pope and some of his adherents by means of wax images and incantations—though he had not intended to neglect ordinary poison as well. A number of Jews and converts from Judaism had been involved in the case. One of them, Bernard Jourdain of Toulouse, had manufactured the images of the pope and the two cardinals who were marked for death with him. For the extraordinary story and the part Jews played in it see E. Albe, *Hughes Géraud*, Cahors, 1904, esp. pp. 58, 65, 178; cf. *Histoire littéraire de la France*, vol. 34, p. 409; Mollat, *Les Papes d'Avignon*, pp. 44–5.

In another case of a man tried for the crime of practicing magic, the name of a convert from Judaism actually figures in a papal letter. This was Johannes de

Foresio (Jean de Forez), *conversus, qui ante conversionem suam Abraam de Perpiniano vocabatur* (cf. Vidal, *Bullaire*, pp. 99 f., no. 60, Pope John's letter to the king of France, September 13, 1324). He was wanted as a witness *non obstante ratione vilitatis sue et facinorum suorum tam ante baptismum quam post* (*ibid.*, pp. 77–83, no. 46).

V   June 5, 1318

To Mary, Queen of France:[1]

EXIGIT TUORUM . . . Her petition stated that, after the general expulsion of the Jews from France, she had come into a large sum, amounting to ten thousand pounds (*parvorum Turon.*) from the Jews of the territories which had been given her as her marriage portion or as gifts. Since she does not know from whom the money had been exacted—the original owners may have died or cannot be found[2]—(*cumque ignores personas eorum ex quibus huiusmodi exactio facta est ac etiam aliorum a quibus dicti Judei exegerunt pecunias huiusmodi nomine usurarum cum forte sunt morti aut nequeant reperiri*), she asks permission to retain the sum. The pope grants the request on condition that part of the money be given to Philip, king of France, in support of his planned voyage to bring aid to the Holy Land.[3]

Dat. Avin., Non. Junii, anno secundo.

Mollat, no. 7384.
Reg. Aven. 12, fol. 23a.

1. Mary of Brabant, 1254–1321, widow of Philip III of France. A similar letter had been addressed to her by Pope Clement V on January 3, 1306 (*Regestum Clementis Pape V*, I, no. 461).

2. According to the agreement with King Louis X, the returned Jews could reclaim their communal property and their debts, provided two-thirds of the latter were turned over to the treasury (see Graetz, *Geschichte*, VII, pp. 275 f.). Possibly the queen sought justification for not returning property confiscated or debts collected before the return.

3. This was the usual arrangement whereby such money could be retained by the princes (cf. Grayzel, pp. 233–9, nos. 90, 91, 92, 93).

VI   February 24, 1319

To William, Bishop of Paris:

CUM SICUT . . . The pope orders the bishop of Paris to see that the churchmen, monasteries and convents of France make proper provision,[1] in accordance with his person and his status, for John Salvati of Villeneuve-le-Roi, a cleric of the diocese of Beauvais, a convert from Judaism and a scholar in Hebrew and Aramaic (*qui olim de judaice cecitatis errore ad fidem catholicam se convertit, in linguis tam ebrea quam chaldea sufficienter instructus existat*), and desirous of translating books from these languages into Latin and of instructing Christians in these languages[2] so that they in turn might convert others[3] (*possint Altissimo reddere gratum fructum*).

Dat. Avin., vi Kal. Martii, anno tertio.

H. Denifle, *Chartularium Universitatis Parisiensis*, II, p. 228, no. 777.

1. Denifle, *ibid.*, p. 237, no. 786, dated February 2, 1320, is a receipt given to a monastery in Dijon for 12 denarii paid as its share of the money being collected by the bishopric of Lingones for the support of John Salvati.

2. See no. XXIX, below, where the pope seeks to appraise the experiment.

3. The decision to introduce such studies for missionary purposes was reached at the Council of Vienne and proclaimed by Clement V in 1312 (see *Corpus Juris Canonici*, ed. Ae. Friedberg, II, Clementin., Lib. V, tit. 1, c. i: *Inter sollicitudines;* also Denifle, *ibid.*, II, p. 154, no. 695). Clement had done nothing to implement the decision, so that the credit goes to John XXII. Cf. Browe, *Judenmission*, pp. 273 ff; also B. Altaner, "Sprachstudien und Sprachkenntnisse im Dienste der Mission des 12. und 13. Jahrhunderts," in *Zeitschrift für Missionswissenschaft*, 21 (1931), pp. 121–29, where previous efforts at such study are outlined. See also *Histoire littéraire de la France*, vol. 36 (1927), p. 363; H. Denifle, *Die Universitäten des Mittelalters bis 1400*, Berlin, 1885, pp. 306 ff.

VII   November 11, 1319

To All Faithful Christians:

VIRGO VENUSTISSIMA . . . The pope grants a special indulgence to those who, during a period of sixty days, will visit the chapel dedicated to the

Holy Mary of Nazareth in the city of Tarragona. A resident of this city, named Arnaldus Raymundi, had erected this chapel within a former synagogue[1] (*in synagoga que fuit olim Judeorum*).

Dat. Avin., iii Idus Novembris, anno quarto.

Mollat, no. 10365.
Reg. Vat. 70, fol. 133v, no. 165.

1. The background is given in Baer, *History of the Jews in Christian Spain* (Hebrew), I, p. 258. The reason given for the destruction was that it had been built without permission; actually the destruction was connected with the same incident which lay behind the upheaval in Majorca indicated in no. III, above. Cf. Baer, I, pp. 204 f., no. 166 and p. 239, no. 180.

VIII   April 7, 1320

To the Abbot of Murbach and the Deans of Colmar and Basel:

SUA NOBIS . . . The burgomaster and the consuls of the city of Strasbourg asked that the ban imposed upon them by the provost of the Church of All Saints in Friburg be lifted. Rudolph, marquis of Baden, had charged that David (*senior*), called Walch, and his son Aaron, Jews of Strasbourg, had been extorting and continued to extort from him large sums as usury.[1] At the request of the marquis, the provost had haled the Jews before his court. They refused to appear[2] and the provost decided in favor of the marquis and forbade Christians to have any dealings with them (. . . *pro dicto nobili definitivam sententiam promulgaret et pro eo quod ipsi Judei eidem definitive contumaciter parere contempserant publice inhibuerat ne aliquis fidelium communicaret eisdem*). On the ground that the burgomaster and consuls continued to have dealings with the Jews, the marquis prevailed upon the provost to place them under the interdict. The provost, the burgomaster asserts, had not sought nor could he have found any proof for this charge. Hence they appealed to the pope, who asks the above to investigate.[3]

Dat. Avin., vii Idus Aprilis, anno quarto.

Urkundenbuch der Stadt Strassburg, II, pp. 346-7, no. 393.

1. The case is discussed in A. Glaser, *Geschichte der Juden in Strassburg*, Strassburg, 1924, pp. 45-7.

2. Since the Jews of Strasbourg enjoyed the privilege of appearing only before the city magistrate's court, they naturally refused to answer the summons of the provost and were, no doubt, supported in their refusal by the burgomaster and the consuls. The interference by an ecclesiastical court was predicated on the new attitude towards money-lending. The right of the Jews to lend money at interest had been recognized throughout the 13th century. The Church's reluctant recognition that this was beyond its jurisdiction was implied in the IV Lateran Council's warning on the subject issued to the secular rulers (Grayzel, pp. 312-3). The Council of Vienne (1311-2) introduced a new viewpoint, including the Jews in the general prohibition of usury expressed in the canon *Ex gravi* (Clementin., Lib. V. tit. V, c. 1). Christian borrowers were quick to take advantage of the new situation so that the money of Jewish lenders was quickly tied up in litigation (cf. Baer, *The Jews in Christian Spain* (Hebrew), I, p. 139). The Jews refused to accept such an application of church law to themselves (see no. XVII below), and the secular authorities, as evident here, sided with them. For Spain, see Baer, II, nos. 121, 133, 138, 139, 142, 144. For a general discussion of the effects of this canon see Benjamin N. Nelson, *The Idea of Usury*, Princeton, 1949, esp. p. 23 note. For Germany, see Kober, pp. 243 ff. See also Georg Caro, *Sozial und Wirtschaftsgeschichte der Juden* ..., II, pp. 198-200. That civil law continued to enforce the rights of the Jews in this respect is evident from the discussion of the subject in Guido Kisch's *The Jews in Medieval Germany*, Chicago, 1949, pp. 223-41.

3. The continuation of the case in *Urkundenbuch der Stadt Strassburg*, II, nos. 406, 408.

IX   June 19, 1320

To All Government Officials of the Comtat Venaissin and of other Territories Belonging to the Papacy:

Ad futuram rei memoriam.

CUM SIT ABSURDUM . . . Since it is absurd, unjust and unreasonable (*juri contrarium et obvium rationi*) that Jews upon conversion should be deprived of their property and thus be worse off than they had been as Jews,[1] government officials of the Comtat and of other territories belonging to and dependent upon the Apostolic See are ordered that such converts and those to be converted in the future shall not be disturbed in their property, but shall, on the contrary, be protected from every injury and violence (. . . *in possessionibus et bonis aliis . . . que conversionis tempore obtinebant . . . non perturbent vel impediant nec permittant ab aliis molestari, sed ipsis se favorabiles exhibentes ipsosque ab injuriis et violentiis protegant et defendant).*

Dat. Avin., . . . , anno quarto.[2]

Coulon, no. 1106.
Reg. Vat. 110, fol. 229v, no. 805.

1. The problem was one of long standing. To the princes the conversion of a Jew meant loss of property taxable and subject to confiscation at will. The matter was attacked at the III Lateran Council in 1179 and repeatedly thereafter (see Grayzel, pp. 19, 96-9, 224-5, 296-7, 298-9 §10). Apparently the Church regulation had until this time been unobserved even in papal territory. For a thorough discussion of the subject see Browe, *Judenmission*, pp. 186-95, esp. p. 189. According to Noel Valois (in *Histoire littéraire de la France*, vol. 34, p. 422 note 1), the desired result was not achieved till 1393.

2. There is no doubt about the date. Some give it as June 18.

X   June 19, 1320

To the Archbishop of Narbonne and His Suffragans:[1]

CUM DIFFICILE PROCUL . . . Reports have reached the pope that shepherds (*porcorum et ovium aliorumque custodes animalium rusticani qui se nominant pastorellos*) have gathered in large numbers, among them youngsters and women (*impuberibus ad hoc et mulieribus imprudenter assumptis*), on the pretense of going on a crusade to the Holy Land, though they are unarmed for the most part and ill prepared and lacking proper leadership. They resort to offensive and detestable actions, killing and robbing (*quamplures immaniter gladiis trucidarunt, diversorum quam laicorum et etiam Judeorum bona[2] temporis oportunitate captata violentia predatione subripiunt et ea in usus proprios . . . convertentes*). They thus cause grave injury to many nobles and officials.[3] The archbishop and his suffragans are therefore instructed to persuade or compel the shepherds and their adherents, whether lay or clerical,[4] to desist from their evil actions and to wait until King Philip of France is ready to redeem his promise to go on a crusade.[5]

Dat. Avin. xiii Kal. Julii, anno quarto.

Coulon, nos. 1104, 1107, 1113.
Vidal, "L'Émeute des Pastoureaux en 1320," in *Annales de St. Louis des Français*, III (1898), pp. 145 ff.
L. Guerard, *Documents Pontificaux sur la Gascogne*, I, pp. 197-9.
Reg. Vat. 70, fol. 27v.

1. Letters in practically the same terms were sent, on June 23, to the Archbishop of Toulouse and his suffragans, to the Archbishop of Arles and his suffragans, and to the vicar of the Bishopric of Avignon; and to the seneschals of Beaucaire, Toulouse, and others (on June 29: Reg. Vat., *ibid.*, fol. 27r).

2. It was not a question of the property of Jews, but of their lives (cf. Baluze, *Vitae Paparum Avenionensium*, ed. G. Mollat, I, pp. 179, 191; Vidal in the article cited above). A further example of the effects of the Shepherds' Crusade may be seen in Joachim Miret, "Le Massacre des Juifs de Montclus," in *REJ*, vol. 53, pp. 255 ff.

3. According to chroniclers of the period (cf. L. Guerard, *ibid.*, p. 198 note) the disorders by the shepherds began in Paris and rapidly spread southward, attracted especially by such places as had a Jewish population. Bernard, Viscount of Lomagne, in defending himself for his failure to appear on time in connection with the famous case of Clement V's inheritance, excused himself by saying that he had to stay at his post because he had to defend the Jews of his territory against the shepherds: *quia Judei pro baptizando seu convertendo ad fidem catholicam vel si baptizari nollent pro interficiendo non tradebantur eisdem* (Vat. Archives, Collect. 467, fol. 108v–109r: Instrumenta Misc. 703). The pope himself, in a letter to several cardinals in connection with the same case, on July 1, 1320, expressed surprise that the king had been less active than he should have been: *Miramur quod providencia regia scandalosis excessibus et perniciosis exemplo illorum qui se pastorellos nominant, qui utique lupi rapaces et homicide potius possunt dici, omittat occurrere, cum processus eorum offendat divine magestatis occulos, honori regio non leviter detrahant, ac toti regno graviora quam possit exprimi . . . pericula continentur* (L. Guerard, *ibid.*, p. 201).

4. The shepherds found many sympathizers among the Christian population of the towns. Vidal (*ibid.*, p. 138) points out that the need for sending a copy of this letter to the vicar of Avignon indicates the existence of such sympathizers in the papal territory as well.

5. The days of crusades to the Holy Land on a large scale were over, although various princes of Western Europe occasionally still toyed with the idea. Philip IV (the Fair) of France had promised to go and had used his vow as an excuse to raise an extra tithe. At his death, his son, Philip V, took the Cross (1314). In 1318 he appointed Louis, Count of Clairmont, captain of the crusading forces. The act seems to have had an effect on the peasantry but did not result in a crusade then or later. Cf. Louis Bréhier, *Les Croisades*, Paris, 1928, pp. 266 f.

XI   June 1320.[1]

To the Archbishop of Toulouse:

PER TUAS LITTERAS . . . The pope acknowledges the receipt of a letter from the archbishop informing him of the excesses of those who call themselves Shepherds, and who claim to want to go on a crusade, against the persons and property of the Jews. The archbishop further says that some people request that he take steps against these shepherds and their associates (. . . *quod ab aliquibus ut tam contra eos quam contra fautores adjutores et receptatores eorum procederes extiteras requisitus*). Concerned about saving himself and the Church the expense in men and money involved in such action, the archbishop turned to the pope for advice (*Tu vero, que tibi et ecclesie tue dispendia in personis et bonis ex huiusmodi processu poterant provenire considerans, ab eodem abstinere processu proinde studuisti, nos quid agendum a te super hoc existeret per dictas litteras consulendo.*) The pope informs the archbishop of the letters sent him and various others[2] a few days before, letters that must have reached him already. In these he had tried to impress the ecclesiastical and secular authorities with the fact that King Philip was diligently preparing to keep his crusader's vows and to warn them of the danger that experience shows is bound to arise from disorganized mobs (. . . *multis scandalis variisque periculis que frequenter in diversis partibus ex inordinatis congregationibus talium, sicut manifeste docet magistra rerum experientia, provenerunt*). Each and everyone of those to whom he had written must try to impress the shepherds and their associates with the importance of waiting for King Philip's signal. The warning is to be given in the pope's name (*ex parte nostra*), making use of ecclesiastical restraints and enlisting the support of the secular powers.[3] As to the city and province of Toulouse itself, the pope replies that the archbishop should adjust his actions to the time and the persons concerned, using suasion with some, threats with others, and public exhortation with the masses (. . . *aliquos populares de quolibet vico . . . ad tue facias presentiam evocari . . . set ex ipsorum tolerantia sola perferri diligenter ostensis . . . ipsos nunc secrete, nunc publice . . . nunc generaliter universos verbo publice predicationis monendo, exhortando et etiam increpando . . . nunc per spiritualium penarum comminationem . . . nunc per publice preconisationis edictum*). It is suggested that he take stronger measures where he has temporal authority. The pope asks to be kept informed (*nobis per litteras tuas quicquid feceris in premissis et qualiter dicti pastorelli et congregationes disponuntur ipsorum sepius rescripturus*).

Dat. Avin., . . . Kal. Julii, anno quarto.

Coulon, no. 1114.
Vidal, *ibid.*, pp. 149 f.

---

1. All the date indicates is that the letter was sent before the first of July; the general contents indicate that it was sent after June 19th. The seneschal's letter

must have arrived at the same time and been answered at the same time (cf. no. XII, below).

2. The phrase used—. . . *universis senescallis et officialibus aliis ac nobilibus regni Francie*—seems to indicate further that the Shepherds' movement was not confined to the south of France.

3. See the next document.

XII   June 1320.[1]

To the Seneschal of Toulouse:

SIGNIFICASTI NOBIS . . . The seneschal sent letters informing the pope of the grave excesses performed by those who call themselves Pastorelli against the persons and property of the Jews, not without injury to the king of France.[2] The seneschal asked for advice how he might proceed in the matter. The pope replies that he had heard about the shepherds some days ago and had written to various prelates and to the other seneschals and officials of the king in France,[3] asking and urging the prelates to use spiritual means and the officials to use secular force to disband the shepherds (. . . *ut ipsi per spirituales, tu vero ac senescalli, officiales et nobiles supradicti per temporales penas curaretis Pastorellos eosdem ab eorum congregationibus cohibere*). He had also advised the Archbishop of Toulouse, in response to his letter, how to deal with the problem, as the seneschal can see from the said response[4] (. . . *prout in litteras responsionis poteris intueri*).

   Dat. Avin . . . . Kal. Julii, anno quarto.

Coulon, no. 1115.
Vidal, *ibid.*, p. 151.

1. See above, XI, note 1.

2. The Jews and their property being taxable by the king and under his special protection. Cf. no. X. above, note 3, end.

3. See no. XI, above, note 2.

4. Perhaps a copy of the reply to the archbishop was sent along for the information of the seneschal.

XIII   July 9, 1320

To All Christian Princes, Nobles, Seneschals, Bailiffs, Communities, Castles, Villages, and All Other Places Where These Letters Reach:

DECET SEDIS APOSTOLICE . . . It is but fitting that the piety of the Apostolic Throne should, when necessary, guard the Jews all the more readily as they are in a special sense preserved to bear witness in favor of the Catholic faith (. . . *ut eo promptius tueatur, cum expedit, sua defensione Judeos, quod specialius sunt in testimonium catholice fidei reservati*).[1] A group of evildoers (*congregatio malignorum*), calling themselves Pastorelli and pretending to want to go to the aid of the Holy Land, have cruelly and without cause given over to slaughter a multitude of Jews in various places and provinces, wickedly stealing their property and proclaiming their wicked efforts so that they might be able to kill others with equal cruelty (. . . *et ut alios valeant simili severitate necare perversos eorum conatus exponant*).[2] We, desirous of maintaining unharmed the Jews who live in our Comtat Venaissin, Bédarride, Châteauneuf and the diocese of Avignon and who are dependent upon the Church of Avignon, and of defending them from the rage of the above-named Pastorelli, request all of you and urge you in the name of Jesus Christ the Lord, for the sake of our reverence and that of the Holy See, to grant such ready aid (*vestre adesse velitis presidio*) to the Jews, individually and collectively, who live in the Comtat and in these places, that none of them shall be harmed in goods, property and person by the hands of the above-named Pastorelli, so that we may thereupon be able to commend your devotion.[3]

Dat. Avin., vii Idus Julii, anno quarto.

Reg. Vat. 70, fol. 408v, no. 952.
Vidal, in *Annales, ibid.*, pp. 152 f.

1. The introductory sentence is reminiscent of the motivation given in letters of protection by earlier popes: Innocent III (cf. Grayzel, p. 92, no. 5); Gregory IX (*ibid.*, p. 226, no. 87), *quod quasi ex archivis ipsorum Christiane fidei testimonia prodierunt;* Innocent IV (*ibid.*, p. 260, no. 110), *specialius sunt in testimonium orthodoxe fidei reservati.*

2. By announcing the prospect of booty they obtained the aid of the inhabitants of places they planned to attack.

3. He was asking for help to defend his own Jews, but he was also setting an example for others. For the entire incident of the Shepherds, see Graetz, *Geschichte*, vol. VII, pp. 277–9. See especially Robert Anchel, *Les Juifs de France*, Paris, 1946, pp. 79–82.

XIV   July 22, 1320

Ad perpetuam rei memoriam.

DIGNUM ARBITRANTES[1] . . . We consider it proper and in consonance with right that those who, having given up the blindness of Judaism, are reborn in the baptismal font should enjoy favor and grace more abundantly than before (*amplioribus favoribus ac gratiis quam antea abundare*), and improper and absurd that believers (*fideles*) should be forced to beg like those who abound in disbelief[2] (*ut qui in perfidia abundarent*). We therefore order and command each and every rector and other official of the Comtat Venaissin and of the other counties and territories belonging to the Apostolic See that such converts and those who may be converted in the future shall not be harmed in their property or goods, by whatever name these are called, which these converts had at the time of their conversion or may obtain in the future, nor permit such harm to be caused them by others. They must, on the contrary, show themselves well inclined towards the converts and protect them from injury and molestation, so that they may be aware of having passed from servitude to liberty and not be compelled by reason of odious poverty to return to the disbelief which they had abandoned (. . . *ut sic de servitute ad libertatem se transisse percipiant nec redire pretextu mendicitatis odibilis ad dimissam perfidiam compellantur*).

Dat. Avin., xi Kal. Augusti, anno quarto.

Mollat, no. 12205.
Coulon, no. 1131.
Vidal, in *Annales*, p. 153 f.
Reg. Vat. 70, fol. 38r, no. 115.

1. In somewhat different form it has already been given above no. IX; cf. the notes there. In this form it was taken over into the *Corpus Juris Canonici*, Extravag. Lib. V, tit. ii, c. 2, where it is dated July 23. See also no. XV, where it is applied to a specific case. It seems to have been repeated on July 31 with slight verbal changes (Reg. Vat. 70, fol. 429v, no. 1003b).

2. Vidal, *ibid.*, suggests that the issuance, and presumably the repetition, of this order was connected with the events of the Shepherds' crusade. Those converted through fright or compulsion might be less likely to return to Judaism if there were some prospect of having their property restored to them.

XV   July 31, 1320

To the Rectors and Officials of the Comtat Venaissin and of Other Countries and Territories Dependent upon the Bishopric of Avignon Spiritually or Temporally:

DIGNUM ARBITRANTES . . . [as in no. XIV above, down to "in disbelief"]. Therefore, since our dear son Peter Arnaldi of Sarrians in the diocese of Avignon, bearer of these presents,[1] detesting recently the ancient Jewish impiety (*vetustatem nuper judaice impietatis detestans*), accepted sacred baptism and became a convert to the Catholic faith, we order and command each and every one of you that the said Peter . . . [as in no. XIV above, but in singular].

> Dat. Avin., ii Kal. Augusti, anno quarto.

Coulon, no. 1131.
Reg. Vat. 70, fol. 429v, no. 1003.

1. See above, no. XIV note 2. While this letter was given into the hands of the convert, the pope sent another, addressed to the vicars, judges, baliffs etc., in which he repeated in general terms and without mention of Peter, the order of no. XIV (Mollat, no. 11842; Reg. Vat., *ibid.*, no. 1003b).

XVI   September 4, 1320

To the Archbishop of Bourges[1] and His Suffragans:

DUDUM FELICIS RECORDATIONIS . . . Some time ago, Clement IV,[2] of happy memory, fully recognized the innumerable blasphemies of the Jews, their many wrongful practices, and the detestable blasphemies against the Savior and Lord Jesus Christ and the lofty and glorious everlasting Virgin Mary, his mother, which are to be found in a certain book of theirs. Later, Honorius[3] of pious memory, also a Roman pontiff and one of our predecessors, heard it truthfully averred that through the damnable instigation of Jewish unbelief (*Judeorum damnata suggerente perfidia*) some followers of the Christian faith, both men and women, judaized[4] in certain respects along with the Jews (*in certis articulis cum Judeis judaizabant eisdem*) and that there are other enormities which Jews commit against Christian men and women, all these being gravely insulting to our Redeemer and derogatory of the Catholic faith. These our predecessors thereupon directed formal letters (*sub certa forma*) against the Jews: that is, Clement to the archbishop of Tarragona[5] and Honorius later on to the archbishop of York.[6] Moreover, Odo, bishop of Tusculum,[7] apostolic legate to the Kingdom of France, upon finding that certain books of the Jews, called Talmutz—these having been inspected by himself and other men zealous in the faith—contained numberless errors, abuses and blasphemies, is known to have pronounced sentence against the said Jews, as may be seen from his letter of condemnation which we have caused to be appended to these presents.

We, therefore, whose special duty it is to defend the orthodox faith, after having given the matter careful consideration (*in debite considerationis scrutinio recensentes*), have decided that such a plague, such a pernicious disease which has continued to rage in various lands, is not to be estimated lightly (*tam pestilens, tamque perniciosus morbus . . . non est aliquatenus contemnendus*), lest it grow in the course of time and infect still others; but rather to pull out those pestiferous twigs by their roots so that they be not spread by that faith's lack of discrimination (*ne indiscrimen ipsius fidei dilatentur*). Following in the footsteps of our above-named predecessors, we strictly order Your Fraternity, by the virtue of obedience, that each and every one of you must carefully warn all Christian men and women in your provinces and dioceses, by preachments and sermons which you shall preach or cause to be preached. This we want and order to be done frequently—in the cathedrals and in other churches—by yourselves or by those whom you may appoint for this purpose, taking care to warn and to restrain them most strictly to try wholeheartedly to abstain from all and every one of the matters contained in the said writings. You shall hold the people in check and keep them away from these things by such spiritual punishments as you may see fit to impose, appeal denied, and by such others as you may impose, in accordance with canonical statutes, upon Christian men and women as well as upon the Jews so that these may desist from the above-named blasphemies, errors, curses, falsehoods and other evils mentioned in the said letters. You must find fitting and opportune remedies for all the above.

Moreover, you shall make the Jews who live in the said provinces and dioceses assign to you whole the said law, or book, which they call Talmutz, and all their other books with their additions and commentaries (. . . *legem seu librum quem talmutz predicitur vocant, omnesque alios ipsorum libros cum additionibus et expositionibus eorundem faciatis vobis integraliter assignari*), compelling them to do this by whatever canonical punishments may seem to you expedient. After having subjected the Talmutz and books to careful examination along with some Franciscan and Dominican friars and with other men of good sense and learning whom you know to be versed in God's law, you shall burn by fire those of the books which you shall find contain the said blasphemies, errors, falsehoods and curses, calling in the secular arm, if necessary, for this purpose.[8] You shall arrange matters with foresight, so that you can proceed with this business in the said consultation simultaneously and with such care and caution that our order regarding the total delivery of the Talmutz and the other books in your provinces and dioceses shall emerge into full execution quickly and at one and the same time, lest the deceptiveness of the Jews be enabled in some fashion to hide them[9] (*attentius provisuri ut una simul in dicto consilio sic provide, sic consulte in huiusmodi negotio procedatis quod in eisdem civitatibus et diocesibus vestris mandatum nostrum huiusmodi vobis integre faciendum uno eodemque tempore celeriter effectum in executionis debite sortiatur, ne Judeorum ipsorum fallacia dictos libros quomodolibet valeat occultare . . .*)

Dat. Avin., ii Non. Septembris, anno quarto.

Raynaldus, *Annales Eccl.,* 1320 24 ff.
Mollat, no. 12238.
Ripoll, *Bullar. Praedicatorum,* II, p. 149, no. 28.

1. Raynaldus, *ibid.,* says that a similar letter was sent to the Archbishop of Toulouse and his suffragans, and, under date of October 9, also to the Bishop of Paris. Baluze, *Vitae Paparum* etc., ed. Mollat, II, pp. 243 ff. mentions only Bourges; cf. R. L. Poole, in *English Historical Review,* III (1891), p. 372.

2. Clement IV, 1265–1268.

3. Honorius IV, 1285–1287.

4. The term *judaizare* was used in a very broad sense. Cf. Louis I. Newman, *Jewish Influence on Christian Reform Movements,* New York, 1925, pp. 1–3.

5. Clement's letter, *Damnabili perfidia,* was addressed to the Archbishop of Tarragona, July 15, 1267, and a similar one to James I of Aragon. Potthast nos. 20081–2; Ripoll, *Bullar. Praed.,* I, p. 487; Sbaralea, *Bullar. Francisc.,* III, pp. 123 ff. The letters were carried from Rome to Aragon by the convert Pablo Christiani, who had instigated their writing as a result of his disputation with Nahmanides. The charges there enumerated by Pope Clement no doubt represent the charges made by Pablo. The disputation of 1263 therefore serves as the background for Clement's letter. For a Christian view of the disputation see H. Denifle, "Quellen zur Disputation Pablos Christiani mit Mose Nachmani zu Barcelona," in *Historisches Jahrbuch,* vol. VIII (1887), pp. 225 ff.; for a Jewish

view see I. Loeb, "La Controverse de 1263 à Barcelone," in *REJ*, XV (1887), pp. 1 ff. Cf. further, Peter Browe, *Die Judenmission* etc., pp. 19, 72 ff.

6. Honorius' letter, *Nimis in partibus*, was addressed to John Pecham, Archbishop of Canterbury, November 18, 1286. Potthast no. 22541 (gives the date as Nov. 30); Prou, *Les Registres d'Honorius IV*, col. 513, no. 869; Raynaldus, *Annales Eccl.*, 1286, §25; Sbaralea, *ibid.*, pp. 590-1. The writing was probably instigated by the English clergy in an attempt to increase the pressure on the Jews which yielded a harvest of converts and ended in the general expulsion a few years later. Cf. Cecil Roth, *A History of the Jews in England*, Oxford, 1941, pp. 68-80; Browe, *ibid.*, pp. 294 f., 303.

7. For Odo of Châteauroux and his part in the condemnation of the Talmud in France (1242-8), see Grayzel, pp. 275-9.

8. H. C. Lea, *A History of the Inquisition in the Middle Ages*, I, p. 555, says that Philip the Fair in 1299 ordered the extermination of the copies of the Talmud which seem to have become numerous again, and that again in 1309 three cartloads of books were burned in Paris. These must have been books confiscated or left behind when the Jews were expelled in 1306. Bardinet, "Les Juifs du Comtat Venaissin au moyen age," in *Revue Historique*, XIV (1880), p. 13 n. 5, speaks of two cartloads of Jewish books burned by the inquisitor of Toulouse during the interregnum between Clement and John. Even before this letter was sent by John XXII, the zealous inquisitor Bernard Gui (c. 1261-1331), had taken steps against the Talmud. His *Practica Inquisitionis Heretice Pravitatis* (ed. Douais, Paris, 1886, pp. 67-71) contains a series of formulae for requisitioning copies of the Talmud, excommunication of those who refuse to permit a search for them and of those who hide such books etc. In all likelihood, Bernard Gui turned for aid to the royal superintendent of Jewish affairs, since the Jews were under royal protection. This letter of the pope was the result of Bernard's urging. The fresh crop of converts resulting from the Shepherds' crusade and, now that the danger was over, desirous of resuming their former faith, would naturally persuade an inquisitor of the need for such action as this letter commands. On the effect which the Talmud was supposed to have on the Jews, see Gregory IX's letter of June 9, 1239 (Grayzel, p. 240, no. 96). Cf. Browe, *Judenmission*, p. 120.

The orders of the pope were carried out. Copies of the Talmud and other Jewish books were burned in Bourges and Toulouse. In Pamiers the burning was presided over by Jacques Fournier, the future Benedict XII. In Paris the Talmud was burned during the Lent season of 1321. Cf. Noel Valois in *Histoire littéraire de la France*, 34 (1914), p. 424.

9. The advice to plan surprise raids on Jewish homes and houses of study was not new. Gregory IX suggested it in the letter cited above, and also Clement IV in the letter referred to here.

XVII   December 24, 1320

To the Rector of the March of Ancona:

SIGNIFICARUNT NOBIS . . . The community of Macerata, which is subject to the Roman Church, and some individuals of the city complained that, as a result of rebellions against Church authority which had taken place there, they had become heavily burdened by debts to Jews living there and in the neighborhood (. . . *necessario sunt coacti magna debitorum onera contrahentes maximas pecuniarum summas a nonnullis Judeis qui in eadem civitate Maceraten. et convicinis partibus moram trahere dinoscuntur sub usuris receperunt mutuo communiter et diversim*). They so worded the public instruments of indebtedness as to provide for three times the amount of the debt. Since these Jews do not consider themselves bound up with the edicts against usury issued by Pope Clement V and other popes[1] (*cum . . . Judei usurarum intenti voragini . . . Clementis pape V et aliorum predecessorum nostrorum . . . constitutionibus contra usurarios editis se asserunt non ligati*), they try to collect from the said community and individuals sums beyond the principal, subjecting them to annoyance and expense. The pope orders that the Jews, satisfied with the principal, shall abstain from the exaction of usury (. . . *sua sorte contenti, ab usurarum exactione desistant*). The rector must make the canonical statute apply to them (*faciens quo ad eos statutas canonum observari* [sic]).

Dat. Avin., viiii Kal. Januarii, anno quinto.

Mollat, no. 12776.
Reg. Vat. 72, fol. 155r, no. 1191.

1. For the new attitude towards moneylending by Jews see above, no. VIII, note 2. In the March of Ancona, where the pope was also secular ruler, the new attitude could be made to prevail sooner than elsewhere. This may be why the complainants took care to indicate that the Jews involved lived in the neighborhood.

XVIII   January 14, 1321

To the Archbishop of Toulouse:

CLEMENS ET MITIS . . . Guyard Gui, seneschal of Toulouse,[1] transmitted a petition containing the following recital: Rainerius of Montgeard, a cleric of the diocese of Toulouse, mentally unbalanced (*vesanio flatu ductus*), said and even proclaimed in Montgeard and elsewhere that, for the sake of God, blessed Mary and the Shepherds—whom the pope had for good reason condemned[2]—all the Jews should be killed and their property taken, he himself having killed three Jewish men and one Jewish woman and taken their property (. . . *dixit et etiam proclamavit quod omnes ex parte Dei et Beate Marie ac quondam Pastorellorum . . . Judeos interficerent et reciperent bona . . . dictusque clericus tres Judeos et unam Judeam nequiter interemit et bona ipsorum interemptorum extitit depredata*). Thereupon the cleric was brought to trial and confessed without being subjected to torture. Unaware that the man was a cleric, the seneschal ordered him hanged. Conscience-stricken now because of this sin, but unable to appear before the Apostolic See in person, he petitions for forgiveness. The archbishop is ordered to grant him absolution.

Dat. Avin., xix Kal. Februar., anno quinto.

Mollat, no. 12842.
Reg. Vat. 71, fol. 184r–v, no. 364.

1. The same seneschal was addressed in no. XII, above.

2. See nos. X, XI, XII.

XIX   A February 20, 1321.[1]

Ad Perpetuam Rei Memoriam:

EXTOLLENTES IN SANCTAM . . . The pope announces the establishment in Bedarride of a chapel with three altars, to be served by three chaplains, in the place where a synagogue used to be when the Jews still lived in the town[2] (. . . *in castro Bidaride,*[3] *Avinionen. dioc., in loco ubi sinagoga extitit hactenus Judeorum dum ipsorum congregatio moraretur ibidem, ea funditus diruta, cappellam, . . . ut, omni de loco ipso Judaice superstitionis eliminata spurtitia . . . , in ea majestas Altissimi collaudetur, . . . fecimus edificare de novo*). The pope had it rebuilt so that,

the filth of Jewish superstition having been eliminated, God, the Holy
Virgin and the saints might be worshipped therein.

Dat. Avin., x Kal. Martii, anno quinto.

Mollat, no. 14244.
Coulon, no. 1255.
Noel Valois, in *H.L.F.*, vol. 34, p. 422, no. 3.
Reg. Vat. 71, fol. 56v, no. 158.

B February 22, 1321

Like the above, but with the addition of a list of properties which the
pope had acquired from some of the Jews for the support of the chapel
and the chaplains (. . . *ad opus eorundem capelle et capellanorum a
quibusdam de prefatis Judeis specialiter emi[4] fecimus et acquiri*).

Dat. Avin., viii Kal. Martii, anno quinto.

Mollat, no. 14245.
Reg. Vat. 71, fol. 56v–57r.

C February 22–September 4, 1321

To Rostagnus Dadons; Bertrand Lamberti; and Bertrand de Narbona:

DIGNE AGERE CREDIMUS . . . Three separate Bulls, granting to each of the
above, respectively, a perpetual chaplaincy in the new chapel, so that, the
filth of Jewish superstition having been eliminated from that place, they
might worship etc.

Dat. Avin., . . . anno quinto.

Coulon, nos. 1285–7.
Reg. Vat. 74, fol. 20v.

1. The date assumed for this expulsion from the Comtat Venaissin by Graetz
(*Geschichte*, VII, p. 285), Is. Loeb (*REJ*, XII, pp. 47 f.), and most recently Mossé
(pp. 77–8) is 1322. Since John's enthronement took place on September 5, 1316,
his fifth year ended September 4, 1321. For the importance of this fact see the next
note. What may have misled them is the establishment of a similar chapel out of a
former synagogue in the better-known town of Carpentras in 1323 (see below,
no. XXIV). But that simply means that the establishment of this chapel was
delayed more than two years.

2. The fact of the expulsion is surprising and has caused much speculation. The pope had welcomed the fugitive Jews only a few months before, while defending them against the Shepherds. Most of Is. Loeb's explanations for this change of attitude (*ibid.*) are untenable, since he presupposes the date 1322 as the time of the accusation that the Jews poisoned the wells. Graetz, and after him others, follows the romantic explanation found in medieval Jewish literature (*Shevet Jehuda*, No. 14, ed. M. Wiener, Hanover, 1924, Hebrew, pp. 37 ff. Cf. F. Baer, *Unter-suchungen . . . des Schebet Jehuda*, Berlin, 1923, pp. 23 ff.) about a sister of the pope (Sancha, or Singhesa) who prevailed upon him to expel them. Noel Valois (in *H.L.F.*, vol. 34, p. 422) denies that there was any such sister. He also denies that John was ever especially favorably disposed, as claimed, for example, by Bardinet (*Revue Historique*, XII (1880), pp. 17 ff.) Valois would rather have it that the pope had admitted them in the hope that the refugees would yield to an intensified missionary effort, which is indeed referred to in no. XXIV, below. Since this effort produced no results, he expelled them. The difficulty is, of course, that he now expelled not only the newcomers but also the old residents whom he had previously tolerated. A more credible explanation, offered by both Bardinet and Loeb, is that the sudden increase of the Jewish population due to the fugitives intensified the opposition of the populace and the clergy and resulted in the expulsion. Perhaps the most plausible explanation is that this expulsion, like the attack on the Talmud (no. XVI, above), was due to the existence of converts to Christianity at the height of the Shepherds' persecutions, who, having found a refuge in the Comtat, now reverted to Judaism. The inquisitors, especially Bernard Gui, thereupon became active and stirred the pope to action.

3. The expulsion was limited to the Comtat, and did not affect Avignon. Graetz and others, continuing with the story culled from medieval Jewish sources, assert that the Jews availed themselves of the good offices of King Robert of Sicily and also paid the pope a large sum of money. Valois denies everything. Whether or not the entire story is true, the fact is that Avignon was not yet papal property, as the Comtat already was. It still belonged to the King of Naples and was not sold to the Papacy till 1348 (taken possession of in 1358). King Robert, therefore, had a veto power over the expulsion from Avignon. The additional gift of money may be apocryphal, based on common Jewish experience; but it is not incredible as a thank offering for the pope's failure to insist, as he might have.

4. The fact of purchase is to be noted. It was not usual.

XX   March 7, 1321

To the Dean of the Church of St. Gereon in Cologne:

AD AUDIENTIAM NOSTRAM. . . Salman of Basel,[1] hailing from Mainz, now a resident of Cologne, is said to have extorted usury from John, lord of the castle of Saffenberg, and his wife Sophia. He had made them take an oath, obtained men to go security for them, drew up certain official papers (*confectis quibusdam publicis instrumentis*), and took other measures to insure payment while hiding the fact of usury. If the facts are as stated,[2] the dean is ordered to compel the said Jew to release his debtors from their oath, to absolve the guarantors of the debt, and . . . satisfied with the principal, notwithstanding the abovementioned letters, documents, penalties, securities and renunciations, give back to John and Sophia what he had extorted and in the future refrain from usury (. . . *iuramentum relaxet . . . fideiussores ab . . . fideiussione absolvat . . . sorte contentus, non obstantibus litteris, instrumentis, penis, cautionibus et renunciationibus supradictis, eisdem . . . restituat sic extorta et ab usurarum exactione desistat . . .*).

Dat. Avin., Nonas Martii, anno quinto.

Sauerland, p. 519, no. 1292.
Kober, p. 265.

1. On Salman of Basel, his wanderings and other references to him, see Kober, *ibid.*, pp. 262 ff.

2. John of Saffenberg's appeal to the pope indicates his inability to obtain relief from his creditors' claims in the local secular courts (cf. above, no. VIII and notes). His case dragged on for a number of years, not being finally disposed of until October 17, 1324. The dean's decision could be enforced only in the usual fashion where Jews were concerned, *per subtractionem communionis fidelium.* Cf. Kober, *ibid.*, pp. 258 ff. Salman was ordered to pay costs, return the interest he had collected, and surrender the pledge which was in the form of a silver cup.

XXI   October 6, 1321

To the Dean of the Church of Xanthen:

AD AUDIENTIAM NOSTRAM . . . It has come to our notice that Vivus de Monasterio, Leyfmannus his son, Leyfmannus de Berka, Isahak de Schure, Moyses called Beyn de Stumbele, Godescalus called Mothir, Alexander de Wassemberg, all of them of Cologne, extort usury from the dean and chapter of St. Andrew's of Cologne . . . [1]

Dat. Avin., ii Nonas Octobris, anno sexto.

Sauerland, p. 275, no. 585.

1. The rest of the document is practically identical with no. XX, above. Cf. Kober, *ibid.*, pp. 252–3.

XXII   July 3, 1322.[1]

To the Inquisitors of Heresy in the Kingdom of France:

EX PARTE VESTRA . . . On your behalf we have recently been informed that certain persons, guilty or suspected of depraved heresy or converted from the blindness of Judaism to the Catholic faith and then apostatized from it, flee to churches, not to seek salvation but to evade your grasp and avoid punishment for their crimes (. . . *non ad salutis remedium, sed ut vestras manus effugiant et suorum scelerum vitént judicium ultionis*). You humbly implore the aid of the Apostolic See in this matter. We, therefore, resolved with wholehearted zeal to extirpate the enemies of the orthodox faith and to uproot from the garden of the Lord a plant so noxious and plague-bearing, order Your Discretion by apostolic letters— following the example of our predecessor, Pope Martin IV of blessed memory, who gave the same order to the inquisitors of heresy in the kingdom of France[2]—that you shall freely execute the duties of your office, in accordance with the nature of the offense (*juxta qualitatem delicti*), against those who, as may be clear to you, are guilty of such heresy or against those widely suspected or accused of it, and also against converted Jews who subsequently either clearly or apparently (*patenter vel verisimilibus indiciis*) apostatized, even if such persons have taken refuge in churches or above-named places. And in order that no one may place any obstacles in your way, we, by these[3] our letters, enjoin our venerable brothers, the archbishops and bishops of France, not to interfere with you[4] so that you may be able to fulfill our order unhampered; but rather that they, when requested, come to your aid whenever possible.

Dat. Avin., v Nonas Julii, anno sexto.

Vidal, *Bullaire*, pp. 69–70, no. 38.
Cherubini, I, p. 216.
Coquelines, III, pt. II, p. 154.

1. Cherubini and Coquelines give the date as August 13, 1317. It is not impossible that it was first issued by John then. Both 1317 and 1322 offered occasion for the situation described herein. The former date followed upon the return to France when many who had stayed behind as Christians were tempted to revert to Judaism. The later date was soon after the Shepherds' and the Lepers' incidents. The problem continued to trouble the Church and the State. The substance of this Bull was repeated at the request of King Philip of France on May 25, 1328

(Vidal, *ibid.*, no. 79), where the Jews are not specifically mentioned but may well have been among the *apostatantes* there referred to.

2. The right of asylum had already been cancelled for heretics by Martin IV's Bull, on October 21, 1281, *Ex parte dilectorum*, addressed to the Archbishops and Bishops of France (Reg. Vat. 41, fol. 19v, no. 77), and *Ex parte vestra*, addressed to the Inquisitors (*ibid.*, no. 78; Potthast no. 21806; Raynaldus, a.a. 1281, §18; Ripoll, II, p. 1).

3. Cherubini and Coquelines read *per has nostras litteras;* Vidal has *per alias.*

4. There was no question of the bishop's right to remove the fugitive from the church, but the bishop frequently resented the claims of the inquisitor. The secular power, too, sought the right of entry, as is evident from the request of the king of France mentioned in note 1, above. It was not merely a struggle for power; obviously the one who possessed himself of the culprit had advantages in the situation. In general, John XXII favored the inquisitors (Mollat, *Les Papes d'Avignon*, p. 53), but he did not want them to go too far in weakening the power of the bishops. The three-sided struggle continued for a long time. For the quarrels with the secular authority cf. Vidal, *Bullaire*, nos. 287–8, 289, 290, 303. See also, a case under Urban V, June 26, 1364, in *Lettres secrètes et curiales d'Urbain V* (ed. Lecacheux), no. 1041. For a further discussion of jurisdictional quarrels between bishops and inquisitors see below, no. XXVII.

XXIII   July 4, 1322.

To Angelo, Bishop of Viterbo:

INTER OPERA LAUDANDA . . . Fardus Hugolini, a citizen of Viterbo, had succeeded in converting certain Jews to the Catholic faith and certain women of loose morals to a life of virtue (. . . *Judeos a cecitate Judaice pravitatis ad veritatis semitam ac mulieres que voluptiose viventes scortis se publice exponebant ad honestatis cultum et continentie laudande virtutem . . .*). The bishop is empowered to grant a forty-day indulgence to Christians who give of their substance[1] to the support of these converts and repentant women.

Dat. Avin., Nonas Julii, anno sexto.

Mollat, no. 15749.
Reg. Vat. 73, fol. 362v, no. 1045.

---

1. On the support of converts through charity see Browe, *Judenmission*, pp. 197 ff.; Grayzel, pp. 94–5, no. 6; 96–7, no. 8; 138–9, no. 29.

XXIV August 23, 1322

To the Archbishops, Bishops and other Prelates in the Kingdom of Germany:[1]

INTER ECCLESIASTICOS ORDINES . . . The master and the brothers of the Order of Hospitallers of St. John of Jerusalem complained that certain Jews of Germany usuriously extort sums of money from persons, houses and other places belonging to their Order.[2] The pope orders the clergy here addressed to aid in recovering the money extorted as usury. They are asked not to aid the Jews,[3] since such aid prevents the Order from obtaining justice (*Judeos ipsos in vestris civitatibus et diocesibus constitutos . . . amore justitie . . . vestri suffragio nullatenus protegatis, ut ab ipsis assistencie vestre brachio non protectis iidem magister et fratres effectum debitum justitie consequantur*).

Dat. Avin., x Kal. Septembris, anno sexto.

Sauerland, p. 292, no. 617.
A. Lang, *Acta Salzburgo-Aquilejensia*, no. 50a.

1. With the necessary modifications the letter was sent on the same day to the princes, dukes, counts, marquises, barons, and landgraves, to the knights and other secular officials of Germany; another copy was sent to Louis, King-Elect of Rome.

2. On the financial transactions of the Hospitallers, see Kober, p. 255, and the references there given.

3. That the local powers, secular and ecclesiastical, sided with the Jews was, under the circumstances, not surprising. For a brief discussion of John XXII's reorganization of the finances of this order see Mollat, *Les Papes d'Avignon*, pp. 54 ff.

XXV A May 27, 1323

Ad Perpetuam Rei Memoriam:

INTER OPERA LAUDANDA . . . The Jews of Châteauneuf in the diocese of Avignon had been given repeated warnings in the spirit of charity (*post plures caritativas monitiones et predicationes salubres eis factas*) but had persisted in their stiff-neckedness and been expelled.[1] Thereupon a chapel had been constructed where a synagogue used to be, the latter having been completely destroyed (*in loco ubi synagoga extitit Judeorum, ea omnino diruta*). A certain number of properties, some of them previously Jewish possessions,[2] are set aside for the support of the Chapel.

Dat. Avin., vi Kal. Junii, anno septimo.

Reg. Vat. 82, fol. 1v–2r.

B May 27, 1323

Ad Perpetuam Rei Memoriam:

INTER OPERA LAUDANDA . . . The Jews of Carpentras having been given repeated warnings etc. [as above, but without the enumeration of the property, merely announcing the establishment of the chapel and the three altars therein].

Dat. Avin., vi Kal. Junii, anno septimo.

Coulon, no. 1724.

C July 1, 1323

To William of Chabaud; William Alberti; Francisco Cabrani:

APOSTOLICE SEDIS . . . Appointing each, respectively, as chaplain at the Chapel of the Blessed Mary at Carpentras.

Dat. Avin., vi Kal. Julii, anno septimo.

Reg. Vat. 82, fol. 2r.

D July 9, 1323

Ad Perpetuam Rei Memoriam:

DUDUM, POST EXPULSIONEM . . . After the expulsion of the Jews from Châteauneuf etc. [as in B. above].

Dat. Avin., vii Id. Julii, anno septimo.

Coulon, no. 1756.

E November 5, 1326

Ad Perpetuam Rei Memoriam:

DUDUM DE CIVITATE . . . [Additions to the property of the chapel at Carpentras].

Dat. Avin., Non. Novembris, anno undecimo.

Reg. Vat. 82, fol. 2v–3r.

1. For the background of the expulsion see above, no. XIX, notes.

2. Among the properties enumerated is a hospice which used to belong to Bonifatius Niger, judeus; and a place described as *plateam et locum in civitate predicta qui dicitur Balneam Judeorum;* and the former Jewish cemetery.

XXVI March 5, 1325

To Henry, Archbishop of Cologne:[1]

CUM, SICUT ACCEPIMUS . . . Since—so we have been informed—some Jews of your parts dare to exact and extort heavy and immoderate usury from Christians, we, desiring to give these Christians opportune aid, grant Your Fraternity by these presents the power to enforce (*faciendi . . . observari*) against the Jews in your diocese, or in whatever other places you exercise temporal power in other provinces and dioceses,[2] all the legal enactments against usurers adopted by the sacred councils and by the Apostolic See (*sacrorum conciliorum et alias sedis apostolice constitutiones contra usurarios promulgatas);* also to see that the full measure of justice is done the Christians by the Jews in these matters (*necnon exhibendi et reddendi eisdem Christianis de dictis Judeis super hiis justitie complementum*); and to compel the Jews by removing from them all contact with Christians, as well as all other opponents and rebels against this, by ecclesiastical punishment without appeal . . .

Dat. Avin., iii Nonas Martii, anno nono.

Sauerland, I, p. 349, no. 740.

1. See no. XXX below. Henry II, von Birnenburg (1304–32). It is difficult to say whether this document was the cause or the result of his changed attitude toward the Jews mentioned in Ernst Weyden, *Geschichte der Juden in Köln am Rhein*, Köln, 1867, p. 165.

2. He is addressed here in his capacity as secular ruler. For a discussion of this document see Kober, pp. 253 ff. Cf. above, no. VI, note 3.

XXVII   July 1, 1325

To Mathias, Archbishop of Mainz:[1]

SINCERE DEVOTIONIS . . . The archbishop's petition informs the pope that the Jews living in his city, towns, castles and fortresses, who are the property of and subject to the archiepiscopal Chamber and from whom this Chamber is known to draw the major part of its income (. . . *sunt tue camere peculiares homines et subjecti, in quibus Judeis maior pars reddituum consistere noscatur camere antedicte* . . .), are oppressed by the judges appointed by the Apostolic See and by their agents.[2] These do not admit the appeals of the Jews and their legitimate defenses, although such action is contrary to the privileges and liberties which the Jews enjoy (. . . *per judices a sede apostolica impetratos et subdelegatos eorum ipsorum Judeorum appellationibus et defensionibus legitimis non admissis contra privilegia et libertates eorum opprimuntur*). This results in a serious diminution of the archiepiscopal Chamber's income and to his own loss (*non modicum detrimentum*). The pope grants that all cases affecting the Jews shall be within the archbishop's jurisdiction only. For a period of two years the Jews may not be haled before any other court by authority of papal letters, unless the present document is specifically mentioned.

Dat. Avin., Kal Julii, anno nono.

Reg. Vat. 79, fol. 173.
Mollat, no. 22710.

1. See the next document for a similar situation.

2. Evidently the Inquisition was not involved. The matter at issue was probably moneylending.

XXVIII   May 9, 1326

To Wolfram, Bishop of Würzburg:[1]

SINCERE DEVOTIONIS . . . The pope grants that for a period of two years the Jews residing in the city and the towns belonging to the church of Würzburg and subject to the bishop's temporal jurisdiction, shall not be subject to the jurisdiction of anyone else empowered by papal authority (*nullus Judeus . . . per litteras apostolicas generales vel speciales conveniri vel ad judicium trahi valeat*), unless the present letter is specifically mentioned and as long as the episcopal court and officials are ready to render justice to anyone complaining against the Jews (*dummodo in tua curia patefecit de ipsis conquerentibus . . . in exhibendo justitiam . . . paratos vos exhibeatis*).

Dat. Avin., vii Id. Maii, anno decimo.

Reg. Vat. 81, fol. 44v.
Mollat, no. 25251.

1. See above, no. XXVII, and below, no. XXXIX. Cf. M. Szulwas, *Die Juden in Würzburg während des Mittelalters,* Berlin, 1934, p. 43, which does not mention this document but from which one may conclude that this petition by Bishop Wolfram was part of a broader plan in which imperial claims were likewise involved.

XXIX   July 25, 1326

To the Bishop of Paris:

CUPIENTES UT . . . The bishop is asked for a report on the situation regarding Hebrew, Greek, Arabic and Chaldaic studies in the University of Paris: who is in charge (*qui dictas scolas regunt*) and whether they have pupils (*si scolares auditores habent*), how, by whom and in what sums the expenses are raised.[1]

> Dat. Avin., viii Kal. Augusti, anno decimo.

Denifle, *Chartularium Universitatis Paris.*, II, p. 293, no. 857.

1. See above, no. VI.

XXX   August 1, 1326

To Baldwin, Archbishop of Treves:[1]

CUM, SICUT ACCEPIMUS . . . [identical with no. XXVI above].

> Dat. Avin., Kal. Augusti, anno decimo.

Mollat, no. 26143.
Sauerland, p. 457, no. 1019.
Reg. Vat. 81, fol. 247r.

1. On the same day a similar letter was sent to Henry, archbishop of Cologne (Sauerland, no. 1020) who had been addressed in identical terms a year and a half previously. Kober, pp. 253-5, discusses these letters and points out that this very archbishop of Treves was then using the Jews of his diocese to reorganize and centralize his finances.

XXXI   October 29, 1326

To Odardus of St. Ferreol, Canon of the Church of St. Michael, in Beauvais:

PERSONAM TUAM . . . The canon relates that at the age of ten he had witnessed the execution of a Jew and, along with other bystanders, had thrown stones at the man hanging, head down,[1] on the gibbet. He does not know whether the stone he had thrown, which had struck the man's head, had hastened his death (. . . *cum quidam Judeus propter eius demerita ad ultimum esset judicatum supplicium et suspendio deputatus, dum per pedes in patibulo pendens, lapidaretur a populo, tu, una cum aliis ibidem astantibus, dictum Judeum lapidantibus, lapides perjecisti in eum ipsamque in capite percussisti, ignorans tamen utrum ex ictu huius dicto Judeo mors magis fuit preparata . . .*). When he left the spot, the Jew was still alive, but, weakened by the stones, soon died. The petitioner entered the Church soon thereafter in Soissons, and later was provided with a more lucrative prebend. But his conscience troubles him lest the scene above described had left a stain upon him[2] (*propter factum premissum dubites te irregularitatis maculam incurrisse*). The pope grants him absolution and pronounces him capable of enjoying the fruits of his prebend.

Dat. Avin., iv Kal. Decembris, anno undecimo.

Reg. Vat. 83, fol. 396v.

1. On this manner of executing a Jew see Guido Kisch, "The 'Jewish Execution' in Medieval Germany," in *Historia Judaica*, vol. V, no. 2 (October 1943), pp. 103–32.

2. It may be that his right to it had been questioned.

XXXII   November 4, 1327

To the Archbishop of Trani:

The archbishop is commanded that, if he finds it expedient, he shall unite the church of St. Gervais, which is situated outside the walls of

Trani, with the church of St. Mary in New Trani, where a synagogue used to be.[1]

Dat. Avin., ii Non. Novembr., anno duodecimo.

Mollat, no. 30262.

1. For the background of this reference and of the next document, no. XXXIII, see Joshua Starr, "The Mass Conversion of the Jews in Southern Italy (1290-3)," in *Speculum*, vol. XXI (1946), pp. 208-11. See also M. D. A. Cassuto, "The Destruction of the Academies in Southern Italy in the Thirteenth Century," in *Sefer Zikkaron to the Memory of Asher Gulak and Samuel Klein*, Jerusalem, 1942, pp. 139-51. This very church seems to be referred to *ibid.*, p. 148. Cf. Cecil Roth, *The History of the Jews of Italy*, Phila., 1946, pp. 100-2.

XXXIII   January 26, 1328

To the Inquisitors of Heresy in Apulia:

PETITIO DILECTI FILII . . . Bartholomew, bishop-elect of Trani,[1] complains that Jews residing in Trani, from whom, when they were more numerous, the church's economy used to draw considerable income (*ex quibus dicta mensa consuevit hactenus, quando erant in maiori numero, ampla emolumenta percipere et habere*),[2] have been and continue to be so oppressed by the Inquisition that the few who remain are threatened by want and the church economy can expect little from them[3] (*verum vos tot gravamina retroacto tempore intulistis et continue infertis eisdem quod valde pauci inibi remanserunt et illi qui ibidem supersunt tanta premuntur inopia quod valde tenuis profectus potest deinceps ex dictis Judeis succedere dicte mense*). Similar oppressions are practiced by the inquisitors on the converts from Judaism, more attention being paid to the gain which may be derived from them than to the spiritual edification which should be provided them (. . . *plus ab eis temporalia lucra querentes quam aliquam edificationem facere spiritualem*). The bishop-elect therefore petitions that, since he is ready to administer punishment to Jews and converts when they deserve it, and since they are his subjects, the pope come to his aid against the inquisitors. The pope commands the inquisitors that, for a period of two years, they shall not proceed against

Jews and converts except at the request of the bishop or his vicar or in their presence.

Dat. Avin., vii Kal. Februarii, anno duodecimo.

Mollat, no. 40234.
Eubel, *Bull Francisc.*, V, p. 338, no. 700 n.

1. See no. XXXII for another aspect of the same situation.

2. For a similar claim that the Jews are an important source of income, see above, nos. XXVII and XXVIII.

3. For a discussion of the extent to which the Inquisition could exercise jurisdiction over the Jews see Fritz Baer, *Studien zur Geschichte der Juden im Königreich Aragonien während des 13. und 14. Jahrhunderts*, Berlin, 1913, pp. 60 ff. Such powers were limited and the procedure strictly defined (cf. Vidal, *Bullaire*, pp. xliii ff.). Obviously an organization which drew its personnel from among the most energetic among the friars refused to recognize limitations. Jurisdictional quarrels between inquisitors and bishops began early (cf. no. XXII note 4, above). An attempt to adjust the matter was made at the Council of Vienne by the decretal *Multorum* (included in the *Clementin.* Lib. V, tit. iii, c. 1), which gave both sides equal standing and urged cooperation (cf. Vidal, *Bullaire*, p. xii and 17 n.). John XXII, on the other hand, was inclined to favor the inquisitors. Before long they began to infringe on the royal authority, as well. In 1302, Philip the Fair forbade inquisitional interference with the Jews for any reason (*REJ*, II, p. 31, no. XV). Finke (*Acta Aragon.*, II, nos. 540, 542, 543, 548) offers a number of instances when James II of Aragon showed vehement displeasure over the interference of inquisitors in Jewish affairs. One case (no. 543) is reminiscent of this document.

XXXIV February 19, 1328

To the Deans of the Holy Cross of Liege and Deventer and to the Scholasticus of the Church of Treves:

SIGNIFICARUNT NOBIS . . . Frederick, abbot of the monastery of St. Nicholas at Brauweiler, in the diocese of Cologne, complains that his monastery had been weighed down with debt as a result of a ten-year-long quarrel and lawsuit between two claimants to the office of abbot. The monastery is therefore in such straits that its income does not suffice to pay the usury demanded by Jewish and Christian creditors[1] (. . . *ad solvendas usuras tam Judeis quam aliis Christianis usurariis*). The pope empowers the above-named churchmen to compel the creditors to claim no more than the face value of the debt, all documents, oaths and obligations made on behalf of the monastery being declared void. The Jewish creditors shall be compelled by the threat of a boycott (*per subtractionem communionis*) and the Christians by ecclesiastical punishment.

Dat. Avin., xii Kal. Martii, anno duodecimo.

Sauerland, nos. 1437–8.

1. Cf. Kober, pp. 254–5.

XXXV   March 22, 1329

To All Christians:

GLORIOSUS DEUS . . . King Philip of France[1] informed the pope of the following incident: A certain Jew, having some time ago falsely accepted baptism and adopted the name of William, continued for a long while to practice Judaism secretly though seemingly a Christian (*diutius sub Christianitatis nomine judaizans*). One day, while in the monastery of Cambon of the Cistercian Order, in the diocese of Cambrai, he was moved by a spirit of vileness (*nequam inductus spiritu*) and with a sword he five times wickedly stabbed (*perforavit*) a certain image of the Glorious Virgin painted on one of the walls. Then, because news of this horrible crime had begun to spread among the populace against this Jew, he mendaciously asserted that he was blameless of this act and because of this false denial went unpunished for his crime. It happened that a certain Catholic Christian of praiseworthy and honest life, John Flamens of Lessines by name, a carpenter who lived in that diocese, hearing that no fitting punishment had been imposed for so shameful a crime, challenged the said Jew to a judicial ordeal by duel, though perhaps illegally[2] (*licet forsan illicite*). When he and the Jew entered upon the duel, he, heavenly grace being with him, felled the Jew within a brief time and conquered him. Right there the Jew, vanquished and bound to the stump of a tree preparatory to burning, publicly confessed his guilt of the abominable crime (*et ibidem dictus Judeus devictus et ligatus ad stipitem ut cremaretur publice fuit confessus se predictum scelus abhominabile perpetrasse*). Subsequently a chapel was erected in the monastery in front of the abovementioned image, for the honor and reverence of the Glorious Virgin that she might be the more fittingly and reverently honored in return for the dishonor visited upon her. The pope accedes to the king's request and grants a remission of sins to anyone making a pilgrimage to this chapel.[3]

Dat. Avin., ii Kal. Aprilis, anno tertiodecimo.

Arnold Fayen, *Lettres de Jean XXII,* vol. II (Analecta Vaticana-Belgica, vol. III), Rome, 1909, no. 2404.

---

1. Philip VI, of Valois, 1328-50, was noted for his chivalry and piety, being called "the Very Good Christian," though not for his ability or statesmanship (cf. Lavisse, *Histoire de France,* vol. IV, pt. ii, p. 14). At the very beginning of his reign he won that victory in Flanders which led directly to the Hundred Years's War. Being in the neighborhood of Cambrai, he no doubt heard the story and addressed his letter to the pope. The events described had happened in 1322.

2. Since it was done without the authority of a court of law.

3. For the full story, with its embellishments, see Theophile Lejeune, "La Vierge miraculeuse de Cambon," in *Annales du cercle archaeologique de Mons,* vol. VIII (1866-8), pp. 67-95, and the bibliography there given on p. 68. William the Good, Count of Hainault, had been the Jew's godfather and given him his name. Conversion did not improve the new Christian's economic situation, for he had to appeal for a job (as carpenter?). The convert had been accustomed to stop at the Abbey of Cambon, and the event is supposed to have happened on one of these visits. There was but one witness to the crime, the carpenter-friar Jean Mandidier, who said that he rushed in at the cries of the Jew while stabbing the image. At the instance of the abbot, the Jew was "put to the question" by being hung by his wrists while a weight was attached to his feet. But he persisted in his complete denial and, there being only one witness, he was released. There is also supposed to have been an exchange of letters with the pope at this stage of the story; but none has been discovered and, if it had existed, it would have beeen referred to in the document here presented. Further embellishments speak of Jean Flamens (also a carpenter!) as having been a paralytic who dreamed that the Virgin demanded to be avenged. The Jew, according to the story, of huge size, was easily vanquished by the paralytic. The chapel was erected, the story continues, on the place of combat, not as in the above letter, facing the image. It continued to be the objective of pilgrims down to the French Revolution. Poets and chroniclers told the story often; weavers and painters represented it in their art. The chapel became very wealthy as a result of the pilgrims. In 1559 it was robbed. Cf. Leopold Devillers in *Annales de l'Académie d'Archéologie de Belgique,* ser. I, vol. 19 (1862), pp. 499 ff., where some doubt is cast on the veracity of the story.

XXXVI   April 11, 1330

To the Bishop of Strasbourg:

APOSTOLICE SEDIS . . . The abbot and the monastery of Schwarzach inform the pope of their dire straits. Because of the wars carried on in their neighborhood by Louis the Bavarian, they had become impoverished and indebted to the Jews[1] (. . . *quam propter importabilia onera debitorum in quibus dictum monasterium erga Judeos propter guerras predictas ac sceleritates maximas in eisdem partibus peccatis exigentibus ingruentes est obligatum*). The pope orders that this monastery be joined to the parish churches of Dossenheim and Schwindratzheim.

Dat. Avin., iii Idus Aprilis, anno quartodecimo.

E. Hauviller, *Analecta Argentinensia*, I, Strasbourg, 1900, no. 204.

1. It is to be noted that nothing is said about the debt being usurious.

XXXVII   April 19, 1330

To Rudolph, Duke of Saxony:

EXIMIE TUE DEVOTIONIS . . . The duke complains that his duchy of Saxony and his other lands are frequently placed under the interdict. Such a decree affects all persons living there, including the Jews, although the cause of the interdict is no fault of theirs[1] (. . . *contra singulares personas eorundem ducatus et terrarum, interdum contra Judeos commorantes inibi impetrantur . . .*). The pope grants a relaxation of the interdict so that it shall not affect the guiltless.

Dat. Avin., xiii Kal. Maii, anno quartodecimo.

Schmidt, *Päbstiche Urkunden und Regesten*, Halle, 1886, no. 405.

1. The quarrel between John XXII and Louis the Bavarian kept the entire empire in turmoil. See no. XXXVI above.

XXXVIII   September 24, 1331

To the Bishop of Würzburg:

SINCERE DEVOTIONIS AFFECTUS . . . At the urgent request of the bishop, the pope had some time before[1] granted him that, for a period of two years, no Jew of his province and his cities might be haled before any other judge as long as the Jew is ready to answer before the episcopal curia, and the bishop and his officers are ready to render justice there. The two-year period having expired, the Jews, his subjects, have been made to suffer many molestations (*multipliciter et indebite molestentur*). The pope grants another period of two years.

Dat. Avin., viii Kal. Octobri, anno sextodecimo.

Reg. Vat. 101, fol. 43r.

1. See above, no. XXVIII.

XXXIX   October 18, 1331

To the Abbot of the Cistercian Monastery at Chalon-sur-Saône:

PORRECTA NOBIS . . . A friar by the name of Gaufridus de Dimegneyo asks for absolution for an incident that occurred in his youth. He relates the following: On a certain day, at the time when it was generally believed that the lepers and certain Jews deserved to have secular justice condemn them to the stake[1] (. . . *olim tempore que leprosi et quidam ex Judeis eorum demeritis ut communiter dicebatur comburebantur per justitiam secularem. . .*), a number of men entered the tavern belonging to Gaufrid's father. One of them was seen by Gaufrid hiding a sack of some seeds and, having hidden it, returning to drink with the others. When they left, the man recovered his sack and took it along. Gaufrid voiced his suspicions to someone that the sack contained an evil potion, in which people then generally believed[2] (. . . *que de sacro potionum illis partibus vulgariter dicebatur . . .*). The men were brought back and, as he returned, the same man again hid his sack. Arrested by the local lord and put to the question, the man confessed to being a thief and to carrying with him a sleeping potion which, when put into wine, made drinkers fall asleep and thus easily robbed. He was executed by hanging and the others were freed. Since he participated in all this when he was young and innocent, Gaufrid petitions to be absolved from the sin of having caused a man's death and be made fit for promotion to holy orders. His petition is granted.

Dat. Avin., xiiii Kal. Novembris, anno sextodecimo.

Reg. Vat. 101, fol. 195–196r, no. 546.

1. The Lepers' Persecution occurred in 1321–2. Cf. Graetz, *Geschichte*, VII, 258 f.

2. Apparently the charge was no longer so widely credited. It was to be revived at the time of the Black Death, in 1348.

Bibliography

Manuscripts

Paris

Archives Nationales
    L242, no. 177
    L252, no. 178
    L254, no. 25
Bibliothèque Nationale
    Fond Doat 32, fols. 4r–7r, 11r–15r, 191r–192r, 193r–194r,
        206r–208r, 209r
    Fond Latin 4169, fol. 72
    Fond Moreau 1233, fol. 90, no. 381

Rome

Archivio Segreto Vaticano
    Armarium
        2, tome 38, fols. 22r–24v
        31, tome 72, fols. 231v–232r, 232r, 233r, 247r–v, 307v
    Instrumenta Miscellanea
    Regesta Vaticana
        24, fols. 12, c. 91; 113v, c. 768
        26, fols. 26v, no. 109; 57, anno II, no. 32
        27, fols. 53, no. 2; 88, no. 1
        28, fols. 21, no. 70; 43, no. 145
        29, fols. 198v, no. 975; 202, no. 1005
        29A, fols. 3, no. 13; no. 20; 234, no. 66
        37 (Reg. Curiales), fol. 195, no. 94
        40, fol. 56, no. 10
        41, fols. 19v–20r; 20r, no. 78; 194–198
        43, fols. 29v, no. 93; 25v, no. 92; 208v, no. 42
        44, fols. 2v, no. 4; 45r, no. 185; 25v, c. 106; 47r, c. 194; 117r, c. 50;
            284r–v, no. 783; 284v; 294v, no. 848
        45, fol. 75r, c. 379; 102v, c. 505; 119v, no. 594; 147r, no. 724
        46, fols. 26v, no. 136; 45r, c. 224; 46r, c. 227; 125r, c. 623
        47, fols. 102v–103r, no. 441

48, fol. 314r, no. 452a
49, fols. 140; 175v; 309v–310; 310
52, fols. 84r; 124r, c. 626; 90v, c. 415; 123v, c. 590; 269, c. 1085
59, fol. 126r, no. 598
60, fol. 72v.

Bibliotheca Vaticana
Ottobon. 2546, fol. 12a

Primary Sources

Alberigo, J. *Conciliorum Oecumenicorum Decreta.* Basle, 1962.

Anemüller, Ernst. *Urkundebuch des Klosters Paulinzelle, 1068–1534.* Vol. 7 of *Thuringische Geschichtsquellen.* Jena, 1905.

Aronius, Julius, et al., eds. *Regesten zur Geschichte der Juden im fränkischen und deutschen Reiche bis zum Jahre 1273.* Berlin, 1887–1902.

Auvray, L., ed. *Les registres de Grégoire IX.* Paris, 1899–1908.

Bernard Gui. *Manuel de l'Inquisiteur.* Ed. G. Mollat. Paris, 1927.

Berthelé, Jos., "Les instructions et constitutions de Guillaume Durand, le Spéculateur, d'après le manuscrit de Cessenon." *Academie des sciences et lettres de Montpellier, Mémoires de la Section des Lettres,* 2nd series, 3 (1900): 1–148.

Böhmer, J. F., ed. *Codex diplomaticus Moenofrancfurtanus.* Frankfurt, 1901.

———. *Urkundenbuch der Reichsstadt Frankfurt.* Frankfurt a.M., 1836.

Bouquet, M., et al., eds. *Recueil des Historiens des Gaules et de la France.* Paris, 1737–1904.

Bullarium Romanum, Taurinensis Editio. Rome, 1857–1872.

Bzovius, A. *Annalium Ecclesiasticorum.* Cologne, 1616.

Cadier, Leon, ed. *Bulles originales du XIIIe siècle.* Rome, 1887.

Capes, W. W., ed. *Registrum Ricardi de Swinfield.* London, 1909.

Chavel, Ch. *Kitvei R. Moshe b. Nahman.* Jerusalem, 1971.

Corpus Iuris Canonici. Ed. E. Friedberg. Leipzig, 1879–1881.

Corpus Iuris Civilis. Ed. P. Kruger and Th. Mommsen. Berlin, 1905–1928.

de Gudenus, V. F., ed., *Codex diplomaticus . . . res Moguntinas.* Frankfurt, 1747.

Delaville le Roulx, J. *Cartulaire générale de l'Ordre des Hospitaliers de St. Jean de Jerusalem 1100–1310.* Paris, 1906.

Deloix, Jean, ed. *Speculum Inquisitionis Bisuntinae.* Dôle, 1628.

Denifle, H. *Chartularium Universitatis Parisiensis.* Paris, 1889–1897.

de Susannis, Marquardus. *De Iudaeis et aliis Infidelibus.* Venice, 1558.

Digard, G., et al., eds. *Les registres de Boniface VIII.* Paris, 1904–1939.

Ennen, L., and Eckertz, E., eds. *Quellen zur Geschichte der stadt Köln.* Cologne, 1860–1879.

Fejér, George. *Codex diplomaticus Hungariae ecclesiasticus et civilis.* Buda, 1829–1866.

Felibien, D. Michel. *Histoire de la Ville de Paris.* Paris, 1725.

Friss, Arminius, ed. *Monumenta Hungariae Judaica.* Budapest, 1903.

Gallia Christiana (Nova). Ed. D. de Sainte-Marthe et al. Paris, 1715–1865.

Gay, J., ed. *Les registres de Nicolas III.* Paris, 1898–1938.

Guiraud, Jean, ed. *Les registres d'Urbain IV.* Paris, 1901–1958.

—— and Cadier, L., eds. *Les registres de Gregoire X et de Jean XXI.* Paris, 1892–1906.

Hube, R. *Antiquissimae Constitutiones Synodales Provinciae Gneznensis.* St. Petersburg, 1856.

Jaffé, P., ed. *Monumenta Moguntina.* Vol. 3 of *Bibliotheca rerum Germanicarum.* Berlin, 1864–1873.

John Duns Scotus, *Opera Omnia.* Vatican, 1950.

Jordan, E., ed. *Les registres de Clement IV.* Paris, 1893–1945.

Laborde, J. de. *Layettes du trésor des chartes.* Vol. 3. Paris, 1875.

Lacomblet, T. J. *Urkundenbuch für die Geschichte des Niederrheins.* Dusseldorf, 1840–1857.

Lagumina, G. and B., eds. *Codice diplomatico dei Giudei di Sicilia.* Palermo, 1884–1895.

Langlois, E., ed., *Les registres de Nicolas IV.* Paris, 1886.

La Roncière, C. Bourel de, et al., eds. *Les registres d'Alexandre IV.* Paris, 1895–1959.

Laurière, E. de, et al. *Ordonnances des rois de la troisième race.* Paris, 1723–1849.

Loeb, Isidore. "Bulles inédites des papes." *REJ* 1 (1880): 114–118, 293–298.

Luce, Siméon. "Catalogue des documents du Trésor des Chartes relatifs aux Juifs sous le règne de Philippe le Bel." *REJ* 2 (1881): 15–72.

Mansi, J. D. *Sacrorum Conciliorum Collectio.* Venice, 1779–1782.

Marcus, J. R. *The Jew in the Medieval World.* Cincinnati, 1938.

Martène, E., and Durand, U. *Thesaurus Novus Anecdotorum.* Paris: 1817, 1822.

Martin, Ch. T., ed. *Registrum epistolarum Fratris Johannis Peckham Archiepiscopi Cantuariensis.* London, 1908–1912.

Muratori, L. A. *Rerum Italicarum scriptores.* Milan, 1723–1751.

Olivier-Martin, F., ed. *Les registres de Martin IV.* Paris, 1901–1935.

Posse, O., ed. *Analecta Vaticana.* Innsbruck, 1878.

Potthast, Augustus. *Regesta Pontificum Romanorum*. Berlin, 1875.

Powicke, F. M., and Cheney, C. R., *Councils and Synods with Other Documents Relating to the English Church, A.D. 1205–1313*. Oxford, 1964.

Prou, M., ed. *Les registres d'Honorius IV*. Paris, 1888.

Ptasnik, J., ed. *Analecta Vaticana*. Vol. 3 of *Monumenta Poloniae Vaticana*. Lemberg, 1864–1888.

Raymond de Peñaforte. *Summa de poenitentia et matrimonia*. Rome, 1603.

Raynaldus, O. *Annales Ecclesiastici*. Ed. J. D. Mansi. Lucca, 1738–1756.

Regestum Clementis Papae V. Rome, 1884–1888.

Régné, Jean. "Catalogue des actes de Jaime Ier, Pedro III et Alfonso III, rois d'Aragon, concernant les Juifs 1213–1291." *REJ* 60 (1910): 161–201; 61 (1911): 1–43; 62 (1912): 38–73.

Ripoll,· Thomas. *Bullarium Ordinis FF. Praedicatorum*. Rome, 1729–1740.

Robert, Ulysse. "Catalogue des actes relatifs aux Juifs (1183–1300)." *REJ* 3 (1881): 211–224.

Sawicki, J. T. *Bibliographia synodorum particularium, Monumenta Iuris Canonici*. Series C: Subsidia, vol. 2. Vatican City, 1967.

Sbaralea, J., ed. *Annales Minorum*. Rome, 1650; reprint Rome, 1906.

———. *Bullarium Franciscanum Romanorum Pontificum*. Rome, 1759–1904.

Solomon ibn Verga. *Shevet Yehudah*. Ed. Azriel Shohet. Jerusalem, 1946.

Steinschneider, M. *Sefer Vikhuah ha-Ramban lifné Melekh ve-Sarim*. Berlin, 1860.

Stern, Moritz. *Die päpstliche Bullen über die Blutbeschuldigung*. Munich, 1900.

———. "Papsturkunden: Ein Beitrag zur Geschichte der Juden, aus Archiven mitgeteilt." *Beilage zum Berichte der israelitischen Religionsschule zu Kiel über das Schuljahr 1892/3*. Kiel, 1893.

———. *Urkundliche Beiträge über die Stellung der Päpste zu den Juden*. Kiel, 1893.

Tangl, M. *Die Päpstlichen Kanzleiordnungen von 1250–1500*. Innsbruck, 1894; reprint 1959.

Tatu, Aloysius L., ed. *Acta Alexandri IV*. Rome, 1952.

Teulet, Alexandre, et al., eds. *Layettes du Trésor des Chartes*. Vols. 1–2. Paris, 1863–1909.

Theiner, A. *Codex diplomaticus dominii temporalis S. Sedis*. Rome, 1861–1862.

———. *Monumenta Historica Hungariae*. Rome, 1859.

Thomas Aquinas. *Aquinas, Selected Political Writings.* Ed. A. P. d'Entrèves and trans. J. G. Dawson. Oxford, 1948.

Tovey, D'Blossiers. *Anglia Judaica.* Oxford, 1738.

Vidal, J. M. *Bullaire de l'Inquisition française.* Paris, 1913.

Wagenseil, Johann Christoph, ed. *Tela ignea Satanae.* Altdorf, 1681.

Wilkins, W. W. *Concilia Magnae Britanniae et Hiberniae.* London, 1737.

Secondary Sources

Adler, M. *Jews of Medieval England.* London, 1939.

Agus, Irving A. *Rabbi Meir of Rothenburg.* Philadelphia, 1947.

Amador de los Rios, J. *Historia social, politica y religiosa de los Judios de España y Portugal.* Madrid, 1876; reprint Buenos Aires, 1943.

Anchel, Robert. *Les Juifs de France.* Paris, 1946.

Arbois de Jubainville, H. d'. *Histoire des ducs et des comtes de Champagne.* Paris, 1859–1869.

Baer, Y. *A History of the Jews in Christian Spain.* Philadelphia, 1966.

———. *Die Juden im Christlichen Spanien.* Berlin, 1929–1936; repr. Farnborough, Eng. 1970.

Baras, Z. "Persecution of Jews in Brabant in 1309." *Zion* 34 (1969): 111–116.

Baron, S. W. *A Social and Religious History of the Jews.* 18 vols. 2nd ed. New York, 1952–1983.

Bevan, E. R., and Singer, Charles, eds. *The Legacy of Israel.* Oxford, 1927.

Blanchet, J. "Les Juifs à Pamiers en 1256." *REJ* 18 (1889): 139–141.

Blumenkranz, Bernhard. *Juifs et Chrétiens dans le monde occidentale.* Paris, 1960.

Bondy, G., and Dworský, F. *Zur Geschichte der Juden in Böhmen, Mähren und Schlesien von 906 bis 1620.* Prague, 1906.

Brandão, F. *Monarchia Lusytana.* Alcobaça, Portugal, 1597–1727.

Browe, Peter. "Die Eucharistenwunder des Mittelalters." *Breslauer Studien zur historischen Theologie,* n.s., 4 (1938): 128–139, 162–165.

———. "Die Hostienschändungen der Juden im Mittelalter." *Römische Quartalschrift* 34 (1926): 167–197.

———. *Die Judenmission im Mittelalter und die Päpste.* Rome, 1942.

———. "Die religiöse Duldung der Juden in Mittelalter." *Archiv für Katholisches Kirchenrecht* 118 (1938): 1–76.

Camau, Émile. *La Provence à travers les siècles.* Paris, 1908–1940.

Cassuto, D. A. "The Destruction of the Yeshivot in Southern Italy in the Thirteenth Century." In *Studies in Memory of Asher Gulak and Samuel Klein.* Jerusalem, 1942.

Chazan, Robert. "The Barcelona Disputation of 1263: Christian Missionizing and Jewish Response." *Speculum* 52 (1977): 824–842.

Cohen, Jeremy. *The Friars and the Jews*. Ithaca, 1982.

Cohen, Martin A. "Reflections on the Text and Context of the Disputation of Barcelona." *HUCA* 35 (1964): 157–192.

Coulton, G. G. *Medieval Panorama*. New York, 1955.

Demaitre, Luke. *Doctor Bernard de Gordon: Professor and Practioner*. Toronto, 1980.

Denifle, H. "Quellen zur Disputation Pablos Christiani mit Moses Nachmani zu Barcelona, 1263." *Historisches Jahrbuch* 8 (1887): 225–244.

Douie, Decima. *Archbishop Pecham*. Oxford, 1952.

Dubnow, Simon. *History of the Jews in Russia and Poland*. Philadelphia, 1916.

Dufeil, M.-M. *Guillaume de Saint-Amour et la polémique universitaire parisienne, 1250–1259*. Paris, 1972.

Eisenstein, Aron. *Die Stellung der Juden in Polen im XIIIten und XIVten Jahrhundert*. Cieszyn, 1934.

Emery, Richard. *The Jews of Perpignan*. New York, 1959.

Esposito, M. "Un Procès contre les Juifs de la Savoie en 1329." *Revue D'Histoire Ecclésiastique* 34 (1938): 785–801.

Ferorelli, N. *Gli Ebrei nell'Italia meridionale*. Turin, 1915.

Fita, Fidel. "Privilegios de los Hebreos Mallorquinos." *Boletin de la Real Academia de la Historia* 36–37 (1900): 16–18; reprinted from *España Hebrea*. Vol. 2. Madrid, 1891.

Fliche, A., Thouzelier, C., and Azais, Y. *La Chrétienté romaine, 1198–1274*. Vol. 10 of *Histoire de l'Église*. Ed. A. Fliche and V. Martin. Paris, n.d.

Friedenwald, Harry. *The Jews and Medicine*. Baltimore, 1944.

Gauthier, Léon. "Les Juifs dans les deux Bourgognes." *REJ* 48 (1904): 208–229.

———. "Les Juifs dans les deux Bourgognes: Étude sur le commerce de l'argent aux XIIIe et XIVe siècles." *Mémoires de la Société d'émulation du Jura*, 9me serie, 3 (1914): 57–232.

Germania Judaica. Pt. I (to 1238), ed. I. Elbogen, A. Freimann, and H. Tykocinski; Pt. II (to 1350), ed. Zvi Avineri. Tübingen, 1963–1968.

Graetz, H. *Geschichte der Juden*, 2nd ed. Leipzig, 1873.

Grayzel, Solomon, *The Church and the Jews in the XIIIth Century*. Philadelphia, 1933; New York, 1966.

———. "The Confession of a Medieval Jewish Convert." *Historia Judaica* 17 (1955): 89–120.

———. "Jewish References in a 13th Century Formulary." *JQR* 46 (July, 1955): 50–53.

———. "Jews and Roman Law." *JQR* 59 (1968): 93–117.

———. "The Papal Bull *Sicut Judaeis*." In *Studies and Essays in Honor of Abraham A. Neuman*, pp. 243–280. Ed. Meir Ben-Horin et al. Philadelphia, 1962.

———. "Popes, Jews, and Inquisition from 'Sicut' to 'Turbato.'" In *Essays on the Occasion of the Seventieth Anniversary of Dropsie University*, pp. 151–188. Ed. Abraham I. Katsch and Leon Nemoy. Philadelphia, 1979.

———. "References to the Jews in the Correspondence of John XXII." *HUCA* 23, 2 (1950–51): 37–80.

Gregorovius, Ferdinand. *History of the City of Rome in the Middle Ages.* Trans. Annie Hamilton. New York, 1967.

Gross, H. *Gallia Judaica.* Ed. S. Schwartzfuchs. Amsterdam, 1969.

Grunzweig, A. "Les incidences internationales des mutations monetaires de Philippe le Bel." *Le Moyen Age* 59 (1953): 117–172.

Güdemann, Moritz. "Zur Geschichte der Juden in Magdeburg." *MGWJ* 14 (1865): 241–256, 281–296, 321–335, 361–370. Reprinted Breslau, 1866.

Guiraud, Jean. *Histoire de l'Inquisition au Moyen Age.* Paris, 1938.

Guttmann, J. "Guillaume d'Auvergne et la littérature Juive." *REJ* 18 (1889): 243–255.

Hefele, Karl. *Histoire des Conciles.* Trans. and aug. Henri Leclerq et al. Paris, 1907–1949.

Holtzmann, Walther. "Zur päpstlichen Gesetzgebung über die Juden in 12ten Jahrhundert." In *Festschrift Guido Kisch.* Stuttgart, 1955.

Horowitz, Elliot. *Jewish Confraternities in Seventeenth Century Verona: A Study in the Social History of Piety.* Ph.D. Diss., Yale University, 1982.

Jordan, Édouard. *L'Allemagne et l'Italie aux XIIe et XIIIe siècles.* Vol. 4 of *Histoire du Moyen Age.* Ed. Gustave Glotz. Paris, 1939.

———. *De mercatoribus camerae apostolicae saeculi XIII.* 1909.

Jordan, W. C. "Christian Excommunication of Jews in the Middle Ages." *Jewish History* 1 (1986): 31–38.

———. *Louis IX and the Challenge of the Crusade: A Study in Rulership.* Princeton, 1979.

———. "An Unpublished Enquête from Picardy." *REJ* 138 (1979): 47–55.

Jusselin, Maurice. "Documents financiers concernant les mesures prise par Alphonse de Poitiers contre les Juifs (1268–1269)." *Bibliothèque de l'École des Chartes* 68 (1907): 130–149.

Juster, Jean. *La condition légale des Juifs sous les rois visigoths*. Paris, 1912.

Kahn, Zadoc. "Étude sur le livre de Joseph le Zélateur." *REJ* 1 (1880): 222–246; III *REJ* 1–38.

Kayserling, M. *Geschichte der Juden in Portugal*. Leipzig, 1867.

Kedar, B. Z. "Canon Law and the Burning of the Talmud." *Bulletin of Medieval Canon Law* 9 (1979): 79–82.

———. "Notes on the History of the Jews in Palestine in the Middle Ages [Hebrew]." *Tarbiz* 42 (1973): 401–418.

Kemp. J. A. "A New Conception of the Christian Commonwealth in Innocent IV." In *Proceedings of the Second International Congress of Medieval Canon Law*, pp. 155–159. Vatican City, 1965.

Kisch, Guido. *The Jews in Medieval Germany*. Chicago, 1949.

———. *Zasius und Reuchlin*. Constance, 1961.

Kracauer, I. *Geschichte der Juden in Frankfurt a. M.* Frankfurt, 1925.

Kriegel, M. "La juridiction inquisitoriale sur les Juifs à l'époque de Philippe le Hardi et Philippe le Bel." In M. Yardeni, ed., *Les Juifs dans l'histoire de France*. Leiden, 1980.

Langmuir, G. "Tanquam servi: The Change in Jewish Status in French Law about 1200." In *Les Juifs dans l'histoire de France*. Ed. M. Yardeni, Leiden, 1980.

Lazard, L. "Les Juifs du Touraine." *REJ* 17 (1888): 210–234.

Lea, Henry Charles. *A History of the Inquisition*. New York, 1922.

Le Blanc, François. *Traité historique des monnoyes de France*. Amsterdam, 1690.

Lichtenstein, Hans. "Der Vorwurf der Hostienschändung und das erste Auftreten der Juden in der Mark Brandenburg." *Zeitschrift für die Geschichte der Juden in Deutschland* 4 (1932): 189–197.

Linehan, Peter. *The Spanish Church and the Papacy in the 13th Century*. Cambridge, 1971.

Loeb, Isidore. "La controverse de 1263 à Barcelone." *REJ* 15 (1887): 1–18.

———. "Les négociants Juifs à Marseille au milieu du XIIIe siècle." *REJ* 16 (1888): 73–83.

Lopez, Robert. *The Commercial Revolution of the Middle Ages, 950–1350*. Englewood Cliffs, N.J., 1971.

Meeks, W., and Wilken, R. *Jews and Christians in Antioch*. Missoula, Montana, 1978.

Milano, A. "The Church and the Jews of Rome in the Thirteenth and Fourteenth Centuries [Hebrew]." *Eretz Yisrael (Sefer Yovel L'Moshe D. Cassuto)* 3 (1954): 223–239.

———. *Storia degli Ebrei in Italia*. Turin, 1963.

Mollat, G. *The Popes at Avignon*. New York, 1963–1965.

Morey, J. "Les Juifs en Franche-Comté au XIVme siècle." *REJ* 7 (1883): 1-39.

Morrison, K. F. *Tradition and Authority in the Western Church, 300-1140*. Princeton, 1969.

Nahon, G. "Le crédit et les Juifs dans la France du XIIIe siècle." *Annales* 24 (1969): 1121-1148.

Pirenne, H. *Histoire de Belgique*. Brussels, 1929; reprint 1972-1975.

Rabello, A. M. *A Tribute to Jean Juster*. Jerusalem, 1976.

Rankin, O. S. *Jewish Religious Polemics*. Edinburgh, 1956.

Régné, Jean. *Étude sur la condition des Juifs de Narbonne*. Narbonne, 1912.

Richardson, H. G. *The English Jewry under Angevin Kings*. London, 1960.

Robert, Ulysse. "Catalogue des actes relatifs aux Juifs (1183-1300)." *REJ* 3 (1881): 211-224.

Rosenthal, J. "The Talmud on Trial." *JQR* 47 (1956): 58-76, 145-169.

Roth, Cecil. "The Disputation of Barcelona (1263)." *HTR* 43 (1950): 118-144.

———. "Forced Baptisms in Italy." *JQR* 27 (1936-1937): 117-136.

———. "The Forced Baptisms of 1783 at Rome and the Community of London." *JQR* 16 (1925-1926): 105-116.

———. *History of the Jews in England*. Oxford, 1941.

Runciman, Steven. *A History of the Crusades*. Cambridge, 1954.

Saige, Gustave. *Les Juifs de Languedoc, antérieurement au XIVe siècle*. Paris, 1881; repr. Farnborough, Eng., 1971.

Scherer, J. E. *Die Rechtsverhältnisse der Juden in den deutsch-osterreichischen Länder*. Leipzig, 1901.

Schwartzfuchs, S. "The Expulsion of the Jews from France, 1306." In *JQR Seventy-fifth Anniversary Volume*, pp. 482-490. Ed. A. Neuman. Philadelphia, 1967.

Seppelt, F. X. *Papstgeschichte*. Munich, 1940.

Shatzmiller, Joseph. "L'Inquisition et les Juifs de Provence au XIIIe siècle." *Provence Historique* 93/94 (1973): 327-338.

———. "Jews 'Separated from the Communion of the Faithful in Christ.'" In *Studies in Medieval Jewish History and Literature*, pp. 307-314. Ed. I. Twersky. Cambridge, 1979.

Starr, J. "The Mass Conversion of Jews in Southern Italy." *Speculum* 21 (1946): 203-211.

Stengers, Jean. *Les Juifs dans les Pays-Bas au Moyen Age*. Brussels, 1950.

Stokes, H. P. "The Relationship between the Jews and the Royal Family of England in the 13th Century." Transactions of *JHSE* 8 (1918): 153-170.

Stow, Kenneth R. *Catholic Thought and Papal Jewry Policy, 1555–1593.* New York, 1977.

———. *"Gishat ha-Yehudim le-'Apifiorut ve-ha-Doktrinah ha-'Apifiorit shel Hagannat ha-Yehudim ba-Shanim 1063–1147."* Studies in the History of the Jewish People and the Land of Israel 5 (1980): 75–90.

———. "Papal and Royal Attitudes toward Jewish Lending in the Thirteenth Century." *AJS Review* 6 (1981): 161–184.

———. *The "1007 Anonymous" and Papal Sovereignty: Jewish Perceptions of the Papacy and Papal Policy in the High Middle Ages.* Cincinnati, 1984.

Tardif, A. *Privilèges accordés à la Couronne de France par le Saint-Siège.* Paris, 1885.

Tierney, B. *The Crisis of Church and State.* Englewood Cliffs, N.J., 1964.

Trachtenberg, Joshua. *The Devil and the Jews.* New Haven, 1943.

———. *Jewish Magic and Superstition.* New York and Philadelphia, 1961.

Ullman, S. *Histoire des Juifs en Belgique.* Anvers, n.d.

Vicaire, M.-H. "La prédication nouvelle des prêcheurs méridionaux au XIIIe siècle." In *Le crédo, la morale et l'Inquisition*, ed. M.-H. Vicaire. *Cahiers de Fanjeaux* 6 (1971): 21–64.

Vogelstein, H., and Rieger, P., *Geschichte der Juden in Rom.* Berlin, 1896.

Watt, J. A. "The English Episcopate, the State and the Jews: The Evidence of the Thirteenth Century Conciliar Decrees." In *Thirteenth Century England.* Ed. P. R. Cross and S. D. Lloyd. Newcastle-upon-Tyne, 1988.

———. "'Plenitudo potestatis' in Hostiensis." In *Proceedings of the Second Congress of Medieval Canon Law*, pp. 161–187. Ed. S. Kuttner. Vatican City, 1965.

Weyden, Ernst. *Geschichte der Juden in Köln am Rhein.* Cologne, 1867.

Williams, A. Lukyn. *Adversus Judaeos.* Cambridge, 1935.

Yerushalmi, Y. H. "The Inquisition and the Jews of France in the Time of Bernard Gui." *HTR* 63 (1976): 317–376.

Index

Names of ancient and medieval individuals are alphabetized by their first names.